BACK FROM BATTLE

The Forgotten Story of Pennsylvania's Camp Discharge and the Weary Civil War Soldiers It Served

JIM REMSEN AND BRAD UPP

SUNBURY PRESS
Mechanicsburg, PA USA

Published by Sunbury Press, Inc.
Mechanicsburg, PA USA

www.sunburypress.com

FIRST SUNBURY PRESS EDITION: August 2021

Set in Adobe Garamond | Interior design by Crystal Devine | Cover by Lawrence Knorr | Edited by Abigail Henson.

Publisher's Cataloging-in-Publication Data
Names: Remsen, Jim, author | Upp, Brad, author.
Title: Back from battle : the forgotten story of Pennsylvania's Camp Discharge and the weary Civil War soldiers it served / Jim Remsen and Brad Upp.
Description: First trade paperback edition. | Mechanicsburg, PA : Sunbury Press, 2021.
Summary : As the Civil War raged in the South, hundreds of weary Union troops were funneled to a special post near Philadelphia on their way back to civilian life. *Back From Battle* reclaims the forgotten history of this post, named Camp Discharge, and of the Pennsylvania volunteer soldiers who passed through its gates.
Identifiers: ISBN : 978-1-62006-539-6 (softcover).
Subjects: HISTORY / Military / United States | HISTORY / United States / Civil War Period (1850-1877) | HISTORY / United States / State and Local / Middle Atlantic.

Product of the United States of America
0 1 1 2 3 5 8 13 21 34 55

Continue the Enlightenment!

COVER ILLUSTRATION: Detail from "The Soldier's Dream," artist unknown, from the MOLLUS-Massachusetts Collection, courtesy of US Army Heritage & Education Center, Carlisle, Pa.

Contents

Map by George Lonsdorf

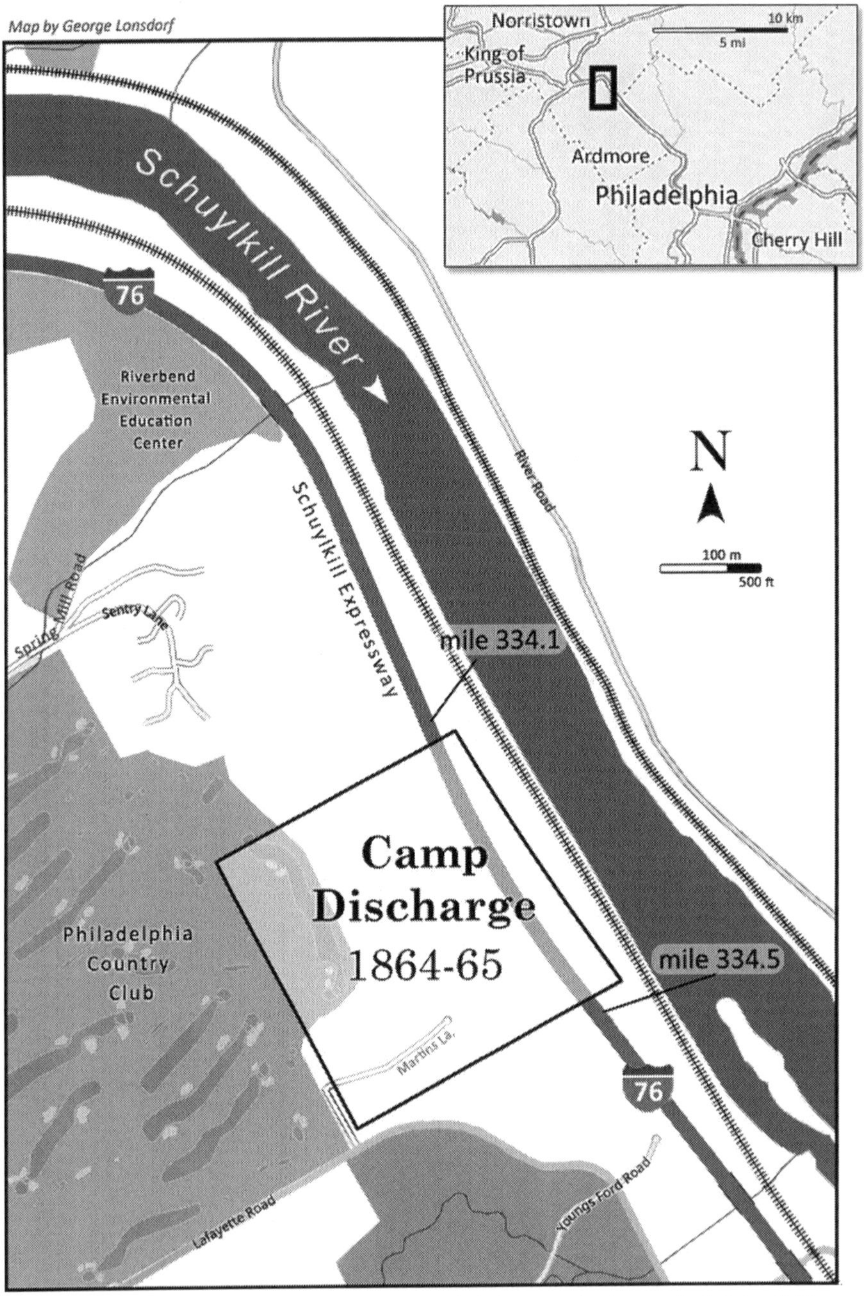

Camp Discharge was situated on a remote wooded slope overlooking today's Schuylkill Expressway (Interstate 76). The highway mile markers locate the site for passing motorists.

Introduction

PRIVATE Aaron E. Bachman of the First Pennsylvania Cavalry was nearly home again. After surviving combat, captivity, and a daring escape north, he was instructed to report to a special new Union Army base outside Philadelphia to await discharge back to civilian life. It was May 1865, a month following the Confederate surrender. As Bachman entered the base filled with other waiting combat veterans, he must have been both numb and elated. We know this because, decades later, he would author a memoir about his odyssey of war. It was a story filled with drama and horror—not unlike the personal testimonies the other weary Union servicemen who had made their way to that same military base could have provided.

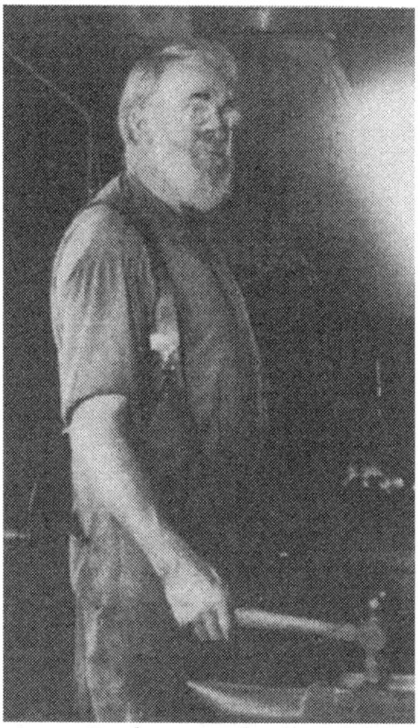

Aaron Bachman in his later life. (Courtesy Dwight Lindsey)

As Aaron Bachman told it, when the Civil War had broken out back in April 1861, he was 18 and learning the blacksmith trade in his German-speaking community of Lititz, Lancaster County. That July, a cavalryman in a handsome outfit came to town to enlist recruits. "I got the 'war fever' like the rest of the boys," Bachman would recall. Off he went to Reading to be mustered into the cavalry. The teenager was trained, assigned horse and weaponry, and found

Camp Discharge as seen from across the Schuylkill River (top), in a period photograph taken by W. B. Powell. It is the only photo of the camp known to still exist and is in the holdings of the Historical Society of Pennsylvania. The bottom image is a cropped, enhanced close-up that highlights the camp's barracks, flagpole, and stockade fence. ("Camp Discharge Opposite Spring Mill," photo by W. B. Powell, Small Graphics Collection, Historical Society of Pennsylvania.)

himself in Maryland and Virginia engaged in drilling, marching, mounted maneuvers, and occasional skirmishes. Then, on June 9, 1863, the First Pennsylvania and other Union horse soldiers launched a mass attack on Confederate general J. E. B. Stuart's cavalry forces at Brandy Station, Va. The Battle of Brandy Station was the Civil War's largest primarily mounted clash—and Private Bachman was thrown into the thick of it.

The experience still gripped him a half-century later.

> The cutting and slashing; the firing from pistol, carbine and cannon; the neighing of horses; the yelling of men; the falling of dead and wounded men and horses, made a scene that beggars description. The enemy's battery fired grape and canister into us, and the smoke was so thick that we could see only a few feet ahead. I fired seven shots out of my carbine and pistol. Men and horses fell in every direction; some forwards, some backwards, others sideways; some horses reared and fell, others plunged forward and rolled over, carrying their riders with them. Surely these were the jaws of death.

Bachman survived that crucible intact, but six months later, his luck turned when he was surrounded and captured while on sentry duty near Culpepper, Va. A hellish year of imprisonment would follow. He and two hundred others caught that day were taken by train to Belle Island, a lice-infested Rebel prison in Richmond. During three winter months there, he wrote, scores of young soldiers captured with him died of exposure and disease.

In March 1864, Bachman was jammed into a boxcar and transferred to southern Georgia—to the most notorious Confederate prison of all, the teeming and filthy stockade known as Andersonville. More than fourteen thousand Union soldiers, men in the prime of life, would waste away and die there. The Northern public was outraged once the scale of deprivation, abuse, and death became known. The Andersonville death toll rose from a few per day to nearly three hundred every day by that August, he wrote. "They died from different causes; some from the heat, some from scurvy, some from diarrhea and fever; most were overcome by the heat, but many died from pure starvation."

The sights Bachman witnessed were hideous. Mouths were so rotted by scurvy that prisoners plucked out their teeth and tongues on their way to dying. Legs and feet were swelling until the skin would burst and become infested with maggots; gangrene followed, so extreme the feet would fall off. Whimpering young men would curl up in the muck and

Issuing rations inside the teeming Andersonville prison in August 1864. (Courtesy Library of Congress)

filth and die. Others provoked the guards to shoot them dead to end their agony.

"It was awful to hear the moaning and the cursing and to see these horrible sights; some prayed and sang, some laughed, some were deranged and performed crazy tricks. Some of those who died had wives and children at home, but said very little about them. Some would, however, call for their mothers before they died. I often thought that if my mother could see or know my condition she would lose her mind." Bachman had grown so emaciated—having lost nearly half his body weight—that his arm above the elbow was a mere an inch and a half in diameter. However, he was determined "that they shouldn't bury my bones in that place."

Abruptly, in mid-September, his surviving group of ninety was ordered to depart Andersonville on a prisoner exchange. They were taken to Charleston and on to another deplorable prison at Florence, S.C. The exchange never happened. But by telling his handlers he was a blacksmith and promising not to flee, Bachman got himself reassigned to Macon, Ga. There he earned a small wage as a smithy and began to recover. On April 14, 1865, Bachman made a break for liberty and headed toward Alabama. A stealthful, zigzag journey ensued. By May, he made it safely to the Union garrison at Nashville and from there to Louisville, Indianapolis, Pittsburgh, and Harrisburg. He expected to be discharged from the service in Harrisburg but was told that because he'd mustered in at Reading, he had to go to Philadelphia to be properly mustered out. So he traveled on to Philadelphia—where he was told that because his papers were not in order, he would have to go to the new Army base nine miles up the river and join the others waiting there to have their cases sorted out.

THAT NEW BASE sat on a ridge overlooking the Schuylkill River in what is today Gladwyne, Pa. Seen from across the river, it resembled a mountaintop stronghold, with ranks of wooden buildings jutting above the treetops and spilling down the slope like a lava flow. An immense flagpole towered above the grounds, a landmark for miles around. By the time Aaron Bachman arrived there in mid-May 1865, the place was at its peak of operation. Bachman called the camp "Spring Hills," a local reference that others also used. The Army gave it a more utilitarian name, the name that stuck: Camp Discharge.

If you've never heard of Camp Discharge, you're hardly alone. The base was quickly erected in 1864 and just as rapidly disassembled and gone by early 1866. The original property is in private hands today and nearly off-limits to the general public. The only way you can access a bit of it is via a remote walking trail that we describe at the end of Chapter 4. There have been no plaques or historical markers about the camp along that trail, or on the ridgetop in present-day Lower Merion Township or down along the Schuylkill Expressway. Hardly a word about the place appears in Civil War histories or annals of the region.

Alas, Camp Discharge's special role in our military history deserves to be known and commemorated. During the fleeting months of its existence, the camp carried out an essential function processing a particular category of Pennsylvania volunteers—castaways like Aaron Bachman who had become separated from their regiments due to capture, injury, or other grim happenstances of war. Although their three-year tours of duty were up, they had to wait to be mustered out of their regiments,

The Philadelphia Brigade repulsing Pickett's Charge. (Courtesy Library of Congress)

often for weeks, until their missing papers were retrieved and updated. The discharges' pace picked up dramatically once Robert E. Lee surrendered his Confederate forces in April 1865. The Union Army launched a sweeping demobilization effort to send most of its million-member force home. By the end of 1865, more than eight hundred thousand Northern soldiers had been mustered out. More than eleven hundred castaways and others from eighty-nine Pennsylvania regiments were part of that tally at Camp Discharge.

The pages that follow will delve into the camp's administrative challenges and sometimes-tangled interactions with the high command. Yet, the essence of the place resided not in its headquarters but in its barracks and hospital. The footsore veterans who were sequestered there are our primary focus. They were from volunteer regiments that had fought in the most famous battles of the war: Antietam, Gettysburg, Fredericksburg, the Wilderness, Chancellorsville, Cold Harbor, Petersburg, even Sherman's March to the Sea. They reflected the social mix of the Union Army. Nearly one-quarter of Union servicemen were foreign-born immigrants, primarily from Ireland and Germany. Many had been thrown into war as rural farmboys. Others were young city dwellers with occupations as varied as a weaver, boatman, puddler, painter, stonemason, and laborer. Though their religions, languages, and customs might differ, one thing that bound them together was the overwhelming experience of war and loss. These men had "seen the elephant," military slang for the shock of full-on combat. One soldier recalled being haunted long afterward by "the shrieks of the wounded and groans of the dying . . . the neighing of wounded horses, the roar of artillery, the rattle of musketry, the yells of deadly charges, and the shouts of victorious hosts." The 72nd Pennsylvania Infantry, which had thirty-one members pass through Camp Discharge, lost fifty men killed or wounded in thirty horrible seconds while defending against Pickett's Charge at Gettysburg. The 69th Pennsylvania Infantry, which had two dozen men at Camp Discharge, had endured a massive Confederate cannonade at Gettysburg that, as the regiment's chronicler wrote, left "guns shattered into splinters, horses disemboweled, their flesh and entrails scattered, men beheaded, limbs torn and bodies most horribly mangled into shapeless and unrecognizable masses of human flesh."

The Camp Discharge men had survived that roulette of combat. In time, once they were mustered out of the military, the more fortunate among them would manage to fold back into their waiting lives and become productive citizens. They were the ones who were physically well, or who embraced their service as noble and necessary, or who managed to keep the worst memories at arm's length. Others, though, grieved for their old selves and would face lifelong psychological struggles. Along with witnessing death, many had perpetrated it, causing what is today termed "moral injury." As one researcher has written, "abandoning the precepts of peace for the rigors of war—learning how to kill and maim—is psychologically demanding even for soldiers who emerge from battle victorious. Afflicted with guilt, sorrow, and purposelessness, Union soldiers considered homecoming a task as onerous and demanding as any military campaign." One soldier warned his wife of the "despondency which will creep over me at times." There was no professional help for the haunted ones. Post-traumatic stress disorder was still unknown. Its symptoms were grouped as "nervous disorders" but were left untreated.

Another huge issue was lost physical health. However young they still were, amputees and the infirm had good reason to worry that they would become burdens to their families. The rampant "camp sicknesses" of the war had debilitated even more men than shot and shell. Historian Brian Jordan notes that military statistics showed Union vets "were twice as likely as adult civilian males to suffer from consumption [tuberculosis] and rheumatism; nearly seven times as likely to develop heart disease; and some fifty-five times more likely to contract diarrheal diseases." It was often said that veterans "aged so early."

As you will learn in the pages ahead, some Camp Discharge men were so psychologically broken by their war experiences that they would go on to abandon their families and wander the land as roustabouts or vagrants. The Wild West became a draw, where some sought providence and peace of mind in its open spaces while others embraced violence as antisocial gunslingers. Many slid into battles with the bottle or narcotics and would waste away in coming years.

No group of veterans was more traumatized than former prisoners of war like Private Bachman. We have compiled a list of four hundred and ninety-two Camp Discharge men whom the Confederates had captured. While some were held for only a few days, most spent months of misery in Southern prison pens. Two-thirds of them—three hundred and thirty-one men—were imprisoned at Andersonville like Aaron Bachman. While fighting off death, they had seen countless emaciated comrades expire inside its gates or, later, on their precarious return journeys north.

Sergeant John Faller (Courtesy Dan Convery)

The 36th Pennsylvania Infantry had an astonishing seventy-one Andersonville survivors turn up at Camp Discharge. One of them was 23-year-old Sergeant John Faller, who would write of Andersonville, "Much has been said about the sufferings and horrors of the place but a great, great deal will remain unsaid. No tongue can explain, no pen can describe the terrible sufferings that were inflicted on our men." Many ex-POWs carried an added burden inside. Once back home, they knew they would have to bring shattering news to neighbors. Some of the boyhood friends they had marched off to war with had died abject deaths during captivity. The survivors knew they might well be the first ones to return home with that dread information.

CAMP DISCHARGE offers no shortage of compelling human stories. We will present them chronologically in chapters beginning with 1864. That was the year the camp was ordered and constructed and when the first soldiers arrived to be processed. We also weave in the germane events from the battlefront during 1864, when many future arrivals were still immersed in combat. Same with 1865, when the camp's population peaked, and events in the South crescendoed. With 1866 and beyond, we cover the camp's closing and the fates of the officers and enlisted men we have tracked. You also will learn what is at the site now and how the camp has been remembered, or not, over time, and what artifacts have been unearthed there. The book concludes with a regiment-by-regiment roster that identifies all the men at Camp Discharge, either because they were sent there to await muster out or were posted there as garrison guards. By our count, the garrison force totaled six hundred forty-four men from three regiments stationed at the camp in sequence. They would keep a loose guard over eleven hundred nineteen soldiers, the vast majority infantrymen, from eighty-nine regiments who straggled into the camp to be discharged.

Our work is based on information found in history archives, period newspapers, military files, regimental histories, war memoirs, census books, genealogy records, the writings of academic historians, and other sources. For our research, we visited the National Archives repositories in Washington, D.C., and Northeast Philadelphia, as well as the US Army Heritage and Education Center in Carlisle, Pa., the Pennsylvania State Archives in Harrisburg, the GAR Museum and Library in Philadelphia, the Montgomery County Historical Society in Norristown, Pa., the Delaware County Historical Society in Chester, Pa., and the Hagley Museum in Wilmington, Del.

We wish to acknowledge the generous assistance of Anthony Waskie, Bonnie Brice Dorwart, Don Ernsberger, Herb Kaufman, Ann Corson, George Lonsdorf, Rick Bates, James Mundy, Barry Singer, Ted

Goldsborough, Ken Brier, Jack Tomarchio, Alan Wood, Carole Adrienne Murphy, Bridget Guiles, Richard Fernley, Mike Palmer, Harry Eichman, Craig Williams, Richard Colin Ringwood, John Pickard, Christopher Waddell, Jason Wells, and, from the Philadelphia Country Club, Ted Barry, Michael McNulty, Daniel Biehl, and Robert Wiley.

We are forever grateful to our wise and patient partners, Harriet Katz and Jean Schaller.

Finally, our utmost gratitude goes to Jerry Francis. During his tenure as president of the Lower Merion Historical Society, he championed this project and provided the wherewithal to make our research journey possible.

Because our work is written for a general audience rather than academicians, we have not laden it with footnotes. Instead, a listing of the sources we consulted appears at the end.

The Lower Merion Historical Society has developed a special Camp Discharge section on its website, lowermerionhistory.org, that contains illustrations and a complete, searchable roster of the men associated with the camp. We are indebted to LMHS board member George Lonsdorf for his stellar work on the project. You are invited to check it out.

Faces of Camp Discharge

Private John Vanderslice of the 8th Pa. Cavalry won the Medal of Honor for bravery at Hatchers Run. He became a state leader of the Grand Army of the Republic.

Private Jesse Humer was a clerk prior to joining the 36th Pa. Infantry. He was one of that regiment's 71 Andersonville survivors at Camp Discharge. (Courtesy Ronn Palm's Museum of Civil War Images)

Private John J. Rhoades of the 186th Pa. Infantry was a camp guard and spent time at the camp hospital. (Courtesy Quentin Schuetz)

Sergeant James J. Foy of the 106th Pa. Infantry survived captivity but never recovered his full health. He died in a home for disabled soldiers in California. ("History of the One-Hundred and Sixth Regiment")

Private George A. Campbell of the 2nd Pa. Heavy Artillery survived five months in Southern prisons, including being shot during an escape attempt. At Camp Discharge, Campbell was hospitalized for scurvy. After the war, he became a Mennonite preacher. (Courtesy Tom Myers)

Private Nicholas E. Bloom was a 21-year-old shoemaker in Philadelphia when he joined the 3rd Pa. Cavalry early in the war. He would spend sixteen months in Southern prisons including Andersonville before being paroled at war's end. (Courtesy Ken Bloom)

Private Tobias Eshleman of the 118th Pa. Infantry was wounded and captured at the Battle of the Wilderness. He was sent to Andersonville prison, and would be one of 5 Andersonville survivors from the 118th to make it alive to Camp Discharge. (Courtesy Ronn Palm's Museum of Civil War Images)

Private Jonathan Keiser was a member of the 105th Pa. Infantry, known as the Wildcats, that saw heavy action in the battlefields of Virginia. According to regimental records, Keiser was wounded May 5, 1864 ("slightly in hand"), and June 3 ("severe in thigh") somewhere between the Wilderness and Petersburg. By September, he was at Camp Discharge. (Courtesy Ronn Palm's Museum of Civil War Images)

Corporal Arthur Paul was one of a dozen men of the 118th Pa. Infantry, known as the Corn Exchange Regiment, to transit Camp Discharge. ("History of One-Hundred Eighteenth Pa. Volunteers")

Corporal Charles Rubright of the 106th Pa. Infantry was captured at Petersburg and sent to Andersonville prison, where he spent many months. The painting above depicts him following his release. After Camp Discharge, Rubright (also seen below) went on to join the Veteran Reserve Corps. (Courtesy of Sharon E.)

Private John A. Whiteman (seated, center, with his family years after the war) was one of 22 Andersonville survivors from the 19th Pa. Cavalry who went through Camp Discharge in the spring and summer of 1865. He went on to become a Methodist Episcopal pastor in Fulton County, Pa. (Courtesy Marlene Whiteman Payne)

Private Darius Thomas (left) and Corporal John Koons also both survived Andersonville. Thomas was in the 19th Pa. Cavalry, Koons the 36th Pa. Infantry (7th Reserves). (Courtesy GPoppa, Sherry Keefer Bonham)

CHAPTER ONE

1864

On Break Neck Hill

ON June 1, 1864, just as the bloody battle of Cold Harbor was erupting in Virginia, the US War Department issued an urgent order to build a new Union Army base near Philadelphia. "Temporary barracks will be erected in the vicinity of Philadelphia sufficient for the accommodation of two thousand (2000) men," the quartermaster general's office was told. "You will cause them to be constructed with as little delay as possible . . . if possible, some distance from Philadelphia."

That summer of 1864 was shaping up as a pivotal time in America's Civil War. General Ulysses S. Grant was waging the grueling Overland Campaign to close in on the Confederate capital of Richmond. Farther south, General William Tecumseh Sherman set his sights on Atlanta. Ahead lay Petersburg, Nashville, Sherman's March to the Sea—another frightful year of combat. The new camp near Philadelphia was set up not to muster in and train reinforcements to *join* the hot war. It was there to reduce ranks—to muster a particular set of Union soldiers *out* of the service.

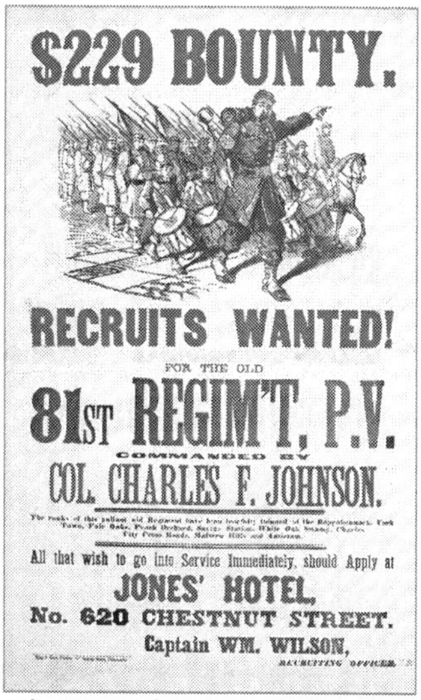

The 81st Infantry would have a dozen of its men sequestered at Camp Discharge. (Courtesy Library Company of Philadelphia)

Most of the troops in question were hard-luck cases from the military jurisdiction of Eastern Pennsylvania. They'd proudly volunteered for three-year enlistments back in the summer and fall of 1861, so their discharge dates were coming due. These men had committed themselves to serve and believed the government, which had federalized them under US Army command, had a reciprocal duty to release them from their contracts on time. Numerous three-year regiments were being mustered out of the service en masse around that time, but as fate would have it, the men of Camp Discharge were generally absent from those ceremonies. They had gotten waylaid from their regiments much earlier—because they'd been sent on detached duty elsewhere in the field or, worse, been captured and locked in a Southern prison, or been wounded in action and left behind to linger in a medical ward somewhere. By the time they straggled into Philadelphia, alone or in small groups, many were in failing health and in no shape for further action. As John Billings notes in *Hardtack and Coffee*, his classic of Civil War Army life, gravely wounded and ill soldiers were frequently desperate to return home before their final hours arrived, to be nursed by "the more loving hands of mother, wife, or sister." Other Camp Discharge men, wounded or not, actually opted to extend their time in the military as members of the Invalid Corps, later known as the Veteran Reserve Corps. The camp also handled a few dozen deserters who showed up seeking mercy and reassignment to qualify for honorable discharges and pay. Yet the vast majority of the Camp Discharge men were honorably serving "three-year men" who had been tossed off course by events and had had enough of war.

The quartermaster general's office in Philadelphia was aware of the time pressure and moved promptly. By June 13, its staff had already chosen a site for the new base. It was in rural Lower Merion along the Schuylkill River, on a property a bit more than a quarter-mile square. An inspection report described the site as "situated on the west bank of the Schuylkill River about nine miles above the City." Three of its 56 acres were located directly on the river flats, where they abutted the Reading Railroad line, a busy link to Philadelphia that would be central to the camp's operation. From that lowland, the property sloped steeply upward across 18 acres—a rocky, wooded incline that locals called Break Neck

Hill—before rounding off at the top. On the slope were a stone farmhouse, a barn, an uphill wagon path, and "numerous springs of pure, excellent water" that the site inspector believed could be pumped to any part of the property.

John McArthur Jr

A lease agreement was reached with the owner, farmer Joseph Kirkner. Once that was signed (granting Kirkner $41.66 rent per month for up to three years), quartermaster architect John McArthur Jr. and his staff produced schematic drawings. McArthur was a notable figure who would design the Schuylkill Arsenal and twenty-four temporary military hospitals, including the enormous Mower Hospital in Chestnut Hill. After the war, he achieved fame as the architect of Philadelphia's landmark City Hall. For Camp Discharge, McArthur punched out a straightforward design. He situated the bulk of the facility at the upper end of the property. There, a large parade ground would be surrounded by a quadrangle of imposing wooden structures. Ten two-story barracks buildings would wrap around three sides of the open parade ground. A line of officers' quarters and administrative and supply buildings would comprise the fourth side. Interspersed in McArthur's layout were two infirmary buildings, a guard house for detainees, storehouses, cookhouses, stables, and a scattering of latrines. From river to ridge top, the entire perimeter would be enclosed by a stockade fence twelve feet high and more than four thousand feet long. All the buildings and the fence would be painted an ocher yellow. Two swinging gates provided access to the premises, one of them down by the railroad tracks, the other one opening onto a local road at the camp's upper end.

Construction began over the summer. With a budget of $61,000, the quartermaster purchased a forest of lumber—almost three hundred thousand board feet—from two nearby lumber yards and hired crews of local craftsmen and laborers to begin leveling the upper ground and erecting the buildings. In this lightly populated corner of Lower Merion, two miles from the village of Merion Square (today's Gladwyne), the

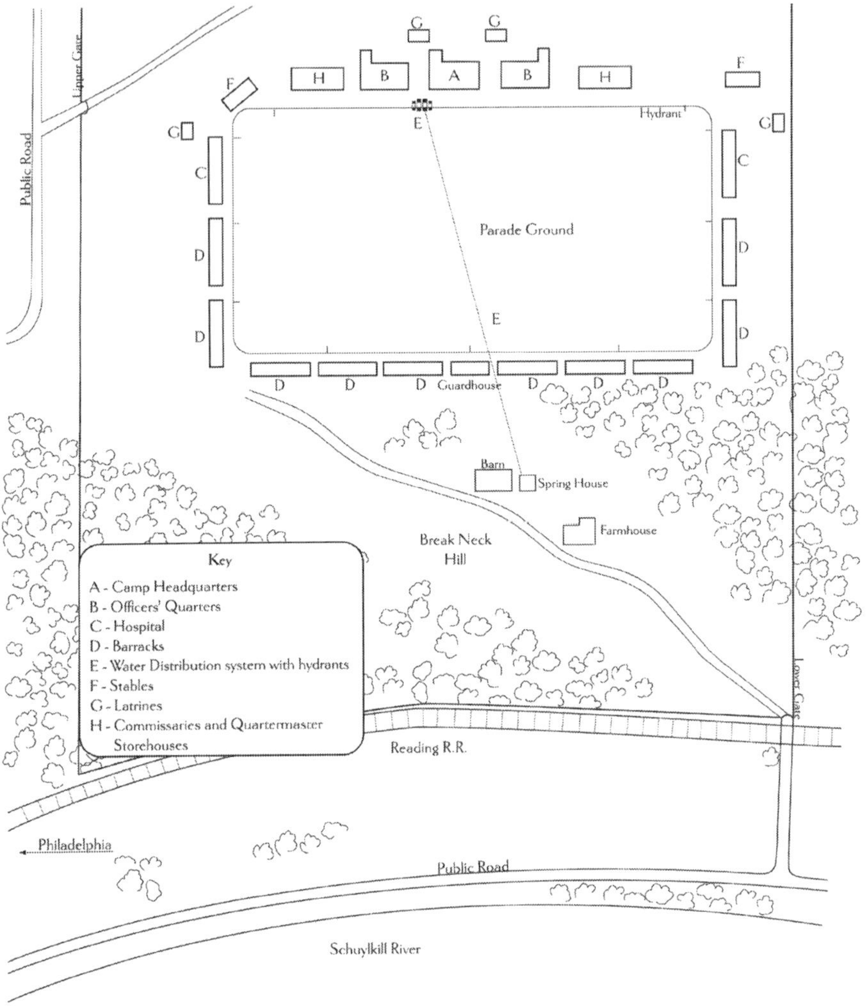

Image by Cassandra Brown

This modern drawing of the Camp Discharge layout follows the specifications laid out in Army architect John McArthur's initial site plan. The details have been enhanced for clarity. McArthur's original, faded sketch is in the holdings of the National Archives.

operation became a local curiosity. In mid-September, Plymouth Meeting doctor Hiram Corson noted in his diary that he was in the vicinity and "went to Kirkner's place below Spring Mill to see the new United States Barracks being built there. They are quite a show." A correspondent for the *Norristown Herald & Free Press* also visited the base and remarked, "The location of the barracks is high and airy, and certainly ought to secure freedom from infection."

The worry about infection helps explain why the camp was purposely placed in a remote locale miles away from the city. Contagion was a constant concern for soldiers and civilians alike. Philadelphians had been weathering outbreaks of deadly smallpox in those years—and smallpox was among the "camp diseases" that ill servicemen might bring back from the war front. In Harrisburg, where a similar rendezvous post was being located to discharge Pennsylvania soldiers, residents expressed anxiety. Camp Curtin was a well-used Union hub there, but many people wanted a new site created across the Susquehanna River to handle the incoming troops. As the *Harrisburg Telegraph* put it, "The condition of the ground at Camp Curtin is such, after being so long occupied, that the location of large bodies of men thereon, might tend to the engendering of disease—the spread, perhaps, of an epidemic which would prove fatal to the citizens of Harrisburg. A camp on fresh ground would escape such dangers." Having a camp be off the beaten path provided other benefits as well. It kept at bay "the whiskey and lager beer influence" of corner saloons, as well as the swindlers and prostitutes who hovered around established Army camps. Philadelphia's crowded Camp Cadwalader was one such place. The *Philadelphia Press* noted in 1865 that newly discharged soldiers, "upon reaching the outside of the Camp, are immediately beset by gangs of sharpers, ready to rob them whenever an opportunity offers." According to one veteran, Cadwalader was notorious for "filthy quarters, miserable diet, embezzlement of money belonging to soldiers, and utter disregard for the welfare and comfort of the men." One soldier who spent time at Camp Discharge called it "a heaven" compared to Cadwalader.

CAMP DISCHARGE'S HILLSIDE BARRACKS were not even completed before soldiers began arriving for processing. To get there, they had to undergo a set Army procedure. After reaching Philadelphia, typically by train or ship, the men reported to the office of the regional Chief Mustering Officer, Major Charles Champion Gilbert, at 1114 Spruce Street. There, any orders they were carrying were inspected and retained. Each man was handed new orders to report to Camp Discharge, along with a pass to travel there via the Reading line. Gilbert's office staff then began the process of reconciling the soldier's paperwork—meaning contacting each one's regiment to obtain a full "descriptive list" of his time served; dates of any detached duty, capture, or injury; possible debts he owed for supplies; and back pay and bounty due him. Since many regiments were disbanding and others were still in the field of battle hundreds of miles away, this information-gathering could take weeks to complete.

Meanwhile, the three-year men got themselves to Camp Discharge to begin their enforced waiting periods. After traipsing uphill from the train stop, they reported to the brand-new headquarters building to be logged in and assigned to a barracks. If they were carrying weapons, the camp would store them for safekeeping. The fresh barracks featured coal stoves, kitchens, mess halls, whitewashed walls, sash windows, shingled roofs, and rows of wooden bunks—luxuries compared to the humble dog tents that had been the men's home for months. Many of the soldiers were there solo, unaccompanied by their officers or even sergeants, so the barracks had superintendents who could step in to help promote discipline and group cohesion.

The very first arrivals were entered into the ledger on Sept. 20, nearly a month before the camp would formally open. It was a batch of six men from six different regiments—an indication of the heterogeneous mix that would come in the following months. Sergeant Thomas Murphy was a sergeant in the 72nd Pennsylvania Infantry, part of the famed Philadelphia Brigade (see box, "First Up, a Hero"). Private A. B. Rosenberger of the Second Pa. Cavalry had been a prisoner of war and missed his regiment's muster-out on Sept. 9; he would be discharged Sept. 27. Private John Zeiber of the 88th Pa. Infantry had been wounded at Antietam and separated from his comrades; gaps in his paperwork would keep him at Camp Discharge until Nov. 30. Private Samuel J. Hart of the 147th Pa. Infantry would remain at the camp until Dec. 22 even though his three years had been up Sept. 17. Private William A. Powers of the 95th Pa. Infantry would be discharged more or less on time on Sept. 28. Sergeant

FIRST UP, A HERO

As it happened, Camp Discharge's entry number one on Sept. 20 was especially notable—a war hero to many. Thomas Murphy, 25, was a sergeant in the 72nd Pennsylvania Infantry, part of the famed Philadelphia Brigade. He'd distinguished himself at the Battle of Gettysburg during Pickett's Charge on the climactic final day of July 3, 1863. As the remnants of the Confederate charge reached the Union stone wall and began close combat, Sergeant Murphy's 72nd Regiment moved up from its reserve position but balked at orders to enter the tumult. When one of the regiment's color bearers was hit and fell, Murphy grabbed the flag staff and charged forward. At that point, he, too, was hit by rifle fire. Accounts differ on whether Murphy reached the wall, but his bravery inspired his regiment to surge forward with a cheer and join a counter-thrust that turned the tide against the Confederates.

The 72nd Pennsylvania, also called the Fire Zouaves, had been officially mustered out as a body on Aug. 24, 1864, in Philadelphia. Murphy was not among them. Being the first of thirty-one Fire Zouaves to pass through Camp Discharge, Murphy would receive his muster-out papers on Sept. 23 and returned to live in Philadelphia.

Major Charles E. Fellows of the Eighth Pa. Cavalry also managed to be discharged with little delay on Sept. 22.

By Oct. 1, the ledger had steadily grown to one hundred fifty-two men, representing thirty-three infantry, seven cavalry, and three artillery regiments. Forty-four of the men bore battle wounds, and seven had been prisoners of war.

By mid-October, the adjutant general received assurance that the Reading Railroad would install a new siding at Camp Discharge's lower gate and add "about 10 House Cars, fitted up with Benches . . . as large bodies of men will be required to be moved at short notice." That month the War Department also assigned a full command staff to administer the camp. Colonel John Hancock of Norristown was appointed as commandant, the man in charge, with the added title of assistant adjutant general of volunteers for the Eastern Division of Volunteers. Hancock had angled for the commandant's position and assumed command on Oct. 20. Although only 33, he had distinguished himself in the Richmond

Campaign as a member of the 49th Pa. Infantry. He also had considerable pull—being the younger brother of one of the war's most illustrious generals, Winfield Scott Hancock. In a Sept. 13 letter, General Hancock recommended that the colonel command the new "Spring Mill Depot" (Camp Discharge). The War Department immediately consented.

Colonel Hancock's new staff hailed from far and wide. The post adjutant was Captain George W. Hooker of the 4th Vermont Infantry, who had won a Medal of Honor for valor at the Battle of South Mountain, Md., in 1862. The quartermaster was Captain Albert S. Ashmead of the 29th Pa. Infantry, with Captain Damon Y. Kilgore of the Wisconsin Volunteers as assistant quartermaster. The inspector general was Captain Henry Clay Pike of the 2nd Veteran Ohio Cavalry. In time the camp would get a small medical staff headed by Dr. Rush Van Dyke, a contract surgeon who had been a lieutenant colonel in the 26th Pa. Volunteers. He was assisted by another contract surgeon, Dr. Joseph K. Corson of Plymouth Meeting, a Medal of Honor winner for his rescue of a wounded soldier under fire at Bristoe Station, Va., in 1863, while with the 35th Pa. Infantry.

On Oct. 24, the command staff was buttressed by a detail of provost guards. Company H of the 187th Pa. Infantry reported from the Hestonville Barracks in present-day West Philadelphia and took up duty guarding the camp gates and policing the grounds. Colonel Hancock and his forces must have felt like jail wardens at times as they began to corral a disparate and sometimes disorderly conglomeration of men. The barracks rang with Gaelic, Yiddish, German, Cockney, and other tongues. High-born Protestants brushed up against foreign-born Catholics and Eastern Orthodox. The pious ones preached prayer and temperance while carousers cussed and stalked about for a drink. The upcoming November election was firing up Lincoln loyalists arguing for Honest Abe and Democrats making noise for "Little Mac" McClellan.

Some men, the severely traumatized ones, likely lay low to nurse their psychological and perhaps physical wounds. Many had seen combat and mass death up close. It might have been at the Wilderness, "a blind and bloody hunt to the death, in bewildering thickets." At Mechanicsville, where Pennsylvania Reserves stood their ground against six hours

Colonel John Hancock (shown above left in 1896) took command of Camp Discharge after letting his famous brother, General Winfield Scott Hancock (right), know of his wishes. (Courtesy US Army Heritage and Education Center, Carlisle, Pa., Library of Congress, and Ancestry.com)

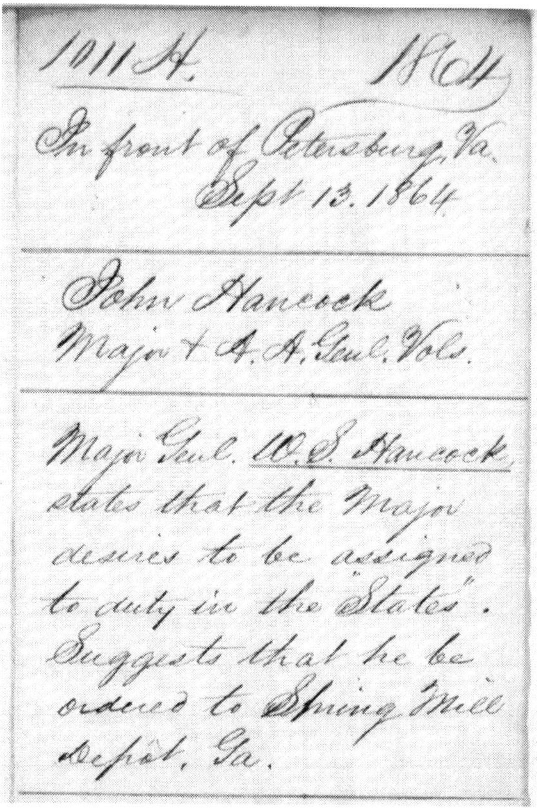

1011 H. 1864

In front of Petersburg, Va.
Sept 13. 1864

John Hancock
Major + A. A. Genl. Vols.

Major Genl. W. S. Hancock, states that the Major desires to be assigned to duty in the "States". Suggests that he be ordered to Spring Mill Depot, Ga.

of relentless Rebel attacks. Or at Charles City Cross Road, a scene of "a sanguinary hand-to-hand bayonet conflict" that lasted from morning until dark. Scores of the Camp Discharge men had fought at Spotsylvania, where the attacks and counterattacks caused Union General Horace Porter to write, "Rank after rank was riddled by shot and shell and bayonet thrusts, and finally sank, a mass of torn and mutilated corpses. Trees over a foot and half in diameter were cut completely in two by the incessant musketry. . . . We had not only shot down an army, we had shot down a forest. . . . Even the darkness failed to stop the fierce contest, and the deadly strife did not cease till after midnight."

A man's loss could be agonizingly intimate. At Antietam, Sergeant John I. Faller of the 36th Pa. Infantry saw a shell burst take out five men in his company—including his brother. Faller managed to bury brother Leo on the spot and move on to a future that would include much more fighting and then months of captivity at Andersonville. The bunks at Camp Discharge must have afforded a quiet respite to vets like Faller as they learned to bear the weight of their worst memories. Others among them, though, became brawlers spoiling loudly for a fight—men whose combat flashbacks could set them off at any moment.

It was standard for discipline to be imposed on the ranks through a routine morning roll call and light duty, such as gathering firewood and water and clearing the grounds. That left the men plenty of downtime for writing letters, playing cards, telling yarns, and generally commiserating. Many no doubt brooded alone or caught up on sleep as the days ticked past. The humdrum bred irritability, making the place what was known as "a growler's paradise."

One welcome break in the monotony was the arrival of the daily train transporting a mustering officer from Major Gilbert's staff in Philadelphia. For the fortunate ones, that train brought liberation. The mustering officer was there to attend to the discharge of men whose paperwork had been successfully adjusted and completed. Each lucky soldier would be summoned and, in a brief ceremony, presented with an honorable discharge certificate, any bounty owed him, and his final pay in cash. By that point in 1864, a private's pay had risen to $16 per month, multiplied by the months he was owed. If a man still had his gear, his knapsack and canteen were his to keep, and he could buy his service musket for $6 or carbine for $8. The state would pay for his rail journey home, a welcome benefit for the more distant travelers. A common custom, at least for the able-bodied ones, was to head into the city first to celebrate a bit and perhaps buy a fresh homecoming outfit.

Unfortunately, Colonel Hancock learned, the roll call quickly revealed that dozens of men had been stealthily discharging themselves from the base for days at a time. The commandant's October monthly report to the adjutant general listed forty-nine men present and awaiting discharge, no men mustered out—and ninety-two men AWOL (away without leave). Most of them weren't deserting outright but just absenting themselves for an unauthorized fling on the town or perhaps a visit to their families since home might be only a few miles away. If they were ill, they might be turning to their families for homespun remedies. In reaction, the adjutant ordered a lockdown at the camp between 8 a.m. and 6 p.m. That would require everyone to sit tight during the day in case a mustering officer came with questions about particular cases. Men still could and did take off in the evening—the gentleman-officers by horse and wagon to dinner parties and ice-cream parlors, the enlisted men on foot to the taverns and nightlife in Spring Mill, Conshohocken, and Norristown—as long as they were present for the next morning's roll call or had a signed pass granting extended leave. When the provost guards starting detaining violators in the guardhouse, the AWOL count dropped. Best of all for the general morale, by the end of November, two hundred men had received their official discharges and exited the camp free and clear. Their departures would have been a kind of release valve that kept the others' hopes up and irritation down.

Hancock's early reports also flagged a second problem at the camp, a more serious one: thirty-four men sick and three dead in October including a typhoid victim, forty-six men sick in November, and no medical staff yet in place.

THAT CHANGED IN MID-NOVEMBER when Dr. Rush Van Dyke reported for duty as camp surgeon (that period's term for a physician), and Dr. Joseph K. Corson followed as his assistant. They would soon have the aid of a trained hospital steward, Samuel F. Poorman, a veteran of the 8th Ohio Infantry. In his memoir years later, Dr. Corson called Dr. Van Dyke "an elderly man" who "contented himself with signing the morning report each day and I did the work. There was a collection of broken down men who required a great deal of work for a doctor but I was young and strong and did not mind it." In his own diary, Dr. Corson's physician father Hiram called Dr. Van Dyke "good for nothing"—though that may have been unduly harsh. Rush Van Dyke was a seriously ill man at the time. As an officer in the 26th Pa. Infantry, he had contracted "acute dysentery" in Maryland in late 1861. His pension file at the National Archives includes an affidavit from his brother-in-law attesting that "malarial trouble with his bowels" caused by bad water afflicted Dr. Van Dyke regularly at Camp Discharge and would lead to his death in 1882. "Many times he would curse the War," said the family maid, Mary.

Under Dr. Van Dyke's intermittent guidance, young Dr. Corson and Poorman soldiered on in the camp's hospital, which consisted of two matching infirmary buildings, each holding thirty inpatient beds. A special ambulance wagon had been assigned to the camp and could be deployed to ferry the more disabled men up the hill from the train stop. The hospital's Register of the Sick and Wounded reveals a formidable caseload from its very first page on Nov. 13: Four officers sick, eighty-eight enlisted men sick, fifteen men wounded, eighteen transferred from other hospitals, ninety "taken on here." The average number on the daily sick report would be thirty. Van Dyke would triage his patients to a hospital bed or, just as often, send them back to their quarters as outpatients with daily dosages and instructions in hand. Most of the infirm would do anything to be outpatients since hospitals were considered pestilent places where one went to die. The Camp Discharge hospital

Dr. Joseph K. Corson (Courtesy Historical Society of Montgomery County, Pa.)

benefited from late-war improvements such as high ceilings for ventilation, sitting porches, and bathrooms with cast iron bathtubs and wash sinks—yet men still had good reason to avoid the premises. Between Nov. 13 and the following Aug. 29, the register would list a litany of infectious diseases there: four cases of smallpox (recorded as variola); nine cases of cowpox (vaccinia); four cases of typhoid; six cases of unspecified "miasmatic disease" (perhaps cholera); two cases of diphtheria; two cases of pneumonia; five cases of influenza; two cases of scrofula (neck tuberculosis); sixty-nine cases of ecthyma (a serious skin infection), and eighteen cases of scabies (another skin disease). There also were dozens of cases of diarrhea and catarrh (a head cold or bronchitis), either of which could spread easily.

On top of that, the cures could be as troubling as the diseases. The eight hundred and forty men handled at the Camp Discharge hospital were subject to medical treatments that might have been conventional for their time and place but can seem appalling today. According to Bonnie Brice Dorwart, M.D., of Bala Cynwyd, Pa., an expert on Civil War medicine, physicians of the era prescribed medicines containing gradations of mercury—a poison—for a variety of ills because they regarded mercury as a key "alterative" that changed the course of diseases. In addition, patients many times underwent treatments to excrete body fluids in an attempt to cleanse "noxious ingredients" from their blood. "Saliva treatment" and other such regimens targeted tears, sweat, and urine, Dr. Dorwart said. The camp's medical books also show periodic use of cupping, a procedure that would suction blood into a large blister in the false hope of purging noxious material.

The modern germ theory of disease, which holds that microbes cause infectious diseases, was circulating in Europe but had yet to take root in America. Most US doctors had been taught that the culprit was "mal air," poisonous fumes arising from decaying vegetation and swampy areas. The noxious air was termed miasma—and indeed, the Camp Discharge hospital ledger listed a substantial caseload of so-called miasmatic diseases.

Another Civil War medicine expert, Herb Kaufman of the Civil War Institute at Manor College in Langhorne, Pa., says doctors of the era often misunderstood basic human functions. For example, he notes, a soldier with nausea might be subjected to a "nutritive enema" of liquefied

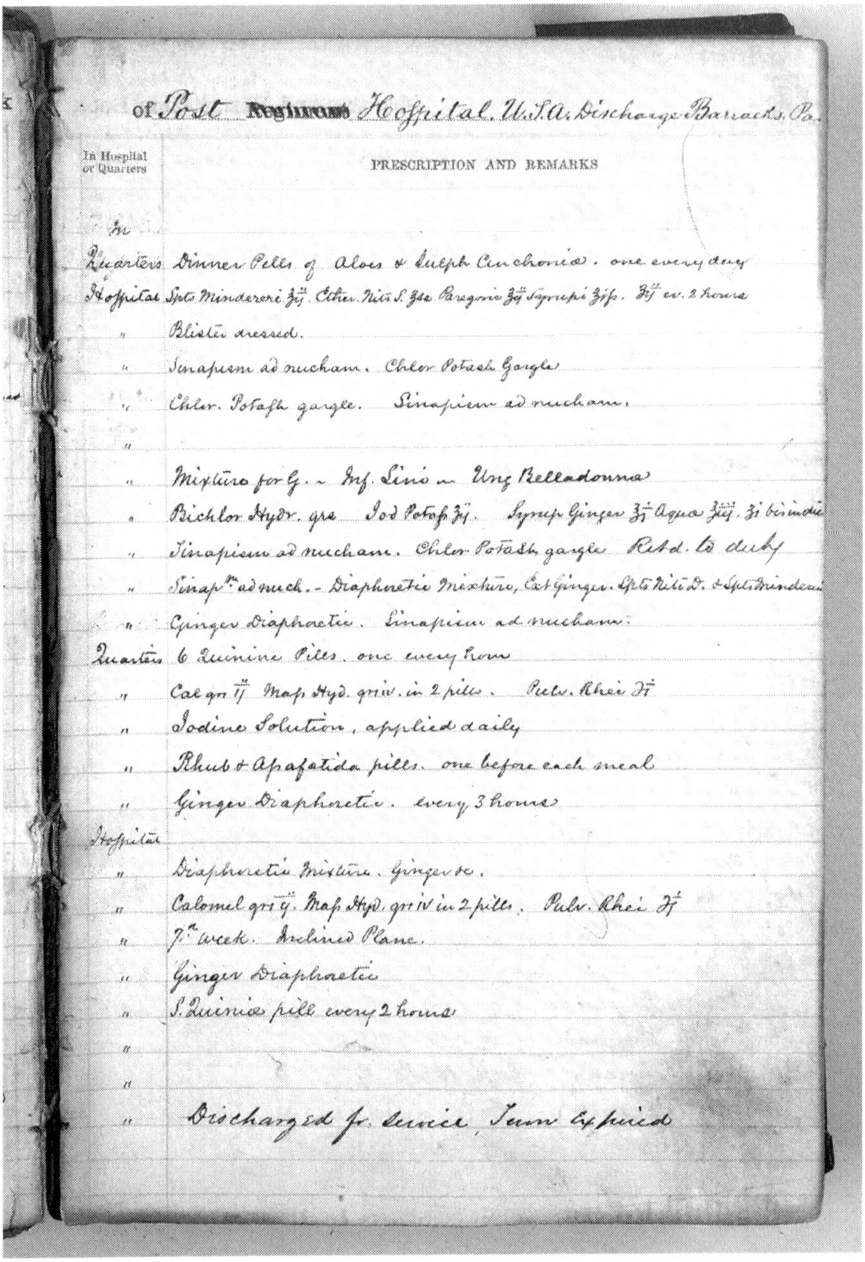

of Post Regiment Hospital. U.S.A. Discharge Barracks, Pa.

In Hospital or Quarters — PRESCRIPTION AND REMARKS

In
Quarters Dinner Pills of Aloes & Sulph Cinchonia. one every day
Hospital Spts Mindereri ℥ij. Ether. Nitr S. ℥ss Paregoric ℥ij Syrupi ℥iss. ℥ij ev. 2 hours
" Blister dressed.
" Sinapism ad nucham. Chlor Potash Gargle
" Chlor. Potash gargle. Sinapism ad nucham.
"
" Mixture for G. – Inf. Lini – Ung Belladonna
" Bichlor Hydr. grs Iod Potash ℥j. Syrup Ginger ℥i Aqua ℥iij. ℥i bis indie
" Sinapism ad nucham. Chlor Potash gargle Retd. to duty
" Sinap. ad nuch. – Diaphoretic Mixture, Ext Ginger. Spts Nitr D. & Spts Mindereri
" Ginger Diaphoretic. Sinapism ad nucham.
Quarters 6 Quinine Pills. one every hour
" Cal grs ij Mass Hyd. grs iv. in 2 pills. Pulv. Rhei ℈i
" Iodine Solution, applied daily
" Rhub & Assafœtida pills. one before each meal
" Ginger Diaphoretic. every 3 hours
Hospital
" Diaphoretic Mixture. Ginger &c.
" Calomel grs ij. Mass Hyd. grs iv in 2 pills. Pulv. Rhei ℈i
" 7th week. Inclined Plane.
" Ginger Diaphoretic
" S. Quinia pill every 2 hours
"
"
" Discharged fr. Service, Term Expired

The camp hospital's Prescription Book recorded patients receiving treatments with ingredients as benign as rhubarb and quinine and as toxic as the mercury-infused calomel (Courtesy NARA).

food in the misguided belief that his body could digest food inserted upwards toward his intestines.

After analyzing a segment of the Camp Discharge medical staff's Prescription Book, Mr. Kaufman explained the treatments it contained. He found the following: for catarrh (the common cold or bronchitis)—"a cough mixture of opium and wine or opium and another flavor like licorice"; for stomach ailments—calomel (liquid mercury chloride), which was also the major ingredient in a commonly used pill called "blue mass"; for debility ("a catchall word for any illness they didn't understand")—the potent astringent known as catechu; for diarrhea—calomel, catechu, and farina (a soft oatmeal); for boils—"Fowler's solution," whose base ingredient was arsenic; for syphilis—wet applications of an opium compound; for gonorrhea—"usually a treatment of silver nitrate solution inserted into the penis with a rubber syringe (hopefully but not necessarily under anesthesia)." Jarring as many of those "curatives" may seem, less drastic medicines such as castor oil (oil of ricini) and quinine also were being dispensed freely, if ineffectually, for a variety of conditions.

In a 2016 article titled "Medical and Surgical Care During the American Civil War, 1861–1865," Dr. Robert F. Reilly of Dallas had a blunt assessment:

> There were few useful medications at the time, and about two thirds of all drugs were botanicals. In 1860 Oliver Wendell Holmes stated at the annual meeting of the Massachusetts Medical Society, 'I firmly believe that if the whole materia medica, as now used, could be sunk to the bottom of the sea, it would be all the better for mankind,—and all the worse for the fishes.' Medications that were helpful included quinine for malaria, morphine, chloroform, and ether, as well as paregoric. Many others were harmful. Fowler's solution was used to treat fevers and contained arsenic. Calomel (mercurous chloride) was used for diarrhea. Mercury is excreted in high concentration in saliva. This led to excessive salivation, loss of teeth, and gangrene of the mouth and cheeks in some patients. There were several famous cases of calomel toxicity.

Toxic or not, calomel was in regular use at Camp Discharge because of the incidence of chronic diarrhea and, especially once released prisoners began arriving in force, of bloody dysentery. Looseness of the bowels, however ignoble, was a common Civil War camp disease that killed more than fifty-seven thousand men on the Union side alone. Curiously, the camp's medical records show the opposite ill, constipation, also occurring with frequency. That might have been due to an overuse of astringents to stop diarrhea. Opiate treatment for pain might have accounted for some of the cases. Dr. Dorwart makes the added point that a Civil War soldier's diet—heavy on beans and biscuits, short on greens, fiber, and water—was guaranteed to promote constipation.

Another inglorious affliction that appeared with regularity at the camp was venereal disease. That was evident on the very first page of the hospital registry on Nov. 23. Fifteen soldiers, nearly all camp guards, were admitted as inpatients for diagnoses including jaundice, lumbago, skin infections, fever, and coughs. But among them were one camp guard

"SERIOUS MENTAL DERANGEMENT

One of the most heart-rending medical cases at Camp Discharge was a young infantry private named Collum Duffy. In October 1861, Duffy left his home in Wilmington for West Chester to sign up for the 97th Pa. Infantry and join the fight. He was only 16 and stood a mere 5-foot-3.

In August 1864, Duffy was taken prisoner during action at Deep Bottom, Va. His captors shipped him to the Belle Island prison in Richmond, where a painful staph infection attacked both of his eyes. A health ordeal began that would end up consuming his life. In late September, he was paroled by the Rebels and made his way with help to the Union hospital in Camp Parole, Md. By late November, he was at Camp Discharge and admitted to the camp hospital, blind in one eye and barely seeing out of the other. The diagnosis of the right eye was staphyloma, in which interior tissue protrudes out of a damaged spot of the eyeball. His left eye suffered from amaurosis, a form of blindness caused by damage to the optic nerve. The camp doctor, Dr. Rush Van Dyke, persuaded the commandant, Col. John Hancock, to make a special request to ship their young patient to an eye infirmary to save his eyesight. Hancock wrote to the adjutant general that Duffy "has entirely lost the sight of one eye, and has symptoms of rapidly approaching blindness in the other," adding that "it would be but an act of justice to forward his papers with syphilis and a second with gonorrhea. The guards' unit, the 187th Pa. Infantry, had transferred from Philadelphia, where they would have had ready access to prostitutes.

In coming months the hospital would receive a stream of venereal disease victims, peaking with thirty-one treated in May 1865. However stigmatized those men might have found themselves, they were hardly alone. More than one hundred thousand Union soldiers contracted gonorrhea during the war, and more than seventy-three thousand got the more deadly syphilis. The prevailing treatment for syphilis was mercury—salts of mercury, in this case—which gave rise to the bitter maxim, "A night with Venus, a lifetime with Mercury." In addition to handling the pain of sexually transmitted diseases, with their rashes and boils and discharges, and the harshness of the treatments, the camp's V.D. patients were probably gripped with anxiety about having to soon admit to their loved ones they had indulged in what was then called "vicious habits."

with the least practicable delay." A few days later, on Dec. 2, Duffy was discharged from the service and headed home to Wilmington.

Duffy immediately applied to the government for an invalid pension and was approved. It began at $6 per month and rose to $10 by 1884. Over the years, he was able to find some work as a laborer, although his health would deteriorate. According to an 1877 pension examination, Duffy's eye pain was constant, and he had become "paralyzed in consequence of hardships while in prison" during the war.

By 1890, his mental health had failed as well. An examiner found "serious mental derangement requiring aid and attendance." In September 1890, the *Wilmington Evening Journal* reported that "Collum Duffy was arrested yesterday while wandering about Pleasant Hill and Jackson Streets. He is insane and will probably be sent to the Delaware Hospital for the Insane."

Two years later, a pension examiner tried to visit Duffy and was shocked. "I found him too violent to approach, and all the information I could gain was from the neighbors. He seems tractable and controllable by his mother, but vicious to all others. He attempted to assault me and had I not taken the precaution to take another party with me, would probably have accomplished it." Afterward, a guardian was appointed to handle Duffy's affairs.

Eventually, Collum Duffy was committed to the state mental hospital. That is where he died on Aug. 14, 1909. He was 69.

Thomas B. McCord (left) and Franklin Finnecy were privates in the camp's first provost guards, Company H of the 187th Pa. Infantry. While at the camp, both contracted vaccinia (cowpox) and were treated for skin infections. McCord, who had enlisted at age 14 as a musician, also found himself in the camp hospital for long periods due to syphilis and "general debility." (History of the 187th Regiment)

Dread diseases continued to appear. In early December, a guard from the 187th Pa. Infantry and a man from the 99th were admitted to the hospital with signs of typhoid fever. Two other guards from the 187th came down with smallpox. (The first, on Dec. 9, was Private George Nichols, a 21-year-old private from Susquehanna County. He pulled through, but his skin was left "fearfully pitted and his face marred," according to pension records. Two weeks later, Pvt. Jeremiah Flegle fell ill and began a two-month stay in the camp hospital. He became a farmer in Somerset County, though a comrade attested that the smallpox greatly impaired Flegle's eyesight.) Then, nine guards contracted the cowpox virus right after Christmas and began extended stays in the camp hospital.

Military camps could be breeding grounds for contagions spread by what Dr. Dorwart terms "the four Fs"—flies, fingers, feces, and food. By late 1864, the Army of the Potomac had taken steps to improve sanitation and hygiene through rules that would have extended to Camp Discharge. Among the reforms was that camps should burn or bury refuse daily. Drainage ditches had to be dug and maintained as a way to limit mud and pooling water. Latrine pits had to have a six-inch layer of dirt or lime added daily. Only designated cooks could prepare the meals. And all soldiers should bathe twice a week.

At Dr. Van Dyke's urging, Colonel Hancock asked to have a bathhouse built for the troops' general use. In a Nov. 27 letter to the Adjutant General's office in Washington, he requested "a sufficient number of tubs to afford them facility for a thorough bath each, twice a week in summer. Regular bathing is essential to health . . . the post surgeon remarks a great want of personal cleanliness on the part of those who are awaiting discharge, and is persuaded that the general health of that class of persons is suffering for bathing arrangements."

WAS THE BATHHOUSE EVER BUILT? The camp's final property inventory shows no sign of it. Several other buildings were being added, though, ones that didn't appear on the architect's original drawings. These included a carpentry shop, a blacksmith shop, an icehouse, a band room, and an engine house.

The engine house was needed to help fix an unexpected problem with the camp's water supply. By December, it was noticed that the hillside springs were yielding only half their expected volume, one theory for this being that water was evaporating because overhanging foliage had recently been cleared away. A proposal to dig a series of deep wells was rejected due to the rockiness of the terrain. Instead, water was pumped in from a nearby creek via a surface pipe running across a neighbor's property. For $100 per year, the neighbor, Thomas G. Rose, let the Army install a steam engine, pump, and piping to move the creek water five hundred yards overland to the camp's engine house. There, another steam engine pumped the water into four large holding tanks, from where it could be distributed to a series of hydrants for camp use.

The newly installed band room, for its part, was a pet project of the commandant's. He had it placed at the foot of another pet project,

The flagpole of the 1864 Great Central Sanitary Fair was moved to Camp Discharge. (Library of Congress, Music Division)

a spectacularly tall flagpole. Colonel Hancock arranged to have the 170-foot-high flagpole brought up from Philadelphia's Logan Circle, where it had graced the US Sanitary Commission fairgrounds the prior summer. It was erected next to the Camp Discharge parade grounds. A pair of bronze cannons known as Napoleons were emplaced at two corners of the parade grounds and used for reveille, taps, and special occasions.

The commandant had grand hopes for those parade grounds. One of his first requests was for extra horses and carts to speed up the grading and terracing of the uneven grounds. He hired ten musicians from Philadelphia, at $12 each per month, to be the camp band, and pushed the railroad to grant the musicians free passage. Such a band would be featured at Sunday dress parades to perform while ranks of soldiers—or at least the provost guards—would march smartly and stand for inspection. To draw audiences, Colonel Hancock even persuaded the Reading line to add a "Sunday visitation train" beginning in mid-November "for the convenience of soldiers and others visiting Camp Discharge." (Although he anticipated wide interest, the railroad would soon discontinue the Sunday runs for lack of ridership.)

Colonel Hancock also kept an eye out for the less showy, everyday needs of the enlisted men. In November, he pressed the adjutant general to have the barracks be better insulated against the cold. He complained

(Courtesy Dianne Stackhouse)

(Courtesy Frank E. Masland IV)

Among the soldiers arriving at Camp Discharge during its early phase in 1864 was Private Charles Masland of the 6th Pa. Cavalry (shown above, in uniform and then in later life). The 6th Cavalry was known as Rush's Lancers because of its use of 9-foot-long lances. Twenty of its men would pass through Camp Discharge. The 1864 arrivals also included (below, from left) Captain Bernard T. Janney and 2nd Lieutenant Thomas H. Berry, both officers of the 197th Pa. Infantry, and Private John Q. A. Nycum of the 186th Pa. Infantry. Nycum, whose Company G was posted as the camp guard for a time, spent his Christmastime in the Camp Discharge hospital due to ecthyma, a serious form of skin infection.

(Courtesy Companions of the Military Order of the Loyal Legion of the United States)

(Courtesy Gordon Brett Echols)

(Courtesy Clifton Simes)

to the Reading superintendent that bread shipments were being tossed so carelessly off the trains that they missed the siding and landed nearby, "entirely covered with coal dust." That month he also arranged to have a poll set up at the camp to allow soldiers sequestered there to vote in the Lincoln-McClellan presidential election. Only one vote was recorded, for Lincoln.

As the commandant saw to the outfitting of Camp Discharge during that period, it should be remembered that many of the men who would eventually arrive into his care were still embroiled in the ongoing war down south. On November 30, an entire company of German-speaking soldiers from the 75th Pennsylvania Infantry was cut off and captured during the Battle of Franklin in Tennessee. Twenty-two of them—including nineteen Andersonville survivors—would make it to the camp the following May and June.

Sherman's March to the Sea would be in full stride almost until Christmas of 1864. The boys in blue marauding across Georgia included one hundred and nine men from six different regiments bound for Camp Discharge. And in mid-December, the 19th Pennsylvania Cavalry successfully clashed with Rebel forces in the Battle of Nashville. Thirty-two of its horsemen would reach the Discharge barracks the following spring. Nine had been captured in the last stages of the fighting at Nashville and sent to Andersonville, where they were enduring a long winter of exposure and hardship.

BY THE END OF 1864, Colonel Hancock had taken up residence in the stone farmhouse on Break Neck Hill and seemed generally pleased with conditions inside the camp. He told the adjutant general's office in Washington as much in a letter dated Dec. 25: "I visited the Barracks and found them in fair condition taking into consideration the stormy weather experienced during the past week. The Arms, Accoutrements, Equipments, Clothing, and appearance of the troops are very good. Instruction also is very much improved. The Quarter Master and Commissary Departments are in good order. The stables and horses are well attended to. The hospital is in good order, and the sick well cared for. The Guard House contains but five prisoners. Discipline is strictly enforced."

Not everyone sounded cheery that holiday season, however. On Dec. 15, a letter of complaint—no, of outrage—was issued from the barracks by a horse soldier from the 6th Pa. Cavalry. Sergeant John J. Huntzinger, a 32-year-old from Reading, sent the letter to his congressman, Myer Strouse, with a plea that three-year men like himself whose terms of service had expired be released from their bureaucratic limbo at the camp. Though he'd been there for only a week when he wrote to Strouse, Huntzinger was including the complaints of others sequestered far longer.

The letter, laced with invective and misspellings, began,

> I have been urged by my friends to call your attention to facts concerning my case. I was mustered into the Service at Phila. Nov. 29, 1861, to serve for the period of 3 yrs. Consequently my term of enlistment expired Nov. 29, 1864. But for reasons unknown to me I am still retained in the service. My papers where examined in Washington prior to my leaving and pronounced correct. An order and Transportation where given me ordering me to report to Maj. Gilbert US Mustering office in Phila. & be mustered out. I did so. He also examined my papers & pronounced them correct ordering me to report to his clerk in another room where my papers were retained and Transportation furnished me to this Camp where I have been ever since awaiting my discharge. There are 60 of us here and many of them 2 3 4 5 & 6 months over their time. I feel confident the Dept. knows nothing of it. I have been in many Camps but this is without any exception the most miserably conducted camp I ever saw. The officers in charge are constantly drunk to drunk to attend to business. I have served faithfully my three years & 3 months & am now entitled to my discharge. I am anxious to go Home on Christmas. Will you please assist me to that and Bro. George & others desire me to add you feeling confident that what you could you would do. Maj. Nichols Paymaster USA. No. 27 Indiana Avenue knows all about my affairs has the Rolls and all that is due me. This is a money making machine. Seldom ever is

> a man discharged from here but 2 & often 4 mos. Pay taken off of him. It is outrageous. We are treated worse than Dogs once in here & you cannot get out 2 company of home. Cowards guard the camp. . . . It is so bad I can scarcely endure it. You have [no] idea of the amt. of Red Tape. I think one word from you to the President, Sec. of War or the adjutant General would settle all. I will be forever & forever indebted to you for anything you may do for me in the Premises. With my best wishes for your health happiness and prospect.

If Huntzinger figured that appealing directly to a congressman would prompt rapid attention from the brass, he was right. Within three days, his paperwork was finalized and he was mustered out of Camp Discharge in plenty of time to be home for Christmas. Also, the adjutant general's office in Philadelphia dispatched an aide-de-camp, Lieutenant George Ripley, to look into Huntzinger's barrage of grievances. Ripley worked through the holidays and quickly had his inspection report on the desk of Major John S. Schultz, Major Gilbert's newly installed successor as regional mustering officer in Philadelphia.

Ripley's report had a measured tone. While some of the three-year men had indeed been subject to "painful delays," he wrote, the commandant and his camp staff were not to blame because their duty was merely to watch over the men and record their presence. The report was accompanied by a chart analyzing the Philadelphia mustering office's handling of thirty-four soldiers awaiting discharge at Camp Discharge on Dec. 30. Six of the soldiers had been waiting since September, three since October, two since November, and eight since the first half of December, with the remainder arriving at the camp more recently. Enough cases were finalized that discharges moved along at the rate of five a day in December, Ripley reported.

The chart provides a window into the difficulties of resolving soldiers' paperwork, usually meaning their pay and clothing accounts. Consider the cases of two men on the chart, Corporal Ira Kennedy of the 2nd Pa. Cavalry and Private James Thompson of the 106th Pa. Infantry. Kennedy had reported to the mustering office in Philadelphia on Sept.

5, just as his three-year term of duty was ending. Three weeks later, the mustering office had written for and received Kennedy's Descriptive List from his cavalry commander. A second exchange of letters clarified that Kennedy had not been discharged in the field. Although that news came on Nov. 7, Kennedy would not be mustered out until Jan. 6, 1865, nearly two months later. Here the chart provides an important clarification—Kennedy had been AWOL from Camp Discharge from Oct. 28 until Dec. 17, "which accounts for the delay in his muster-out of service." James Thompson, meanwhile, had arrived at Camp Discharge on Nov. 10 from Camp Parole, Md. He had been captured by the Rebels the prior June but was fortunate to be released three days later, unlike dozens of his comrades who ended up in Andersonville. The mustering office wrote to Thompson's commanding officer seeking his Descriptive List on Nov. 30, got no reply for five weeks, wrote again, and finally received the required papers on Jan. 16. One day later, Thompson was mustered out.

"I am of the opinion," Ripley concluded, "that the painful delays to which these men have been subjected have induced them to exaggerate their grievances. I discovered no evidence of the bad conduct complained of on the part of the officers at the Camp as will appear from the report. I had no facilities to discovering frauds, had they been practiced in the discharging of enlisted men. . . . The Barracks were in good order, but from defects in construction afford insufficient protection in inclement weather. Men awaiting discharge are employed on light duty. In other respects they are subjected to the same requirements and discipline as the regular garrison of the Camp."

Ripley closed with a special note of compassion. "Although the incidental grievances of these soldiers have been exaggerated, it is evident from the foregoing facts that their position is one of uncommon hardship," he wrote. "The Records show that they are usually men who, from sickness and wounds, the effects of faithful service, have been separated from their commands, and they have failed to be mustered out with the organizations to which they belong. It would thus seem that they are entitled to peculiar consideration, and to the exertion on their behalf of every means to secure their speedy release from the service."

The report was forwarded to the adjutant general's office in Washington, which issued a statement brushing off Huntzinger's complaints. "It is thought that although there may be some incidental inconveniences to which these soldiers may be subjected that there are no real causes that could be avoided upon which the complaints of Sgt. Huntzinger are founded. But in view of the defective state of the Barracks at that camp it is respectfully recommended that the Quarter Master General be directed to cause them to be properly repaired so that they will afford comfortable quarters for such soldiers as may be detained there for muster out and other purposes."

Washington was silent on Ripley's call for compassionate care. As 1865 arrived and the pace of arrivals accelerated—especially of hundreds more ragtag prisoners of war—such "peculiar consideration" would be sorely needed.

CHAPTER TWO

1865

Boom and Bust

NO sooner did the new year 1865 arrive than a holiday gun accident caused a stir. The victim was Private Richard J. Gibbs of the 6th Pa. Cavalry. Gibbs had arrived at Camp Discharge in late October. Two months later, he was in Philadelphia with a friend for the public festivities on New Year's Eve. The two were at the Union Volunteer Refreshment Saloon, a popular USO-like establishment near the Delaware River wharf, and joined the crowds milling outside. Just before midnight, as the revelry reached a peak, Gibbs suddenly felt a shock in his right arm. From out of nowhere, a bullet had torn into his elbow and down to his wrist, where it lodged. The incident bore the hallmarks of a reckless holiday custom—making merry by firing guns overhead, the downward trajectory of the bullets be damned. The *Philadelphia Inquirer*, in an item two days later, noted that the 21-year-old Gibbs "has been in the service since the commencement of the Rebellion; was at South Mountain, Chancellorsville, Antietam, Gettysburg, Sheridan's raid, and wounded five times, and of all his wounds this is the most painful to him. There is always much danger in the practice of firing off the old year."

Back at Camp Discharge, the random shooting of a compatriot may have struck the men in the barracks, at least the superstitious ones, as a bad omen for their new year. Beyond that, the *Inquirer* item about young Gibbs serves as a reminder of the multiple battles that warriors like him had fought in and the injuries so many sustained in combat. In Virginia,

The Union Volunteer Refreshment Saloon was a hub of wartime activity. (Courtesy Library of Congress)

Gibbs had been thrown into heavy fighting the previous May at the Battle of Old Church. In one afternoon, he was shot through the throat and neck, through the left arm near the shoulder, and then through the right arm near the elbow.

Gibbs spent months recovering at various hospitals, including, finally, the one attached to Philadelphia's Refreshment Saloon. In that regard, he may have been an exception. Curiously, most of Camp Discharge's other war-wounded never went to the camp hospital. Overall, one hundred of the sequestered men had been shot or otherwise injured in action—but only thirty-seven of them sought treatment from the camp's medical staff. Why might that have been? For some, the injuries occurred during the early years of the war and had already healed or at least stabilized. Others who were still recovering had learned to treat themselves with poultices and other remedies. And, just as with the ill soldiers, many of the wounded men no doubt stayed away due to a deep fear of diseases lurking in the hospital wards.

The shot and battle-scarred men who did seek care from Dr. Van Dyke and his medical team would generally have their wounds dressed, soothing (but mercury-laden) poultices applied, and painkillers administered.

It was a common practice of the day to give wounded soldiers morphine to ease their pain. Rather than use a syringe, doctors might sprinkle morphine onto the wound. Amputees and others would be given "aqueous opium" or laudanum—a course of treatment that led many disabled veterans into addiction. The Camp Discharge hospital register lists six amputees admitted for the care of their stumps and skin flaps. One was Corporal Cyrus Baldwin, 32, who arrived at the camp in late January, the eldest of four brothers in Company H of the 58th Pa. Infantry. Doctors had amputated Baldwin's mangled leg right after the Battle of Cold Harbor the previous June. He would live until 1891 and was relatively lucky: his brother James died of combat wounds in October 1864 at age 20. The camp medical team also did what they could for amputees James Foley of the 61st Pa. Infantry (loss of right arm), Thomas Christie of the 69th Pa. Infantry (partial left arm gone), John Brady of the 71st Pa. Infantry (left leg amputated at the thigh), John Snyder of the 87th Pa. Infantry (right forearm gone), and William G. Large of the 90th Pa. Infantry (loss of right leg at the thigh). The camp register also lists dozens of cases of gunshot wounds, usually to the men's legs and arms but also to the fingers, toes, face, scalp, shoulder, hip, gut, and groin. In due time those men would be discharged back into civilian life.

The winter weather failed to hinder the camp staff's operations. Their report for January listed eighty-five men being discharged that month, with one hundred and two others in the process. Former prisoners of war were an ever-larger part of the mix. Forty-nine freed POWs showed up fresh at the camp gates in January, including twenty-eight Andersonville survivors. Many came in pairs or small clusters, suggesting they had managed to stay together in captivity and travel back north together.

A good example is the 3rd Pa. Cavalry, which had ten of its released POWs arrive in January, five of them out of Andersonville. The regiment's history book details the following misfortunes of those five Andersonville men. In summer 1863, as Lee's army retreated from Pennsylvania in defeat after Gettysburg, the 3rd Pa. Cavalry had kept up a pursuit into northern Virginia terrain "infested with irregular bands of guerillas." Parties of Union horsemen found themselves harassed, ambushed, shot, and sometimes captured. One scouting party that was captured included two of the Andersonville five, Privates John W. Artley and John S. Smith. They would endure confinement at Libby, Belle Island, and Andersonville prisons before reaching Camp Discharge. Three months later, near Warrenton, Va., another 3rd Cavalry party was ambushed as it returned to base, with every horseman "either shot or sabred mercilessly and then taken prisoner." Among those captives were Privates William Frost, Willis Brown, and James Johnston, who were sent to Richmond prisons and then Andersonville before being released back into Union hands. Private Artley had been a 19-year-old shoemaker when he enlisted in the 3rd Cavalry back in 1861. By the time he reached Camp Discharge, he was suffering from jaundice and was immediately admitted to the camp hospital. Artley would go on to write an account of his service for regimental history. After seven months of misery at Andersonville, he wrote, he was sent to Savannah in September 1864, then to Millen, Ga., and exchanged with five hundred other prisoners. On Nov. 17, Artley "wept tears of joy to see the dear old Flag at the masthead of our ship as we were brought down the Savannah River for exchange. My clothing at this time consisted of a worn-out pair of pants and an old blouse minus one shoulder and the greater part of a sleeve. Yet, with all our privation and suffering, I am proud to claim my share of service in the Third Pennsylvania Cavalry in an endeavor to reunite our country and put down slavery and secession."

THE 3RD PA. CAVALRY CONTINGENT also had two soldiers from another category in the mix at Camp Discharge—deserters. The ledgers show sixty-one men passing through the camp who had the black mark of desertion on their records. Information about most of them is sketchy. All we know about Privates John Briscoe and Thomas Hurdle of the 3rd Cavalry is that both had deserted and then returned, dates and circumstances unspecified. It is estimated that nearly two hundred thousand enlisted men overall deserted during the Civil War and that more than a third of them returned to the ranks, either voluntarily or because they'd been apprehended. Their reasons for bolting were varied. For some, it might have been fear or cowardice (known as "showing the white feather"). For others, it was to slip away and help their struggling families back home, at least temporarily, or to have their families nurse them if they were sick or wounded. For others, it might be a belief that the military had dishonored them—and effectively broken their enlistment contracts—by providing inadequate equipment or officers.

Deserters risked execution, although that was rarely carried out. More likely, an offender would be sentenced to time in the brig, hard labor, a fine, or perhaps branding with a letter "D" on his hip. In the field, a single officer could judge and punish a deserter in a brief regimental court-martial. In posts like Camp Discharge, "garrison courts martial" were convened with panels of three officers to judge cases. The Camp Discharge records list a dizzying variety of desertions and summary adjudications. Private John Elliott, for example, was an Irish-born shoemaker who joined the 31st Pa. Infantry in October 1861. Elliott deserted in July 1863, returned a year later, and was transferred to the 191st Pa. Infantry. On April 10, 1865, he reported to Camp Discharge, where a desertion charge was withdrawn May 24 with no explanation recorded. He was mustered out five days later. Private Thomas Caden deserted in July 1864, near the end of his three-year enlistment in the 96th Pa. Infantry. When he reported to Camp Discharge that October, he was immediately arrested and thrown into the brig. His desertion charge was withdrawn, but not until late February 1865, and he wasn't discharged from the camp until April 1, without explanation. Five privates in Co. D of the 197th Pa. Infantry took off in Philadelphia on July 28, 1864, and then showed up at Camp Discharge three months later. All were charged with desertion, although the charge was dropped for three of them—Stewart Smith, William Jordan, and James Albany—and replaced with "absence without proper authority." All five were mustered out by the end of the year, even the two who still stood charged, Charles Shaw and Robert Wharton.

Union authorities balanced the stick with a carrot by enticing deserters back with amnesty offers if they returned to their units within a certain time period. Doing so would restore the men's eligibility for honorable discharges, pay, and even government pensions. In March 1865, President Lincoln offered a full pardon to deserters who returned by May 10, 1865, served out their terms of service, and made up any lost time. At least one Camp Discharge man was among the many who accepted Lincoln's offer. Private John Cox of the 186th Pa. Infantry, the provost guard unit, had deserted in February 1865 but returned in April "under presidential proclamation." Cox was able to muster out with his company.

OPERATIONS CONTINUED at an even clip that February and March. The camp's monthly report for February lists eighty-eight men discharged and ninety-six others approved for muster out. The March totals were ninety-two discharged and seventy-five more approved. The AWOL and misbehavior problems had apparently lessened. The camp's inspector general, Captain Henry Clay Pike, reported on Feb. 3: "I visited the Guard several times through the day and found them very well instructed. I made the Rounds at 2 o'clock. Sentinels on the Alert and very Vigilant." Two weeks later, Captain D. P. Billington of the 186th Pa. Infantry, one of the provost guard units, made the rounds as officer of the day. He told the commandant he "found eight prisoners in the guard-house one was released by order from Head Quarters to report to Court-Martial at Philada. Visited the guard-house and sentinels on post several times during the day and night, made the rounds about 1 o'clock, and found the sentinels vigilant."

In early March, a contingent of the camp's guards was dispatched to Norristown to participate in the funeral of Corporal Joseph Cornog of the 51st Pa. Infantry, who'd been killed at Petersburg the prior June and whose remains were being belatedly returned to his hometown. According to the *Norristown Herald & Republican*, the men marched into Montgomery Cemetery with reversed arms and fired a salute over the 20-year-old's fresh grave. A month later, the paper reported, a Camp Discharge squad returned to the cemetery to serve as a funeral escort for Ethan Dooley of the 2nd US Cavalry, who had made it north from a Rebel prison but died suddenly at a hotel in Norristown.

The *Herald & Republican* also reported on another incident involving the camp, this one in mid-March. It seems a train was running late and going at high speed. Near Spring Mill, the engine's fire door flew open, and embers and sparks blew free. The car behind it, filled with clothing and other goods, became enveloped in flames. The newspaper remarked sardonically that "the soldiers at Camp Discharge and the people of the neighborhood were soon on the ground and with the generosity which generally characterized the American people in such affairs reaped a good harvest by rescuing clothes, dry-goods, etc., and running off with them. One gentleman triumphantly exclaimed that he had clothes enough to last him through the rebellion if it lasted forever."

LATE WINTER OF 1865 BROUGHT a historic turnaround by the two warring militaries that would end up straining the capacity of Camp Discharge. North-South prisoner exchanges, which had ended in rancor in 1863, were resumed in full force. Thousands of Yankee captives were released from Andersonville, Millen, Florence, and other Rebel prisons and made their way to distant exchange points. Carts and litters were rigged up to carry the infirm, but many others had to walk the entire way because the South had no mules or horses to spare. "Local hospitals and doctors' offices along the transfer route were filled to overflowing with sick prisoners, most of which would eventually die," author Edward F. Roberts writes in *Andersonville Journey: The Civil War's Greatest Tragedy*. "Many Southerners sincerely felt sorry for the ragged prisoners of war and tried to aid the cadaverous-looking men by bringing them food, water and medicines. Many small community cemeteries would become the final resting place of former Andersonville inmates."

One particularly crowded gathering point was Wilmington, N.C. In his book *Civil War Medicine*, Robert Denney wrote of one woman's shock at encountering prison survivors. "Those who could walk were walking skeletons, repulsive with the ugly running sores of 'prison pox,' a skin disease attributed to exposure, starvation diet, and rat bites. The stretcher cases suffered from worse ills, such as septic wounds." The men carried epidemic diseases, which spread into the civilian population. Two Northern "lady nurses" fell ill and succumbed there, as did a chaplain and several medics. The US Sanitary Commission staff provided urgent care to more than nine thousand men at Wilmington that winter and spring. Charles J. Stille, in his 1866 report on the commission's relief effort, described how the workers managed to steer surplus supplies from the Army. "Four thousand suits of woolen clothing were at once issued, and the sufferers were supplied with proper food during a period of nearly three weeks. Army rations were abundant, but it was, of course, necessary to provide men who were emerging from a state of starvation with a diet of quite a different kind, and nourishing broth and vegetable food, staple articles in the Commission's supply list, were, fortunately, just as their condition required."

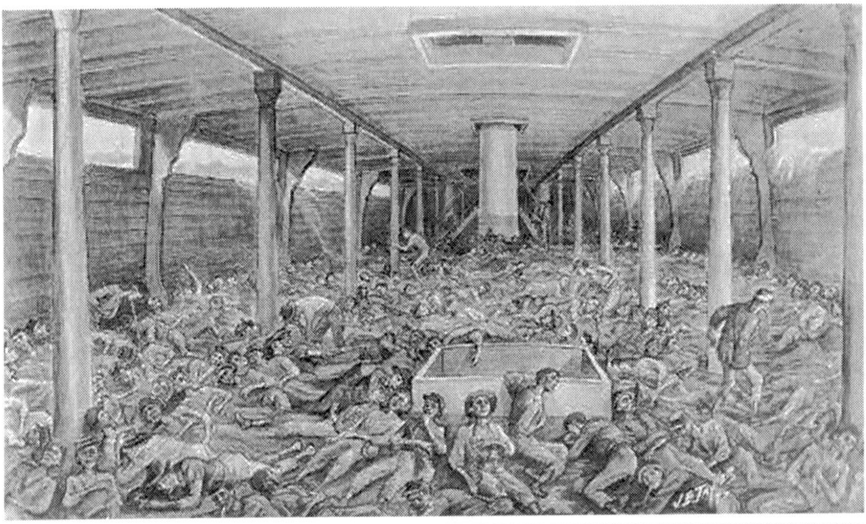

The 1897 watercolor above depicts Union soldiers newly released from Florence prison in South Carolina being transported north by ship in 1865. (Courtesy Library of Congress, Florence Military Prison Series)

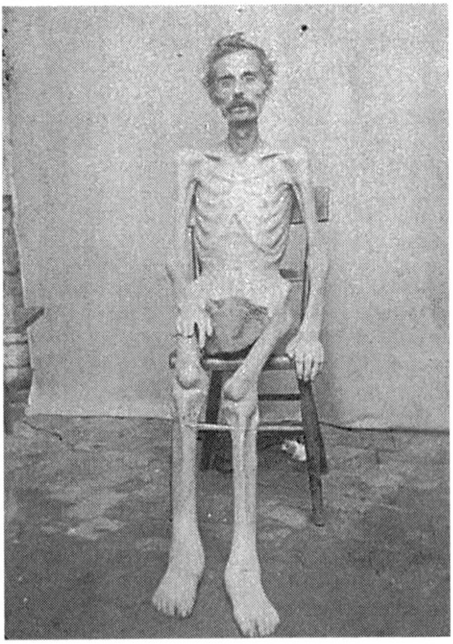

At right is Philip Hattle, who survived Andersonville only to die in a Maryland hospital on his return journey north. A German immigrant, Hattle was living with his family in Whitemarsh, Pa., when he enlisted in the 51st Pa. Infantry. He was 41 and left behind his wife and four children. (Courtesy Library of Congress)

Private Shadrach L. Hagenback of the 36th Pa. Infantry arrived safely in Wilmington after walking the final ten miles from Florence. He was "almost famished from hunger and weighed only seventy-five pounds with no shoes on his feet." Hagenback was one of fifty-nine men from the 36th regiment who'd been captured en masse at the Battle of the Wilderness, survived Andersonville, and in time would be mustered out at Camp Discharge.

For many of the released POWs, the next stop on the difficult journey north was Annapolis, Md., the site of Camp Parole and its large military hospital. Dozens of the Camp Discharge men had been transported there. One of them was Phoenixville native James A. Cornett, a corporal in the 5th Pa. Cavalry, known as the Cameron Dragoons. The Historical Society of Pennsylvania has a pair of wartime letters that Cornett wrote to his sister Jane from the field. One was sent in early June 1864 during the Petersburg Campaign, just prior to his capture. In it, he described how he was erecting breastworks and "our gunboats are throwing heavy shells in the direction of Petersburg . . . all hands are ready to repair to the ramparts at the sound of the bugle." Two weeks later, during the First Battle of Reams Station, Cornett fell into Confederate hands. He would spend half a year imprisoned in Andersonville and then Florence before being released in December.

His next letter home to Jane was dated Jan. 24, 1865, from "1st Ward, Section A, Camp Parole Hospital." Despite having swollen feet and a cough, he sounded encouraged:

> I coff very little, get as much to eat as i want two or three cups of oyster soop half oysters night and morning toast and butter every meal, mutton soop for dinner potato's and rump roast mutton. My appetite is pretty good i throw up no more and am getting rite by degrees the doctor prescribed three glasses ale per day, have a comfortable bed and large hot stove within four feet of the foot night and day. I cannot tell when i may leave here, they have sent to the Regiment for my descriptive list, i will try and get them to turn me over to Pa. . . .

Cornett was far sicker than he let on. During his time in captivity, he'd been pressed into duty as a nurse for the ill, and that hands-on work may have been his undoing. Upon arriving at Camp Discharge in late February, he was hospitalized with chronic diarrhea. A month later, he was mustered out of the service—and a month after that, on April 29, he died. Cornett's headstone at Great Valley Presbyterian Cemetery in Tredyffrin bears a plaque stating "he came home and died from disease contracted while a prisoner."

Two days before James Cornett wasted away, another POW tragedy occurred down on the Mississippi River, an epic one known as the Sultana Disaster. On April 27, a badly overloaded steamboat called the Sultana carried more than two thousand Union soldiers, most of them Andersonville survivors, north for mustering out when its boiler exploded, engulfing the vessel in flames. Eighteen hundred passengers died of injury, burns, or drowning. "Hundreds of men who had passed safely through many bloody battles and the horrible suffering of Southern prison life perished within but a few days' journey of home and friends," wrote one of the Sultana survivors, Private Michael Dougherty of the 13th Pa. Cavalry.

Dougherty had lost fifty pounds during twenty-three months in prison, primarily at Andersonville. By his own account, he was the sole survivor of the one hundred twenty-seven men from the 13th Cavalry who'd been captured together. After Sultana, Dougherty managed to continue north and arrived at Camp Discharge in late May. He was mustered out a month later and returned to his mother and sisters in Bristol, Pa. "I am more dead than alive after all my trials of suffering and hardships, with shattered constitution and crippled with rheumatism and scurvy," he would write in his diary afterward. "I placed myself under the care of Dr. E. J. Groom, and in less than one year he had me in a fair condition, and was able to go to work. I cannot stand much yet, for the disease contracted in those prisons is in my system, and will be, I suppose, as long as I live."

IN ADDITION TO THE SULTANA DISASTER, two other momentous events occurred that April: Lee's surrender and the Lincoln assassination. On April 9, Confederate General Robert E. Lee met with the

"GIVE THE TRAITORS TO THE ROPE"

The more the Northern public learned about the sufferings of Union POWs, the more the emotions boiled. On May 4, 1865, the *Norristown Herald & Republican* ran this poem, written under the pen name "Eudora."

Now let the Eagle of the Nation rise,
The Dove hath played her part too long.
With sweeping wings and piercing eyes,
Be firm, and vigilant, and strong.

For those who sought to pierce her breast,
Why should the judgment hour delay? . . .
Who soiled her pinion, robbed her nest,
And tore her cherished young away.

Now that the stormy clouds have fled,
Let her not stoop to pity guilt;
The Noblest of the land lies dead,
Why should not traitor blood be spilt?

From every soldier's bloody shroud,
From every desperate battle spot,
A voice goes up to Heaven aloud,
"For you we died—Forget us not!"

From every southern prison hell,
Whereon those fearful words are carved,
"For you midst traitor fiends we fell,
For you were beaten, cursed, and starved.

"For you a lingering death we died.
For you were shut from life and hope.
Now will you all our wrongs deride?
No! Give the traitors to the rope.

Union commander, General Ulysses S. Grant, at Appomattox Court House in Virginia and signed terms of surrender, effectively ending the war. The North exulted in victory. The adjutant general's office for the Department of Pennsylvania immediately issued a directive that "a Salute of Two hundreds (200) Guns will be fired at every Post and Arsenal in the Department." Thus did Camp Discharge's two brass cannons, the Napoleans, issue a volley that resounded over and over across the Schuylkill Valley. "We celebrated by a salute and much rejoicing at Camp Discharge," Joseph K. Corson, the young physician, noted in a diary entry. A 1905 article about the camp added that "most of the patriots got drunk" for the occasion.

Then, six days after Appomattox, the jubilant North was whipsawed by the shocking news that President Lincoln had been assassinated in Washington. Private Dougherty, the Sultana survivor, was still in the South when the word came. His war diary entry for April 20 read, "Just heard of the assassination of President Lincoln. Our boys are furious over the sad news, saying it is a Rebel plot." Across the North, anger mixed with grief. In Philadelphia, some soldiers, even newly discharged ones, agitated to return south on a campaign of revenge. Lincoln's body was taken by train to Philadelphia on April 22 and lay in state at Independence Hall before proceeding on its slow rail journey home to Illinois. The military escort that had the honor of accompanying the body back to the train in Philadelphia included the 187th Pa. Infantry. The same regiment comprised most of Camp Discharge's provost guards.

Although sporadic skirmishing would continue down south for several weeks, Lee's surrender prompted officials at the War Department in Washington to prepare for de-escalation. The winding down of the war brought calls to reduce expenses and shut down excess operations as soon as possible. Simultaneously, military officials faced a countervailing need to *expand* their capacity to demobilize the Union's vast force of

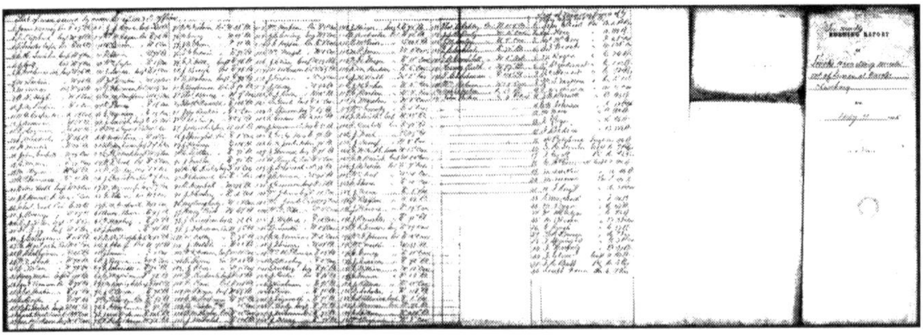

This roster sheet from May 1865 records the surge of new arrivals at Camp Discharge. (Courtesy NARA)

federalized state volunteers—and do it quickly, as the soldiers and their families were demanding. Camp Discharge was caught in that administrative dilemma. On April 10, the Quartermaster General's Office in Washington asked the Philadelphia quartermaster, Captain William McKim, whether the camp should be kept active or broken up. In reply May 3, McKim wrote that General George Cadwalader, commander of the Army's Department of Pennsylvania, notified him that he had been ordered to send extra guards to Camp Discharge,

> from which he concludes it is intended to use it as a rendezvous while the troops are being mustered out of service. If it is not the intention of the War Dept. to avail of it for that purpose, he can see no reason why it should not be abandoned and the property sold. Camp Discharge is inconveniently located, but if there are to be large numbers of troops sent here [to Philadelphia] to be mustered out, there are not sufficient quarters and it would be better to defer breaking up the camp if it is likely to be wanted for that purpose.

Thus, Camp Discharge's life was extended into the busy spring and early summer of 1865, which coincides with the peak of the Union's mass demobilization campaign. The camp's monthly reports show a clear intensification of mustering-out activity there. The tally for April was sixty-eight men discharged, fifty-six approved for discharge, and thirteen others waiting. In May, the numbers swelled to eighty-five men discharged, two hundred seventy-eight approved for muster-out, and one hundred sixty-one waiting. The numbers peaked in June, at two hundred fifty-two men discharged, fifty waiting—and twenty-seven AWOL. The largest single contingent was made up of freed prisoners, nearly all of them three-year men who'd enlisted back in 1861. But by this point, the rolls also contained three-year men from 1862 and some stray one-year men who'd only joined the Army late the prior summer. With the war over, these one-year regiments—the 198th, 199th, and 203rd Pa. Infantry and others—were being mustered out early, beneficiaries of the War

Department's postwar edict to move state volunteers out of the federal service as quickly as possible.

Hancock, the commandant, had been trying for some time to get a larger force of guards stationed at his post to handle the expected hustle-bustle. He even floated the idea of using Confederate deserters for that purpose. In a letter on April 1, Hancock asked the Adjutant General in Washington for permission "to recruit and organize 2 to 3 companies of Rebel Deserters, and others, without bounty, or under such restrictions as you may deem advisable, for garrison duty at this Post. . . . I may add that I have but one Company now performing here and that, in my opinion is entirely insufficient to protect the public property without referring to the necessary guard required around the camp." A month later, after that request went nowhere, Hancock asked to have four companies of the 187th Pa. Infantry transferred from Camp Cadwalader to be his garrison guards. That request was granted, and Companies C, H, G, and K trekked up from Philadelphia and reported for duty on May 13.

Their trip turned out to be a rough one. As the men marched along the west bank of the Schuylkill River, a downpour began that lasted most of the night. These hardened veterans had survived a murderous fire at Petersburg the prior year, but their night march was remembered as an ordeal. According to the regiment's 1906 history, "they had not done any marching for several months, and in addition to that they were loaded down with extra clothing, so before the march was half over, the men were pretty well fagged out. When the storm broke on them they were given orders to seek shelter wherever they could find it. Some found it in barns, some in a large covered bridge, while others plodded on to camp, arriving there covered with mud and wet to the skin."

THE NEW GARRISON GUARDS were put to work "digging down the hill in order to make a level parade ground." They joined a large force of men, both uniformed and civilian, who were already on that daily assignment. Hancock, it seems, was still fixated on his parade ground. He'd been trying to improve drainage and obtain cinders (from local iron furnaces) and sand to cover the parade ground to address winter and spring mud problems. He also was angling to have at least ten more carts and horses sent to the camp to hasten the grading and drainage work.

Hancock's fixation would put him at cross purposes with the higher command. On May 4, US Quartermaster General Montgomery Meigs ordered all of his field officers to pursue "the greatest possible reduction of expenditure consistent with the efficiency and comfort of the troops now about to be withdrawn from active operations in the field." The order called for a sunset provision for civilian employees, meaning they were to be let go if their jobs could be taken over by soldiers. The order would put Camp Discharge's quartermaster staff, especially Captain Damon Y. Kilgore, at odds with the proud and testy Hancock.

Damon Y. Kilgore, who drew Hancock's wrath. (Courtesy J. T. Kilgore, Jr.)

The Kilgore-Hancock drama is recorded, blow by blow, in a protracted exchange of letters held at the National Archives. Pitting two top officers and involving the fate of the camp's workforce, it must have been the talk of the camp. A seemingly minor matter kicked it off. On May 4, a soldier on duty for the quartermaster failed to carry out Hancock's direct order to remove a pile of wood and scantling from the parade ground. Even though Kilgore had been absent that day, the post headquarters sent him a letter on May 9 saying Hancock wanted an explanation for the soldier's "neglect." Kilgore offered a curt reply. He didn't know what had happened that day, he wrote, but "I shall be pleased to have executed all proper orders issued by you when cognizant of the same."

That same day, Kilgore received a note from the unlucky soldier involved, Corporal Thomas C. Kirkwood of the 186th Pa. Infantry. Kirkwood wrote that Hancock had called him in and "threatened to have me punished by Court Marshal [*sic*] if I refused or neglected to obey his orders in the future. As I wish to do my duty I want to know whom I shall obey in the future." Kilgore immediately wrote back to say that "while you remain in your present capacity and so long as I remain in charge of the Quartermaster Department at this post, or in other words while we sustain our present official relation to each other it is your duty to obey my orders. No other officer has any right to give you orders except through the proper channel." Kilgore also shot off a letter to Hancock saying he wanted "all orders given to men detailed for duty in the Quartermaster Department at this Post be hereafter given through me."

That was a brazen statement. The chain of command placed Kilgore beneath Hancock, so he was risking a charge of insubordination, but his dander was up. Deploying Meigs's sunset provision, Kilgore dismissed one of Hancock's preferred civilian employees, Patrick O'Reilly, the camp's foreman of laborers.

The combustible Hancock had enough. On May 11, the commandant issued Special Order No. 75, declaring that Kilgore:

> Is hereby forbidden to interfere in any of the plans or in any way with the employees engaged in the work of drainage and grading within the Camp without consulting the Col. Commdg. All orders he may deem necessary to be issued to them for the purpose of correctly keeping the accounts relative to the disbursements for labor etc. will first be submitted to the Col. Commdg. All instructions relative to carrying out the work will be given by the Col. Commdg. P. O'Reilly who is in charge of the work will be taken up on the rolls from the day he was dropped.

On May 11, Kilgore wrote directly to Meigs in Washington to protest "the many acts of improper interference" including Hancock's order to reinstate the foreman. Kilgore asked for an appeal of the order, saying he'd dismissed O'Reilly both because he was absent from the job for most of April and because the grading work could proceed adequately without him. Hancock issued a snorting reply: "P. O'Reilly is an expert at this business and is here at the request of the Col. Commanding to Superintend and carry on the work economically and properly. He under the circumstances is the judge of the times his services are required in the Camp. When he was employed it was so understood."

On May 13, the same day the waterlogged guards from the 187th arrived at camp, Hancock placed Kilgore under arrest. Kilgore promptly "broke his arrest," the details of which are not recorded.

On May 16, Hancock formally asked that Kilgore "may be at once relieved from duty at this post." As his letter to the adjutant general's office stated, "I base this request upon the insubordinate and refractory conduct of Capt Kilgore—upon his efforts to promote a mutinous spirit in my command—upon his repeated disobedience of orders—upon his scandalous conduct in promoting and encouraging profanity in his own son [Arthur Kilgore, 12, a messenger at the camp] to the great scandal of the command—upon his breaking his arrest—all of which will be the subject of charges and forwarded to Maj. Genl. Comdng Depmt at once."

The adjutant general denied the request, telling Hancock that "the services of Capt. Kilgore will be required at Camp Discharge, Phila., as troops will be mustered out at that Rendezvous."

Two tense weeks later, higher authorities stepped in. On May 27, the adjutant general in Philadelphia notified the Secretary of War that the quartermaster general's office in Washington wanted Hancock "to be directed to have the grading and drainage at that post done by troops." Finally, on May 31, Hancock received a clear order from the adjutant general's office in Washington. "The Secretary of War directs that you cause all labor connected with the grading and drainage of Camp Discharge to be performed by troops—the Quartermaster General US Army having reported that he ordered the discharge of all employees of his Department whose services are no longer required, and cessation of all expenditures for grading."

Hancock complied, but not without taking a potshot the same day in the form of Special Order 95. It stated: "Capt. D. Y. Kilgore A.G.M. Vols has with persistent contumacy refused to transfer the rolls of the laborers employed with grading &ct this Post to Capt. H. Clay Pike 2nd Ohio notwithstanding repeated orders to him commanding him to do so." Hancock ordered Pike to bypass Kilgore and get the information directly from the foreman so the laborers could get their final pay.

At some point in June, Hancock convened a garrison court-martial of Kilgore. Dr. Hiram Corson noted in his diary that his son Joseph, the camp doctor, had attended the proceeding. "It seems to be an attempt on the part of Col. Hancock, who commands the camp, to rid himself of Kilgore who is a very thorough officer and honest man," the senior Corson wrote. No court-martial record and its outcome could be found, but camp records note that Kilgore was ordered to report to General Cadwalader afterward. Kilgore must have pleaded his case effectively because a special order was issued July 7th, freeing him from arrest and "restoring him to duty."

That order returned Kilgore to the camp headquarters—an outcome that proved unbearable to the two combatants. Both began pleading to have Kilgore reassigned. On July 17th, a missive from General Cadwalader's Department of Pennsylvania urged the adjutant general to do just that. "The relations existing between Lieut. Col. Hancock and Capt. Kilgore are of such a nature," the letter stated, "that the interests of the service would be benefitted by relieving this officer."

On July 22, Kilgore was relieved of duty at Camp Discharge. With that, the rancor was brought to a ragged ending.

WHILE THE HANCOCK-KILGORE FIREWORKS were going off, much else of significance had been happening at Camp Discharge. Throughout April and May, the Philadelphia newspapers reported the arrivals of thousands of wounded and sick soldiers into the city, by rail and ship, from both the battlefront and the prison camps. The Reading train had been running hundreds of them out to Camp Discharge. The numbers notably surged in mid-May. Twenty-three men arrived on May 20th, four on May 21st, and then forty, twenty-seven, twenty-nine, twenty-seven, and twenty-five on the succeeding five days. Many came in cohort groups. Five were from the 28th Pa. Infantry captured in combat in North Carolina and released two months later near Savannah. Ten arriving comrades of the 19th Pa. Cavalry had it harder, captured in Nashville the prior winter and sent right to Andersonville. Fourteen men of the 106th Pa. Infantry, also all Andersonville survivors, showed up together at the camp. They were among sixteen hundred Yankees

The 36th Pa. Infantry (7th Reserves) had sixty-six men pass through Camp Discharge – fully fifty-nine of whom were Andersonville survivors. Fourteen of the men were from its Co. H, pictured above early in the war. Below are three individuals of the 36th who got to Camp Discharge in 1865. From left, they are Private George W. Palmer of Co. H and Private John A. Hunter and Corporal George Garman, both of Co. K. All three men enlisted in 1861, were captured at the Battle of the Wilderness, and went to Andersonville. (Courtesy Library of Congress)

(Courtesy Ronn Palm's Museum of Civil War Images)

(Courtesy Carol Sneddon)

(Courtesy Joe Wilson)

captured the prior June 22 when Rebel forces outflanked their brigade at Petersburg.

At least eighty-four of the arriving POWs, including sixty Andersonville survivors, had been kept in Confederate hands for weeks *after* Lee's April 9th capitulation. Finally, the Confederates let fifty-six of them go as part of a large prisoner release on April 28-29. Seventeen others who were bound for Camp Discharge were not freed by the Rebels until May. According to camp records, the last of them was a 22-year-old private named John Keltner of the 11th Pa. Cavalry, who had endured more than six months at Andersonville. The Rebels didn't set him free until May 9, a full month after the Appomattox surrender. Keltner would spend two weeks at Camp Discharge before heading home to his farm in Franklin County.

The camp hospital hit its peak during this period. The population of inpatients and outpatients surged in May from its customary total of about a dozen men per day. The daily figure hit thirty-three on May 14, seventy-one on May 24, and a record eighty-seven on May 29. It would

TWO UNANSWERED QUESTIONS

In his official history of the 187th Pa. Infantry, published in 1905, author James M. Gibbs touches on two aspects of Camp Discharge that still beg for solid confirmation.

First was this statement: "The camp was a healthy one and the good people of the surrounding country were good and kind to the boys while there." What was Gibbs recalling? Another 1905 article by local historian S. Gordon Smyth also noted that "the camp was enlivened socially by the presence of the families of some of the officers, and by a continuous visiting of friends and others." We were unable to find elaboration. A check of period newspapers and the archival records of nearby churches turned up no evidence of friendly visits, prayer meetings with the sequestered soldiers, or the like, let alone "continuous visiting." A women's aid society existed in Norristown, but its aim was sending care packages down to the war front. Perhaps Camp Discharge's hired laborers shared food with the soldiers and were companionable. But if anything, the locals would have had reason to keep their distance for fear of disease.

Second, Gibbs wrote this: "A large number of men were sent there that had been confined in the various Rebel prisons for months. Some of them were in such a feeble condition that they could hardly walk, and a never fall beneath the forties through June 12, the last day aggregate figures were recorded.

With the end of the war, and the sudden hyperactivity at the camp, came unruliness. The AWOL problem resumed. Some men awaiting discharge went on benders and had to be rounded up. Troublemakers burgled the camp stables. Two guards were delivered to the commandant in May for court-martial for "high-way robbery." In late May, a pair of men being held in the guardhouse refused orders to work. In his report on that incident, Colonel Hancock complained that he'd detained the pair in the first place "to enable me to produce them when called on [by a mustering officer from Philadelphia]. I find the prevailing opinion among these men is that because their terms of service have expired they are not subject to any military rules or regulations and in consequence I am compelled to use severity. I have been instructed by the Secretary of War to use these men for guard duty when necessary but on account of their unreliability from my experience have not made use of them except on one or two occasions."

number of them never reached their homes. They died at the camp and were buried in the little cemetery just outside of the camp."

There is no physical or documentary evidence of a soldier cemetery or individual graves close to Camp Discharge. Nor is it clear how many men died there. The camp's monthly reports list five deaths, but only three can be confirmed. The December report stated that Private Richard W. Derr, Company H of the 187th Pa. Infantry, "died Nov. 30th at Post." In February, Private James H. Jeffers, Company F of the 188th Pa. Infantry, was admitted to the camp hospital on the 17th complaining of variola (smallpox). He died there nine days later, according to an adjutant general report.

Private Calvin Morrison, Company G of the 19th Pa. Cavalry, was admitted to the camp hospital on May 22, "very much prostrated with Chronic Diarrhea." He would remain there for weeks, getting heavy doses of calomel and oatmeal. When Col. Hancock asked for an update in late June, Dr. Van Dyke replied that Morrison "is now measurably better but is not cured and is not fit to be forwarded to his Regiment." Morrison grew worse and died July 8.

The disposition of the men's bodies is not known. In those days, death and burial records were not yet required.

Hancock was under orders to make do with less and less. He had lost his crew of paid employees working on the grounds. His headquarters staff of three officers and five enlisted men (recording clerks and others) were reduced by one officer in June. It was down to only himself, another officer, and one enlisted man in July. The medical team lost Dr. Corson in mid-May and the main hospital steward, Samuel Poorman, in July. The four companies of the 187th Pa. Infantry that had composed the camp's garrison force, three hundred and fifty-eight in number, departed for Harrisburg in mid-July to be mustered out. They were replaced July 19 by two companies of the 7th US Veteran Volunteers. According to camp records, the new garrison force totaled only one hundred and forty-two men, and many were absent or sick.

As the camp's capacity shrank in the disjointed final weeks, the staff kept at the task of logging in the new arrivals and working in tandem with the Philadelphia mustering office to speed the outflow. Teams of mustering officers shuttled up to the camp over and over with packets of discharge papers and final pay. Two hundred and fifty-two men were discharged in June and sixty-three more in July. New men arrived well into July, though the ledger entries for most of the final ones state that they were simply forwarded to another location: Camp Cadwalader.

Before doffing their uniforms, some of the discharged men likely went into Philadelphia to join the victory parade that the city held on June 10. It came on the heels of the huge "Grand Review" that had taken place over two days in Washington in late May. The Philadelphia parade proceeded from Camp Cadwalader to the Refreshment Saloon at the wharf. As the *Philadelphia Inquirer* reported, General George Gordon Meade and his staff were at the head, followed by detachments of cavalry and artillery. Next came infantry regiments, "each regiment followed by the wounded and disabled sailors and soldiers in carriages," then "discharged men, on foot, who may be disposed to join."

FINALLY, ON JULY 19, came the inevitable order from the Adjutant General's office in Washington. Special Order 381 directed that Camp Discharge "be broken up immediately and turned over to the Quarter-master's Department for auction, under Paragraph 2, General Orders 113.

General Staff Officers on duty at the Camp are directed to repair to their places of residence and report thence by letter to the Adjutant General." With that, Hancock departed with his wife and children from the old stone house they'd inhabited on Break Neck Hill and awaited his next assignment. The 7th US Veteran Volunteer contingent remained on duty as garrison guards and Capt. James Dunne, who led its Company B, received official command of the premises for the duration.

Corporal Frank B. Hastings was one of the 7th US Veteran Volunteer guards at the camp. He'd been wounded in action at Gettysburg in 1863. (Courtesy Lester Letson)

The camp's last monthly report was filed on July 31. It listed the final fifty-one people "disposed of" and fourteen others, unnamed, who had gone AWOL.

The camp hospital would remain open for a time, although with a new staff and a changing patient population. As part of its downsizing campaign, the War Department laid off thousands of contract surgeons, volunteer doctors, and medical assistants. Dr. Joseph Corson wrote that on May 15, "my contract was annulled and an Assistant Surgeon of the Regular Army took the place for the short time that the Camp lasted." Similarly, in May, the Army had ordered that final pay and discharge papers be issued to "all convalescent soldiers in hospitals," with an immediate goal of fifty-thousand dismissals.

Some convalescents weren't in shape to be released right away. For instance, at Camp Discharge, Private James Handlin of the 1st Pa. Cavalry, an Andersonville survivor, remained in the hospital throughout July with ecthyma before being discharged. The hospital ledger also showed Private James Robb of the 147th Pa. Infantry was hospitalized with scrofula from July 20 to July 31, and Private James Buskirk of the 1St Pa. Cavalry was hospitalized with a fractured ankle, also until July 31. But once July led into August, the camp hospital became the sole domain of the garrison guard that remained on duty. The newly assigned Army doctor would handle sixty-five visits from those men of the 7th US Veteran Volunteers. They came with complaints of coughs, constipation, and gonorrhea until the ledger's final entry on Aug. 29.

The War Department's order decreeing a reduction of expenses had also called for an inspection of all military posts. Sometime over the summer, before Hancock's departure as commandant, General George S. Dodge of the quartermaster's office visited Camp Discharge for that purpose. His inspection report, submitted on Sept. 14, was one last blow to Hancock.

> The Camp is situated on a very high, steep hill and on ground in my opinion certainly unsuitable. There is but one avenue of approach, directly up this hill, rendering access difficult and increasing greatly the cost of all the transportation for supplies and material. I am at a loss to conceive how any officer in his right senses should have selected the site. The camp, of which I enclose the plan, extends over about fifty-six acres.
>
> I should say that about two thirds of this ground is for the use of the command; the remaining one-third seems to be reserved for the convenience of the commander, Lieut. Col. Hancock, who reports, I believe, to the Adjutant General of the Army.
>
> The residence of the Commanding Officer is enclosed by a picket fence made of such material as is generally used in constructing a 'hennery.' The price paid for the slats or pickets was 23½ cents apiece for oak and 12½ for hemlock. The residence itself was formerly used as a slaughterhouse which has been remodeled, tastefully fitted up with green window blinds and other modern conveniences until it has been a very comfortable residence for a gentleman of wealth.
>
> The camp is supplied with water flowing through long pipes into large and expensive tanks; a costly bakery has been built and many other improvements made at an expense of several thousand dollars without any corresponding benefit to the Govt. whatever.

> A large flag-staff has also been erected, with a band room at the foot, at a cost of about $2,000. The room for the band has been roofed with Hospital and Wall-Tent flies (new) and the same material has been used in making shades at the windows of the Commanding Officer's Head-Quarters.

Back in May, amid the Hancock-Van Dyke blowup, the cannibalizing of the tent flies had prompted the camp adjutant to convene a special hearing. Several garrison guards testified that Hancock had ordered them to cut up and repurpose the tent flies as described above. The hearing's outcome was not recorded, but the situation was later brought to Dodge's attention—and did not sit well with him.

"I am informed that but very few troops have at any time been stationed at Camp Discharge," he seethed, "and this renders the expense incurred in constructing and beautifying it still more inexcusable."

Dodge noted that $61,000 had been allocated to build the camp—but he estimated the actual final outlay at $200,000. The best option for the mothballed buildings, he wrote, was "that they be sold at public auction as they stand, as in my opinion the Govt. will realize as much in that manner, as if they were disposed of in any other manner."

A carpenter was sent to inventory the contents of the camp. His list, submitted on Oct. 4, was detailed and voluminous. For instance, "148,681 feet Hemlock Joist, 143,077 feet of Flooring boards, 397,662 Shingles, 373 Doors with locks etc., Fence 4,148 feet long."

The Philadelphia quartermaster had already been selling off other surplus property in its jurisdiction. Local newspapers ran classified ads that August announcing the auction of nine hundred government mules and thirty-nine "extra good government horses" and the sale of the buildings and fixtures of Haddington Hospital in West Philadelphia.

Camp Discharge would get its turn. In December, the newspapers carried a notice that a public auction would be held at the camp midday on Dec. 28. The list of contents ran particularly long (see illustration on following page). It was an everything-must-go proposition, from the thirty-nine frame buildings to the sentry box to the horse trough. Apparently, everything did go.

sale. C. SUTHERLAND,
Surgeon U. S. A., Med. Purveyor.

SALE OF GOVERNMENT BARRACKS, CAMP Discharge, near Spring Mills, Montgomery county, Pennsylvania.—Office Assistant Quartermaster Philadelphia Depot, TWELFTH and GIRARD Streets.

Will be sold at Public Auction, for account of the United States, at Camp Discharge, near Spring Mills, Montgomery county, Penna., on Thursday, December 28, 1865, at 12 o'clock M., all the buildings belonging to the Government, known as Camp Discharge, as follows:—

39 Frame Buildings.
9 Frame Sinks.
7 Iron Sinks.
1 Sentry Box.
1 Flag-Staff.
131 Benches.
31 Tables.
186 Trussels.
19 Wash-Troughs, lined.
1 Dough Trough.
1 Horse Trough.
1 Carpenter's Bench.
1 Oval Iron Pot.
1 Dresser, with Drawers.
1 Meat Table.
2 Butcher's Blocks.
1 Large Clothes Press.

ALSO,

5 Wooden Tanks, holding from 800 to 12,000 gallons each.

7228 feet of Fencing, containing 905 Posts, 21,498 feet of Rails, 196,996 feet of Laths, 17,250 Bricks.

The buildings contain about
116,692 feet of Flooring Boards.
286,997 feet of Rough Boards.
525 feet of Tongued Boards.
280,670 feet of Hemlock Scantling.
6,792 feet of Hemlock Plank.

The 8 A. M. train of Philadelphia and Reading Railroad, and 8.35 A. M. train of Philadelphia, Germantown and Norristown Railroad will arrive at the Camp in time for the sale.

Plans and specifications of the property can be seen upon application at this office.

The property must be removed within twenty (20) days from the day of sale.

Terms, Cash, in Government funds.

By order of Col. WM. W. McKIM,
Chief Quartermaster,
Philadelphia Depot.
HENRY W. JANES,
Captain and Asst. Quartermaster,
Brevet Major U. S. Army.

This notice appeared in the Philadelphia Inquirer *on Dec. 28, 1865. (*The Philadelphia Inquirer, *Newspapers.com)*

CHAPTER THREE

1866

Onward

THE quartermaster's auction went off without a hitch that chilly Thursday. By midday, the bidders and their agents were on the vacant camp premises and got down to business. They would have twenty days to haul their purchases away, board by board, nail by nail.

Among the successful bidders was Dr. Hiram Corson, who had already visited the camp several times while in operation. His impression was that the government took a financial bath that day. Corson's diary entry for Jan. 9, 1866, says he

> Drove over to the Barracks to see the men taking down the barn I bought for $100.00 about a week ago at a public sale of all the Barracks. Thirty-four immense buildings only brought about $8,000 which cost about 120,000 Dollars. I gave only $100 for a stable 80 feet by 30, 15 feet high, well boarded all round, shingle roof, large doors at each end that carriages might drive in. The whole base planked, also a lean-to 80 feet long, 14 feet wide roof first of board, then covered with shingles. There is an immense amount of lumber in it. The cost to government was $1,600. I will bring it home and use it as needed in building.

Another man who saw a hot opportunity was George Bullock, proprietor of the Balligomingo Mills woolen factory in nearby West

Conshohocken. A week before the auction, the *Norristown Herald & Republican* noted that Bullock "contemplates the erection of additional buildings at his already extensive woolen mills," which, the item said, "are now engaged in the manufacture of a fine quality of doeskins." Bullock proceeded to purchase camp barracks, knock them down, and repurpose them as dwellings for his mill workers. Entrepreneur Samuel Fulton "did practically the same in Conshohocken," according to a 1905 article by local historian S. Gordon Smyth. Bullock topped off his barracks purchase by buying Camp Discharge's landmark flagpole and installing it at his Balligomingo factory. It towered there until 1889, "when the destruction of the wool room by fire partially consumed it as well," Smyth wrote.

By the planting season of 1866, the Camp Discharge site would revert to the hands of farmer Joseph Kirkner, who had leased it to the Army back in 1864. The property would change hands several times over the next century but would keep its bucolic character as a mix of cropland, pasture, and woods.

By early 1866, the servicemen who had spent time at Camp Discharge were scattered to the winds. The three-year men had, by and

The Balligomingo Mills in West Conshohocken in 1875, when it sported the camp's flagpole. (Courtesy Library Company of Philadelphia)

large, headed back into civilian life, some to the bosom of family and community, others to fend for themselves alone. The camp's guards had been reassigned elsewhere or been mustered out of the service en masse. Some men chose to re-up and join the Veteran Reserve Corps for the continuing structure and certain income it provided.

Unfortunately, a weak economy awaited the homeward-bound servicemen. "War-related manufacturing had sputtered to a halt, shuttering factories throughout the North that had once hummed with activity," historian Brian Matthew Jordan writes in *Marching Home: Union Veterans and Their Unending Civil War.* In addition, "supposing that returning soldiers could 'do nothing hereafter for a living but fight,' many employers refused to hire veterans."

Fortunately, the vets had some advocates on the employment front. No sooner had the war ended than a civic group known as the Patriotic Order of Washington formed in Philadelphia to encourage job preferences for honorably discharged veterans. According to a *Philadelphia Inquirer* article, the group's position was that returning servicemen had earned the right to "be sustained by those for whom they have fought and toiled. These soldiers would scorn to ask the removal of another to make way for themselves, but when vacancies occur justly claim precedence over those who have not shown so great and practical a devotion to their country and her institutions."

In addition to homecoming parades and banquets, there were other early expressions of goodwill and practical support. A network of a dozen orphan asylums and schools was quickly set up across Pennsylvania to care for the state's many orphans of war. Those institutions would be sorely needed; the number of young orphans kept increasing because men were dying even days after returning home. That sad phenomenon was reported over and over by one coal-region newspaper, the *Miner's Journal* of Minersville, Pa. John C. Hoskins of the 129th Pa. Infantry—eleven months a POW, wounded in action at Fredericksburg—died back home in Minersville at age 25. Henry Clay Graeff of the 48th Pa. Infantry died at age 21 "from disease contracted in rebel prisons." Then, "a soldier of the 95th, William Boyd, a returned prisoner from Andersonville, dropped dead on Center Street. The cause was apoplexy." Joshua Reed "died at his father's residence, age 30 years, 8 months. He died from the effects of starvation at Salisbury, N.C." Then, Walter P. Aims of the 48th Pa. Infantry succumbed to "the effects of starvation and brutality which he endured in rebel prisons. His age at the time of his death was 21 years 6 months."

To be sure, numerous returning veterans went on to raise families and be productive, valued citizens. A crucial factor in that regard was the man's health status. Unfortunately, in the case of Camp Discharge, hundreds of men re-entered civilian life in woeful health—and would confront futures that were more precarious than the average veteran faced. Researcher Dora L. Costa put it this way in a 2012 article about "mortality selection" among men who had been Civil War POWs: "By limiting men's ability to work and to climb the occupational ladder, poor health upon discharge from the Army would increase their chances of being laborers rather than farmers or artisans and decrease wealth, likelihood of owning property, and likelihood of being married. Their lower socioeconomic status might then place them at greater risk of developing cardiovascular disease through greater exposure to disease, worse/lesser nutrition, or stress. Too, POW status in itself could also have an effect on later life heart disease."

As they struggled upon re-entry, some of the more physically impaired veterans sought relief, if only transitionally, from local officials known as Overseers of the Poor. These officials might grant individual stipends—but of as little as $4 a month, far less than the $44 per month that laborers were averaging at the time.

In addition, thousands of war vets turned to the federal government for disability pensions. Since 1862, the US Pensions Commission had provided payments to individual enlisted men for incapacities they'd contracted in the service. The stipend for a "total disability" from manual labor began at $8 per month in 1862 and rose to $20 in 1866 and $24 in 1872. Partial amounts might be granted to those who had lost a single hand in battle, for instance, or been blinded in one eye, or had episodic illnesses such as rheumatism. Qualifying for a pension was no sure thing. An applicant had to provide a written record of his wound or disease, or, barring that, an affidavit from the military doctor who had treated

THE INSATIABLE GLUTTON.

1882 cartoon reflects a public wariness of pension abuse. (Courtesy Social Security Administration Archives)

him, provided he could track the man down years later. Testimonials from neighbors, family, or employers also were expected. The vet would be interviewed by a pension examiner and, over the years, might have to submit to follow-up medical exams to determine if he was still entitled to the pension.

On top of those bureaucratic challenges was the social stigma of being a so-called "pension beggar." Many people of the era opposed the public dole and did not want to sanction dependency. Seeing veterans they had once welcomed home from the war malinger as drunkards and wastrels left them appalled. "Most civilians wanted the 'piteous' sight of the one-armed soldier begging in the streets, like the memory of the war, to just go away," historian Jordan writes.

Family life was a haven of rest and understanding for many veterans. For others, though, it brought new challenges. Where wives had run the household in their absences, the men had to navigate the domestic power dynamic anew. The roles could be even more strained when the veteran's ill health or addiction impaired him as a breadwinner. Many would find succor in the nearest post of the Grand Army of the Republic (G.A.R.), the Union Veteran Legion, and the Union Veteran League. There also were POW survivors' groups. The Scranton lodge of the Ex-Union Prisoners of War Association, for instance, had forty-seven members by the mid-1880s. Those spaces provided ongoing fellowship, material support for struggling households, and the promise of a dignified burial when the time came.

THE MEN OF CAMP DISCHARGE represent a cross-section of the veteran experience. A look at pension files, diaries, biographies, newspaper accounts, census records, and other documentary evidence showed that some of the men went on to become leading citizens of their communities while others were wanderers. Some had abundant family lives while others languished on society's margins. Some died young. Others lasted well into their eighties. The profiles that follow begin with the officers posted in the camp headquarters and proceed to a sampling of the enlisted men who had inhabited the barracks.

By the end of January 1866, **John Hancock** was in Baltimore presiding over a busy military court-martial panel. His brother, the famous general, also made him one of his staff officers for the "Great Parade" held that July Fourth in Philadelphia. Two months later, Hancock was mustered out of the service. He went on to be a railroad ticket agent in Washington, D. C., and a post office inspector in Florida before settling in Washington and taking up law as a profession. He died there of pneumonia in 1912, at age 83, surrounded by his son and three daughters. According to an obituary in the *Washington Herald*, Hancock found success as a lawyer but "steadily declined offers of public service." He is buried in Arlington National Cemetery.

Hancock's nemesis at Camp Discharge, the assistant quartermaster **Damon Y. Kilgore**, also went on to practice law, but there the similarity ended. Whereas Hancock slipped into a conventional life, Kilgore was an outspoken nonconformist and social reformer. In his postwar years, he was a member of the Liberal League of Philadelphia, advocated for women's rights, and petitioned to exclude the Bible from public schools. His wife was Carrie Kilgore, a suffragist who became the first woman admitted to Penn Law School and the bar in Pennsylvania. (She is the namesake of Penn's Kilgore House and the law school's Kilgore Society.) Furthermore, Damon Kilgore was the first person to be voluntarily cremated in Philadelphia. He was a devotee of Spiritualism, a movement whose adherents, including numerous war widows, gathered for seances to communicate with the dead. Kilgore believed his spirit would live on after death. His will specified that his remains—his "mortal garment"—be cremated and that his wife and children not wear black for him. When death came in 1888, his funeral drew a throng. According to a reporter for the *Philadelphia Times*, the eulogy was given by a Spiritualist medium "who spoke for over an hour with his eyes tightly closed." The mourners proceeded to the newly opened Philadelphia Crematorium in Germantown for the final rites. At the end, family and friends "took their last look at his burning body through a little glass peep-hole in the door and the funeral was over." Kilgore believed he would return to "the scenes of his life" after death, and his spirit was said to haunt the crematorium, which is still in operation in the city's Chelten Hills Cemetery.

Rush Van Dyke, the camp's contract surgeon, moved to New Brunswick, N.J., and tried to practice medicine while coping with a chronic illness. According to pension files, when Van Dyke was in the army in 1861, he contracted "malarial trouble" from bad water. Diarrhea worsened to "acute dysentery." The affliction led to his death in 1882, at age 69. Brother-in-law Thomas J. Williamson said Van Dyke "looked like a man of 80, dilapidated, broken down, sickly . . . when he died he had dwindled away to his bones." He died a bitter man. The *New Brunswick Fredonian* obituary remarked how he had "indulged in severe and caustic criticism upon the follies of the day."

Van Dyke's assistant surgeon, **Joseph K. Corson** of Plymouth Meeting, practiced medicine with his father for a time but soon rejoined the Army. He was a military surgeon until 1897, serving at Army posts around the country. From New York City, he was transferred to Carlisle, Pa., then Wyoming, Nebraska, and back to Wyoming. From there, in order, to Alabama, upstate New York, Arizona twice, Missouri, and Washington, D.C. Corson's western exploits included fossil digs with visiting paleontologists. He even had three fossils named after him, "my only chance for immortality," he quipped in his memoir. He also played a part in the improved training of the medical corps. Corson retired with the rank of surgeon, and in 1899 was awarded the Medal of Honor for bravery in combat back in 1863. He wrote his memoir in 1910 and died three years later, at age 76.

Meanwhile, **Albert Ashmead**, the assistant quartermaster who organized the Camp Discharge auction, left the military and became a real estate agent in West Philadelphia. He later moved his family to Lower Merion, where he was an "oil merchant," then to Norristown. Because he'd suffered rheumatism and a hernia during the war, Ashmead was getting a monthly pension that was $30 by the time he died in 1916 at the advanced age of 92. The camp's adjutant, **George W. Hooker**, had been badly wounded at the Battle of Cold Harbor. By 1866, Hooker was out of uniform and back in his native New England, where he became a banker, G.A.R. leader, and Republican politician. He served in the Vermont legislature and was sergeant-at-arms in the US House of Representatives. He died at age 64 in 1902, a decade after receiving the Medal of Honor for wartime bravery. **John McArthur Jr.**, the architect of Camp Discharge, became the Navy Department's official architect and designed several prominent structures.

Albert Ashmead
(Courtesy Melissa Applegate)

Chief among them was Philadelphia's monumental City Hall, the tallest public building in the country at the time. McArthur died at age 66 in 1890, a decade before his ongoing masterwork was completed.

THE ENLISTED MEN OF THE BARRACKS, especially the former prisoners, were often beset with chronic disabilities and personal challenges in their postwar years. Sixteen of their cases follow. They are a solemn representation of the whole.

Jeremiah J. Stailey was among the fifty-nine men of the 36th Pa. Infantry (7th Pa. Reserves) who made it to Camp Discharge alive after the long ordeal of capture at the Battle of the Wilderness and imprisonment, first at Libby Prison and then at Andersonville. Stailey was discharged from the service in May 1865 after spending three weeks at Camp Discharge. From there, he returned home to Liverpool, north of Harrisburg, where he was one in a long line of Staileys who were tinsmiths. He had enlisted in Liverpool in 1861 as a private, giving his age as 18, and would die there suddenly in 1878 at age 32. A tribute in the *Perry County Democrat* said that "on the previous afternoon he was on the street appearing well, but took ill about 5 o'clock in the evening and never spoke again. His disease was contracted in Libby Prison, he having been a Union soldier during the rebellion. His death has cast a gloom over our town, for he was a good citizen and faithful husband. He leaves a widow and two small children to mourn their loss."

Wilson Long
(Courtesy Sandra Daniels)

Another veteran of the 36th Pa. Infantry was **Wilson Long**, who had enlisted in 1861 at age 23 and served as a corporal. Like Stailey, Long was captured at the Wilderness and spent harrowing months at Andersonville. After being released into Union hands in Charleston, S.C., and spending a week in Camp Discharge, Long returned to his native Luzerne County, restored his health, and settled into a full life. He became active in Republican politics and both the GAR and the Union Veteran League. For several years he was the county's jury commissioner. A series of strokes paralyzed him and led to his death in 1899 at age 61. The turnout for Long's funeral was overwhelming, according to the *Wilkes-Barre Record.* "The church was packed to suffocation and more than 400 people were unable to gain admission," the correspondent remarked. "Wilson Long was a popular man in every sense of the word: an heroic soldier, a good neighbor and his dealings with his fellow men were never questioned. He ever had a kind, encouraging word for the struggling ones."

One of the struggling ones Long could have counseled was **John Kemp** of nearby Hazleton. Kemp had been a newcomer to the war, a miner who enrolled at age 19 in February 1865, just two months before Lee's surrender. As his 8th Pa. Cavalry unit engaged Lee's forces during the Appomattox Campaign, Kemp was shot twice and suffered a contusion of the pelvis, a common falling hazard for horsemen. After convalescing for two months at Camp Discharge, Kemp returned to Hazleton in July 1865. He found work as a boilermaker, but by the 1880s, his health was slipping. He applied for a disability pension in 1885, citing not his battle wounds but a heart ailment he said resulted from the strain of a forced march. "In working I have trouble with my heart and fall down," he attested. "At times I have to be carried home." By 1890 he was confining himself to his house and losing weight. A neighbor said Kemp was suffering from "a general breaking down, with incontinence of bowel and spends almost all his time in a reclining position. He is not able to do any work and is not able to leave his home to be examined." His $4 monthly pension was increased to $16. Kemp died in 1892, at age 46, from what a physician termed "apoplexy induced by a severe attack of influenza aggravated by disease of long standing. . . . He was a broken down man."

And then there was **Mark McCusker**, whose trials rivaled the biblical Job's. The Irish-born weaver had enlisted in the 69th Pa. Infantry in 1861, at age 26. A year later, during the Battle of Antietam, an exploding shell wounded him in the right hand, back, and thigh. The hand was left partially paralyzed. In June 1864, McCusker was captured during action at Petersburg, Va., and shipped to Andersonville. There he would suffer permanent eye damage that doctors later diagnosed as "atrophy of the optic nerves." Another survivor who had known McCusker at Andersonville told a pension examiner that countless prisoners suffered swollen eyes from lying on the damp, cold ground without shelter. The problem was exacerbated by caustic wood smoke from the cooking fires they would tend. McCusker was freed from Rebel hands in April 1865 and discharged from the army two months later. He returned to Philadelphia, married, and found work as a weaver—but he would find no peace. In 1880, his employer told a pension examiner that McCusker's eyes "gradually became diseased, a greenish blue scum coming over the balls of each eye," and said his work deteriorated. By 1883, McCusker lived in an almshouse in South Philadelphia, a jobless alcoholic with "the appearance of a tramp." Because the Camp Discharge medical team had treated him as an outpatient, they'd kept no records on him—so the pension examiner decided there was no conclusive evidence his impairment was due to his service. McCusker's application was still pending when he died in 1885, at age 51, of "dilatation of the heart." By the end, the treating doctor said, "he lived mostly on bread and water and rum. He was a poor old broken down man." McCusker's wife had died two years earlier, the cause listed as alcoholism. They left behind two destitute children who were put under the care of Orphans Court.

After the war, **Michael Dougherty**, a veteran of the 13th Pa. Cavalry, transited Camp Discharge en route back to Bristol, Pa. A long imprisonment at Andersonville had hobbled him with scurvy and rheumatism. Yet, the Irish-born Dougherty would marry and have eight children and operated both a bakery and a pool hall in Bristol. His war record—of "distinguished gallantry" under fire in 1863 and then surviving Andersonville—gave him "considerable prominence" and helped elevate him to elected office as the clerk of Bucks County Orphans Court, according to an 1887 article in the *Philadelphia Times*. The article was occasioned by Dougherty's disappearance that year and his wife's desperate search for him. Drinking might have been the cause, the paper suggested, because Dougherty "would occasionally indulge in a spree, at times being absent from home for several days." It might have been a spree—or a descent into melancholia. Dougherty, in a prison diary, called himself the lone

Michael Dougherty as a young man, and later in life. At right is his Medal of Honor for valor. (Courtesy Jim Lawler)

survivor of his regiment's captives. The memory of leaving some men to die in Andersonville haunted him. "They would stretch out their wasted hands and implore us by word and signs to give them water, but the glassy stare of their eyes telling us they would soon be out of their misery, we leave them to die; we have all the sick comrades we can care for and we must not neglect them for those we cannot save with the means at hand." Congress awarded Dougherty the Medal of Honor in 1897 for his bravery in battle. Despite his ills, Dougherty would live until 1930, when death took him, by then a widower, at age 87.

Among the infantrymen who spent extended periods in the Camp Discharge hospital was **Jeremiah Fleegle**, a married farmer from Somerset County. Fleegle (listed by the military as Flegle) returned home to his family in 1865 and persevered for years as a farmer, but he was not the same man. Neighbors noticed how he labored and walked with a stoop. He'd done two tours of duty during the war and been battered by both. During the first, a nine-month enlistment with the 133rd Pa. Infantry, he contracted typhoid fever while marching from Antietam to Fredericksburg in late 1862. According to his pension paperwork, he was hospitalized for that and recovered. Fleegle went on to join the 187th Pa. Infantry and returned to the field. A comrade in his Company H, John Wolford, testified that at the outset of the Battle of Cold Harbor in

June 1864, Fleegle was injured when a cannonball struck a tree, causing a large limb to fall on him and break his right shoulder blade. Fleegle refused to leave the action and had to be ordered to a hospital. Then, at Camp Discharge in December 1864, Fleegle was hospitalized for a cold and contracted variola (smallpox). Wolford, who was with him at the camp, said smallpox permanently damaged Fleegle's eyes and spine. In 1895, Fleegle applied for disability from manual labor but lost; the pension examiner was not convinced the injuries were contracted in the service. He won on appeal and was given $12 per month for a shoulder injury, lumbago, and heart disease. Fleegle would die in 1918, a widower for decades.

Marshall Houck, a native of Fulton County, enlisted at age 31 in the 31st Pa. Infantry (2nd Pa. Reserves) in August 1861. His Company F, the Governor's Rangers, saw action in seventeen battles, including Antietam, Fredericksburg, Gettysburg, and the Wilderness. In one of the regiment's last engagements, at Spotsylvania Courthouse, Houck was shot in the left forearm. The wound must have been shattering because field surgeons felt Houck could only be saved by amputating his arm at the elbow. By early 1865, he was in Camp Discharge and hospitalized for cephalalgia, a general term for pain in the head. In December 1865, following his honorable discharge, Houck got an $8 per month invalid pension due to the amputation. He tried to get on with his life, entering Millersville State Normal School for training as a schoolteacher. He moved west, married a woman in Nebraska, and settled down in Des Moines, Iowa. Pension examiners had increased his stipend to $36 by 1892. But something went very wrong along the way. In 1892, Houck was admitted to the Iowa Hospital for the Insane. The next year, the hospital's superintendent notified the pension bureau that Houck had died there of "paralysis." He left behind his wife Alice and two minor children.

Another wounded veteran who hit the road from Pennsylvania was **George T. Barnes**. He had been an early recruit, signing up as a private in the 28th Pa. Infantry in June 1861. A 25-year-old clerk in Philadelphia at the time, he took to army life and was promoted to sergeant by the end of the year. He was commissioned a second lieutenant in May 1863—the same month he led his men into combat at Chancellorsville

The Dayton home housed over 7,000 men at its peak. (Courtesy Library of Congress)

and was shot in the right knee and the left hip. After recuperating at a hospital in Washington, he returned to action and was shot in the right leg again, this time in Tennessee in April 1864. Barnes also sustained an inguinal hernia during the war, according to his pension records. In January 1865, after spending three months at Camp Discharge, Barnes left the service and moved to New York. From there, he migrated west to San Francisco and became a "ranchman." By 1889, however, Barnes found himself unable to earn a living by manual labor. He moved to the National Home for Disabled Volunteer Soldiers in Dayton, Ohio, one of a dozen such homes the government created after the war. He would spend the rest of his life there. A $10 monthly invalid pension had been raised to $15 by the time Barnes died of "cardiac dilatation" in June 1908. His body was laid to rest among other veterans in the Dayton National Cemetery. Having never married, he left only one survivor, a sister, back in Philadelphia.

George Cartwright also served in the 28th Infantry with Sergeant Barnes and also would pay a heavy price in combat. A Philadelphia draftee, Cartwright mustered in at age 34 on July 1863, two weeks after the Battle of Gettysburg, and was shipped south to the fighting. A pension report summarized what befell him: "wounded, Face, severe, at battle of Pine Knob, Ga., June 15, 1864: treated June 18 & 19, 1864, G.S.W. [gunshot wound] Side Face, fract.: June 20 to July 18, 1864, G.S.W. Left chest; furloughed July 18, 1864: Aug. 15 to Dec. 12, 1864, G.S.W. Of Face:

rtd [returned] to duty: Apl 7&8 1865, malarial fever: Apl 9, 1865, Typ Mal. Fever; Apl 16 to 19, 1865, Chronic Rheumatism: Apl 24 to May 9, 1865, Convalescent; discharged from service May 9, 1865." Cartwright spent an extra month convalescing at Camp Discharge before returning to Philadelphia in June 1865. He married, found work as a laborer, and lasted until November 1880, when pneumonia killed him. He left behind his wife, Sarah, and a son eleven days old. Little more is known about Sarah except that she applied for a widow pension a decade later.

Bizarre best describes the case of **John Nester**, a private in the 69th Pa. Infantry. Nester lived in Phoenixville, a thirty-year-old pig-iron "puddler," when he enlisted in October 1861. According to War Department records, he went into battle at Gettysburg and, on July 3, 1863, was wounded in the left leg while defending against Pickett's Charge. Then he was shot in the abdomen and both thighs during the fight at the Wilderness on May 6, 1864. Nester returned to duty and was mustered out Dec. 1, 1864, after spending a month at Camp Discharge. At least, that's the official record. Decades later, in 1911, a disability claim was filed in Nester's name by an elderly fellow in Pittsburgh. A pension examiner paid a visit to the claimant's residence, "a squalid tenement," where he lived with his adult son. As identification, the claimant presented a peddler's license and Nester's apparent discharge certificate, but he had no supporting witnesses. Under questioning, the old man changed his story entirely. He told the examiner he had served under the name John J. Hanlon in the 1st US Cavalry, Co. C, in 1861, and had a finger severed by a saber at First Bull Run, then jumped to the 38th Pa. Infantry (9th Reserves) Co. E, as Nester, and then to the 4th Pa. Cavalry, Co. E, as Hanlon, from which he deserted. As the examiner reported, "He now specifically denies that service [in the 69th] and that he was in the battle of Gettysburg and that he was ever wounded in the leg in service. He exhibited however a scar in the right groin about three inches long and a half inch wide, which he claims was the result of a bayonet thrust at Malvern Hill." The man kept going in an affidavit, claiming he was born in Ireland, lost both parents, was taken to England by his sisters, and arrived in New York just as the war broke out. "I was a wild young fellow and did not care what happened," he stated. "I was not raised the same as

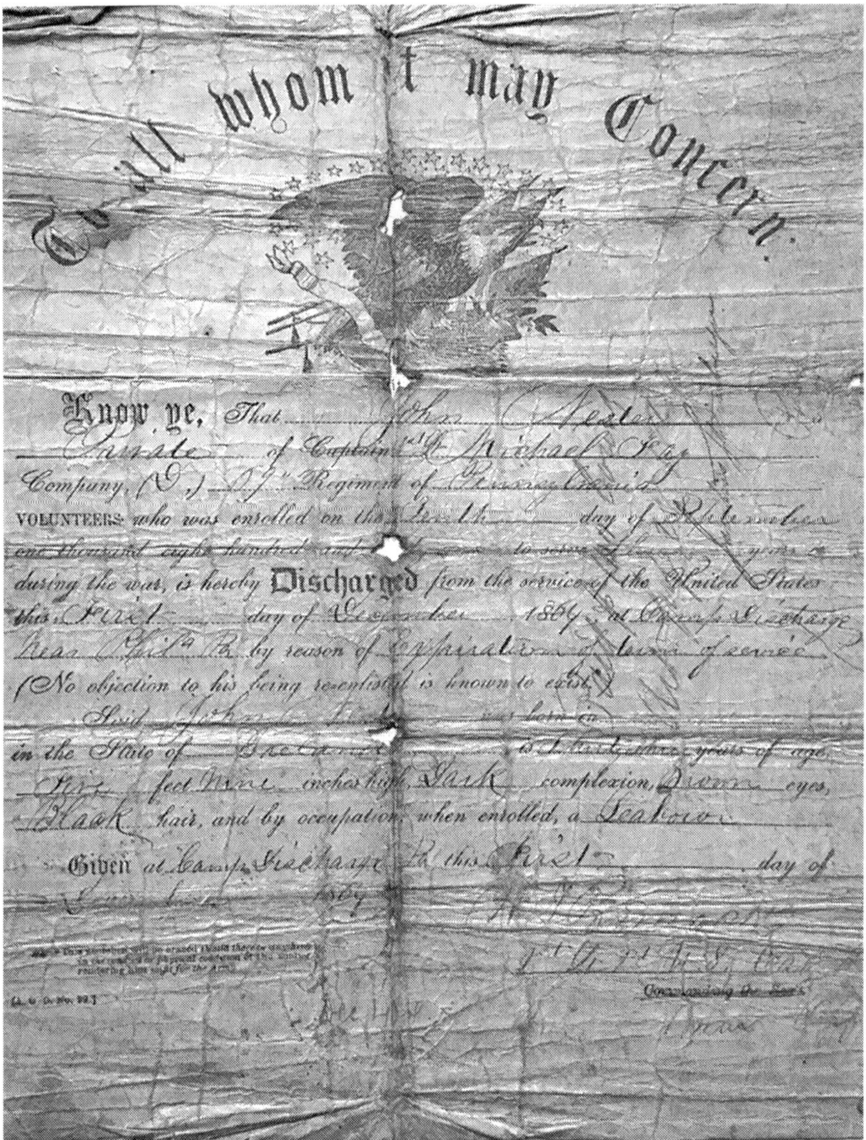
To all whom it may Concern.

Know ye, That John Nester
Private of Captain [illegible] Company, (D) 97th Regiment of Pennsylvania
VOLUNTEERS who was enrolled on the [illegible] day of [illegible]
one thousand eight hundred and [illegible] to serve [illegible] years or
during the war, is hereby Discharged from the service of the United States
this First day of December 1864 at Camp Discharge
near Phil'a Pa by reason of Expiration of term of service
(No objection to his being reenlisted is known to exist.)
Said John [illegible] was born in
in the State of [illegible] is thirty three years of age
five feet nine inches high, dark complexion, brown eyes,
black hair, and by occupation, when enrolled, a [illegible]
Given at Camp Discharge Pa this First day of
December 1864

Commanding the Post.

This is the Nester discharge certificate that was confiscated from the suspicious claimant by the pension bureau. Originally issued at Camp Discharge, it remains in the Nester pension file at the National Archives in Washington, D.C. (Courtesy NARA) anybody else was, I had no parents." His adult son, who went by Patrick Hanlan, said his father "was always of a roaming disposition." The examiner was less generous: "to use a slang term, he is nutty." The pension bureau rejected the man's claim due to his own recanting and his admitting to having deserted his unit. The examiner confiscated the Nester discharge paper from him. A member of the pension bureau's review board, Rev. B. A. Chaplin, expressed pity and urged outreach workers to seek old comrades or neighbors to step in. "This is one of the peculiar cases for which the Special Examination Division was established and it should do everything to assist in placing this unfortunate old fellow where he belongs," the reverend wrote. "He is surely irresponsible for anything he states." This case remains a puzzle. The rosters of the three other regiments the man named contain no soldiers named Nester or Hanlon. Their fates remain unclear to us, as do their very identities.

The Dayton old soldiers' home ended up taking in **Joseph Peffley** of Lebanon County—although his time there is as hard to track as the rest of his fractured postwar life. Peffley was a cigar maker when he'd enlisted in the 36th Pa. Infantry (7th Pa. Reserves) at age 19 in early 1862. He may have been wounded at Antietam, and there's no doubt he was swept up in his regiment's mass capture at the Wilderness. Nine months of imprisonment followed at Andersonville and Goldsboro, N.C. After leaving Camp Discharge in July 1865, Peffley returned to Lebanon and went to work in a rolling mill. In time, he supplemented his wages with a $12 disability pension for rheumatism and chronic bronchitis. He also became active briefly in Republican circles. But in 1892, Peffley found himself disgraced and in prison. The crimes were bigamy and perjury—for keeping one wife in Lebanon and another forty miles north in Ashland. According to news reports, he'd pulled off the duplicity for a while until the Ashland wife found out and pressed charges. As the *Pottsville Republican* remarked, "The man is said to be weak-minded, according to letters received by the judges. Peffley is a resident of Lebanon and the father of 7 children, and one died since he has been in jail. He was sentenced to $1 and cost and four months in prison. . . . The charge of perjury was overlooked on account of his menial condition." Peffley stayed around Lebanon and found work as a quarry laborer, puddler, and railroad brakeman. That was until 1899, when he was admitted into the disabled soldiers' home in Dayton. A year later, the home expelled him, notating the cause as "dishonorably." Returning home, he hit bottom. The *Lebanon Daily News* ran an item in January 1903 headlined "A Union Soldier on the Pension List Goes to the Poor House." It said Peffley "will pay the county for his support and treatment" in the almshouse. But he somehow got back into the Dayton home in 1905 and was still living there in 1912, or so he told the *Lebanon Courier* during a visit that year. Peffley's life story is confounding. There's no record of his being wounded at Antietam or the Dayton home taking him back. We only have his word for both. In the 1870 census, he was listed in Lebanon with a wife, Katherine, and a son; in 1880, in Lebanon with a wife, Sallie, and three other children; in 1900, in Lebanon and widowed; and in 1919, in Dauphin County with a wife, Sarah. The war had loosened other men's moorings and morality and may have undone Peffley, too. He survived until September 1919, when apoplexy killed him at age 77 in Harrisburg. In the end, Sarah got the widow's pension.

Peffley and **Samuel B. Trafford** were both from Lebanon, joined Company C of the 36th Pa. Infantry (7th Reserves), survived combat and imprisonment, and lived long lives. But whereas Peffley fell into suspect ways over time, Trafford became a leading light in his hometown. In 1922, the Lebanon County Historical Society even commissioned a written tribute to the aging Trafford. It told of the perils of battle he and his colleagues underwent at Seven Days, Antietam, Fredericksburg, Gettysburg, and the Wilderness. Trafford was among forty-two men of Company C taken to Andersonville—twenty-two of whom succumbed there. Trafford made it out from Andersonville and Florence prison and would spend five days at Camp Discharge en route back to civilian life. He returned to his trade as an iron maker, tending and then operating forges. He also married and started a family that grew to

Samuel B. Trafford (Courtesy Lebanon County Historical Society)

eight children. In civic affairs, Trafford became active in the local G.A.R., Masons, and other fraternal groups. After his wife died in 1888, he was appointed warden of the Lebanon County jail, a position he held for twenty-one years until retiring. When Trafford died in July 1927 at age 87, the *Lebanon Semi-Weekly News* ran a lengthy obituary. It said, in part, "He had a cheerful word for those he met on the street in daily contact, and had optimistic helpfulness for those in distress. He could not look on the dark side of anything even when it concerned his own affairs. He was known far and wide and was liked by everybody."

E. Haze Swisher was part of the surge of Andersonville survivors who made it to Camp Discharge in May 1865, many of them in dire shape. A tailor by training, Swisher had signed up for the proud 7th Pa. Reserves back in October 1861. He was 24 at the time and slight in stature at 5-feet-4 and 140 pounds. The regiment was federalized as the 36th Pa. Infantry, and Swisher was mustered as a corporal in Company H, a contingent of Cumberland County men. They saw more than their share of combat. Swisher was shot in the left calf at Charles City Crossroads, Va., in June 1862. The minie ball lodged in his leg, a sergeant in his company recalled years later: "He refused to leave the battle line, as he might have done, but being a brave soldier and full of grit, would stand at his post as long as he was able, although the blood was flowing from his wound in a stream, and did fight on until night closed the battle." Later that year, at Antietam, Swisher was shot in the finger. Then, in May 1864, he was captured at the Wilderness. Hellish imprisonment followed until he was freed in April 1865—afflicted with scurvy and rheumatism. Swisher left Camp Discharge for home and found work first as a laborer and then as a railroad watchman. In the mid-1870s, he moved to the oil region of northwestern Pennsylvania to try his luck. That's where he first applied for an invalid pension in 1879. Affidavits in support of the claim describe Swisher's tenuous health. Joseph Egolf, who went through

E. Haze Swisher (Courtesy Mike Fitzpatrick)

the war (and Camp Discharge) with Swisher, told a pension lawyer of their time together at Andersonville. As the lawyer summarized: "Both Swisher and deponent contracted the bone scurvy, were together in the same bunk, and suffered greatly from this painful disease, 'helping each other as we could in our affliction.' Swisher was very bad with the disease, and deponent often wondered that he survived to get through." A boss at a well site said Swisher's feet "gave him great deal of trouble the flesh seemed not right frequently and [he] would remove his boots and put his feet in water." A medical exam in 1890 gave a grim picture: "disease of mouth with loss of teeth result of scurvy . . . has no teeth at all in upper jaw and front teeth loose in lower jaw . . . excessive flow of saliva, gums ulcerated at times. Has rheumatism all through body." In 1899, he was still toiling in the oil fields as best he could. Neighbors attested that he was blind in one eye, short of breath, and "so broken down and disabled that he could not work over half his time." The first pension examiner denied his claim, saying there wasn't enough proof his disabilities were war-related. Swisher kept trying and was eventually ruled 8/18th disabled. This got him a paltry monthly stipend of $6 in 1897. It had risen to $12 by February 1904, when Swisher died. His wife Mary was granted a monthly widow pension of $8 that year. Swisher's struggle with the pension bureau led Joseph Egolf, his old comrade, to write, "I think it very strange we prisoners mus have so much trouble to get what is justly doo to us. All we ask for is justis befor we all quit this hard fight for life."

Some former prisoners of war, at least those who managed to regain their health and footing, seemed to burn with purpose. **Albert Thalheimer** was one of them. His German Jewish family had brought him to the United States as a boy, leaving the murderous anti-Semitism of the old country behind, and settled in Philadelphia. In July 1861, when he was 19, Thalheimer joined the 23rd Pa. Infantry, the colorful "Birney's Zouaves." Three years later, he fell into Rebel hands at the Battle of Cold Harbor, Va. Nine months of privation at Andersonville followed, during which he lost nearly one hundred pounds. He began to recuperate at a Union hospital in Vicksburg, then spent three weeks at Camp Discharge before returning to his family in Philadelphia. From there, a renewed

Albert Thalheimer (Courtesy Reading Eagle*/newspapers.com)*

Thalheimer migrated to Reading to establish himself as an entrepreneur. He opened a dancing school first, then an organ factory. The breakthrough came when he set up a business manufacturing cigar boxes. That brought wealth and prestige, plus seats on Reading's Board of Trade and Chamber of Commerce. But Thalheimer never lost touch with fellow veterans. Newspapers reported his leadership in the local Andersonville survivors association and his hiring of a half-dozen aging or disabled Civil War vets for light work at his factory (a number that grew to fifty men). He lobbied senators on behalf of an 1890 bill broadening veterans' pension rights, saying that "he himself is not dependent on the bill but he speaks for many who are." Further, he offered his G.A.R. post a tract of land and the stones to erect a soldiers monument on the western slope of Reading's Mount Penn and donated another tract to house an "old man's home." Thalheimer retired in 1911 and died twelve years later at age 81. His obituary in the *Reading Times* lauded him as "one of the city's public spirited citizens."

Back in 1861, **Henry H. Cloud** and his kin were fired up with patriotism. Five of the Clouds hiked to Camp Wayne near West Chester that autumn, some from as far as Wilmington, Del., to sign up for the 97th Pa. Infantry's Company D, known as the Concordville Rifles. Henry, 19, left his job as a fabric spinner in Brandywine Village, Del., to enlist. He would prove to be a determined soldier, overcoming bouts of diarrhea and even life-threatening dysentery to join his comrades in battle. During the Siege of Petersburg in 1864, he paid a hefty toll. On Aug. 16 at Deep Bottom, Va., Cloud's division captured a set of enemy trenches and took up position inside. In the midday heat, the Rebels suddenly counterattacked in force. According to the regimental history, "The division opened a rapid and galling fire, and bravely maintained its position until the enemy, in overwhelming numbers had advanced to the trenches and planted their flags beside our own upon the line of works; then as their flanks began to sweep around to envelop the position capture or retreat became inevitable. Slowly and stubbornly and men retired, fighting from tree to tree, keeping at bay their pursuers. Many were captured, some killed, and many wounded." Henry Cloud was among the casualties. A minie ball had smashed into his left leg above the knee and lodged in his thigh. He also was injured in his head and right hand. The young private was treated at a field hospital and then shipped to the army's huge Mower hospital in Philadelphia. From there, Cloud went to Camp Discharge, separated from his regiment as well as his kin. On Dec. 1, 1864, he was discharged on what the army termed "an individual muster out roll." After the war, Cloud married a Philadelphia woman and moved to Hammonton, N.J. There he worked as a farmer and raised six children until his wife, Ann, passed away in 1888 at age 40. He was receiving a disability pension at the time, but only a meager $4 per month. By 1900, Cloud was in Hilltown, Bucks County, where he lived as a farmer. According to an item in the *Bucks County Gazette*, he died in 1905 at age 62—"an indigent soldier" whose $50 burial expense was picked up by a local GAR representative. He was buried with the minie ball still lodged in his leg.

Isaac F. Horner had been a farmer and produce dealer when, in early 1864, he enlisted in the 72nd Pa. Infantry, part of the vaunted Philadelphia Brigade. Perhaps the 36-year-old farmer was drawn to the brigade's fame or the late war bounty of $575. In any event, Horner ended up doing hard duty—shot in the right hip at the Battle of Spotsylvania, captured at Petersburg, sent to Libby Prison, and on to Andersonville. Horner carried a small "soldier's diary" with him to record his ordeal, though its penciled entries became less legible as it, too, underwent rugged conditions. After nine months at Andersonville, Horner made his way north and was processed through Camp Discharge on July 12, 1865. He rejoined his wife, Lydia, and their five children in Camden, N.J., where he remained until Dec. 12, 1879. At that point, his story takes a sharp turn. With $300 borrowed from his brother and mother, Horner boarded a train and vanished. He sent his family two letters en route, from Harrisburg and Columbus, Ohio, that advised against trying

Isaac Horner in uniform as a young soldier, at left, along with two photos of him in middle age and later that were exchanged by his two families during his remarkable later years. (Courtesy NARA)

to track him down. In an affidavit years later, Horner's brother Lemuel blamed Isaac's compulsion to flee on his Andersonville trauma. Lydia Horner would struggle financially in her husband's long absence, and in 1890 applied to get a widow pension. She was denied because she couldn't establish if he was alive or dead. Unbeknownst to her, Isaac Horner was alive and, after a year of wandering, had taken on a new existence in rural Thornville, Ohio. His whereabouts would only be revealed to her in 1901—in a letter informing her of his recent death. The writer, William Neel, explained that Horner had come to live with the extended Neel family in Thornville in 1881. "Isaac was one among us and perfectly at home at either of our Houses," Neel wrote. Horner worked on the Neel family farms, sawmill, brick and tile factory, and cared for William Neel's aging parents. But then, in the winter of 1901, he fell ill and died of pneumonia. It's not known if Horner had confessed his secret to the Neels or if they stumbled upon it later in his papers. In a round of cordial letters, William Neel and the Horners exchanged photographs of Isaac and invitations to visit one another. The Neels also submitted affidavits in support of Lydia Horner's renewed widow-pension claim. By then, she was being cared for by her adult children and would die in Camden in 1906 at age 78. There is no record of her ever receiving a widow pension.

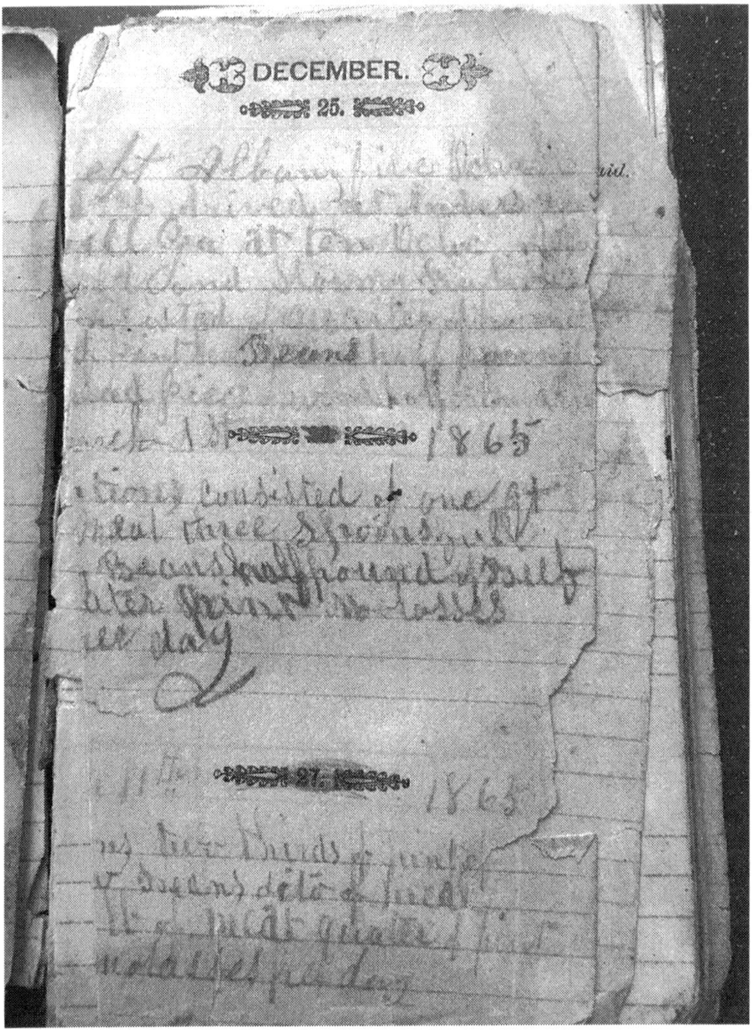

A page from Isaac Horner's diary describes the meager rations at Andersonville. His pension file is what researchers might call "loaded." Not only is his story compelling but the file contains old tintypes of him, the unusual war diary and several personal letters that the pension bureau retained. This was in addition to the customary records of military service, medical exam results, and supporting affidavits. (Courtesy NARA)

AS THE YEARS SLIPPED BY and memories faded, Union veteran groups pressed to keep their legacy of valor fresh for aging comrades and inspiring for the general public. Regimental monuments began going up at battlefields to make the veterans' sacrifices permanently manifest. At Gettysburg, where so many of the Camp Discharge men had fought, monuments were in place even before the grounds became a national park in 1895. Albert Thalheimer's 23rd Pa. Infantry dedicated its monument there in 1886. Two regiments of the heralded Philadelphia Brigade, the 69th Pa. and the 71st Pa., dedicated theirs in 1887, with a third, the 72nd Pa., following four years later.

The Philadelphia Brigade's monuments were placed at the Bloody Angle's stone walls, the famous "high-water mark of the Confederacy" where Pickett's Charge had been repulsed. A nasty legal fight broke out over the exact placements, however. When the 72nd association sought to install its monument directly at the front wall, the 69th association filed suit. According to the 69th, during the heat of battle in 1863, the men of the 72nd "failed to help in the fight at the wall and had stayed out of hand-to-hand combat until the very end," as Don Ernsberger writes in *Paddy Owen's Regulars*, his two-volume history of the 69th. The state

Survivors of the 69th Pa. Infantry dedicate their marker at the Bloody Angle in 1887. At right, the 72nd's monument graces a Pennsylvania coin. (Brief History of the 69th Regiment)

supreme court upheld the 72nd's case, leaving many men of the 69th "unhappy to their dying day." (They might have been apoplectic to know that in 2011, Pennsylvania chose the 72nd monument as the image on the back of the state's "America the Beautiful" quarter coin.)

Elsewhere, regimental monuments were erected at other key battlefields in the early years of the twentieth century. Camp Discharge units were again well-represented. The 77th Pa. Infantry dedicated its memorial at Shiloh in November 1903. At Antietam, the 12th Pa. Cavalry unveiled its monument in September 1904, and the 36th (7th Reserves) dedicated its one in September 1906.

During those years, Union vets encountered dimming memories and a confounding drift in public attitudes towards a forgive-and-forget reconciliation with the South. Many white people in the North were willing to abide by the South's ideology that the Confederate cause had been honorable, even inspiring. The Spanish-American War of 1898 had brought servicemen from the North and South together to fight in far-flung islands as comrades-in-arms—and they, Northerners and Southerners alike, became America's new heroes in uniform. As a counterpoint, Union veteran associations began publishing lavish regimental histories of the Civil War that told about the patriotic Boys in Blue and reminded people of the South's insurrection. A wave of these works appeared in print at the beginning of the twentieth century. They included the histories of regiments that had once trooped through Camp Discharge. The 87th Pa. Infantry published its history in 1903, and the 23rd Pa. Infantry, Albert Thalheimer's unit, in 1904. Among the various authors were two old soldiers who had transited Camp Discharge as enlisted men, James M. Gibbs and John Obreiter. Gibbs's history of his 187th Pa. Infantry, the camp guard unit, was issued in 1905, while Obreiter's chronicle of the 77th Pa. Infantry at Shiloh came out in 1908. Gibbs's book contains the impassioned remarks one comrade, Samuel C. Ilgenfritz, delivered at a meeting in 1899. "It makes a vast difference as to whether we fought for or against Old Glory," Ilgenfritz declared. "The North defended a de facto Government and it was eternally right. The South fought for a de jure Government, which they could not make a fact, and this was a rebellion, and those who engaged therein were Rebels, and hence they were eternally wrong, and being wrong, the sun of the heresy of State sovereignty set in blood in Appomattox forever."

That Yankee pride would rise again at an emotional event held deep inside Dixie, a December 1905 ceremony at Andersonville. Hundreds of Northerners traveled down to the site of the notorious Confederate prison stockade in southern Georgia for a ceremony dedicating Pennsylvania's monument memorializing its one thousand, eight hundred forty-nine soldiers who died there. The G.A.R. Women's Relief Corps had purchased the prison grounds and its vast graveyard and was in the process of turning them into a hallowed memorial. The National Association of Union Ex-Prisoners of War had already dedicated an ornate fountain where Andersonville's famous "Providence Spring" had burst forth—miraculously, survivors said—to provide cold water during the wretched summer of 1864. Pennsylvania was joining a procession of states erecting monuments to their martyred men. Pennsylvania's newly emplaced granite memorial stood thirty-five feet high. At its peak was the bronze figure of a prisoner, "in appearance dejected and sad," overlooking the cemetery that held more than thirteen thousand Union dead. Pennsylvania had provided $25,000 for its monument, as well as $12,000 to defray the travel expenses of any of its honorably discharged Andersonville survivors who wished to attend the dedication. More than four hundred took them up on the offer and traveled by train to Georgia.

The Pennsylvania delegation included thirty-eight survivors who had spent time at Camp Discharge. Seven others registered to attend but were unable to go, one because he died in the interim. The state published a book about the event, titled *Pennsylvania at Andersonville, Georgia*, which identifies the thirty-eight men. John Obreiter, the author, was there. So was Albert Thalheimer, who, fittingly, had stepped forward to organize the Berks contingent. Eleven survivors attended from the 36th Pa. Infantry (7th Reserves), which had lost forty-six men at Andersonville; even Joseph Peffley, the convicted bigamist, was there. Sixteen men came from the cavalry regiments. The bulk of the Camp Discharge contingent represented infantry regiments that had collectively lost well over a hundred comrades at Andersonville.

The Pennsylvania memorial at Andersonville. (Pennsylvania at Andersonville)

According to contemporary news reports, the hosts turned on the Southern charm, giving the arriving Yankees carriage rides and tours of the cotton warehouses, and exchanging niceties. Jim Crow and Southern lynchings (fifty-seven that year alone) were undoubtedly glossed over.

The dedication ceremony drew five thousand people, including the honored survivors, their families, and Union vets who had survived other Rebel prisons. One can only imagine the welter of emotions—grief, anger, pride, perhaps remorse—the Andersonville survivors felt as they gathered in their Sunday best on the ground where they'd once huddled in rags and barefoot, where guards had kept their muzzles pointed at them night and day, where stench and death were suffocating.

"Some men are anxious to hide the fact that they were once in prison," the *Wilkes-Barre News* remarked in an article about the event, "but the brave lads of the sixties who served their country under Southern skies and suffered in the bull-pens of that land are not ashamed to tell of a courage which while manifold at the time yet tested severely the souls of men."

Michael Dougherty, the survivor from Bristol, was in the crowd that day and reflected on that courage, an unsung courage he had witnessed so often during twenty-three months of imprisonment. In his war diary published three years later, he put it this way:

> We point with pride to the thousands of graves and say, these comrades chose the most cruel death rather than dishonor their country in any way by assisting the enemy to destroy it by taking the oath of allegiance, which they often tried to induce us to do. Under the most trying circumstances, naked and starving, and raked with pain and disease, with certain torture and death staring us in the face, did we refuse the oft-repeated offers of relief by enlisting in the Rebel Army or working in their shops. Those young men gave up all their bright hopes and prospects of loving homes and pursuits of happiness and submitted to cruel torture and death, believing that their sacrifices and deeds of heroism would ever be kept fresh in the memory of those who would enjoy the freedom for which this price was paid.

When the dedication ceremony began, a Southern chaplain set a benign tone with an opening prayer of thanks "that the animosities of the past have been obliterated, that the blue and the gray now mingle in fraternal sympathy." A few other speakers gave similar platitudes. But then came Colonel James D. Walker of Pittsburgh, the head of Pennsylvania's monument commission, who stripped away the gloss. His message was, in sum, "That the Confederate authorities were guilty of perpetrating a most iniquitous method of exterminating a mass of helpless and powerless prisoners cannot be gainsaid or successfully controverted, and their action will ever remain a foul, deep, and dark blot upon the humanity and civilization of an enlightened government." General Harry White of

Indiana, Pa., who had survived a series of Confederate prisons, kept it up. His speech decried the new crop of Southern history textbooks that depicted Northerners as aggressors and Southerners as noble victims. Don't be fooled, he said. The rebel doctrines of nullification and secession had been unconstitutional and traitorous. "Let the youth of the land be instructed that while all, North and South, who fought in this war were brave men, there was a difference between the cause for which the men in blue fought and that for which the men in gray fought. One was eternally wrong and the other eternally right."

Aaron Bachman, the Lancaster County blacksmith, also was in the audience. By 1905, he had become ridden with rheumatism and got a one-half disability pension of $8. In his war memoir, Bachman offered some reflections on that Andersonville trip.

> A sadness came over my heart as I viewed the cemetery and recalled the destitute condition, the wasted forms, the haggard looks of distress and sorrow and the pale faces of the thousands of brave boys who were carried there forty years before. The United States government has built a fine marble house over the spring; a large lion's head of marble is placed in the wall, and the water from the spring comes running out over its tongue. What a contrast to the bark of the tree that was used to carry the water away from the deadline when we were guests in Jeff Davis' boarding house. The water is pure but it does not have a very good taste. In front of this spring house stands a post with a board nailed to it in the form of a cross; on which is the following inscription, 'A thunder bolt burst a ring, and forth burst the Providence Spring.' It was a providential supply of water but it came through natural causes, which is the way God usually works. The water had at first come from many points on the hillside, but the boys had covered these places over with the sand taken from the wells that they dug. So all this water was pent up, waiting for a chance to escape, which the heavy thunderstorm gave to it. . . . Is it any wonder that in the face of all this so many died, and others were so reduced in health and vitality that they never recovered, but

> died long before their time? Or that many were so overcome by the sights they saw and the groans, the cursing and swearing, the singing and praying, and the weeping and lamenting of the sick and crippled that they became unbalanced in mind?

HAD ANY VETERANS TRAVELED back to Break Neck Hill in 1906 to install a monument at Camp Discharge, they would have lost their bearings. The Reading trains still ran down along the river, but the camp's rail siding was gone, replaced by a little station nearby named Woodlane. The camp's big perimeter fence was long gone. The slope was tilled in parts and gone to seed elsewhere. Hancock's parade ground had become pasture land where sheep grazed. If a disoriented visitor asked about Camp Discharge, he might be directed to a point in the distance where a large stone house stood on a bluff. It was the summer estate of Howard Wood, operator of the Schuylkill Iron Works in Conshohocken, the predecessor of Alan Wood Steel Co. Beginning in the 1880s, Howard Wood had acquired a cluster of properties totaling nearly four hundred acres that included the site of the old Army base. He placed his family estate prominently on the hilltop and dubbed the premises "Camp Discharge" to keep the name alive.

After Howard Wood died in 1911, his son Clement inherited the hilltop house, and his daughter Marion built an adjacent manse for herself. Their compound expanded over the years with a barn, orchard, tennis courts, swimming pool, and caretaker cottages.

For a time, the property even took on a renewed military purpose. Clement Wood was a member of the First Troop Philadelphia City Cavalry, a prestigious gentlemen's unit that dates to the colonial era and is now part of the Pennsylvania Army National Guard. By 1920 Wood had risen to become the troop's captain, and he opened his hilltop grounds for training and drilling by his members. The troop's official history mentions annual encampments, saber training, and mounted pistol-shooting competitions there during the 1920s and 1930s. For example, the 1929 entry states, "The competition for the Gold Medal of 1828, in the mounted pistol course, was this year combined with a week-end bivouac at Captain Wood's estate, 'Camp Discharge.' Trooper T. Evans Dunn was the winner with a score of 27 hits out of 28. A buffet

Two snapshots from the Wood family collection showing the high life there, circa 1900. (Courtesy Alan Wood)

supper given by Captain and Mrs. Wood was attended by the families of the Active Roll."

For decades, newspaper society pages would follow the Woods' comings and goings and report on the various swimming parties, tennis tournaments, benefit soirees, and other events that happened at their Camp Discharge estate. By the early 1960s, however, the old estate house was gone—razed in the aftermath of a devastating boiler explosion and fire—and the next generation was in the process of divesting the family properties. Marion Wood's house was sold off. Developers bought some parcels. Other acreage was set aside for what became Riverbend Nature Center. And in 1965, the private Philadelphia Country Club expanded its footprint by purchasing eighty-five acres that included the Kirkner land—the actual Camp Discharge site.

Today, most of the old camp property remains in the Philadelphia Country Club's hands, on a remote edge of the club's Centennial Course. The fairway of Hole Four passes along the old parade ground, and the green sits near Colonel Hancock's headquarters. Any ball sliced leftward into the woods risks landing where barracks once stood. Below lie Break Neck Hill, untended woods, and the hum of traffic on the busy Schuylkill Expressway.

Camp Discharge never got its monument. If it weren't for the military records, memoirs, and news clippings, one could think the place never existed. Today's only physical relic is a sentry box in place at the fork of Spring Mill Road and Sentry Lane, at the foot of Howard Wood's old driveway. That, and the collection of artifacts a lone digger has been able to unearth on the slope of Break Neck Hill. This digger, Brad Upp, is a local resident who's been at it for years, rain or shine. With the muscle of a stevedore and the eye of a jeweler, he's managed to excavate and classify bullets, buttons, rifle parts, medicine bottles, scabbards, and other objects that the Camp Discharge soldiers seem to have deposited, willy-nilly, into the camp's scattered latrines and refuse pits.

If you're lucky, you might see Brad slipping into the woods along Hole Four. He'll be laden with gear and purpose—double-timing on his personal mission to honor Camp Discharge and resurrect its remarkable history for posterity.

Clement Wood, shown at near left, with brother Howard in their First City Troop finery, opened his Camp Discharge estate for military exercises. Above, an undated snapshot shows members of the troop at ease during an outing on the hilltop. The man at the center is Sgt. Robert N. Downs, who would go on to succeed Clement Wood as troop captain. (Courtesy First Troop Philadelphia City Calvary)

CHAPTER FOUR

Digging Into History

By Brad Upp

MY relationship with Camp Discharge can only be described as intermittent until about four years ago. An article by "Uncle Ben Kramer" in the May 24, 1979, issue of the *Main Line Times* was my introduction. I was ten years old and generally would flip through the newspaper mimicking my parents, not really reading anything. I did, however, find myself reading the article titled "Civil War Camp in Gladwyne"—and was surprised to learn that the camp was right up the road from our house. I vowed to myself that I would go up and look for evidence of the camp sooner than later.

As it turned out, I wouldn't actively look until 1994. In the interim, I unknowingly spent quite a bit of time at Camp Discharge while hiking through the wooded trails overlooking the Schuylkill River with my brother and other kids from our street. In the early '90s, I had moved back to Lower Merion after living up in New England for about seven years. In relatively short order, I watched the Ken Burns series "The Civil War," re-read my great-great-great-grandfather's Civil War diary (which I had last read in middle school), and purchased a metal detector by the summer of 1994. In addition, I had been making regular trips to Richmond, Va., to visit my girlfriend who was going to school there. I began to include visits to Civil War sites during my commute and before long dragged her on day trips to various historical sites abundant in Northern Virginia. I became obsessed with the Civil War, absorbing everything I could find on the subject, and by the summer of 1995, I was in a reenacting group.

My first Civil War artifact was unearthed in November of 1994. After lunch that day, I left Richmond in a fairly nice outfit: slacks, button-down shirt, and the like. I stopped by one of the Fredericksburg Civil War shops that sold excavated artifacts, metal detectors, books, and various other sundries related to the subject. I asked the proprietor where I could take my new metal detector and look for Civil War artifacts. He took a long look at me and said, "You going out to metal-detect in *that* outfit?" I made some kind of offhanded comment that my metal detector hadn't come with a detecting suit. To which he joshed, "You Yankees will never learn." Finally, he said they didn't normally tell people where to hunt for artifacts, just like he wouldn't tell me where his favorite fishing hole was located. I think he figured that I wasn't going to be putting a major dent in the unfound artifact population judging by my attire and my being a stranger to metal-detecting. Then, he said that there was a former Connecticut campsite across the Rappahannock River that had been occupied by troops before and after the Battle of Fredericksburg and was being cleared for a new housing development. I couldn't wait to get over there and find something.

I pulled up to the site, jumped out of the truck, and saw about fifteen guys dressed in camouflage, swinging metal detectors around. I walked up to one of them, and he immediately said that they had already gotten permission to be there from the contractor. I answered with something along the lines of "that's great news." I didn't realize that he thought I was one of the developers or future homeowners because I was "all dressed up" and was potentially there to give them a hard time. I told him I was there to metal-detect. He looked me up and down, gesturing with his metal detector, "In that, where's your shovel?" I found a stick and said, "This is my shovel." By now, several of the other guys had gathered around and were laughing. I followed up with, "Can one of you guys show me how to use this metal detector?" That also garnered an amused reaction. Finally, one of them took pity and gave me a crash course on setting up the machine, what to listen for, and so on. Finally, after following his instructions closely, I thanked the guy and started what would become one of my greatest passions, excavating relics from the American Civil War. As it turns out, after digging up lots of barbed wire, beer cans and breaking several "shovels," I found a partially melted Civil War bullet and couldn't have been more thrilled. I still have that bullet.

I began to use the metal detector as often as possible throughout the Philadelphia area and started to find quite a few old and interesting artifacts. Although the colonial and other early Americana relics I found were fascinating, they were not Civil War artifacts. It dawned on me that I should make a concerted effort to find Camp Discharge. I tracked down Uncle Ben Kramer's 1979 newspaper article at the Gladwyne library's archives room and examined the picture accompanying the article. It featured an old map of Lower Merion Township shaded to highlight where the camp had been. The shading covered about 300 acres. I thought that that couldn't possibly be accurate—and as I would learn years later, it was not. I ventured out to the area that seemed a likely possibility and didn't find anything indicative of the Civil War era. What I did find were quite a few parcels of private property that did not encourage metal-detecting. I wandered around in a rough effort to find something that I could link to the discharge camp. After several unsuccessful trips to the wooded areas around Spring Mill Road and along the ridge above the Schuylkill Expressway, I gave up on trying to locate the camp for a while. Instead, I directed my attention to Virginia and Georgia to pursue Civil War artifact hunting and have made numerous trips down to both states over the years.

Interestingly enough, I found the first Camp Discharge artifacts along a public trail system near the shaded boundaries on Ben Kramer's map. The items were a carbine sling buckle and an eyehook-shaped carabiner. Initially, I didn't know that these objects were used by the US Cavalry and had placed them in the unidentified-recoveries box. But once time passed and my knowledge of Civil War equipment expanded, I correctly identified these brass items. I flipped through a book from my rapidly growing Civil War library and paused on an old tin-type image of a Union cavalier. This book had been examined many times before, but this time I took a closer look at the cross belt running along his chest. There it was, a carbine sling buckle exactly like the one buried in my unidentified-finds

(Courtesy Craig Williams)

(Courtesy Brad Upp)

Shovelful by shovelful and rock by rock, Brad Upp has managed to excavate two old latrines he located at the Camp Discharge site, including the deep pit pictured right. Above left, he holds a fresh find, a whisky flask, that was in the vicinity of the commandant's quarters. At above right are the carbine sling buckle and carabiner he unearthed, identified, and cleaned for display.

(Courtesy Christopher Waddell)

box. I also noticed that his carbine rifle was dangling from the lower end of the cross belt connected by an eyehook-shaped carabiner to a ring on the wooden stock of his gun. This would be the first of many inadvertent positive identifications. I was ecstatic, and the next day I went right back to where I had found the carbine sling buckle two years prior. To my dismay, two days of searching yielded no other period items. I remember thinking that this was ridiculous; it wasn't even near Uncle Ben's highlighted area, anyway. Our more recent research suggested that this was likely an old path that had been patrolled by the cavalry arm of the Camp Discharge guard to ensure no soldiers were wandering around outside the camp perimeter. Perhaps the cavalier lost it or disposed of it deliberately.

Fast forward to 2016. As I had maintained a waxing and waning connection to Camp Discharge, I had a similar relationship with the Lower Merion Historical Society that had begun in the mid-1990s. It had become clear to me that I wanted to redouble my efforts and be more involved with the Historical Society. The Society's holdings include a large folder filled with a fair amount of information on my old friend Camp Discharge. I was permitted to take the folder home, and I started to read through photocopies of the original documents on the camp. One of the documents happened to be an 1864 contract between the US Army and a Lower Merion farmer, Joseph Kirkner, to lease his land and construct the discharge camp upon it. I was sure I had seen his name before on one of the old maps or atlases at the Historical Society. I pulled out my copy of John Levering's 1851 map and, sure enough, found the 56-acre parcel owned by Kirkner. So there it was, the official location of Camp Discharge with the Philadelphia Country Club's fourth fairway on their nine-hole course running right through the middle of what was once the old property boundary. It occurred to me almost as fast as I had solved the mystery of where the camp had been located; there's no way the Philadelphia Country Club was going to allow me to go traipsing around on their finely manicured golf course. However, I knew some of the people in the neighborhood that ran along the east border of the Country Club and was still within the original Kirkner tract. So I set out on a few metal-detecting excursions within the border properties and, sure enough, started to find Civil War artifacts.

During this time, the Historical Society's President, Jerry Francis, suggested that I consider putting together a brochure or booklet about Camp Discharge. This seemed like the next natural direction to make this a legitimate project. Yet where to start? There is no central storehouse of information about Camp Discharge. The only resources that came to mind were Uncle Ben Kramer's newspaper article, the large binder of camp correspondence, and a few pages about the camp in an old publication called *Historical Sketches* at the Montgomery County Historical Society. So I figured that I would have to perform some legitimate and extensive research to do this right.

Five significant things happened around this time and soon after. A Cadet at West Point Military Academy named Bridget Guiles secured about 62 images of the Camp Discharge roster sheets, listing the soldiers, command staff, and other relevant notations, and furnished me with them. These documents proved to be invaluable because I was able to document the personnel and research them. It was suggested that I visit the Historical Society of Pennsylvania on Locust Street in Philadelphia to locate more information. So off I went. I did not have an actual research plan and approached a gentleman seated at a small desk. He happened to be a noted Civil War historian who was coming up from Virginia about once a month. I explained that I was trying to find anything I could about Camp Discharge. We scoured the massive card catalog section together and, to my amazement, found two references to an actual picture of the camp. I immediately filled out the request card, gave it to the reference desk, and waited, with great anticipation, in the hushed research area. A young intern finally appeared with a tray containing a glass negative picture of a couple of soldiers sitting around in a camp setting near Springfield, Ill. She indicated that that was the only thing in the bin with those reference numbers. I left the room feeling a bit defeated. Who should I bump into but the Civil War historian. I explained the situation to him, and he jumped back in. He told the intern to go back upstairs and search all of the bins surrounding the one he had gotten the first image from. After a while, the young intern returned—and placed the game-changing photograph on the research desk in front of me. There it was, a wide-angle shot of the camp taken from across the river in Conshohocken.

The camp was a literal fortress seeming to hang out over the hillside above the Schuylkill River. I couldn't believe I actually saw the place for real, with its large wooden buildings and perimeter fence. I sat there for a long time, took several non-flash pictures with my cellular telephone, and rose to leave. I stopped by the historian's desk and thanked him profusely for his help. He indicated that the picture probably ended up in the wrong bin as far back as the early 1900s. That seemed very plausible because, more than likely, no one had been looking for it.

I have to emphasize the importance, assistance, and perseverance of Dr. Daniel Rolph, the Civil War historian who helped me find that picture.

At that point, I spilled outside onto Locust Street to get myself together, basking in the excitement of this wonderful discovery. I hesitate to add this next portion of the picture discovery story, but it seems strangely relevant. As I was leaning against the outside wall of the Historical Society's building, daydreaming and savoring the endorphin rush, a rough-looking, disheveled individual stumbled up and essentially asked me if I wanted to buy crack cocaine and "kick it" together with him. In a flash, I grabbed his shoulder and uttered, "Kick it!? Oh no, no, no. Are you aware of the incredible discovery I just made in there?" My thumb gesticulating back behind me for emphasis. "I'll have you know that a long-lost picture of Camp Discharge was just unveiled after about a century of being misfiled in the wrong bin!" He blanched and said, "Please, sir, man, I don't want any problems." I assured him that this was anything but a problem and we should be rejoicing with one another. He wrenched free of my grasp and stumbled away. I headed for my car and called Jerry Francis to give him the good news. So, now I not only knew where the camp was located—I had a visual aid. Some had speculated that the camp was a small affair with a couple of tents set up for the soldiers. This new image dashed that. The camp had clearly been a going concern.

The next critical hurdle was to gain permission and access to the Philadelphia Country Club property to conduct exploratory excavations. This was not the kind of thing one can handle with a couple of inquisitive emails. For starters, I was not a member of the club. To the best of my knowledge, neither were any board members of the Lower Merion

Historical Society. Jerry Francis is a rainmaker and ever-persistent; however, and with the assistance of Colonel Ken Brier (Retired), we secured a meeting with the Country Club's vice president at the time, Ted Berry, and his assistant in their elegant Bistro Room. Following an exchange of pleasantries, we agreed to some understandable conditions; they did not want to run the risk of me unearthing human remains. I was pleased to assure them that the US Army had leased the property from a private citizen and that anyone who had perished during the camp operations would have been removed from Mr. Kirkner's land for burial. In some instances, I had read where soldiers that died in the field would sometimes be buried in a family cemetery that happened to be nearby. In the case of the Kirkner property, there was no such family cemetery on the premises. Mr. Berry said that any excavation activities would be handled by the grounds superintendent, Mike McNulty. So, we arranged to meet with Mike McNulty and Dan Beal, the second in command of the grounds. These gentlemen were extremely accommodating and specified that access to the camp location would be granted in late November, after the golf season. Naturally, I couldn't be more thrilled with this pending excavation opportunity.

Enter my colleague and friend, Jim Remsen, who would become the primary author of this Camp Discharge book. Jerry Francis brought Jim to my attention shortly after our first meeting with Mr. Berry and suggested that he could help develop this book. So Jim and I got together at the Historical Society and launched what became the epic journey of putting together a detailed accounting of Camp Discharge. He brought the means of writing an actual book to the table, having already written two history books and had a career in journalism at the *Philadelphia Inquirer*. So we started compiling all available resources that could be ferreted out about what might be considered a footnote in the grand scheme of the American Civil War.

I had already created an overall roster file with the names that Bridget had provided, adding entries once I could make out a soldier's name in the colorful cursive writing in the 1860s. Also, soldiers' names might be spelled slightly differently in different months, and their rank, regiment, and company sometimes didn't jibe with entries found in other reference works. We were conducting a forensic assembly of historical facts that had occurred in 1864-65 regarding a specific, almost forgotten discharge camp. I had not ventured into anything quite like this before. When you google "The Battle of Gettysburg," 10,100,000 results pop up in .71 seconds. Jim was invaluable as we wended forward as he is a practiced researcher. We took day trips to various places in the greater Philadelphia area, Harrisburg, and Delaware, to locate sometimes small morsels of information. However, I felt that any discovery was a victory.

The Lower Merion Historical Society financed three overnight trips to Washington D.C. for us, and it was at the National Archives where we would make some significant discoveries. I had learned that John McArthur Jr. was the noted Philadelphia architect who had designed and drawn the blueprints for Camp Discharge and other military facilities around eastern Pennsylvania. I searched high and low through Pennsylvania's state repositories and beyond for a copy of the camp plans but to no avail. During our second visit to Washington, we had a random conversation with a researcher in the basement café at the National Archives. I was lamenting that locating the blueprints of our subject matter seemed to be a lost cause. He asked if we had checked the Archives' annex building out in College Park, Md. I didn't even know there was an annex building. He went on to say that there was a section dedicated to land holdings and architectural records. All one needed to do was take the hourly shuttle bus to the annex, So the next morning, Jim headed into the National Archives, and I headed to the shuttle. The ride to College Park was an adventure in itself. This utilitarian vehicle rode like an old stagecoach—slow, bumpy, and loud. Honestly, I would have ridden on the roof because I felt the euphoric recall of my photo find at the Historical Society of Pennsylvania. I believed that if the camp blueprints were not at the annex building, then they weren't going to be anywhere. Inside, I regaled each security personnel with the tale of how exciting the sheer gravity of this potential discovery was going to be. One or two likely took a second, security risk type look at me because I was acting like I was heading to my front-row seat at the 2017 Super Bowl. Finally, I arrived at the reference area and, as had happened on other occasions, stood wondering where to begin.

Finally, one of the research assistants asked me if I needed help. Within 15 seconds, she had grabbed a binder out of a sea of identical binders from a gigantic bookshelf and flipped it open. She said that it would be about an hour until they made the next "pull" from the records department—and that the blueprints of Camp Discharge would be delivered to the big table near the back of the room. I said, "You mean the blueprints are really here?" She confirmed that they were. I couldn't believe my good fortune. This was monumental. I hovered near the door like a dog waiting for its owner to get home. The door finally opened, and the woman pushing a cart with a giant blue-grey cardboard folder on it said, "Well, this is the most interesting thing I've pulled today." She proceeded to place the folder on the table and said that I could leave it there when I was finished with it.

I opened the folder, and there before me were four prints drawn onto very fine-threaded muslin cloth. A massive piece of the Camp Discharge puzzle was staring up at me, and I was overwhelmed with emotion. I was able to arrange for copies to be made, and just like that, we had the overall footprint of the camp along with additional detailed renderings of the camp buildings. I went outside and immediately called Jerry Francis with the good news. I rejoined Jim Remsen back at the National Archives building following another harrowing ride on the shuttle, with the cat who ate the canary expression on my face.

Amid our travels to Washington, I had begun to make regular site visits to Camp Discharge and slowly built up a collection of artifacts. The .58-caliber, three-ringed Minie ball and Williams cleaner type-three bullets were the most common finds. The Williams cleaner bullet was included in a pack of 25 paper-cartridge bullets issued to the soldiers. It is unique because there was a thin zinc edge around the base of this round that would serve to clean the residue from the musket as it was fired following the first 24. Often the soldiers would throw away the Williams cleaners because they were difficult to push down the barrel with the ramrod. I also found several eagle buttons, which were the standard issue for a soldier's coat, vest (if he had one), and kepi (cap). These were other fairly common items lost by the soldiers. I also discovered some shallow burn pits that the enlisted men had likely used for warmth and possibly heat water for coffee. It was interesting to discover that the men were using coal rather than wood to build these fires. Late in the war, some of the established camps were using coal as the primary fuel source. When looking through the supply manifests, I noticed that large quantities of coal were delivered to Camp Discharge. Something else should be highlighted about this site. The land is extremely rocky, and the soil is hot, which means that the dirt is highly mineralized. The average VLF (very low frequency) metal detector does not perform well in these conditions. I have used both a VLF and pulse induction metal detectors on the property. A pulse induction machine cuts out the mineralized soil but is less able to discriminate among the iron objects. Consequently, I recovered a fair number of horseshoes, chunks, and iron pieces that were once part of a larger object, along with hundreds of hand-forged square nails. Often whole and broken bricks were scattered throughout the area that had been used in a variety of ways at Camp Discharge.

All the familiar symptoms of a once-bustling Army post are present if you look hard enough. I wondered if anyone else had metal-detected this site over the years. Others had likely discovered the camp in one fashion or the other at some point. Perhaps they had been able to search the area before the nine-hole golf course was developed. Ideally, that would have been the best time to explore the entirety of the camp before any major changes to the landscape. After conducting a significant amount of surface hunting, I felt that I should focus my efforts on finding a trash pit or one of the nine "sinks" (latrines) reported to have been constructed at the camp. Often various interesting artifacts are thrown into these pits. To date, I have located and excavated two sinks. The first I sort of found by accident while digging an object near a tree. It became obvious that the rocks were loose and devoid of an equal amount of soil, so I started digging. The privy yielded numerous animal bones, iron objects, and one soda water bottle. A regulation sink was 12 feet long, 5 feet wide, and 10 feet deep, and this was every bit of those dimensions. I was a little disappointed that it had not been filled with artifacts. To the average person, this must seem like a feeble return for the amount of effort required to dig this large hole out completely. For me, however, this is the zenith of the search because you never know what lies beneath the next shovelful of dirt.

The second sink was a bit more interesting. After finding the first one, I was encouraged and thought there must have been another one at the bottom end of the interior camp wall. So I set out looking for a relatively level spot on the ground. Did I mention that a fair portion of the searchable area is on a slight slope? I continued to walk over the area and settled on what appeared to be a level plateau roughly meeting the regulation sink dimensions. I started to dig a test hole, removing two cubic feet of dirt and rocks in hopes of determining that it was not merely undisturbed, virgin ground. The slope is filled with large, cumbersome rocks, and after considerable effort, I was thinking of giving up. I lifted what I figured would be one more rock when suddenly the loose dirt between the rocks fell away into a void. This was at the very least an indication that the ground had been disturbed at some point, similar to what I had found at the first sink. I widened the hole and went deeper into what became loose and supple soil. Before long, I uncovered the jawbone of a pig and some broken pieces of brick. I had arrived.

The excavation of this second sink took several days at great physical expense, and I had some associates come out and intermittently assist me. Each layer of earth and rock had to be carefully removed so as not to miss any artifacts. The rest of the pig gradually materialized, along with what appeared to be an array of cow bones. Then, another soda water bottle, made by the Johnston company in Philadelphia, likely manufactured in 1864-65. Another interesting item was lime, chunks of it. This made sense. I had read in one of the military regulation books that a layer of lime and or dirt was to be thrown into the privy to help break down the materials and keep the smell to a minimum. To me, the most interesting and personal item found at the very bottom of the sink was a round eyeglass lens. I had my eye doctor look at it during my next appointment, and he said that it had been ground and polished for a farsighted prescription. Five bottles were recovered when all was said and done, the most interesting one being a Schenck's Pulmonic Syrup bottle manufactured in Philadelphia. I found an advertisement for Dr. Schenck's Pulmonic Syrup in the *New York Times*, dated April 10, 1865. "This syrup will search through every blood vessel, equalizing the circulation, preventing hemorrhage, separating the bile from the blood,

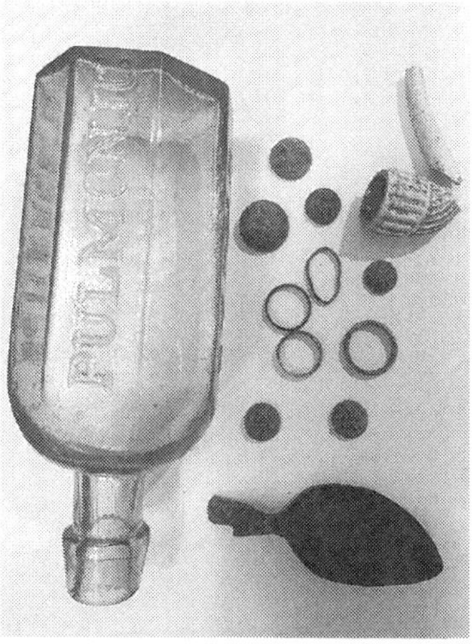

Brad Upp has found hundreds of Civil War artifacts at or near the Camp Discharge site: bullets, rifle gear, uniform parts, eating utensils, and more. At left are a medicine bottle, eagle buttons, wedding rings, a tobacco pipe, and a soldier's spoon. (Courtesy Brad Upp)

making it healthy and the circulation natural. With the aid of seaweed Tonic and Mandrake Pills, the system resumes its healthy condition, the purulent matter, abscesses, and all ulcerations of the lungs must yield to their power. . . . Victims of consumption have descended to their graves, who might have been cured if they had come to Dr. Schenck's in time and placed themselves under his directions. It is not denied that some who take Dr. Schenck's Pulmonic Syrup die also. They commence too late." This is the added benefit when unearthing artifacts from the past. It's exciting to find an object, but when you can expand that discovery into a more thorough understanding, it becomes fascinating. I found myself wondering which one of our Camp Discharge residents had thrown the bottle into the privy. What had been his ailment, and did Dr. Schenck's cutting-edge elixir help him?

The sink yielded other artifacts such as four horseshoes, some pewter underwear buttons, pieces of a small stove, and a quantity of broken glass. While the sink didn't prove to be a gold mine of relics, it secured another piece of the camp puzzle. The remaining elusive trash pit(s) would likely hold larger quantities of discarded items. I can't help but wonder if the soldiers hauled much of the camp trash off-site and threw it in the river. Again, the Army was leasing the property from Joseph Kirkner and maybe didn't want to leave too much evidence of their presence there. Perhaps the US Sanitary Commission, which regulated camp cleanliness later in the war to reduce health problems, had pushed to have anything that couldn't be burned to be removed elsewhere. We have no specific references to the sanitation procedures at Camp Discharge, so I am speculating.

Meanwhile, my metal detector has continued to unearth artifacts, including several personal items. The current count of wedding rings is four. Each is a simple brass ring that may have had a light silver or gold wash that has long since faded or chipped off the surface. Naturally, I wonder who the owners of these rings were and what circumstances led to the separation from their owners. Every 1864-65 period artifact is relevant in this journey. I have spent many days at Camp Discharge and found nothing, but the pursuit does not waver. Recently I found a Native American spear point while digging a test hole. It was about two feet in the ground and was discovered by sheer chance. The most important aspect of finding this stone-chipped tool of the Lenape, a regional Native tribe, was to confirm their presence at this location. As it turns out, I have been fortunate to find artifacts highlighting the many facets of history left behind through the centuries as this location has gone through a series of inhabitants.

I hope that the land will continue to disclose more of its secrets in the future. Another hope is that a historical marker is eventually installed along the trail that winds around the camp location (see next page) to inform people that this was once more than just a footpath. An official roadside marker along one of our nearby roads also would be well-deserved. Having spent a good deal of my adult life studying the Civil War, visiting battlefields as far away as Arizona, reenacting it, excavating it, and learning to play the music of the era, I regard Camp Discharge as a culmination of my involvement. Although the camp may have left a light footprint in our historical awareness, the humanity of those who passed through remains just below the surface.

The camp's old sentry box sits near the entrance to a hiking trail that leads to Camp Discharge. (Courtesy Brad Upp)

How to Catch a Glimpse

The Camp Discharge site is on private property today and off-limits to the general public—except for a lone, legal avenue of access for the hardy hiker. If you're interested, plan for an hour's walk, wear sturdy footwear, and consider a walking stick to negotiate occasional stretches of uneven terrain.

The access is via Sid Thayer Trail, a narrow but blazed path of Lower Merion's Bridlewild Trail system. The best entry point is from Riverbend Nature Center, at the eastern end of Spring Mill Road in Gladwyne. As you drive down Spring Mill Road, bear left at the fork with Sentry Lane—where the old Camp Discharge sentry box has been relocated. Continue into Riverbend's visitor lot and park there. A few steps farther down the road, on the right, is the entrance to Sid Thayer Trail, marked with a sign.

The trail will curve you across the wooded hillside as it heads south, roughly paralleling the Schuylkill River below. The forest and the birdsong are lovely to behold, although the Schuylkill Expressway also makes its noisy presence known. Above the trail, on the right, are a few private homes and the Philadelphia Country Club golf course. Also, on the right, a long stone wall will soon appear. Local lore claims that the wall was built by Camp Discharge soldiers, although we could find no solid proof of that. After about a half-mile, another path merges into the trail from the right side. You have crossed into the Camp Discharge grounds at that point. The camp barracks once stood above you, along the top of the wood line, and Brad Upp has done much of his excavating up there. Continue on the trail for a hundred yards, and a tumble-down stone foundation appears in front of you. These are the ruins of a settler's barn that predated Camp Discharge. Below the ruins, to the left and barely visible, are the foundations of a springhouse and the farmstead that once housed the camp commandant and his family—another site of Brad's digging.

The trail curves uphill from the barn, roughly following the road that the soldiers hiked from the rail stop below. As you ascend, you'll see a few more private homes off to the left that fall within the camp's footprint. At the top, look to your right and imagine the camp headquarters, hospital, and parade grounds that once stood there, overlooked by an enormous flagpole. From there, you can either retrace your steps or follow the service road that loops to the right, safely below the fairway. At all points, you are advised to stay on the trail, avoid wildlife and rashes, and respect the private property that the trail traverses. By all means, stay off the golf course.

Camp Discharge Roster of Enlisted Men

September 1864-September 1865

The lengthy roster that follows is divided into two sections. The first section identifies the 1,119 men from 89 Pennsylvania regiments recorded as present at Camp Discharge during their mustering-out process. Their names were drawn from a series of monthly roster sheets compiled by the Camp Discharge staff. The vast majority of them—784 men—were infantry foot soldiers from 72 volunteer regiments. The remainder came from 13 cavalry and four artillery regiments. Their regiments are presented in numerical order.

The second section is a compilation of the provost guards assigned to Camp Discharge to keep order. A total of 644 men from three regiments were posted there at different times as garrison guards. (NOTE: The camp's records list the guard units but not the guards' individual names. We list all of their names here unless there was strong evidence that an individual was no longer with his unit in that period of time.)

The entries about individual soldiers are summaries of duplicative information from various sources. Our primary sources were: Samuel P. Bates' official *History of Pennsylvania Volunteers, 1861-5*; the Civil War veterans' card file maintained by the Pennsylvania State Archives; patient records from Camp Discharge hospital and other Union hospitals; prisoner of war lists compiled by the National Park Service; and soldier records posted on the military website fold3.com. The information recorded by Civil War mustering officers could vary, so you will find recruits' ages and occupations listed for some regiments but regrettably not for most.

For men in the 69th and 97th Pa. Infantries, we were able to add details drawn from their regimental histories (*Paddy Owen's Regulars: A History of the 69th Pennsylvania "Irish Volunteers,"* by Don Ernsberger, and *History of the Ninety-Seventh Regiment, Pennsylvania Volunteer Infantry, During the War of the Rebellion, 1861-65,* by Isaiah Price).

Camp Discharge was attached to the military jurisdiction of Eastern Pennsylvania, meaning that it served regiments organized in the eastern end of the state or had drawn its recruits from eastern counties. Nevertheless, 26 of its 89 regiments had also recruited a smattering of men from counties west of the Allegheny Ridge. The number of Western Pennsylvania men associated with the camp may have been as high as 100.

If you desire fuller information about an individual soldier or unit, contact the authors at LMHistory@comcast.net

Private Orin M. Fletcher was a farmer in Troy, Pa., before enrolling in the 11th Pa. Cavalry in 1861. He re-enlisted in 1864, and during action was captured and shipped to Andersonville prison. A prisoner exchange in April 1865 brought him north to Camp Discharge, where he arrived as one of 16 Andersonville survivors from his regiment. (Courtesy Jim Mayo)

Private Isaac Rantz (above) served in the 187th Pa. Infantry, which saw action in Virginia before being assigned garrison duty at Camp Discharge. (Courtesy Deborah Himes)

John F. Morrison of Cumberland County joined the 7th Pa. Reserves at age 19 and earned promotion to corporal. Captured in battle, he spent months in Andersonville. He was one of 71 Andersonville survivors from his regiment to make it north to Camp Discharge. (Courtesy August Marchetti)

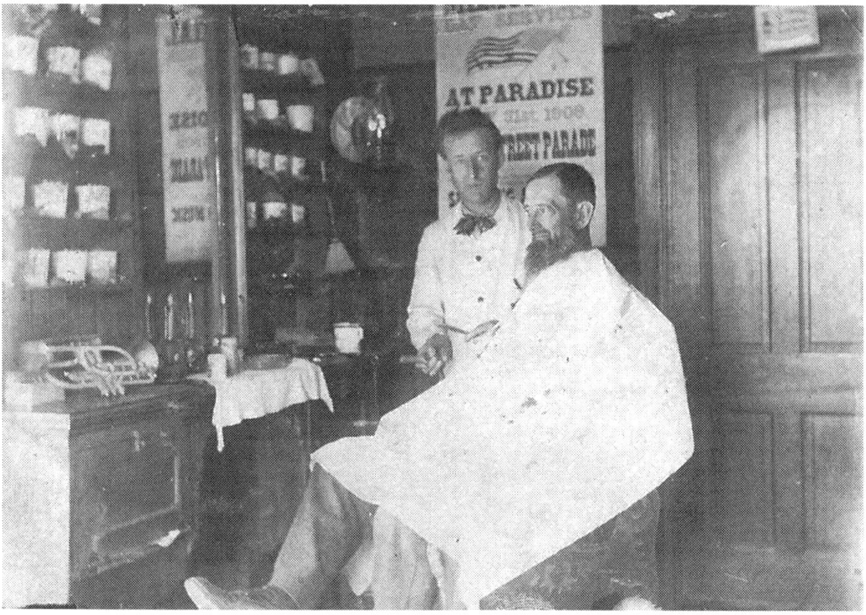

Private Amos M. Benner enlisted at age 18 in the 2nd Pa. Cavalry. He fought in multiple engagements in Virginia before being captured in 1862 and surviving Richmond's Libby Prison. After Camp Discharge, Benner returned home to Strasburg, Pa., became a carpenter, and raised five children. This 1909 photo shows him getting a trim from his son Harry, a barber in Paradise, Pa. (Courtesy Glenn Benner)

Private Adolphus H. Palmer of the 104th Pa. Infantry arrived at the camp in December 1864 and would spend four months there before being discharged. (Courtesy Ashley Killian)

Private William Shade of the 73rd Pa. Infantry spent 18 months in captivity. He was among scores of Andersonville survivors to reach Camp Discharge in May 1865. (Courtesy Christopher Neapolitan)

INFANTRY REGIMENTS

1st Battalion Pa. Infantry (100 Days Men)

The regiment was organized in July 1864 in Philadelphia, Pittsburgh, and Harrisburg. Its men were mustered out on Nov. 14, 1864. *One man passed through Camp Discharge.*

Private Andrew Lightner, Co. E – Mustered in July 1864. Mustered out November 1864. Present at Camp Discharge Nov. 22, 1864-Dec. 5, 1864. Then mustered into the 149th Pa. Infantry (100 Days), Co. I, March 22, 1865, in Carlisle at age 17. Mustered out June 24, 1865.

11th Pa. Infantry

The regiment was organized in 1861 with men from Allegheny, Dauphin, Cumberland, Westmoreland, Clinton, Lycoming, and Carbon Counties. Known as "the Bloody Eleventh," it was part of the Army of the Potomac (first I Corps, then V Corps). Its men took part in 16 engagements, including Second Bull Run, Antietam, Fredericksburg, Chancellorsville, Gettysburg, Wilderness, Spotsylvania CH, Cold Harbor, and Petersburg. Four hundred seventeen enlisted men and officers died from injuries or illnesses during service. Nineteen died at Andersonville. The regiment took part in the Grand Review in D.C., then mustered out in July 1865. *Nine of its men passed through Camp Discharge.*

Private John H. O'Neil, Co. B – Mustered in on Jan. 7, 1862, in Phila. at age 31. Absent, sick at regimental muster out. Arrived at Camp Discharge Jan. 31, 1865. Discharged by general order Feb. 2, 1865.

Private Ambrose Sourwalt, Co. G – Mustered in on Feb. 4, 1862, at age 20. Re-enlisted Feb. 4, 1864, in Phila. Absent, sick at York. Entered Camp Discharge Feb. 13, 1865. Discharged March 3, 1865.

Private Henry Jewell, Co. D – Mustered in on Feb. 14, 1862, in Phila. at age 40. Absent, sick. Recorded present at Camp Discharge Feb. 16. Discharged by general order Feb. 24, 1865.

Sergeant Hugh Sterling, Co. D – Mustered in on Feb. 16, 1862, in Phila. at age 28. Wounded April 30, 1863, details unknown. Entered Camp Discharge March 7, 1865, and discharged the same day, expiration of term.

Private John K. McChesney, Co. E – Mustered in on April 26, 1862, in Phila. at age 24. Absent, sick. Entered Camp Discharge April 28, 1865. Discharged May 2, 1865.

Private James Quigley, Co. E – Mustered in on March 7, 1862, in Phila. at age 22. Arrived at Camp Discharge May 10, 1865. Discharged by general order May 11, 1865.

Private Lawrence Baker, Co. A – Enrolled September 1861 in Carlisle at age 19. Wounded at Battle of Gettysburg. Present at Camp Discharge Sept. 23-Oct. 5, 1864. Discharged Sept. 30, 1864.

Private Horace B. Hauser, Co. K – Mustered in on Jan. 18, 1862, in Phila. at age 19, a farmer. Transferred from 90th Pa Infantry Nov. 26, 1864. Entered Camp Discharge Jan. 20, 1865. Discharged Jan. 28, 1865.

Private David N. Steward, Co. A – Mustered in on April 16, 1862, in Phila. at age 29. Absent, sick in the hospital. Recorded present at Camp Discharge April 14, 1865. Discharged April 20, 1865.

23rd Pa. Infantry

The regiment, also known as 'Birney's Zouaves,' recruited men in Philadelphia. They became part of the Army of the Potomac (first IV Corps, then VI Corps). Its men were involved in 8 combat engagements, including Fair Oaks, Fredericksburg, Gettysburg, Cold Harbor, and Petersburg. One hundred seventy enlisted men and eight officers dead in battle or disease. Four of its men died at Andersonville. The regiment mustered out in September 1864. *Eleven of its men went through Camp Discharge, including five Andersonville survivors.*

Private Louis/Lewis Evans, Co. F – Mustered in August 1861 in Phila. at age 26, a carter. Admitted to Cuyler Hospital, Germantown, December 1862. Entered Camp Discharge Oct. 4, 1864. Mustered out Dec. 1, 1864.

Musician George W. Blanck, Co. B – Mustered in April 1861 in Phila. Prisoner of war Sept. 21, 1863-Dec. 10, 1864, details unknown. Entered Camp Discharge Feb. 21, 1865. Discharged March 15, 1865.

Private Alexander Powell, Co. F – Mustered in on Aug. 2, 1861, in Phila. Captured at Cold Harbor, Va., June 1, 1864. Imprisoned at Andersonville. Released March 1, 1865, at Wilmington, N.C. Recorded present at Camp Discharge April 3, 1865. Discharged April 12, 1865.

Corporal John J. Howe, Co. K – Mustered in August 1861 in Phila. at age 20, a pasteboard maker. Re-enlisted Dec. 26, 1863. Captured at Cold Harbor, Va., June 1, 1864. Held at Andersonville prison. Exchanged April 15, 1865. Arrived at Camp Discharge May 22, 1865. Hospitalized there for ecthyma May 25 and May 31, 1865. Mustered out June 20, 1865. Joined Veteran Reserve Corps.

Private Albert Thalheimer Co. B – Mustered in August 1861 in Phila. at age 19. Captured June 1, 1864, at Cold Harbor, Va. Imprisoned at Andersonville. Released March 27, 1865. Recorded present at Camp Discharge May 22, 1865. Discharged June 10, 1865.

Corporal John McCabe, Co. C – Mustered in September 1861 in Phila. Promoted to corporal Oct. 8, 1861. Captured at Cold Harbor, Va., June 1, 1864. Present at Camp Discharge Oct. 4-6, 1864. Mustered out Oct. 7, 1864.

Private John B. Ulrich, Co. B – Enrolled July 17, 1861, in Phila. at age 21. Mustered in on Aug. 2, 1861, in Phila. Absent, sick in Sandy Hook (Md.) Hospital, at regimental muster out. Recorded present at Camp Discharge Sept. 30, 1864. Discharged Oct. 5, 1864.

Private Robert Davenport, Co. A – Mustered in on Aug. 8, 1861, in Phila. at age 27. Absent, sick in hospital, at regimental muster out. Recorded present at Camp Discharge Oct. 3, 1864. Discharged Oct. 11, 1864.

Private John Lant, Co. H – Mustered in September 1861 in Pittsburgh at age 18. Transferred to Co. E Aug. 23, 1864, to serve out the term. Recorded at Camp Discharge Sept. 27, 1864. Mustered out Nov. 11, 1864.

Private John Kock, Co. C – mustered into service Sept. 1, 1861, in Phila. Captured June 1, 1864, at Cold Harbor, Va. Imprisoned at Andersonville. Entered Camp Discharge Feb. 21, 1865. Discharged Feb. 25, 1865.

Private Alexander Pitts, Co. E – Mustered into service Aug. 14, 1861, in Phila. at age 19. Captured June 1, 1864, at Cold Harbor, Va. Imprisoned at Richmond and Andersonville. Paroled Nov. 30, 1864, at Savannah, Ga. Entered Camp Discharge Jan. 27, 1865. Discharged Jan. 31, 1865. Did additional service with 9th US Veteran Volunteers.

26th Pa. Infantry

The regiment was recruited in 1861 solely in Philadelphia. It became part of the Army of the Potomac (III Corps, then II Corps). Its men were involved in 17 combat engagements, including Seven Days, Savage Station, White Oak Swamp, Malvern Hill, Second Bull Run, Fredericksburg, Chancellorsville, Gettysburg, Wilderness, and Spotsylvania. Two hundred twenty-two of its enlisted men and officers died from injuries or illness. Thirteen men died at Andersonville. The regiment mustered out in June 1864. *Twelve of its men went through Camp Discharge; four had been POWs, including one known Andersonville survivor.*

Corporal John O. Drain, Co. K – Mustered in May 1861 in Phila. at age 18. Promoted to corporal July 1, 1863. Captured at Battle of Wilderness, Va., May 5, 1864. Entered Camp Discharge Jan. 28, 1865, and hospitalized there for catarrh the next day. Discharged Jan 31, 1865.

Private William Arbuckle, Co. A – Mustered in May 1861 in Phila. at age 18. Deserted May 27, 1864, at Wilderness, Va. Recorded at Camp Discharge Jan. 11, 1865. Forwarded to the provost marshal. Date of discharge May 13, 1865.

Private Levi Flight, Co. G – Mustered in February 1864 in Norristown at age 48, a cooper. Transferred to 99th Pa. Infantry May 29, 1864. Wounded at Spotsylvania Court House, Va., May 12, 1864. Lost by desertion from 153rd Pa. Infantry. Transferred to Veteran Reserve Corps Aug. 18, 1864. Recorded present at Camp Discharge Feb. 13, 1865. Discharged March 22, 1865.

Private William H. Miller, Co. K – Transferred to 4th N.Y. Artillery May 1862. Entered Camp Discharge Feb. 16, 1865. Discharged March 18, 1865.

Private John A. Porter, Co. C – Mustered in January 1862 in Phila. at age 31, a druggist. Transferred to 99th Pa. Infantry May 29, 1864. Recorded present at Camp Discharge April 12, 1865. Discharged April 20, 1865.

Private Andrew J. Marshall, Co K – Mustered in June 1861 in Phila. at age 21. Transferred to 99th Pa. Infantry May 30, 1864. Absent, sick at regimental muster out. Discharged May 13, 1865.

Private Otho Greib, Co. G – Mustered in July 1863 in Norristown at age 19. Deserted Oct. 14, 1863, near Beverly Ford, Va., on the line of march. Captured that day. Imprisoned at Andersonville. Freed April 28, 1865. Arrived at Camp Discharge May 31, 1865. Mustered out July 14, 1865.

Private John Scott, Co. E – Mustered in February 1863 in Phila. at age 23. Prisoner of war Oct. 14, 1863-March 8, 1865, circumstances not recorded. Entered Camp Discharge June 15, 1865. Mustered out July 17, 1865.

Private John Ferguson, Co. E – Mustered in on March 8, 1864, in Phila. at age 30. Transferred to 99th Pa. Infantry May 29, 1864. Wounded Oct. 27, 1864, at Petersburg, Va. Discharged per general order May 3, 1865.

Private Robert White, Co. D – Mustered in on June 1861 in Phila. at age 20. Captured at Battle of Wilderness May 6, 1864. Released Feb. 26, 1865. Mustered out May 18, 1865.

Private James Ferguson, Co. C – Mustered in May 1861 in Phila. at age 21. Entered Camp. Discharge Jan. 27, 1865. Hospitalized there for bronchitis Jan. 28-Feb. 3, 1865. Discharged June 18, 1865.

Private Samuel Mitchell, Co. B – Mustered in on Jan. 22, 1862, in Phila. at age 21. Transferred to 99th Pa. Infantry May 24, 1864. Entered Camp Discharge Jan. 23, 1865, and discharged two days later. Did additional service with 7th US Veteran Volunteers.

27th Pa. Infantry

The regiment was recruited in 1861 only in Philadelphia. It became attached to the Army of the Potomac (II Corps, I Corps, XI Corps), then the Army of the Cumberland. Involved in 11 combat engagements, including First Bull Run, Second Bull Run, Chancellorsville, Gettysburg, Lookout Mountain, Missionary Ridge, Knoxville, and Atlanta Campaigns. It lost 134 enlisted men and officers to injuries or illness. Ten died at Andersonville. The regiment mustered out in June 1864. *Four of its men went through Camp Discharge, three of them Andersonville survivors.*

Private George Mueller, Co. A – Mustered in on Aug. 1, 1861, at Roaches Mill, Va., at age 26, a "Morocco dresser" (specialty leatherworker). Transferred to 109th Pa. Infantry June 1864. Recorded present at Camp Discharge Oct. 4-Dec. 5, 1864, then absent. Discharged March 3, 1865.

Private Florence Matrony, Co. D – Mustered in June 1861 in Phila. at age 28, a laborer. Captured July 2, 1863, during Battle of Gettysburg. Imprisoned at Andersonville (listed as Sigmund Matrony). Recorded present at Camp Discharge Dec. 29, 1864. Hospitalized there for diarrhea Jan. 20, 1865. Discharged from service by general order Jan. 21, 1865.

Private Sigmund Warburg, Co. D – Mustered in June 1861 in Phila. at age 26, a merchant. Captured July 2, 1863, during Battle of Gettysburg. Imprisoned at Andersonville. Recorded present at Camp Discharge Dec. 29, 1864. Hospitalized there for catarrh Jan. 6, 1865. Discharged from service Jan. 23, 1865.

Private Christopher Ernst, Co. E – Mustered in June 1861 in Phila. at age 32, a farmer. Captured Nov. 25, 1863, during Battle of Missionary Ridge, Tenn. Held at Andersonville prison. Paroled at Jacksonville, Fla., April 29, 1865. Recorded present at Camp Discharge June 6, 1865. Mustered out by general order June 14, 1865.

28th Pa. Infantry

The regiment was organized in 1861 with men from Philadelphia and Luzerne, Westmoreland, Carbon, Northampton, Allegheny, and Huntingdon Counties. It became known as 'the Goldstream Regiment.' Part of the Army of Virginia, Army of the Potomac (XII Corps), Army of the Cumberland. It was involved in 19 combat engagements, including Second Bull Run, Antietam, Chancellorsville, Gettysburg, Lookout Mountain, Missionary Ridge, Atlanta Campaign, Kennesaw Mountain, Peachtree Creek, Sherman's March the Sea, and the Carolinas Campaign. It lost 284 enlisted men and officers to injuries or disease. The regiment mustered out in July 1865. *Twenty-four of its men went through Camp Discharge, twelve of them ex-POWs.*

Sergeant George T. Barnes, Co. D – Mustered in July 1861 in Phila. at age 25. Promoted to corporal, then sergeant December 1861. Commissioned 2nd lieutenant May 1863 but not mustered. Wounded at Battle of Chancellorsville May 3, 1863. Recorded at Camp Discharge Oct. 5, 1864. Discharged Jan. 4, 1865.

Private John Smith, Co. I – Mustered in on Aug. 29, 1863, in West Chester at age 32, a substitute. Wounded in jaw May 8, 1864, at Battle of Rocky Face Ridge, Ga. Recorded present at Camp Discharge Oct. 31, 1864. Discharged by general order June 23, 1865.

Private William H. Gabriel, Co. C – Mustered in October 1861 in Point of Rocks, Md., at age 18, from Phila. Recorded present at Camp Discharge Oct. 24, 1864. Hospitalized there for gonorrhea on Dec. 17, 1864. Discharged Dec. 28, 1864, expiration of service. Did additional service with 147th Pa. Infantry and 22nd Pa. Infantry.

Private Montreville Young, Co. K – Mustered in on Feb. 14, 1865, in Easton at age 19, a blacksmith. Captured near Raleigh, N.C., April 9, 1865. Paroled at Durham April 29, 1865. Entered Camp Discharge May 23, 1865. Discharged June 27, 1865.

Private Thomas Flinn, Co. D – Mustered in on Jan. 10, 1864, in Troy, Pa., at age 21, a substitute. Captured at James Island, S.C., July 3, 1864. Paroled at Jacksonville, Fla. April 29, 1865. Recorded present at Camp Discharge May 24, 1865. Mustered out June 27, 1865.

Private Charles Neale, Co E – Mustered in February 1865 in Easton at age 24, a substitute. Captured March 31. 1865, in South Carolina. Paroled May 5, 1865, at Savannah, Ga. Arrived at Camp Discharge May 20, 1865. Discharged by general order June 27, 1865.

Private Jackson Anderson, Co. B – Mustered in March 1864 at Harrisburg at age 18, a laborer from Westmoreland County. Captured March 28, 1865, at Snow Hill, N.C. Paroled at Savannah, Ga., May 5, 1865. Entered Camp Discharge May 20, 1865. Mustered out June 5, 1865.

Private Tilman F. Layman/Lemon, Co. B – Mustered in March 1864 in Harrisburg at age 18, a laborer from Westmoreland County. Captured March 28, 1865, at Snow Hill, N.C. Paroled at Savannah, Ga., May 5, 1865. Arrived at Camp Discharge May 20, 1865. Discharged June 22, 1865.

Private Henry Martin, Co. B – Mustered in March 1864 in Harrisburg at age 27, a laborer from Westmoreland County. Captured March 26, 1865, at Snow Hill, N.C. Paroled at Savannah May 5, 1865. Arrived at Camp Discharge May 20, 1865. Mustered out June 5, 1865.

Private Peter Keely, Co. H – Drafted and mustered in September 1863 in Frankford at age 23. Taken prisoner at Sister's Ferry, Ga. Paroled and returned to his company. Recorded present at Camp Discharge May 31, 1865. Mustered out with company July 18, 1865.

Private George Cartwright, Co. F – Drafted, mustered in on July 17, 1863, in Phila at age 34. Wounded in chest and face at Battle of Pine Knob, Ga., June 15, 1864. Admitted to Cumberland Hospital, Tenn., June 20 to treat wounds. Furloughed July 18, 1864. Arrived at Camp Discharge March 11, 1865. Mustered out by general order June 9, 1865.

Private John Shriver, Co. A – Drafted, mustered in December 1864 at Hollidaysburg at age 21. Absent, sick since April 8, 1865. Recorded present at Camp Discharge May 25, 1865. Mustered out June 9, 1865.

Private William H. Thomas, Co. E – Drafted; mustered in December 1864 in Hollidaysburg. Absent, sick since March 17, 1865. Recorded present at Camp Discharge May 25, 1865. Discharged June 9, 1965.

Sergeant David F. Ghrist Co. B – Mustered in June 1861 in Phila. at age 21. Re-enlisted Dec. 12, 1863. Captured March 27, 1865, at Snow Hill, N.C. Paroled at Savannah, Ga., May 5, 1865. Recorded present at Camp Discharge May 22, 1865. Mustered out June 22, 1865.

Private William H. Nicholas, Co. I – Mustered in February 1865 in Easton at age 18, a clerk. Captured April 9, 1865. Paroled at Durham, N.C., April 29, 1865. Recorded present at Camp Discharge May 23, 1865. Mustered out June 22, 1865.

Private John Welsh, Co. G – Mustered in July 1861 in Phila. at age 24. Transferred to Veteran Reserve Corps Sept. 18, 1863. Recorded present at Camp Discharge May 24, 1865. Hospitalized there for acute diarrhea on June 3, 1865. Discharged June 28, 1865.

Private John Walsh, Co. E – Mustered in on Jan. 27, 1865, in Scranton, at age 19, a substitute. Captured in South Carolina April 1, 1865. Paroled at Savannah, Ga., May 5, 1865. Discharged by general order June 28, 1865.

Private William McDonald, Co. I – Mustered in on Feb. 14, 1865, in Norristown at age 30, a seaman. Captured in South Carolina April 1, 1865. Released at Sister's Ferry, Ga., May 5, 1865. Recorded present at Camp Discharge May 19, 1865. Discharged June 29, 1865.

Private George Curtis, Co. E – Mustered in on Feb. 4, 1865, in Phila. at age 24, a substitute. Captured in South Carolina April 1, 1865. Paroled at Sister's Ferry, Ga., May 5, 1865. Recorded present at Camp Discharge June 8, 1865. Hospitalized there for dislocation and fracture of thumb June 13, 1865. Discharged by general order June 29, 1865.

Private John Ribble Jr., Co. D – Mustered in July 1861 in Phila. at age 21. Re-enlisted Dec. 24, 1863, at Wanhatchie, Tenn. Absent at muster out, sick, since May 3, 1864. Recorded present at Camp Discharge July 13, 1865. Joined Veteran Reserve Corps.

Private George Townsend, Co. C – Mustered in on Jan. 27, 1865, in Frankford at age 22, a clerk. Recorded present at Camp Discharge June 30, 1865. Discharged by general order Aug. 24, 1865.

Private John A. Ferguson, Co. D – Mustered in on July 10, 1861, in Phila. at age 27, a paper hanger. Re-enlisted Feb. 20, 1864, at Phila. Recorded at Camp Discharge Sept. 23, 1864. Hospitalized there for "debility from miasma disease" Nov. 18, 1864. Detailed to post hospital for duty Dec. 9, 1865. Absent, on detached service, at regimental muster out. Did additional duty with Veteran Reserve Corps.

Private Thomas Watt, Co. C – Mustered in on July 3, 1861, in Phila. at age 24, a weaver. Wounded at Battles of Resaca, Ga., May 15, 1864, and Pine Knob, Ga., June 15, 1864. Recorded present at Camp Discharge Sept. 26, 1864. Discharged Oct. 8, 1864.

Private Charles Wright, Co. C – Mustered in on July 3, 1861, in Phila. at age 23. Entered Camp Discharge Dec. 5, 1864, and discharged the same day. Did additional service with 147th Pa. Infantry.

29th Pa. Infantry

The regiment was organized in 1861 with men from Philadelphia, Montgomery (Cos. C & F), Franklin, and Erie Counties. It was attached to the Army of the Potomac (V Corps, XII Corps), Army of Virginia, Army of the Cumberland. Its men were involved in 21 combat engagements, including First Winchester, Chancellorsville, Gettysburg, Lookout Mountain, Missionary Ridge, Atlanta Campaign, Kennesaw Mountain, Peachtree Creek, Atlanta Siege, Sherman's March to the Sea, and the Carolinas Campaign. They lost 187 enlisted men and officers to injuries or illness. One of its men died at Andersonville. The regiment mustered out July 1865. *Fourteen of its men went through Camp Discharge; sevem had been POWs, including one Andersonville survivor.*

Private Francis R. Wylie, Co. B – Enrolled July 1861 in Phila. at age 18, a shoemaker. Recorded present at Camp Discharge Sept. 24, 1865. Discharged by general order Dec. 3, 1864.

Private James Connerton, Co. C – Enrolled May 14, 1861, mustered in on July 1, 1864, both at Phila., age 19. Recorded present at Camp Discharge Sept. 22, 1864. Discharged by general order Dec. 3, 1864.

Private Thomas Cox, Co. H – Mustered in January 1865 in Frankford at age 24. Prisoner of war March 10 to May 5, 1865. Arrived at Camp Discharge May 23, 1865. Discharged by gen. order June 27, 1865.

Private Robert M'Cormick. Co. G – Mustered in on Feb. 10, 1865, in West Chester at age 37, a coachman born in Ireland. Absent, sick in hospital since April 9, 1865. Entered Camp Discharge May 12, 1865. Discharged by general order June 14, 1865.

Private Gottlieb Deitz, Co. G – Mustered in January 1864 in Phila. at age 20, a rope maker born in Germany. Captured at Goldsboro, N.C., March 28, 1865. Paroled at Savannah, Ga., May 5, 1865. Arrived at Camp Discharge May 22, 1865. Mustered out June 8, 1865.

Private Benjamin Smith, Co. B – Mustered in January 1865 in Troy, Pa., at age 19. Captured in Jefferson County, Ga., Feb. 20, 1865. Paroled at Savannah, Ga., May 5, 1865. Recorded present at Camp Discharge May 25, 1865. Discharged by general order July 5, 1865.

Private John A. Ward, Co. B – Mustered in February 1864 in Phila. at age 21. Captured at Dallas, Ga., May 25, 1864. Imprisoned at Andersonville. Paroled. Arrived at Camp Discharge May 26, 1865. Discharged by general order June 26, 1865.

Private Michael Rogers/Rodgers, Co. C – Mustered in on Oct. 18, 1864, in Phila, age 42, Irish-born laborer. Hospitalized in New Bern, N.C., since March 1865. Recorded at Camp Discharge May 11, 1865. Discharged by general order May 22, 1865.

Private John Rodney/Runey, Co. D – Mustered in on Jan. 17, 1865, in Reading at age 23, a substitute. Captured at Adais Run, S.C., Jan. 28, 1865. Paroled at Savannah May 5, 1865. At Camp Discharge May 20, 1865. Discharged May 23, 1865.

Private Peter Garegan, Co. I – Mustered in on Jan. 16, 1865, in Pottsville, at age 19, a substitute. Captured and escaped, circumstances not given. Entered Camp Discharge May 20, 1865. Discharged by general order July 28, 1865.

Private Henry Rementer Sr., Co. E – Mustered in on Sept. 1, 1862, in Phila. at age 45. Recorded present at Camp Discharge July 31, 1865. Discharged by general order Oct. 13, 1865.

Private William Rutter, Co. I – Mustered in February 1864 in Phila. at age 18, a recruit. Recorded present at Camp Discharge June 7, 1865. Mustered out with company July 17, 1865.

Private Henry M. Reuter, Unassigned – Mustered in on Jan. 5, 1865, in Williamsport at age 19; a substitute. Captured at Salkehatchie, S.C., March 10, 1865. Paroled at Savannah, Ga., May 5, 1865. Arrived at Camp Discharge June 7, 1865. Discharged by general order Aug. 9, 1865.

Private David B. Olmstead, Co. B – Enrolled May 1861 in Phila. at age 19, one of three Olmsteads in Co. B. Wounded at Resaca, Ga., May 15, 1864. Entered Camp Discharge Sept. 24, 1864. Discharged by general order Sept. 26, 1864.

30th Pa. Infantry (1st Pa. Reserves)

The regiment was recruited in 1861 in Chester, Delaware, Lancaster, and Cumberland Counties. It was attached to the Army of the Potomac (I Corps, V Corps). The men were involved in 17 combat engagements, including Seven Days, Mechanicsville, Savage Station, Malvern Hill, Second Bull Run, Antietam, Fredericksburg, Gettysburg, Wilderness, Spotsylvania, and Cold Harbor. The regiment lost 175 enlisted men and officers to injury and sickness. It mustered out on June 10, 1864. *Twelve of its men went through Camp Discharge; seven were Andersonville survivors.*

Private George Laird, Co. F – Enrolled May 30, 1861, in Phila. at age 27, a farmer. Mustered in on July 26, 1861, in Baltimore. Captured Feb. 14, 1864. Imprisoned in Richmond. Arrived at Camp Discharge Feb. 17, 1865. Mustered out March 3, 1865, by order of Maj. Hayden.

Private William Moudy, Co. I – Enrolled May 10, 1861, in West Chester at age 26. Mustered in on July 26, 1861, in Baltimore. Deserted May 4 and captured May 5, 1864, at Wilderness, Va. Imprisoned at Andersonville. Recorded present at Camp Discharge Feb. 20, 1865. Hospitalized there for catarrh Feb. 22-27, for rheumatism March 11-15. Mustered out March 21, 1865, by order of Maj. Harper.

Private Passmore W. Hoopes, Co. A – Mustered in on Sept. 20, 1861, at Washington, D.C., at age 21, one of 4 Hoopeses in Co. A. Transferred to 190th Pa. Infantry May 31, 1864. Taken captive, circumstances not given. Imprisoned at Andersonville. Present at Camp Discharge June 14-28, 1865. Muster-out date not recorded.

Sergeant Abraham D. Heiser, Co. H – Enrolled July 17, 1861, in West Chester at age 34. Mustered in on July 24 in Washington, DC. Transferred to 190th Pa. Infantry June 1, 1864. Hospitalized at Camp Discharge for colic pains for cold Dec. 22, 1864. Joined Veteran Reserve Corps.

Private William R, Paull, Co. A – Mustered in on Dec. 1, 1861, in Pierpont, Va., at age 19. Transferred to 1st Pa. Rifles May 31, 1864. Entered Camp Discharge Dec. 7, 1865. Discharged Dec. 27, 1864.

Private Franklin Aument, Co. E – Mustered in on Feb. 5, 1864, in Lancaster at age 20, a laborer. Captured May 30, 1864, at Bethesda Church, Va. Transferred to 190th Pa. Infantry May 31, 1864, to serve out his time. Held at Andersonville prison. Exchanged April 1865. Arrived at Camp Discharge May 23, 1865. Muster out date not recorded. Joined Veteran Reserve Corps.

Private Calvin Harbaugh, Co. K – Enrolled June 19, 1861, in West Chester at age 19, a laborer. Mustered in July 1861 in Baltimore. Re-enlisted February 1864 at Bristoe, Va. Transferred to 190th Pa. Infantry May 31, 1864. Captured, circumstance not given. Held at Andersonville prison. Exchanged at Millen, Ga., October 1864. Recorded at Camp Discharge May 21-June 2, 1865. Joined Veteran Reserve Corps.

Corporal Hanford H. Rigg, Co. A – Mustered in May 1861 in Baltimore at age 19, a blacksmith from Chester. Re-enlisted February 1864 at Bristoe, Va. Transferred to 190th Pa. Infantry May 31, 1864. Taken prisoner, circumstance not given. Held at Andersonville. Sent to Millen, Ga., Nov. 11, 1864. Recorded present at Camp Discharge May 21-June 30, 1865. Mustered out June 28, 1865. Joined Veteran Reserve Corps.

Corporal Gottleib Hildwine, Co. I – Mustered in July 1861 in Baltimore at age 25. Captured May 30, 1864, at Bethesda Church, Va. Held at Andersonville prison. Exchanged. Arrived at Camp Discharge May 29, 1865, and mustered out two days later. Joined Veteran Reserve Corps.

Private Miller Brady, Co. D – Enrolled June 8, 1861, in West Chester at age 42, a mason tender. Mustered in July 1861 in Baltimore. Absent, wounded, in hospital since May 10, 1864. Recorded present at Camp Discharge Sept. 23, 1864. No discharge date listed.

Private Joseph Garret, Co. H – Mustered into service Sept. 6, 1861, at age 20. Entered Camp Discharge Jan. 23, 1865, and mustered out two days later.

Private John Elliot, Co. E – Mustered into service July 26, 1861, in Baltimore at age 30, a farmer. Captured Nov. 27, 1862, circumstance not given. Imprisoned at Andersonville. Entered Camp Discharge Feb. 2, 1865. Discharged Feb. 8, 1

31st Pa. Infantry (2nd Pa. Reserves)

The regiment was organized in 1861 with men from Philadelphia, Huntingdon, Blair, and Lancaster Counties. It was part of the Army of the Potomac (I Corps, V Corps). The men were involved in 17 combat engagements, including Seven Days, Mechanicsville, Savage Station, Malvern Hill, Second Bull Run, Antietam, Fredericksburg, Gettysburg, Wilderness, Spotsylvania, and Cold Harbor. It lost 151 enlisted men and officers to injury or illness. The regiment took part in the Grand Review in D.C., then mustered out June 16, 1864. *Five of its men went through Camp Discharge, including one Andersonville survivor.*

Private John Elliott, Co. B – Enrolled Oct. 3, 1861, in Harrisburg at age 30, a shoemaker born in Ireland. Mustered in on Oct. 29, 1861, in Harrisburg. Deserted July 9, 1863, at Bull Run, Va. Transferred to 191st Pa. Infantry June 6, 1864. Recorded at Camp Discharge April 10, 1865. Charge of desertion withdrawn May 24, 1865. Discharged from service May 29, 1865.

Private James Maines, Co. D – Mustered in September 1862 in Phila. at age 25. Deserted from Falmouth, Va., Dec. 19, 1862. Recorded at Camp Discharge July 3, 1865. Muster-out date not given.

Private Thomas G. Burns, Co. H – Enrolled May 27, 1861, in Phila. at age 33. Mustered in on Aug. 1, 1861, at Sandy Hook, Md. Wounded at Gettysburg July 1863. Missing in action Nov. 28, 1863, at New Hope Church, Va. Taken prisoner May 6, 1864, at Charles City Cross Roads. Imprisoned at Andersonville. Released April 28, 1865. Mustered out May 20, 1865, by order of Maj. Hayden.

Private Marshall Houk/Houck, Co. F – Mustered in on Aug. 27, 1861. Wounded at Spotsylvania Court House, Va., May 10, 1864. Transferred to 191st Pa. Infantry June 6, 1864. Entered

Camp Discharge Feb. 27, 1865. Hospitalized there for cephalalgia Feb. 28-March 1, 1865. Discharge date not recorded. Did additional service with 1st D.C. Infantry.

Sergeant William Brighton, Co. G – Enrolled Feb. 2, 1862, in Lancaster at age 23, a farmer. Mustered in on June 25, 1862, in Harrisburg. Promoted from corporal. Taken captive at Fredericksburg, Va., Dec. 13, 1862, and from May 5, 1864, to April 1, 1865. Recorded present at Camp Discharge June 16, 1864. Discharged June 22, 1865.

32nd Pa. Infantry (3rd Pa Reserves)

The regiment formed in 1861 with men from Philadelphia, Bucks, Berks, and Wayne Counties. It became part of the Army of the Potomac (I Corps, XXII Corps). The men took part in 11 combat engagements, including Mechanicsville, Malvern Hill, Second Bull Run, Antietam, Fredericksburg, and Winchester. They suffered 127 fatalities from injuries or illness. The regiment mustered out June 17, 1864. *Eight of its men went through Camp Discharge, including three Andersonville survivors.*

Private Charles H. Barber, Co. D – Enrolled June 7, 1861, in Reading at age 20, a boatman. Mustered in on July 28, 1861, in Harrisburg. Re-enlisted Nov. 23, 1863. Transferred to 54th Pa. Infantry July 4, 1864, by re-enlistment. Wounded in legs. Captured, circumstances not known. Held at Andersonville prison. Exchanged April 1865. Recorded present at Camp Discharge May 26-June 1, 1865. Did extra duty with Veteran Reserve Corps.

Private John H. Babb/Bobb, Co. A – Enrolled June 7, 1861, in Berks County at age 19, a clerk. Mustered in on July 28, 1861, in Harrisburg. Wounded and captured at Battle of Cloyd's Mountain, Va., May 9, 1864. Held at Andersonville prison. Paroled May 28, 1865. Recorded present at Camp Discharge May 26, 1865. Mustered out May 30, 1865.

Private John M. Yohn, Co. A – Enrolled June 7, 1861, in Easton at age 18, a farmer. Mustered in on July 28, 1861, at Harrisburg. Transferred to 5th Pa. Infantry June 4, 1864. Wounded in leg and captured, circumstance not known. Held at Andersonville prison. Exchanged April 1, 1865. Recorded present at Camp Discharge May 26-June 1, 1865. Did additional duty with Veteran Reserve Corps.

Private Edmund W. Frill, Co. D – Enrolled June 11, 1861, in Berks County at age 21, a machinist. Mustered in on July 28, 1861, in Harrisburg. Deserted Oct. 30, 1862, at Berlin, Md. Entered Camp Discharge June 20, 1865, and hospitalized the next day for "Deb. M. Dis." (debility from miasmatic disease). Mustered out by order of Maj. Love June 23, 1865.

Corporal Henry Bennett, Co. C – Enrolled May 10, 1861, in Bucks County at age 22, a farmer. Mustered in on July 29, 1861, in Harrisburg. Recorded present at Camp Discharge Jan. 16, 1865. Mustered out by order of Maj. Hayden Feb. 8, 1865.

Private Samuel M. Adair, Co. K – Mustered in July 1861 in Camp Washington, Pa., at age 21. Transferred to 54th Pa. Infantry July 4, 1864. Recorded at Camp Discharge Sept. 29, 1864, arriving from Cumberland, Md. Admitted to Camp Discharge Hospital with "Pterygium Gran dis" (an eye disease) Nov. 27, 1864. Discharged from the military by general order Jan. 7, 1865.

Private John Wentzel, Co. F – Mustered in July 1861 in Harrisburg at age 30, a laborer from Berks County. Transferred to 54th Pa. Infantry July 4, 1864. Recorded present at Camp Discharge Nov. 3, 1864, forwarded from Harrisburg. Hospitalized at camp for constipation Nov. 30, 1864. Did additional service with Veteran Reserve Corps.

Private Jeremiah C. Hunsburger (Hansberger), Co. D – Mustered in on July 26, 1861, in Harrisburg at age 28, a miller. Wounded and taken prisoner at Battle of Cloyd's Mountain, Va., May 9, 1864. Imprisoned at Andersonville. Recorded present at Camp Discharge Oct. 15-Nov. 22, 1864.

33rd Pa. Infantry (4th Pa. Reserves)

The regiment was raised in 1861 with men from Philadelphia, Montgomery (Co. C), Chester, Lycoming, Monroe, and Susquehanna Counties. It joined the Army of the Potomac (I Corps, V Corps). Involved in nine combat engagements, including Mechanicsville, Malvern Hill, Second Bull Run, Antietam, and Fredericksburg. It had 139 enlisted men and officers die from injuries or illness. Two died at Andersonville. The regiment mustered out June 17, 1864. *Five of its men went through Camp Discharge, including 1 Andersonville survivor.*

Private Joseph H. Mehaffey, Co. D – Mustered into service July 17, 1861, in Harrisburg at age 20, a farmer. Wounded and captured May 9, 1864, at Battle of Cloyd's Mountain, Va. Released Dec. 10, 1864, at Charleston, S.C. Entered Camp Discharge Feb 16, 1865. Discharged March 7, 1865.

Private Francis Sanville, Co. I – Mustered in on Feb. 3, 1862, in Phila. at age 21. Captured May 9, 1864, at Cloyd's Mountain, Va. Imprisoned at Andersonville. Transferred to 54th Pa. Infantry June 8, 1864, by general order. Held captive until March 1, 1865. Recorded present at Camp Discharge March 23, 1865. Hospitalized there for catarrh April 14-21, 1865. Discharged from military May 4, 1865.

Corporal William Warren, Co. B – Mustered into service July 17, 1861, in Harrisburg at age 26. Promoted to corporal Jan. 1, 1862. Wounded and taken prisoner May 9, 1864, at Battle of Cloyd's Mountain, Va. At Camp Discharge Oct. 3-7, 1864.

Musician Benjamin Franklin Houck, Co. K – Enrolled June 6, 1861, in Chester County at age 22, a lawyer. Mustered in on July 17, 1961, in Harrisburg as a musician. Deserted Dec. 1, 1862, at Brooks Station, Va. Apprehended Jan. 9, 1864, and found absent on account of sickness. Recorded at Camp Discharge Oct. 14, 1864. Charge of desertion removed Oct. 18, 1864. Discharged, to date June 17, 1864.

Private Frederick Weaver, Co. E – Mustered in on July 17, 1861, in Harrisburg at age 22. Wounded, absent in hospital, at regimental muster out. Entered Camp Discharge Nov. 29, 1864. Discharged Dec. 3, 1864.

36th Pa. Infantry (7th Pa Reserves)

The regiment was recruited in 1861 with men from Philadelphia, Cumberland, Perry, Lebanon, Clinton, Luzerne, and Berks Counties. It was attached to the Army of the Potomac (I Corps). The men were involved in 13 combat engagements, including at Mechanicsville, Malvern Hill, Second Bull Run, Antietam, Fredericksburg, Wilderness, Spotsylvania, and North Anna. They lost 218 enlisted men and officers to injuries or illness – 67 of them at Andersonville. The regiment was discharged on June 16, 1864. *However, 81 of its men passed through Camp Discharge, including 71 Andersonville survivors.*

Private Jacob Hess, Co. H – Enrolled May 8, 1861, in Cumberland County at age 20, a clerk. Mustered in on July 27 in Washington, D.C. Captured at Battle of Wilderness, Va., May 5, 1864. Imprisoned at Andersonville. Entered Camp Discharge Oct. 28, 1864. Discharged Nov. 3, 1864.

Private Thomas Edwards, Co. E – Mustered into service July 27, 1861, in Washington, D.C., at age 29. Absent at muster out, sick in hospital at Washington since April 29, 1864. Entered Camp Discharge Oct. 17, 1864, arriving from Washington. Dropped Dec. 5, 1864.

Private George W. Roat, Co. F – Captured May 5, 1864, at Wilderness, Va. Imprisoned at Andersonville. Released from captivity Dec. 16, 1864. Entered Camp Discharge Feb. 22, 1865. Discharged March 1, 1865.

Private Thaddeus Mealy, Co. K – Mustered in on June 4, 1861, in Phila. at age 27, a paper-hanger. Missing in action at Wilderness May 5, 1864. Entered Camp Discharge Jan. 29, 1865. Hospitalized there for scabies Jan. 30, 1865. No muster-out date recorded. Did additional service with 190th Pa. Infantry, Co.

Sergeant Alexander Bates, Co. I – Mustered into service at Washington, D.C., at age 20. Promoted to sergeant May 26, 1863. Missing in action at Battle of Wilderness Va. May 6, 1864. Entered Camp Discharge Feb. 18, 1865. Discharged Feb. 27, 1865.

Corporal Wilson Long, Co. F – Enrolled June 13, 1861, in Luzerne County at age 23. Mustered in on July 27, 1861, in Washington, D.C. Promoted to corporal Nov. 1862. Captured at Wilderness May 6, 184. Held at Andersonville prison. Released Dec. 16, 1864, at Charleston S.C. Discharged Feb. 27, 1865.

Private Joseph Constercamp, Co. A – Mustered in on July 27, 1861, in Washington, D.C. at age 23, a carpenter from Cumberland County. Captured May 5, 1864, at Wilderness, Va. Imprisoned at Andersonville. Released Dec. 11, 1864, at Charleston S.C. Entered Camp Discharge Feb. 17, 1865. Discharged Feb. 24, 1865.

Private Alex Emmons, Co. F – Enrolled June 13, 1861, in Luzerne County at age 27. Mustered in on July 27, 1861, in Washington, D.C. Captured May 5, 1864, at Wilderness, Va. Held at Andersonville prison. Released Dec. 10, 1864, at Charleston S.C. Entered Camp Discharge Feb. 17, 1865. Hospitalized there for "Marasmus A." Feb. 23, 1865. Discharged from service Feb. 27, 1865.

Private Jacob Holeman (Holman), Co. B – Captured May 30, 1864, at Bethesda Church, Va. Imprisoned at Andersonville. Arrived at Camp Discharge Feb. 17, 1865. Discharged Feb. 27, 1865. Did additional service with 37th US Infantry and 83rd Pa. Infantry.

Sergeant Charles Carson, Co. E – Enrolled May 31, 1861, in Phila at age 32, a bricklayer. Mustered in on July 27, 1861, in Washington, D.C. Promoted to corporal July 27, 1861, to sergeant March 1, 1863. Captured May 5, 1864, at Wilderness, Va. Imprisoned at Andersonville. Released Dec. 10, 1864, at Charleston, S.C. Entered Camp Discharge Feb. 17, 1865. Discharged Feb. 24, 1865. Additional service with 7th Pa. Infantry.

Sergeant M.S. Frederick, Co D – Enrolled April 24, 1861, in Clinton County at age 22, a lumberman. Mustered in on July 27, 1861, in Washington, D.C. Promoted to sergeant, date unknown. Captured May 5, 1864, at Battle of Wilderness. Held at Andersonville. Entered Camp Discharge Feb. 16, 1865. Discharged from military Feb. 25, 1865.

Private Patrick Crook/Croak, Co. D – Enrolled May 20, 1861, in Clinton County at age 19, a laborer. Captured May 5, 1864, at Wilderness, Va. Held at Andersonville. At Camp Discharge, hospitalized for constipation Jan. 16-17, 1865. Discharged from service Jan. 23, 1865.

Private Peter Nostall, Co. G – Enrolled May 27, 1861, in Phila. at age 21, a bolt-nut maker. Mustered in on July 27, 1861, in Washington, D.C. Captured May 5, 1864, at Wilderness. Imprisoned at Andersonville. Discharged from service Feb. 14, 1865.

Corporal Samuel Sites, Co. A – Enrolled Sept. 2, 1861, in Carlisle at age 25. Mustered in on Sept. 16, in Washington, D.C. Promoted to corporal March 3, 1863. Captured May 5, 1864, at Wilderness, Va. Held at Andersonville. Released March 4, 1865, at Wilmington, N.C. Recorded at Camp Discharge March 31-May 31, 1865. Officially discharged April 3, 1865.

Corporal Peter F. Seaman, Co. I – Enrolled July 7, 1861, in Lebanon County, at age 20, a wheelwright. Mustered in on July 27 in Washington, D.C. Promoted to corporal Feb 12, 1863. Captured May 5, 1864, at Wilderness, Va. Imprisoned at Andersonville. Exchanged Feb. 27, 1865, at Wilmington, N.C. Recorded at Camp Discharge March 31-May 31, 1865. Officially discharged April 3, 1865.

Sergeant John J. Faller, Co. A – Mustered in on Aug. 16, 1861, in Washington, D.C., from Carlisle at age 20. Promoted to corporal March 3, 1862, to sergeant Sept. 1, 1862. Captured May

5, 1864, at Wilderness, Va. Held at Andersonville prison. Released from captivity on March 5, 1865. Recorded at Camp Discharge March 31-May 31, 1865. Discharged April 3, 1865.

Private John Otto, Co. A – Enrolled April 21, 1861, in Cumberland County at age 25, a carpenter. Captured at Cold Harbor, Va., May 30, 1864. Imprisoned at Andersonville. Released at Wilmington, N.C., Feb. 27, 1865. Recorded present at Camp Discharge March 30-May 30, 1865. Hospitalized at camp for chronic rheumatism April 6, 1865. Officially discharged from service April 12, 1865.

Private William Monroe, Co. F – Enrolled Sept. 12, 1861, at age 20. Mustered in on Oct. 25, in Washington, D.C. Captured May 3, 1864, at Wilderness, Va. Held at Andersonville prison. Released Feb. 23, 1865, at Wilmington, N.C. Recorded present at Camp Discharge March 29-May 29, 1865. Officially discharged April 1, 1865.

Corporal Henry Miller, Co. I – Mustered in on July 28, 1861, in Washington, D.C., at age 19. Promoted to corporal July 14, 1862. Captured May 5, 1864. Imprisoned at Andersonville. Released March 3, 1865, at Wilmington, N.C. Recorded at Camp Discharge March 29-May 29, 1865. Discharged April 1, 1865.

Corporal Cornelius Carmany, Co. C – Enrolled May 27, 1861, in Lebanon County at age 20, a laborer. Mustered in on July 27, 1861, in Washington, D.C. Captured May 6, 1864, at Battle of Wilderness. Held at Andersonville. Released March 4, 1865, at Wilmington, N.C. Recorded at Camp Discharge March 29-May 29, 1864. Officially discharged April 1, 1865.

Corporal John T. Harris, Co. A – Enrolled June 4, 1861, in Cumberland County at age 20, a grocer. Mustered in on July 27, 1861, in Washington, D.C. Promoted to corporal Sept. 1, 1862. Captured May 5, 1864, at Wilderness, Va. Held at Andersonville. Released March 27, 1865, at Wilmington, N.C. Recorded at Camp Discharge March 29-May 29, 1865. Officially discharged April 1, 1865.

Private Shadrach L. Hagenback/Hagenbaugh, Co. F – Enrolled July 19, 1861, in Luzerne County at age 20, a carpenter. Mustered in on July 27 in Washington, D.C. Captured May 5, 1864, at Wilderness, Va. Held at Andersonville. Released March 27, 1865, at Wilmington, N.C. Recorded at Camp Discharge March 29-May 29, 1865. Discharged April 1, 1865.

Private Francis Green, Co. G – Enrolled May 1861 in Phila., at age 20, a printer. Mustered in on July 27, 1861, in Washington, D.C. Captured May 5, 1864, at Wilderness, Va. Held at Andersonville. Recorded present at Camp Discharge May 19, 1865. Discharged June 21, 1865.

Private Frederick Green, Co. D – Mustered in on June 1, 1861, at Camp Curtin at age 25, a carpenter. Promoted to corporal June 28, 1861. At Camp Discharge, hospitalized for "Delir. Tremens" Jan. 11, 1865. Discharged from service Jan. 22, 1865.

Private William H. Morris, Co. K – Mustered in on June 4, 1861, in Phila. at age 19, a farmer. Captured May 5, 1864, at Battle of Wilderness. Held at Andersonville prison. Entered Camp Discharge March 7, 1865. Discharged March 9, 1865

Corporal John F. Morrison, Co. A – Enrolled May 12, 1861, in Cumberland County at age 19, a coach maker. Mustered in on July 27, 1861, in Washington, D.C. Promoted to Corporal March 1, 1863. Captured May 5, 1864, at Wilderness, Va. Imprisoned at Andersonville. Released Dec. 11, 1864, at Charleston, S.C. Entered Camp Discharge March 16, 1865. Discharged March 21, 1865.

Private Luther F. Dodson, Co. F – Enrolled June 13, 1861, in Luzerne County at age 28. Mustered in on July 27, 1861, in Washington, D.C. Reduced to private, date unknown. Captured May 5, 1864, at Wilderness, Va. Held at Andersonville prison. Released Feb. 24, 1865, at Aikens Landing, Va. Recorded at Camp Discharge March 13, 1865. Hospitalized there for chronic diarrhea two days later. Discharged from service April 7, 1865.

Private P.K. Bartholomew, Co. K – Mustered in on June 4, 1861, in Phila. at age 34, a plasterer. Captured May 5, 1864, at Wilderness, Va. Imprisoned at Andersonville. Released Dec.

13, 1864, at Charleston, S.C. Entered Camp Discharge March 15, 1865. Discharged March 18, 1865.

Sergeant William Eichelberger, Co. H – Enrolled May 8, 1861, in Cumberland County at age 22, a dentist. Mustered in on May 28, 1861, at Camp Curtin. Appointed sergeant Dec. 1, 1862. Captured at Wilderness May 5, 1864. Imprisoned at Andersonville. Released Dec. 11, 1864, at Charleston, S.C. Entered Camp Discharge March 15, 1865. Discharged March 17, 1865.

Private Benjamin F. Tolbert, Co. H – Mustered in on July 27, 1861, in Washington, D.C. at age 21, a puddler. Captured at Wilderness May 5, 1864. Held at Andersonville. Entered Camp Discharge Jan. 24, 1865. Hospitalized there for "syphilis primary" Feb. 5-19, 1865. Discharged from service Feb. 14, 1865.

Private Jacob L. Meloy, Co. A – Enrolled April 21, 1861, in Cumberland County at age 18, a carpenter. Mustered in on July 27, 1861, in Washington, D.C. Captured May 5, 1864, at Wilderness, Va. Imprisoned at Andersonville. Released Dec. 11, 1864, at Charleston, S.C. Entered Camp Discharge March 15, 1865. Discharged March 22, 1865

Corporal John R. Koons, Co. F – Mustered in on July 27, 1861, in Washington, D.C. at age 23, from Luzerne County. Promoted to corporal Nov. 18, 1862. Captured May 5, 1864, at Wilderness. Held at Andersonville prison. Released from Rebel hands Dec. 11, 1864. Entered Camp Discharge March 17, 1865. Discharged March 22, 1865.

Sergeant Samuel Miller, Co. I – Mustered in on July 14, 1861, in West Chester at age 24, a farmer. Promoted to corporal Sept. 14, 1862, to sergeant Dec. 13, 1862. Captured May 5, 1864, at Battle of Wilderness. Imprisoned at Andersonville. Released Dec. 16, 1864, at Charleston, S.C. Entered Camp Discharge March 15, 1865. Discharged March 15, 1865.

Private Jacob Clouser/Clauser, Co. C – Enrolled May 27, 1861, in Lebanon at age 24, a laborer. Mustered in on July 27, 1861, in Washington, D.C. Captured during Battle of Wilderness May 6, 1864. Held at Andersonville prison. Released March 1, 1865, at Wilmington, N.C. Entered Camp Discharge March 23, 1865. Discharged March 27, 1865.

Corporal John H. Fox, Co. C – Enrolled May 27, 1861, in Lebanon County at age 26, a mason. Mustered in on July 27, 1861, in Washington, D.C. Promoted to corporal. Captured at Wilderness May 6, 1864. Imprisoned at Andersonville. Released Feb. 27, 1865, at Wilmington, N.C. Entered Camp Discharge March 23, 1865. Discharged March 27, 1865

Private William H. Myers, Co. G – Enrolled May 27, 1861, in Phila. at age 20, a machinist. Mustered in on July 27, 1861, in Washington, D.C. Captured May 5, 1864, at Wilderness. Held at Andersonville. Released Feb. 2, 1865, in Wilmington, N.C. Entered Camp Discharge March 23, 1865. Discharged March 27, 1865.

Private Samuel B. Trafford, Co. C – Enrolled May 27, 1861, in Lebanon at age 21, a forge runner. Mustered in on July 27, 1861, in Washington, D.C. Captured May 5, 1864, at Wilderness, Va. Held at Andersonville prison. Freed March 1, 1865, at Wilmington, N.C. Entered Camp Discharge March 23, 1865. Discharged March 27, 1865.

Sergeant John B. Burr, Co. G – Enrolled May 27, 1861, in Phila. at age 19, a printer. Mustered in on July 27, 1861, in Washington, D.C. Promoted to sergeant April 1, 1863. Captured May 5, 1864, at Wilderness. Held at Andersonville prison. Released Feb. 26, 1865, at Wilmington, N.C. Entered Camp Discharge March 23, 1865. Discharged March 28, 1865.

Private Evan B. Dodson, Co. F – Mustered in on July 27, 1861, in Washington, D.C., at age 25, from Wilkes-Barre. Captured May 5, 1864, at Wilderness. Held at Andersonville prison. Released March 9, 1865, at Varina, Va. At Camp Discharge, hospitalized for chronic diarrhea March 23, 1865. Discharged from service March 29, 1865.

Private Alvin H. Ford, Co. F – Enrolled June 13, 1861, in Luzerne County at age 24. Mustered in on July 27, 1861, in Washington, D.C. Captured May 5, 1864, at Wilderness. Imprisoned at

Andersonville. Released Feb. 26, 1865, at Wilmington, N.C. Entered Camp Discharge March 25, 1865. Discharged March 30, 1865.

Private Daniel Goodman, Co. F – Enrolled June 13, 1861, in Luzerne County at age 21. Mustered in on July 27, 1861, in Washington, D.C. Captured May 5, 1864, at Wilderness. Held at Andersonville prison. Released Feb. 26, 1865, at Wilmington, N.C. Arrived at Camp Discharge March 25, 1865. Discharged March 30, 1865.

Private Samuel T. Wilson, Co. K – Mustered in on June 4, 1861, in Phila. at age 21, a clerk Captured May 5, 1864. At Wilderness. Sent to Andersonville prison. Released Feb. 26, 1865, at Wilmington, N.C. Recorded present at Camp Discharge April 8, 1865. Discharged two days later.

Corporal William Durnbaugh, Co. H – Mustered in on May 28, 1861, in Harrisburg at age 30, a plasterer Appointed corporal July 27, 1861. Captured at Wilderness May 5, 1864. Recorded at Camp Discharge April 7, 1865. Hospitalized there for "Deb. Fr. M Dis" (debility from miasmatic disease) April 8, 1865. Discharged from service April 10, 1865.

Private William Garman, Co. K – Mustered in on June 4, 1861, in Phila. at age 20, an upholsterer. Captured May 5, 1864, at Battle of Wilderness. Imprisoned at Andersonville. Released Feb. 18, 1865, at Charleston S.C. Recorded present at Camp Discharge April 7, 1865. Discharged April 12, 1865.

Private George W. Palmer, Co. H – Mustered in Oct. 25, 1861, at Camp Pierpont, Va., at age 18. Captured May 5, 1864, at Wilderness. Held at Andersonville. Released Feb. 26, 1865, at Wilmington, N.C. Arrived at Camp Discharge April 4, 1865. Discharged April 8, 1865.

Private Benjamin F. Early, Co. C – Enrolled May 27, 1861, in Lebanon County at age 22, a farmer. Mustered in on July 27, 1861, in Washington, D.C. Captured May 5, 1864, at Wilderness, Va. Imprisoned at Andersonville. Released March 3, 1865, at Wilmington, N.C. Recorded present at Camp Discharge April 4, 1865. Discharged April 8, 1865.

Private Newal (Newell) S. Harrison, Co. F – Enrolled June 13, 1861, in Luzerne County at age 19. Mustered in on July 27, 1861, in Washington, D.C. Captured May 5, 1864, at Wilderness, Va. Held at Andersonville prison. Recorded present at Camp Discharge April 18, 1865. Discharged May 11, 1865.

Private John K. Torbert, Co. F – Enrolled June 13, 1861, in Luzerne County at age 20. Mustered in on July 27, 1861, in Washington, D.C. Captured at Wilderness May 5, 1864. Held at Andersonville. Released at Aikens Landing, Va., Feb. 24, 1865. Recorded at Camp Discharge April 26, 1865. Discharged May 8, 1865.

Private Jeremiah J. Stailey, Co. B – Enrolled May 4, 1861, in Perry County at age 18, a tinner. Mustered in on July 7, 1861, in Washington, D.C. Captured at Wilderness May 5, 1864. Imprisoned at Andersonville. Recorded at Camp Discharge April 25, 1865. Discharged May 11, 1865.

Private Jacob T. Strohecker/Strawhecker, Co. I – Enrolled May 26, 1861, in Lebanon County at age 21, a boatman. Mustered in on July 27, 1861, in Washington, D.C. Re-enlisted Nov. 6, 1863, in Washington. Transferred to 190th Pa. Infantry May 31, 1864. "J.T. Stroobaken, Co. I" held at Andersonville and survived, exchanged April 1, 1865. Discharged at Camp Discharge May 22, 1865. Joined Veteran Reserve Corps.

Private Robert B. Terry, Co. K – Mustered in on June 4, 1861, in Phila. at age 18, a carpenter. Captured May 5, 1864, at Wilderness, Va. Held at Andersonville prison. Released March 1, 1865, at Wilmington, N.C. Recorded present at Camp Discharge April 24, 1865. Discharged April 27, 1865.

Private John A. Natcher, Co. A – Enrolled April 21, 1861, in Cumberland County at age 20, a farmer. Mustered in on July 27, 1861, in Washington, D.C. Re-enlisted Nov. 27, 1863, in Washington. Captured at Wilderness May 5, 1864. Imprisoned at Andersonville. Paroled April

22, 1865, at Jacksonville, Fla. At Camp Discharge, hospitalized for ecthyma May 3-June 1, 1865. Mustered out June 13, 1865. Joined Veteran Reserve Corps.

Corporal Henry D. Hoffman, Co. I – Mustered in June 1861 in West Chester at age 18, a tailor in Lebanon. Re-enlisted Jan. 5, 1864, in Washington. Missing in action at Wilderness May 5, 1864. Recorded present at Camp Discharge May 22, 1865.

Private John Weikamp/Wykamp, Co. I – Enrolled May 26, 1861, in Lebanon County, at age 26, a laborer. Mustered in on June 14, 1861, in Washington, D.C. Recorded at Camp Discharge May 22, 1865.

Sergeant William Vancamp/Weikamp, Co. I – Enrolled May 26, 1861, in Lebanon County at age 31, a laborer. Mustered in on June 14, 1861, in West Chester. Captured May 5, 1864, at Battle of Wilderness. Imprisoned at Andersonville. Exchanged April 1, 1865. Recorded present at Camp Discharge May 22, 1865. Discharged June 16, 1865.

Private Charles McGonnell, Co. I – Enrolled on June 13, 1861, in Phila. at age 19. Mustered in on July 27, 1861, in Washington, D.C. Captured May 5, 1864, at Wilderness, Va. Held at Andersonville. Released March 2, 1865. Recorded at Camp Discharge May 2, 1865. Discharged May 4, 1865.

Private Augustus G. Price, Co. D – Enlisted in July 1861 at age 21, a stage driver. Captured May 5, 1864, at Wilderness. Held at Andersonville prison. Recorded present at Camp Discharge May 9, 1865, and discharged two days later.

Private George W. Stewart/Stuard, Co. E – Enrolled May 31, 1861, in Phila. at age 18, a clerk. Mustered in on July 27, 1861, in Washington, D.C. Captured May 5, 1864, at Wilderness. Imprisoned at Andersonville. Discharged at Camp Discharge May 24, 1865.

Corporal William Cunningham, Co. C – Mustered in May 1861 in Washington, D.C., at age 19, a farmer in Lebanon County. Captured May 6, 1864, at Wilderness. Held at Andersonville. Arrived at Camp Discharge May 11, 1865. Discharged May 18, 1865.

Private Jesse B. Humer, Co. A – Mustered in July 1861 in Washington, D.C., at age 24, a clerk. Captured at Wilderness May 5, 1864. Imprisoned at Andersonville. Recorded present at Camp Discharge June 7, 1865. Discharged June 17, 1865.

Private Joseph Egolf, Co. H – Mustered in May 1861 in Harrisburg at age 20, a blacksmith. Captured May 5, 1864, at Battle of Wilderness. Held at Andersonville prison. Paroled at Savannah, Ga., April 28, 1865. Entered Camp Discharge May 20, 1865. Discharged May 29, 1865.

Corporal E. Haze Swisher, Co. H – Mustered in October 1861 at Camp Pierpont at age 24, a tailor. Captured at Wilderness May 5, 1864. Imprisoned at Andersonville. Exchanged April 1, 1865. Recorded present at Camp Discharge May 20, 1865. Discharged May 29, 1865.

Private Joseph Warner, Co. C – Mustered in August 1862 in Harrisburg at age 39. Captured at Wilderness May 5, 1864. Held at Andersonville prison. Paroled at Jacksonville, Fla., April 9, 1865. Recorded present at Camp Discharge May 26, 1865. Discharged May 30, 1865.

Private Joseph Peffly/Peffley, Co. C – Mustered in January 1862 in Harrisburg at age 19, a cigar maker from Lebanon. Re-enlisted Jan. 29, 1864, at Alexandria, Va. Captured at Wilderness May 6, 1864, and imprisoned at Andersonville. Released Feb. 26, 1865, at Goldsboro, N.C. Arrived at Camp Discharge June 29, 1865. Discharged July 8, 1865.

Sergeant Henry Murray, Co. E – Enrolled May 31, 1861, in Phila. at age 23, a farmer. Mustered in on July 27, 1861, in Washington, D.C. Promoted to sergeant Feb. 2, 1862. Captured at Wilderness May 5, 1864. Imprisoned at Andersonville. Entered Camp Discharge Feb. 1, 1865, and discharged three days later.

Private Isaiah Steigleman, Co. H – Mustered in April 1864 in Harrisburg at age 35, a shoemaker. Captured at Wilderness May 5, 1864. Held at Andersonville prison. Released at Wilmington, N.C., March 1, 1865. Confined at Florence, N.C. Arrived at Camp Discharge July 20, 1865, from Satterlee Hospital in Phila. Mustered out in Harrisburg June 28, 1865.

Corporal Armstrong Noble, Co. H – Enrolled May 8, 1861, in Cumberland County at age 23, a telegraph operator. Mustered in on May 28, 1861, at Camp Curtin. Captured May 5, 1864, at Wilderness. Imprisoned at Andersonville. At Camp Discharge, hospitalized for chronic diarrhea Jan. 8, 1865. Discharged from service Jan. 19, 1865.

Private William Bell, Co. G – Enrolled May 27, 1861, in Phila. at age 19, a bricklayer. Mustered in on July 27, 1861, in Washington, D.C. Captured at Wilderness May 5, 1864. Held at Andersonville. Entered Camp Discharge Jan. 27, 1865. Hospitalized there for catarrh Jan. 28 and scabies Feb. 2, 1865. Discharged from service Jan. 31, 1865.

Sergeant William McManus, Co. K – Mustered in on June 4, 1861, in Phila. at age 20, a carpenter. Promoted to sergeant April 1, 1863. Captured at Wilderness May 5, 1864. Imprisoned at Andersonville. Entered Camp Discharge Feb. 1, 1865, and discharged three days later.

Private Irwin/Edwin Reich, Co. G – Enrolled May 27, 1861, in Phila. at age 28, a molder. Mustered in on July 27, 1861, in Washington, D.C. Captured at Wilderness May 5, 1864. Held at Andersonville. Entered Camp Discharge Feb. 16, 1865, hospitalized for ecthyma Feb. 18-28, 1865. Discharged Feb. 25, 1865.

Private Charles F/J Green, Co. D – Enrolled May 27, 1861, in Lock Haven at age 23. Mustered in on July 27, 1861, in Washington, D.C. Captured May 5, 1864, at Wilderness. Imprisoned at Andersonville. Discharged at Camp Discharge Jan. 23, 1865.

Private Crosby Carlton, Co. I – Mustered into service June 14, 1861, in West Chester at age 23, a teacher. Captured May 5, 1864, at Wilderness. Imprisoned at Andersonville. Recorded at Camp Discharge Jan. 25, 1865, and discharged three days later. Joined 7th US Veteran Volunteers, probably doing garrison duty back at Camp Discharge in August 1865.

Private Daniel Kutz, Co. H – Mustered into service May 28, 1861, in Camp Curtin at age 21, a laborer. Captured May 5, 1864, at Wilderness. Held at Andersonville prison. Entered Camp Discharge Jan. 25, 1865. Discharged Jan. 31, 1865.

Corporal George Garman, Co. K – Mustered into service June 4, 1861, in Phila. at age 18, a blacksmith. Promoted to corporal April 1, 1863. Captured May 5, 1864, at Wilderness. Held at Andersonville and Florence, S.C. Entered Camp Discharge Jan. 27, 1865. Discharged Jan. 31, 1865. Did additional service with 3rd US Veteran Volunteers.

Sergeant Howard Chapman, Co. K – Mustered into service June 4, 1861, in Phila. at age 18, a whip maker. Promoted to sergeant June 1, 1863. Captured May 5, 1864, at Wilderness. Held at Andersonville. Entered Camp Discharge Jan. 27, 1865. Discharged Jan. 31, 1865.

Private John A. Hunter, Co. K – Mustered into service July 23, 1861, in Camp Curtin at age 23, a millwright. Captured May 5, 1864, at Wilderness. Imprisoned at Andersonville. Arrived at Camp Discharge Feb. 3, 1865. Discharged Feb. 8, 1865.

Private Francis Tensure/Transue, Co. F – Mustered into service at Harrisburg at age 20. Captured May 5, 1864, at Wilderness. Held at Andersonville prison. Entered Camp Discharge Feb. 4, 1865. Discharged Feb. 9, 1865.

Private Adison Shafer, Co. H – Mustered into service May 28, 1861, in Camp Curtin at age 18, a blacksmith. Captured May 5, 1864, at Wilderness. Imprisoned at Andersonville. Entered Camp Discharge Feb. 6, 1865, and discharged two days later.

Private William H. Cook, Co. H – Mustered into service May 28, 1861, at Camp Curtin at age 18, a whip maker. Captured May 5, 1864, at Battle of Wilderness, Va. Held at Andersonville. Released Dec. 11, 1864, at Charleston, S.C. Entered Camp Discharge Feb. 18, 1865. Discharged Feb. 25, 1865.

Sergeant Thomas Collins, Co. G – Mustered into service July 27, 1861, in Washington, D.C., at age 20, a silversmith. Promoted to corporal April 1, 1863, to sergeant Aug. 1, 1863. Captured May 5, 1864, at Wilderness. Held at Andersonville. Released Dec. 11, 1864. Entered Camp Discharge Feb. 21, 1865. Discharged Feb. 25, 1865.

Private John C. Scott, Co. K – Mustered into service June 4, 1861, in Phila. at age 24, a jeweler. Captured May 4, 1864. Entered Camp Discharge Feb. 24, 1865, and discharged the next day.

43rd Infantry, US Colored Troops

The regiment was organized in 1864 in Philadelphia. Its men took part in eight actions, including Petersburg, the Crater, and Appomattox. They lost 239 enlisted men and officers to injury or ailments. One died at Andersonville. The regiment mustered out Oct. 20, 1865. *One man passed through Camp Discharge.*

Corporal William S. Green, Co. H – Entered service April 14, 1864, in Meadville at age 29, a laborer, free-born in Clarion, Pa. Promoted to corporal May 17, 1864. Hospitalized Sept. 8, 1864, sent to Willits Points military hospital in New York. Reported to Phila. mustering office May 11, 1865, and ordered to Camp Discharge. Mustered out by special order May 15, 1865.

47th Pa. Infantry

The regiment was organized in 1861 in Harrisburg with men recruited from Northampton, Lehigh, Northumberland, and Perry Counties. Its men engaged in the capture of Jacksonville and battles of Cedar Creek and Opequan. Two hundred ninety enlisted men and officers died from wounds or disease. Took part in the Grand Review in D.C. Mustered out Dec. 5, 1865. *One of its men passed through Camp Discharge.*

Private Sterrett Lightner/Lightier, Co. H – Entered service Sept. 29, 1861, in Harrisburg at age 46, a farmer from Landisburg. Recorded Oct. 3, 1864, at Camp Discharge, sick and sent to Haddington Hospital in Phila. He died Dec. 3, 1864, apparently of typhoid fever.

48th Pa. Infantry

The regiment was organized in 1861 solely with men from Schuylkill County and attached to the Army of the Potomac. Its men were in 19 combat engagements, including Second Bull Run, South Mountain, Antietam, Fredericksburg, Wilderness, Spotsylvania, Cold Harbor, Petersburg, and the Crater. Three hundred one enlisted men and officers died from wounds or disease. The regiment took part in the Grand Review in D.C. and mustered out on July 17, 1865. *One of its men passed through Camp Discharge.*

Private Michael Biron/Byron Co. H – Substitute, mustered in January 1865 in Norristown at age 25, an Irish-born laborer. Wounded in action April 2, 1865, at Petersburg, Va.Hospitalized in Washington, D.C., for treatment. Arrived at Camp Discharge May 20, 1865. Hospitalized there to treat gunshot wound May 21, 1865. Discharged from service by general order May 24, 1865.

51st Pa. Infantry

The regiment was recruited in 1861 in Montgomery (Cos. A, C, D, F, I), Centre, Union, Lycoming, Snyder, and Northampton Counties. It was attached to the Army of the Potomac (IX Corps), Army of the Ohio. The men were in 24 combat engagements, including Second Bull Run, South Mountain, Antietam, Fredericksburg, Vicksburg, Wilderness, Spotsylvania, Cold Harbor, Petersburg, the Crater, and Fort Stedman. The unit lost 314 enlisted men and officers to injuries and illness. Thirteen died at Andersonville, two at Florence. The regiment took part in Grand Review in D.C. and mustered out July 27, 1865. *One of its men passed through Camp Discharge.*

Corporal James Cameron, Co. I – Mustered into service Sept. 28, 1861, in Harrisburg at age 30, a laborer. Re-enlisted at Blaine's Crossroads, Tenn., Jan. 1, 1864. Promoted to sergeant May 21, 1865. Recorded present at Camp Discharge May 25, 1865. Mustered out with company July 27, 1865.

52nd Pa. Infantry

The regiment formed in 1861 with men from Bradford, Clinton, Columbia, Luzerne, Union, and Wyoming Counties. It was assigned to the Army of the Potomac (IV Corp, then X Corps). The men were involved in 4 combat engagements: Williamsburg, Seven Pines, Fort Wagner, and the Carolinas Campaign. From its ranks, 219 enlisted men and officers died of injury or illness. Seven died at Andersonville, thirteen at Florence. The regiment took part in the Grand Review in D.C., then mustered out July 12, 1865. *One of its men passed through Camp Discharge.*

Private Henry Esterbrook, Co. F – Mustered in on Feb. 16, 1865, in Scranton at age 40, a farmer. Recorded present at Camp Discharge May 13, 1865. Hospitalized there for diarrhea May 25, 1865. Discharged from service by general order June 14, 1865.

53rd Pa. Infantry

The regiment was raised in 1861 in Montgomery (Cos. A & B), Chester, Blair, Huntingdon, Centre, Clearfield, Carbon, Union, Luzerne, Potter, Northumberland, Juniata, and Westmoreland Counties. It joined the Army of the Potomac (II Corps). The men took part in 27 combat engagements, including Fair Oaks, Savage Station, Malvern Hill, Antietam, Fredericksburg, Chancellorsville, Gettysburg, Wilderness, and Spotsylvania. Its motto was: "We Might As Well Die Here." The unit saw 394 enlisted men and officers die of injury or illness—22 at Andersonville and seven at Florence. The regiment mustered out on June 30, 1865. *Two of its men passed through Camp Discharge.*

Private Calvin Towner, Co. F – Mustered in February 1865 in Scranton at age 22, a farmer. Recorded at Camp Discharge May 27, 1865. Discharged by general order June 8, 1865.

Private Ashbel Norton, Co. H – Mustered in October 1864 in Towanda at age 17. Absent, sick since March 17, 1865. Recorded present at Camp Discharge May 30, 1865. Discharged by general order June 5, 1865.

54th Pa. Infantry

The regiment was raised in 1861 in Indiana, Cambria, Somerset, Dauphin, Northampton, and Lehigh Counties. The men were involved in six combat engagements, including New Market, Petersburg, and Appomattox. It lost 252 enlisted men and officers to injury and disease. Twenty-seven of its men died at Andersonville. The regiment mustered out at Harrisburg on July 15, 1865. *Four of its men passed through Camp Discharge, including two Andersonville survivors.*

Private Samuel M. Adair, Co. K – Enrolled July 1861 at Camp Washington, Pa., at age 21. Recorded present at Camp Discharge Sept. 29, 1864. Discharged from service by general order Jan. 7, 1865.

Private Henry S. Roberts, Co. F – Mustered in on Aug. 17, 1861, in Baltimore at age 23. Captured June 19, 1864, at Lynchburg, Va. Held at Andersonville prison and survived. Freed Nov. 30, 1864. Recorded at Camp Discharge April 25, 1865, and discharged two days later.

Private William Schleibner, Unassigned – Captured June 20, 1864, ay Lynchburg, Va. Imprisoned at Andersonville. Set free April 6, 1865. At Camp Discharge July 1865, with a charge of desertion withdrawn. Discharged from military by general order July 19, 1865.

Private Franklin B. Howell, Co. A – Mustered in on April 2, 1862, in Harrisburg at age 26. Prisoner of war Oct. 19, 1864, to Feb. 17, 1865. Recorded present at Camp Discharge April 15, 1865. Discharged from service April 27, 1865.

55th Pa. Infantry

The regiment was recruited in 1861 in Cambria, Berks, Bedford, Schuylkill, Indiana, Dauphin, Bedford, and Blair Counties. The men took part in eight combat operations, including Drewry's Bluff, Cold Harbor, Petersburg, and Chaffin's Farm. From its ranks, 479 enlisted men and officers died of injury and illness. Sixty-one died at Andersonville, one at Florence. The regiment mustered out Aug. 30, 1865, in Petersburg. *One of its men transited Camp Discharge.*

Private Patrick McDonough, Co. E – Enrolled September 1861 at Minersville, Pa., at age 40, a miner. Recorded at Camp Discharge Sept. 24, 1864. Hospitalized there for rheumatism Nov. 24, 1864. Mustered out Dec. 10, 1864, to date Sept. 27, 1864, expiration of term.

56th Pa. Infantry

The regiment was formed in 1862 with recruits from Philadelphia, Indiana, Luzerne, Northumberland, Centre, Susquehanna, Schuylkill, and Wayne Counties. It was part of the Army of Virginia, then the Army of the Potomac (I Corps, V Corps). The men took part in 22 combat engagements, including Second Bull Run, Antietam, Fredericksburg, Chancellorsville, Gettysburg, Wilderness, Spotsylvania, Cold Harbor, Petersburg, and Five Forks. They lost 215 enlisted men and officers from injury or illness. Three men died at Andersonville. The regiment took part in Grand Review in D.C., then mustered out July 1, 1865, in Philadelphia. *Three of its men passed through Camp Discharge.*

Private Edward Spaulding, Co. K – Mustered in on Sept. 24, 1863, in Pottsville, at age 20. Discharged June 5. 1865. Discharged by general order June 5, 1865.

Private Adam Robbins, Co. A – Drafted. Wounded March 31, 1865. Absent at regimental muster out. Recorded present at Camp Discharge July 17, 1865, and discharged that month.

Private Martin Curby, Co. A – Mustered into service Oct. 16, 1861, in Harrisburg at age 19, a Tanner. Recorded at Camp Discharge Oct. 17-20, 1864. Mustered out Nov. 1, 1864, expiration of term.

58th Pa. Infantry

The regiment was formed in 1861-62 with men from Philadelphia, Luzerne, Clinton, Northumberland, McKean, Erie, and Tioga Counties. It was attached to the Army of the James. The men took part in three combat operations: Drewry's Bluff, Cold Harbor, and Chaffin's Farm. They lost 217 enlisted men and officers to injury or disease. Two men died at Andersonville. The regiment mustered out on Jan. 24, 1866. *Six of its men passed through Camp Discharge.*

Corporal Cyrus Baldwin Jr., Co. H – Enrolled Dec. 23, 1861, in Otto, Pa., at age 29, one of four Baldwins in Company H. Mustered in on Jan. 23, 1862, in Phila. Promoted to corporal April 1863. Wounded at Cold Harbor June 1, 1864. Recorded present at Camp Discharge Jan. 31, 1865. Hospitalized there Feb. 1, 1865, to treat leg amputation. Discharged by general order Feb. 4, 1865. Joined Veteran Reserve Corps.

Private Daniel F. Vaow, Co. B – Mustered in on Aug. 3, 1864, in Phila. Arrived at Camp Discharge May 9, 1865. Discharged by general order May 13. 1865.

Private Solomon Nittroner/Nittrour, Co. C – Mustered in on Nov. 6, 1861, in Phila. at age 38. Recorded at Camp Discharge Nov. 22, 1864, reporting from Mt. Pleasant Hospital, Washington D.C. Hospitalized at camp for lumbago Nov. 24, 1864. Mustered out Dec. 8, 1864, expiration of term.

Private George Beardsley/Bardsley, Co. C – Mustered in November 1861 in Phila. at age 44. Recorded at Camp Discharge Nov. 25, 1864, reporting from Hammond Hospital, Point Lookout, Md. Hospitalized at camp for liver congestion Nov. 24, 1864. Mustered out Dec. 28, 1864, expiration of term.

Sergeant John Q. Merrick, Co. K – Mustered in on Nov. 23, 1861, in Phila. at age 44. Promoted to sergeant March 1, 1862. Admitted to Camp Discharge Hospital for lumbago Dec. 6, 1864. Discharged Dec. 14, 1864, expiration of term.

Private Joshua/Josiah Palmer, Co. D – Mustered into service Feb. 23, 1864. Entered Camp Discharge Dec. 26, 1864. Discharged from service Dec. 30, 1864.

61st Pa. Infantry

The regiment was recruited in 1861 in Philadelphia, Allegheny, Indiana, and Luzerne Counties. It was attached to the Army of the Potomac. Battle actions included at Fair Oaks, Antietam, Fredericksburg, Gettysburg, Wilderness, Cold Harbor, and Petersburg. The unit lost 338 enlisted men and officers to injury and sickness. *One of its men went through Camp Discharge.*

Private James Foley, Co. H – Mustered in on Sept. 4, 1861, in Phila. at age 25, a Morocco dresser. Wounded at Wilderness May 1864. According to Pa. Veteran Card, Foley died of his wounds Sept. 2, 1864, yet Camp Discharge weekly log recorded him as arriving Nov. 18, 1864, from Broad and Cherry St. Hospital, admitted same day to the camp hospital for treatment of amputated right arm, then discharged from service Dec. 2, 1864. According to Bates, Foley's wound left him absent at expiration of term.

66th Pa. Infantry

The regiment was recruited in 1861 in Philadelphia. It was attached to the Army of the Potomac and consolidated with the 73rd and 99th Pennsylvania Volunteers in March 1862. *One of its men went through Camp Discharge.*

Corporal James Ramage, Co. F – Mustered in June 1861 in Philadelphia. Might have been transferred in 1862 to 73rd Pa. Infantry. Recorded present at Camp Discharge Oct. 25, 1864. Hospitalized there for leg ulcer Dec. 22, 1864. Date of muster out not recorded.

67th Pa. Infantry

The regiment was recruited in 1862 in Carbon, Pike, Wayne, Monroe, Philadelphia, Westmoreland, Indiana, Jefferson, Clarion, Northampton, Allegheny, and Schuylkill Counties. It was attached to the Army of the Potomac. The men saw combat at Wilderness, Spotsylvania, Cold Harbor, Petersburg, and Cedar Creek. They lost 232 enlisted men and officers to injury and sickness. Ten died at Andersonville. The regiment mustered out July 17, 1865. *Sixteen of its men transited Camp Discharge, including one Andersonville survivor.*

Sergeant Noah Benfer, Co. E – Mustered in on March 15, 1862, in Indiana County at age 24. Promoted to sergeant date unknown. Captured at Wilderness May 6, 1864. Held at Andersonville and survived. Released Feb. 27, 1865. Arrived at Camp Discharge on April 26, 1865. Discharged May 5, 1865.

Private Thomas Shaf(f)er, Co. H – Mustered in on Jan. 30, 1862, in Phila. for 3 years. Age 29, from Carbon County. Entered Camp Discharge Jan. 31, 1865. Discharged Feb. 2, 1865, expiration of term.

Private Levi Kresge, Co. G – Enrolled Feb. 11, 1862, in Monroe County at age 28. Mustered in on Feb. 14 in Phila. One of 5 Kresge's in Co. G. Recorded at Camp Discharge Feb. 11, 1865. Mustered out Feb. 15, 1865, expiration of term.

Corporal Thomas Johnson, Co. A – Mustered in Sept. 3, 1861, in Phila. at age 18. Promoted to corporal April 1863. Captured May 6, 1864, at Wilderness, Va. Released Feb. 26, 1865, at Wilmington, N.C. Recorded present at Camp Discharge May 4, 1865. Discharged May 13, 1865.

Private William Thompson, Co. K – Mustered in on Feb. 27, 1865, at age 35, a substitute. Recorded at Camp Discharge May 16, 1865. Discharged by general order July 8, 1865.

Private John Kelley, Co. A – Mustered in Sept. 20, 1861, in Phila. at age 42. Recorded at Camp Discharge Sept. 21, 1864. Hospitalized there to treat gunshot wound of left arm Nov. 15, 1864. Mustered out Dec. 3, 1865, expiration of term.

Private Patrick Carr, Co. A – Mustered in September 1861 in Phila. Transferred from Co. B. Arrived at Camp Discharge Oct. 26, 1864. Hospitalized for a gunshot wound of left leg Nov. 23, 1864. Mustered out Dec. 12, 1864, expiration of term.

Private Joseph B. Cramer/Kramer, Co. D – Mustered in October 1861 in Phila. at age 43, a Stroudsburg native. Recorded present at Camp Discharge Oct. 26, 1864. Hospitalized there for chronic diarrhea Dec. 2, 1864. Mustered out Dec. 9, 1864, expiration of term.

Private Emlen L. Carrolus, Co. K – Mustered in September 1861 in Phila. at age 18, a shoemaker. Captured at Winchester, Va., June 15, 1863, circumstance not recorded. Re-enlisted Jan. 1, 1864, at Brandy Station, Va. Absent, sick at regimental muster out. Arrived at Camp Discharge July 22, 1865. Discharged July 31, 1865. Joined Veteran Reserve Corps.

Private Albert B. Miller, Co. F – Mustered in September 1861 in Phila. at age 20, a laborer. Re-enlisted Jan. 1, 1864. Wounded in action at Battle of Opequan, Winchester, Va., Sept. 19, 1864. Absent, wounded, at muster out. Recorded at Camp Discharge July 14, 1865. Discharged July 31, 1865. Joined Veteran Reserve Corps.

Private Michael Thompson, Co. I – Enrolled March 29, 1865, in Allegheny at age 30, a farmer. Mustered in on April 14, 1865, for one year. Recorded at Camp Discharge June 14, 1865. Discharged by general order that day.

Private George W. Smith, Co. K – Mustered in on Dec. 26, 1864, at age 24, a substitute. Absent, sick in US hospital, at muster out. Recorded present at Camp Discharge July 19, 1865, and discharged in July.

Private Robert Boyce, Co. C – Mustered in on Nov. 25, 1861, in Phila. at age 22. Prisoner June 6-14, 1863, circumstances unknown. Entered Camp Discharge Dec. 21, 1865. Discharged Dec. 24, 1864, expiration of term.

Private Peter Engle/Egl, Co. G – Mustered in on Dec. 4, 1861, in Phila. at age 41. Entered Camp Discharge Dec. 22, 1864. Discharged Dec. 24, 1864, expiration of term.

Corporal David Altman, Co. F – Mustered in on Dec. 19, 1861, in Phila. at age 44. Entered Camp Discharge Jan. 6, 1865. Discharged from military Jan. 7, 1865.

Private Henry D. Skinner, Co. C – Mustered into service Dec. 30, 1861, in Phila. at age 42. Entered Camp Discharge Jan. 21, 1865. Mustered out Dec. 31, 1864, expiration of term.

69th Pa. Infantry

The regiment ('The Irish Volunteers') was raised in 1861 in Philadelphia, part of the famous Philadelphia Brigade. It was part of the Army of the Potomac (II Corps). The men saw action in 13 combat operations, including Second Bull Run, Antietam, Fredericksburg, Chancellorsville, Gettysburg, Wilderness, Spotsylvania, Cold Harbor, and Petersburg. From its ranks, 288 enlisted men and officers died of injury and disease. At least 15 died at Andersonville and one at Florence. The regiment took part in Grand Review in D.C., then mustered out July 1, 1865. *Twenty-eight of its men passed through Camp Discharge, including 10 Andersonville survivors.*

Corporal James Milligan Co. I – Enrolled on Aug. 9, 1861, in Phila. at age 18, a jeweler. Mustered in on Oct. 31, 1861, at Camp Observation, Md. Promoted to corporal Feb. 1, 1862, for bravery under fire. Re-enlisted Feb. 1, 1864, at Stevensburg, Va. Captured at Petersburg, Va., when the unit was flanked June 22, 1864. Held at Andersonville. Exchanged April 15, 1865. Recorded at Camp Discharge May 19, 1865. Discharged by general order June 2, 1865. Joined Veteran Reserve Corps.

Private Patrick H. Anderson, Co. D – Enrolled on Aug. 28, 1861, in Phila. at age 19, a laborer from Norristown. Mustered in on Oct. 31, 1861, at Camp Observation, Md. Captured Sept. 17, 1862, at Antietam and held until Oct. 6, 1862. Captured again July 1, 1863, near Gettysburg. Escaped Feb. 17, 1865. Entered Camp Discharge March 24, 1865. Hospitalized there for debility from "miasmatic disease" March 25, acute laryngitis April 7, and boils April 25. Discharged from military June 15, 1865.

Private Henry Pierce, Co. K – Mustered in October 1861 at Camp Observation, Md., at age 23, a laborer. Re-enlisted Feb. 6, 1864, at Stevensburg, Va. Captured at Petersburg June 22, 1864. Held at Andersonville, then Millen, Ga. Paroled at Jacksonville, Fla., April 28, 1865. Arrived at Camp Discharge May 24, 1865. Discharged by general order June 18, 1865. Joined Veteran Reserve Corps.

Corporal Michael O'Hara, Co. H – Enrolled Sept. 2, 1861, in Phila. at age 19. Mustered in on Oct. 31, 1861, at Camp Observation, Md. Re-enlisted Feb. 19, 1864, at Stevensburg, Va. Promoted to corporal May 1, 1864. Captured June 22, 1864, near Petersburg. Va. Held at Andersonville, then Millen, Ga. Paroled at Jacksonville, Fla., April 28, 1865. Entered Camp Discharge May 24, 1865. Discharged by general order June 8, 1865.

Private Mark McCusker, Co. B – Mustered in on Oct. 31, 1861, at Camp Observation, Md., at age 26, a weaver. Wounded in action at Antietam Sept. 17, 1862. Captured at Petersburg June 22, 1864. Imprisoned at Andersonville, then Millen, Ga. Paroled at Jacksonville, Fla., April 28, 1865. Present at Camp Discharge May 24, 1865. Discharged June 5, 1865.

Private John A. Kane, Co. E – Had been a sergeant in US Marines. Joined 69th as sergeant but demoted in November 1861. Deserted March 25, 1862, in Washington D.C. Recorded present at Camp Discharge Oct. 28, 1864. Hospitalized there for rheumatism on Dec. 14, 1864. Discharged from service Dec. 31, 1864.

Corporal Patrick McAnally, Co. K-B – Enrolled on Aug. 26, 1861, in Phila. at age 32, a stonemason. Mustered in on Oct. 31, 1861, at Camp Observation, Md. Sick during Antietam campaign, deserted hospital. Returned but stripped from sergeant to corporal. Rose to second corporal. Fought at Gettysburg's Bloody Angle. Hospitalized January 1864. Deserted again. Returned, wounded in action at Wilderness, Va., May 6, 1864. Sent to Satterlee hospital, Phila. Recorded at Camp Discharge on Sept. 27, 1864. Hospitalized there to treat gunshot wounds to both legs Nov. 15, 1864. Mustered out Dec. 13, 1864, expiration of term.

Corporal William F. Lantz, Co. K – Enrolled on August 1861 in Phila. at age 18, a printer. Mustered in October at Camp Observation, Md. Fought at Gettysburg's Bloody Angle July 3,

1863. Recorded at Camp Discharge Oct. 25-Dec. 10, 1864. Hospitalized there for tertiary syphilis Nov. 26, 1864. Discharged from service Dec. 10, 1864.

Private Joseph Grover, Co. B –Enrolled on Sept. 2, 1861, mustered in on Oct. 31 at Camp Observation Md. at age 26, a shoemaker. Wounded in left arm and elbow at Gettysburg July 3, 1863. Sent to Phila. Hospital but deserted December 1863. Arrived at Camp Discharge Nov. 1, 1864. Hospitalized there to treat gunshot wound of left arm Dec. 8, 1864. Discharged from service Dec. 22, 1864.

Private James McKenna, Co. D – Enrolled on September 1861 in Phila. at age 30, a Frankford baker. Fought at Gettysburg's Bloody Angle. Arrived at Camp Discharge Sept. 26, 1864, reporting from Haddington Hospital, Phila. Admitted to camp hospital with chronic diarrhea Dec. 9, 1864. Discharged from service on surgeon's certificate March 2, 1865.

Private John Nestor/Nester, Co. D – Mustered in October 1861 at Camp Observation, Md., at age 30, a puddler from Phoenixville. Shot in left leg at Gettysburg's Bloody Angle July 3, 1863. Shot in the same leg at the Wilderness, Va., May 1864. Recorded at Camp Discharge Nov. 3, 1864. Discharged Dec. 1, 1864.

Private James Cavanaugh, Co. H – Mustered in on July 2, 1861, in Phila. at age 19. Absent, sick at regimental muster out. Recorded at Camp Discharge April 29, 1865. Forwarded to Camp Cadwalader and discharged July 28, 1865.

Corporal Richard F. Rea, Co. F – Mustered in March 1864 in Stevensburg, Va., at age 20. Wounded in action May 6, 1864, at Battle of Wilderness, Va. Absent at regimental muster out. Recorded at Camp Discharge July 10, 1865. Discharged July 1, 1865. Joined Veteran Reserve Corps.

Sergeant Robert Stinson, Co. G – Mustered in on May 5, 1861, in Phila. at age 22, a weaver. Transferred from 27th Pa. Infantry, Co. G, Oct. 1, 1861. Shot in right hip at Antietam September 1862. Re-enlisted Feb. 25, 1864, at Stevensburg, Va. Promoted to sergeant date unknown. Captured near Petersburg June 22, 1864. Held at Andersonville, then Millen, Ga. Exchanged April 1, 1865. Recorded at Camp Discharge May 24, 1865. Discharged by general order June 22, 1865. Joined Veteran Reserve Corps.

Private James R. Howard, Co. I – Mustered in on Aug. 9, 1861, in Washington D.C. at age 19, a bricklayer. Re-enlisted Feb. 25, 1864, at Stevensburg, Va. Captured June 22, 1864, at Petersburg. Imprisoned at Andersonville, then Millen, Ga. Recorded at Camp Discharge May 18, 1865. Discharged by general order June 21, 1865. Joined Veteran Reserve Corps.

Private Jacob M. Price, Co. H – Mustered in on July 11, 1861, in Phila. at age 24. Captured June 22, 1864, at Petersburg, Va. Held at Andersonville, then Millen, Ga. Exchanged April 1, 1865. Recorded at Camp Discharge May 19, 1865. Discharged by general order June 17, 1865.

Private William J. Chandler, Co. I – Mustered in on August 1861 in Phila. at age 24, a printer. Deserted Jan. 21, 1863, during the Mud March campaign in Virginia. Caught in Washington Oct. 27, 1863. Sick in Washington hospital for the remainder of the war. Absent at regimental muster out. Recorded at Camp Discharge June 14, 1865. Discharged three days later.

Private James Mooney, Co. C – Mustered in on September 1861 in Phila. at age 22, a baker. Shot in abdomen and hip at Fredericksburg, Va., Dec. 13, 1862. Hospitalized, then served in Invalid Corps. Rejoined 69th Pa. in April 1864. Wounded again and captured at Petersburg, Va., June 22, 1864. Held at Andersonville, then sent to Millen, Ga., Oct. 31, 1864. Recorded at Camp Discharge May 20, 1865. Discharged by general order June 21, 1865.

Private Joseph Noon, Co. K – Drafted and mustered in on July 27, 1863, at age 28. Captured near Petersburg, Va., June 22, 1864. Held at Andersonville—one of only two from 69th left at Andersonville when Union liberated it; 38 others had been transferred (19 others died there). Recorded present at Camp Discharge May 18, 1865. Hospitalized there for ecthyma May 25 and diarrhea June 8, 1865. Discharged from military by general order June 14, 1865.

Corporal Francis Belflow, Co. A – Enrolled August 1861 in Phila., mustered in October 1861 in Camp Observation, Md., age 21, a laborer born in Montreal. Re-enlisted Feb. 9, 1864, at Stevensburg, Va.. Captured June 12, 1864. Released March 3, 1865. Recorded at Camp Discharge May 26, 1865. Hospitalized there for scabies May 31-June 1, 1865. Discharged by general order June 5, 1865. Joined Veteran Reserve Corps.

Private James Flanely, Co. D – Enrolled August 1861 in Phila. at age 21; mustered in on Oct. 31, 1861, at Camp Observation, Md.; Taken prisoner Aug. 25, 1864. Paroled Sept. 25.1864. Recorded at Camp Discharge Nov. 18, 1864, reporting from Camp Parole, Md. Admitted to Camp Discharge Hospital for catarrh Nov. 20, 1864. Discharged from military Dec. 2, 1864.

Private James Hand, Co. F – Enrolled August 1861 in Phila. at age 38. Captured July 3, 1863, at Bloody Angle wall during Battle of Gettysburg. Paroled from Richmond and returned to company. Mustered out Oct. 8, 1864, expiration of term.

Private John Cain, Co. B – Enrolled August 1861 in Phila. at age 27, a watchmaker. Wounded in right shoulder June 5, 1864, during Battle of Cold Harbor, Va. Hospitalized in Baltimore and discharged for wounds received. Recorded present at Camp Discharge Sept. 27-Dec. 5, 1864.

Private Thomas Christie/Christy, Co. B – Enrolled August 1861 in Phila. at age 22; mustered in October 1861 in Camp Observation, Md. Shot in the left arm at Fredericksburg, Va., Dec. 13, 1862. Arm partially amputated. Recorded at Camp Discharge Nov. 10, 1864, reporting from Broad and Cherry Hospital, Phila. Mustered out Dec. 30, 1864, expiration of term.

Sergeant Patrick McMahon, Co. I – Mustered in August 1861 in Phila. at age 26. Promoted to corporal Oct. 1, 1862, to sergeant Feb. 1, 1863. Shot in left thigh twice, at Gettysburg July 3, 1863, and at Spotsylvania Court House May 12, 1864. Admitted to Harewood Hospital in Washington, then Haddington Hospital in Phila. Mustered out Aug. 27, 1864, expiration of term. At Camp Discharge Oct. 18-Nov.12, 1864.

Private Sylvester W. Campbell, Co. I – Mustered in August 1861 in Phila. at age 28; Fell ill at Harpers Ferry, Va., in October 1862 and reassigned to Invalid Corps April 1863. Recorded at Camp Discharge Sept. 23, 1864. Mustered out Nov. 12, 1864, expiration of term.

Private Frank McClarren/McClavant, Co. I – Mustered into service on Aug. 19, 1861, in Phila. at age 21. Captured June 22, 1864, at Petersburg, Va. Imprisoned at Andersonville. Entered Camp Discharge Jan. 30, 1865. Discharged Jan. 31, 1865, expiration of term. Did additional service with 6th US Cavalry, Co. K.

Corporal William F. Moore, Co. A – Mustered into service on July 1, 1861, at age 25. Transferred as a corporal from 71st Pa. Infantry, Co. E. June 1. 1864. Absent at regimental muster out, sick in hospital at Phila. Recorded at Camp Discharge March 13, 1865. Discharged March 22, 1865.

71st Pa. Infantry

The regiment was raised in 1861 in Philadelphia, part of the famous Philadelphia Brigade. It was assigned to the Army of the Potomac (II Corps). It saw action in 23 combat operations, including Balls Bluff, Savage Station, Malvern Hill, Antietam, Gettysburg, Fair Oaks, Fredericksburg, Wilderness, Spotsylvania, and Cold Harbor. In total, 260 of its enlisted men and officers died of injuries or illness. Three died at Andersonville. The regiment mustered out July 2, 1864. *Six of its men transited Camp Discharge, including two Andersonville survivors.*

Private John Brady, Co. C – Mustered in July 1861 in Phila. at age 21. Wounded in action at Battle of Totopotomoy Creek, Va., May 30, 1864. Underwent surgery that day to remove the lower third of the left thigh. Transferred to 69th Pa Infantry, Co. F, June 12, 1864. Recorded present at Camp Discharge Nov. 25, 1864, reporting from Broad and Cherry Street Hospital,

Phila. Hospitalized at camp to treat amputated thigh Dec. 1, 1864. Discharged from service Dec. 5, 1864.

Private Henry Dryedale/Drysdell, Co. E – Mustered in May 1861 in Phila. Deserted Aug. 28, 1862, at Camp Alexandria, Va. On Sept. 28, 1863, underwent surgery for amputation of the right leg at thigh after railroad cars crushed the leg the same day. Arrived at Camp Discharge Oct. 10, 1864, reporting from Broad and Cherry Street Hospital, Phila. Discharged from service March 18, 1865.

Private George C. Moore, Co. I – Mustered in June 1861 in Fort Schuyler, N.Y., at age 21, a farmer. Taken prisoner at Camp Advance, Va., September 1861. Returned to duty Dec. 1, 1862. Wounded Dec. 13, 1862. Wounded July 3, 1863, at Gettysburg. Taken prisoner at Battle of Mine Run, Va., Dec. 2, 1863. Recorded at Camp Discharge June 19, 1865. Discharged by general order July 21, 1865.

Private James Kensella, Co. C – Enrolled July 1861 in Phila. at age 24. Transferred to 69th Pa. Infantry June 12, 1864. Recorded at Camp Discharge Sept. 26, 1864. Discharged Oct. 27, 1864.

Private Bernard Cole, Co. G – Mustered into service on April 15, 1861, in New York. Transferred to 69th Pa Infantry, Co. I, date unknown. Wounded and captured at Spotsylvania Court House May 12, 1864. Held at Andersonville prison. Sent to Millen, Ga., Oct. 31, 1864. Entered Camp Discharge Jan. 21, 1865. Discharged Jan. 25, 1865.

Private John Corcoran, Co. G – Mustered into service on April 15, 1861. In New York. Transferred to 69th Pa. Infantry, Co. I, date unknown. Wounded and captured at Spotsylvania Court House May 12, 1864. Held at Andersonville. Sent to Millen, Ga., Oct. 31, 1864. Entered Camp Discharge Jan. 21, 1865. Discharged from military Jan. 25, 1865.

72nd Pa. Infantry

The regiment was raised in 1861 in Philadelphia, part of the famous Philadelphia Brigade. It was attached to the Army of the Potomac. The men saw action in seven operations, including Balls Bluff, Savage Station, Malvern Hill, Antietam, and Gettysburg. From its ranks, 330 enlisted men and officers died of injuries or sickness. Four died at Andersonville. The regiment mustered out Aug. 24, 1864, in Philadelphia. *Thirty-five of its men were at Camp Discharge, including 22 Andersonville survivors.*

Sergeant Alfred R. Wills, Co. D – Mustered in on Aug. 10, 1861, in Phila. as sergeant. Captured at Petersburg, Va., June 22, 1864. Held at Andersonville and survived. Released from captivity Nov. 21, 1864. Recorded present at Camp Discharge Jan. 7, 1865. Discharged from service March 1, 1865, expiration of term.

Sergeant George Clinton Gordon, Co. C – Mustered in on Aug. 10, 1861, in Phila. at age 26, as first sergeant. Transferred from Co. M on Nov. 1, 1862, by an act of Congress. Prisoner of war details not specified. Recorded at Camp Discharge Feb. 20, 1865. Hospitalized there for chronic diarrhea Feb. 21 and 26, 1865. Mustered out March 1, 1865, expiration of term.

Private John H. Bitting/Baiting, Co. A – Mustered in on Aug. 10, 1861, in Phila. at age 25. Captured May 10, 1864, at Spotsylvania Court House, Va. Held at Andersonville and survived. Entered Camp Discharge Feb. 27, 1865. Discharged from service March 8, 1865, expiration of term.

Corporal Charles F. Hill, Co. C – Mustered in August 1862 in Phila. at age 25. Transferred to 183rd Pa. Infantry, Co. K, July 1864. Captured, date unknown. Held at Andersonville, sent to Millen Ga., Nov. 11, 1864. Recorded present at Camp Discharge May 23, 1865. Discharged June 16, 1865.

Sergeant John E. Cochran, Co. D – Mustered in August 1861 in Phila. Taken prisoner June 22, 1864, at Petersburg, Va. Paroled at Jacksonville April 29, 1865. Recorded at Camp Discharge May 24, 1865. Mustered out June 5, 1865, expiration of term.

Corporal Bernard Mahon, Co. G – Mustered in on Oct. 25, 1861, at Camp Olsen at age 23. Transferred to 183rd Pa. Infantry, Co. K, July 19, 1864. Recorded present at Camp Discharge May 23, 1865. Hospitalized there for diarrhea May 24, 1865.

Private Daniel Culin, Co. H – Mustered in on Oct. 10, 1861, in Poolesville, Md., at age 41. Shot in the right wrist at Po River May 9, 1864. Underwent forearm surgery that day. Transferred to 183rd Pa. Infantry, Co. C, July 19, 1864, to serve out term. Recorded at Camp Discharge Oct. 11, 1864, arriving from York Hospital. Admitted to Camp Discharge Hospital to treat gunshot wound of right wrist Nov. 15, 1864. Discharged from service Dec. 8, 1864.

Private George A. Bakeoven, Co. F – Mustered in August 1861 in Phila. at age 22. Transferred from Co. M Nov. 1, 1862. Mustered out with company Aug. 24, 1864. Recorded at Camp Discharge Nov. 5-11, 1864.

Private William H. Weed, Co. I – Enrolled Sept. 16, 1861, in Phila. at age 28, a carpenter. Mustered in on Oct. 31, 1861, in Phila. Transferred to 183rd Pa. Infantry, Co. F, July 20, 1864, to serve unexpired time. Recorded at Camp Discharge Oct. 25, 1864, arriving from Camp Parole, Md. Discharged Dec. 28, 1864.

Private Thomas Virden, Co. H – Mustered in on Oct. 12, 1861, in Poolesville, Md. at age 21. Transferred to 183rd Pa. Infantry, Co. C, on July 19, 1864, to serve the unexpired term. Recorded at Camp Discharge Nov. 3, 1864, and hospitalized there for shell wound of right heel. Discharged from service Dec. 28, 1864.

Corporal J.P. Barger, Co. E – Mustered in August 1861 in Phila. at age 23, a seaman. Re-enlisted Jan. 1, 1864, at Stevensburg, Va. Captured at Wilderness, Va., May 7, 1864. Held at Andersonville prison, then sent to Millen, Ga., Nov. 11, 1865. Paroled April 21, 1865, at Vicksburg, Miss. Recorded at Camp Discharge May 23, 1865. Discharged by general order July 11, 1865. Joined Veteran Reserve Corps.

Private Joseph Genion, Co. G – Mustered in August 1861 in Phila. at age 30. Captured at Petersburg, Va., June 22, 1864. Imprisoned at Andersonville. Paroled at Vicksburg April 21, 1865. Recorded at Camp Discharge May 27, 1865. Mustered out, June 28, 1865, expiration of term.

Private Robert O'Neil, Co. B (K) – Mustered in August 1861 in Phila. at age 18, a waterman. Re-enlisted March 1864 at Stevensburg, Va. Transferred to 183rd Pa. Infantry, Co. C. Captured at Petersburg, Va., June 22, 1864. Held at Andersonville and survived. Recorded present at Camp Discharge May 18, 1865. Discharged by general order June 26, 1865. Joined Veteran Reserve Corps.

Private Robert Miller, Co. F – Mustered in on Aug. 10, 1861, in Phila. at age 22. Captured at Petersburg June 22, 1864. Held at Andersonville prison. Reached Camp Discharge June 1865. Discharged from service June 23, 1865, expiration of term.

Private Theodore De Young, Co. A – Mustered in on Aug. 10, 1861, in Phila. at age 19. Captured at Petersburg, Va., June 22, 1864. Held at Andersonville. Sent to Millen, Ga., Nov. 11, 1864. Exchanged April 1, 1865. Recorded at Camp Discharge May 18, 1865. Discharged June 16, 1865, expiration of term.

Private Charles Madison, Co. F – Mustered in August 1861 in Phila. at age 26, a brick maker. Re-enlisted Feb. 10, 1864, at Stevensburg, Va. Transferred to 183rd Pa. Infantry July 20, 1864. Captured June 22, 1864, at Petersburg. Held at Andersonville. Sent to Millen, Ga., Nov. 11, 1864. Exchanged April 1, 1865. Recorded at Camp Discharge May 23, 1865.

Private Isaac F. Horner, Co. D – Mustered in on Feb. 9, 1864, in Phila. at age 36, a farmer. Transferred to 183rd Pa. Infantry, July 20, 1864. Captured June 22, 1864, at Petersburg. Held at

Andersonville prison. Exchanged April 15, 1865. Recorded at Camp Discharge May 29, 1865. Discharged July 12, 1865.

Private James M. Hungerford, Co. F – Mustered in on Aug. 10, 1861, in Phila. at age 21, a shoemaker. Captured May 6, 1864, at Wilderness. Held at Andersonville. Released Feb. 27, 1865, at Wilmington, N.C. Recorded at Camp Discharge May 4, 1865. Discharged May 18, 1865, expiration of term.

Corporal John T. Painter Co. E – Mustered in on Aug. 10, 1861, in Phila. at age 22. Captured May 10, 1864, at Po River, Va. Held at Andersonville. Released March 4, 1865, at Wilmington, N.C. Arrived at Camp Discharge May 4, 1865. Mustered out May 5, 1865, expiration of term.

Private William H. Greenman, Co. F – Mustered in August 1861 in Phila. at age 24, a paper hanger. Deserted September 1863. Returned May 10, 1865. Recorded at Camp Discharge May 16, 1865. Discharged by general order May 18, 1865.

Private William M. M. Edgar, Co. E – Mustered in August 1861 in Phila. at age 20. Captured June 22, 1864, at Petersburg. Held at Andersonville prison. Paroled April 9, 1865, at Jacksonville. Discharged May 29, 1865, expiration of term.

Private Michael Kelly, Co. G – Mustered in August 1861 in Phila. at age 21, a porter. Re-enlisted Feb. 20, 1864, at Stevensburg, Va. Transferred to 183rd Pa. Infantry July 19, 1864. Captured, held at Andersonville. Exchanged April 15, 1865. Recorded at Camp Discharge May 24, 1865. Discharged June 5, 1865. Joined Veteran Reserve Corps.

Corporal George W. Lockner, Co. B – Mustered in on Aug. 10, 1861, in Phila. at age 23. Captured June 22, 1864, at Petersburg. Held at Andersonville prison. Paroled at Jacksonville, Fla., on April 29, 1865. Mustered out May 31, 1865, expiration of term.

Sergeant John Stuart, Co. G – Mustered in on Aug. 10, 1861, in Phila. at age 30, as a sergeant. Captured at Petersburg, Va., June 22, 1864. Imprisoned at Andersonville. Paroled at Jacksonville, Fla., on April 29, 1865. Discharged from military May 31, 1865, expiration of term.

Private Thomas Saunders/Sanders, Co. H – Mustered in October 1861 in Poolesville, Md., at age 34. Transferred to 183rd Pa. Infantry July 19, 1864. Recorded present at Camp Discharge Oct. 27, 1864, and hospitalized there for diarrhea. Discharged from service Dec. 6, 1864.

Private Charles Tizzard, Co. B – Mustered in on Aug. 10, 1861, in Phila. at age 25. Taken prisoner June 22, 1864. Held at Andersonville prison. Admitted to Camp Discharge Hospital for "scorbutic rheumatism" Dec. 7, 1864. Mustered out Dec. 12, 1864.

Private James Banfield Co. C – Mustered in on Aug. 10, 1861, in Phila. at age 45. Captured June 22, 1864, at Petersburg, Va. Imprisoned at Andersonville. Released Nov. 21, 1864, at Savannah, Ga. Entered Camp Discharge Jan. 27, 1865. Hospitalized there for rheumatism on Feb. 23, 1865. Mustered out Feb. 24, 1865, expiration of term.

Private William H. Dempsey, Co. A – Mustered in August 1861 in Phila. at age 29. Captured at Wilderness, Va., May 5, 1864. Arrived at Camp Discharge Sept. 30, 1864. Mustered out of service Oct. 3, 1864, expiration of term.

Sergeant Thomas Murphy, Co. G – Enrolled Sept. 27, 1861, in Phila. at age 22; mustered in as sergeant Oct. 25, 1861, at Camp Olsen, Va. Transferred to 183rd Pa. Infantry July 19, 1864. Recorded at Camp Discharge Sept. 20 (arrival #1). Discharged Sept. 26, 1864.

Private James H. Benson, Co. B – Mustered in on Aug. 10, 1861, in Phila. at age 22. Captured near Petersburg, Va., June 22, 1864. Entered Camp Discharge Jan. 9, 1865. Mustered out Jan. 23, 1865, expiration of term. Did additional service with 3rd Pa. Infantry, Co. B.

Private John Allen, Co. F – Mustered into service on Aug. 10, 1861, in Phila. at age 20. Transferred from Co. M Nov. 1, 1862. Captured at Petersburg, Va., June 22, 1864. Held at Andersonville and survived. Entered Camp Discharge Jan. 17, 1865. Mustered out Jan. 25, 1865, expiration of term.

Private Nicholas Weingarden, Co. F – Mustered into service on Aug. 10, 1861, in Phila. at age 20. Captured at Petersburg, Va., June 22, 1864. Imprisoned at Andersonville. Mustered out Jan. 23, 1865, expiration of term. Did additional service with 3rd US Artillery, Co. C.

Sergeant James W. McDonald, Co. F – Mustered into service on Aug. 10, 1861, in Phila. at age 22. Captured at Petersburg, Va., June 22, 1864. Entered Camp Discharge Jan. 23, 1865. Mustered out Jan. 25, 1865, expiration of term.

Private Matthew H. Smith, Co. B – Mustered in on Aug. 10, 1861, in Phila. at age 26, a "core maker." Captured May 6, 1864, at Wilderness, Va. Held at Andersonville prison. Entered Camp Discharge Jan. 24, 1865. Discharged Jan. 25, 1865, expiration of term. Did additional service with 1st Pa. Light Artillery, Co. I; 3rd Pa. Infantry, Co. B; and 17th Pa. Infantry, Co. I.

Sergeant Conrad S. Esher, Co. E – Mustered into service on Aug. 10, 1861, in Phila. at age 27. Captured at Petersburg, Va., and held as a POW from June 22 to Dec. 11, 1864, including at Andersonville. Entered Camp Discharge Feb.20, 1865. Mustered out Feb. 25, 1865, expiration of term.

73rd Pa. Infantry

The regiment was organized in 1861 in Philadelphia. Known as 'The Pennsylvania Legion,' it was part of the Army of the Potomac (II Corps, XI Corps), then Army of Virginia, and Army of the Cumberland. The men were in 14 combat operations, including Second Bull Run, Chancellorsville, Gettysburg, Atlanta, Kennesaw Mountain, Sherman's March to the Sea, and the Carolinas Campaign. By war's end, 216 of its enlisted men and officers died of injuries or illness. Forty succumbed at Andersonville. The regiment mustered out July 14, 1865. *Forty-eight of its men passed through Camp Discharge, 11 of them Andersonville survivors.*

Private Jacob Schaab/Shaube, Co. D – Mustered in on Sept. 7, 1861, in Phila. Prisoner of war Nov. 25, 1863-Oct. 8, 1864. Recorded present at Camp Discharge Jan. 13-May 8, 1865. Hospitalized there for furunculi (skin boils) Jan. 25-27, 1865. Mustered out of service May 16, 1865, expiration of term.

Private Nathaniel Crane, Co. H – Mustered in on Aug. 6, 1861, in Phila. at age 35. Transferred from 66th Pa. Infantry May 1, 1862. Captured at Missionary Ridge, Tenn., Nov. 25, 1863. Held at Andersonville prison. Released Nov. 19, 1864, at Savannah, Ga. Recorded at Camp Discharge Feb. 6, 1865. Hospitalized there for constipation March 15-17, 1865. Discharged from service March 25, 1865, expiration of term.

Sergeant George Kellerman, Co. G – Enrolled Aug. 2, 1861, in Phila. at age 30. Mustered in on Oct. 10, 1861. Arrived at Camp Discharge Oct. 14, 1864. Mustered out Nov. 23,1864, expiration of term.

Sergeant George W. Barlow, Co. E – Mustered in on July 1, 1861, in Phila. at age 30. Promoted to sergeant, date unknown. Captured at Missionary Ridge, Tenn., Nov. 25, 1863. Imprisoned at Andersonville (listed as "Harlow"). Released Dec. 18, 1864, at Charleston, S.C. Recorded at Camp Discharge Feb. 20, 1865. Mustered out March 13, 1865, expiration of term.

Private John Becker, Co. A – Mustered in on Aug. 24, 1861, in Phila. at age 24. Captured Nov. 25, 1863, at Missionary Ridge, Tenn. Imprisoned at Richmond, then Andersonville. Released Dec. 13, 1864, at Charleston, S.C. Recorded at Camp Discharge Feb. 22, 1865. Discharged March 2, 1865, expiration of term.

Private Jacob Daub, Co. H – Mustered in on March 18, 1862, in Harrisburg at age 20. Wounded and taken prisoner at Missionary Ridge, Tenn., Nov. 25, 1863. Held at Andersonville. Released at Venus Point, Ga., Nov. 20, 1864. Entered Camp Discharge March 23, 1865. Discharged April 12, 1865, expiration of term.

Sergeant Charles Ball, Co. A – Mustered in on Aug. 19, 1861, in Phila. at age 44. Promoted to sergeant Sept. 27, 1861. Captured Nov. 25, 1863. Recorded at Camp Discharge April 11, 1865. Discharged by general order April 15, 1865.

Private Lewis Smith, Co. K – Mustered in on July 25, 1861, in Phila. at age 21. Taken prisoner at Missionary Ridge, Tenn., Nov. 25, 1863. Imprisoned at Andersonville. Recorded at Camp Discharge April 17, 1865. Discharged April 22, 1865, expiration of term.

Private Philip Lower/Louar, Co. K – Enrolled Aug. 22, 1861, in Phila. at age 22. Mustered in on Sept. 16, 1861. Transferred from 66th Pa. Infantry, Co. K, March 1862. Captured at Missionary Ridge, Tenn., Nov. 25, 1863. Held at Andersonville and survived. Exchanged April 1, 1865. Entered Camp Discharge May 19, 1865. Discharged June 21, 1865, expiration of term.

Private Alfred O. Hennessy, Co. F – Mustered in September 1861 in Phila. at age 18. Deserted April 24, 1862, at Winchester, Va. Present at Camp Discharge May 20, 1865. No muster-out recorded.

Private William Shade, Co. F – Mustered in September 1862 in Phila. at age 24. Captured at Missionary Ridge, Tenn., Nov. 25, 1863. Held at Andersonville. Exchanged April 1, 1865. Recorded at Camp Discharge May 22, 1865. Discharged by general order June 17, 1865.

Private Charles Nolan, Co. I – Mustered in August 1861 in Phila. at age 24. Captured Nov. 25, 1864, at Missionary Ridge, Tenn. Held at Andersonville and survived. Exchanged April 1, 1865. Recorded at Camp Discharge May 22, 1865. Mustered out June 21, 1865, expiration of term.

Private Samuel Branson, Co. C – Mustered in November 1862 in Phila. at age 21, a brass moulder. Taken prisoner March 28, 1865. Exchanged May 5, 1865. Present at Camp Discharge May 22, 1865. Discharged by general order June 22, 1865.

Private John Hang, Co. A – Mustered in August 1861 in Phila. at age 31. Taken prisoner Nov. 25, 1863, at Missionary Ridge, Tenn. Imprisoned at Andersonville. Exchanged April 15, 1865. Recorded at Camp Discharge May 22, 1865. Mustered out June 21, 1865, expiration of term.

Private George Wilcox, Co. E – Mustered in August 1861 in Phila. at age 20. Captured at Missionary Ridge, Tenn., Nov. 25, 1863. Held at Andersonville and survived. Exchanged April 1, 1865. Present at Camp Discharge May 23, 1865. Mustered out June 14, 1865, expiration of term.

Private Daniel Strain, Co. B – Mustered in August 1861 in Phila. at age 19, a farmer. Re-enlisted Jan. 1, 1864, at Lookout Valley, Tenn. Captured March 21, 1865, at Snow Hill N.C. Paroled at Savannah, Ga., May 5, 1865. Recorded at Camp Discharge May 22, 1865. Mustered out June 8, 1865. Joined Veteran Reserve Corps.

Hospital Steward Charles H. Jacobs – Mustered in on Aug. 3, 1861, at age 24, a druggist. Captured on a forage expedition March 29, 1865, in Goldsboro, N.C. Released May 5, 1865. Recorded at Camp Discharge May 25, 1865. Discharged by general order June 9, 1865. Entered Veteran Reserve Corps.

Musician Valentine Goetz – Mustered in on Aug. 21, 1861, in Phila. at age 32, a shoemaker born in Germany. Taken prisoner at Goldsboro, N.C., March 26, 1865, Exchanged May 5, 1865. Discharged by general order June 9, 1865. Joined Veteran Reserve Corps.

Private Henry C. Smith, Co. I – Taken prisoner near Goldsboro, N.C., March 26, 1865. Absent, no other regimental record. Recorded present at Camp Discharge June 29-July 31, 1865.

Private James Garvin, Co. K – Mustered in August 1861 in Phila. at age 27. Returned from 3rd Regiment Invalid Corps, Feb. 20, 1864. Recorded at Camp Discharge Oct. 5, 1864. Discharged Nov. 30, 1864, expiration of term.

Private James Murray, Co. K – Mustered in on Aug. 6, 1861, in Phila. at age 28. Discharged Aug. 6, 1864, expiration of term. Recorded at Camp Discharge Oct. 28, 1864.

Private Joseph McCorkel, Co. E – Mustered in August 1861 in Phila. at age 47. Admitted July 21, 1864, to Cumberland Hospital, Tenn., with rheumatism. Recorded at Camp Discharge Sept. 23, 1864. Discharged Nov. 22, 1864.

Sergeant John S. Carnes, Co. I/E – Mustered in August 1861 at age 46. Wounded at Chancellorsville, Va., May 2, 1863. Transferred to Veteran Reserve Corps June 1863. Recorded at Camp Discharge Sept. 24, 1864. Discharged at camp Nov. 17, 1864, expiration of term.

Sergeant Charles Bauer/Bower, Co. C – Mustered in on Aug. 19, 1861, in Phila. at age 23. Wounded at Pine Knob, Ga., June 16, 1864. Admitted July 22, 1864, to Cumberland Hospital, Tenn., to treat left foot. Recorded at Camp Discharge Sept. 22, 1864. Hospitalized there for ecthyma Nov. 18, 1864. Mustered out Dec. 3, 1864, expiration of term.

Private William Diver, Co. K – Mustered in August 1861 in Phila. at age 29, from Lancaster. Recorded at Camp Discharge Oct. 30, 1864. Hospitalized there for rheumatism on Nov. 15, 1864. Mustered out Dec. 1, 1864, expiration of term.

Private John Ruff, Co. G/C – Mustered in September 1861 in Phila. at age 40. From Petersburg, Va., sent to US general hospital in Clareyville, Ind., June 1862, then to a hospital in Cumberland, Md., then to convalescent camp near D.C., then to Harwood Hospital in D.C., then to Christian St. Hospital in Philadelphia, then attached to provost guard in Philadelphia until May 1864, then to a hospital in Louisville until term expired, then to Camp Discharge. Recorded present at Camp Discharge Sept. 23, 1864.

Hospitalized there for cephalalgia Nov. 28, 1864. Discharged Jan. 4, 1865, expiration of term.

Private Francis Kelley, Co. F – Enrolled September 1861 in Phila. at age 18. Wounded in right hand May 25, 1864, at Dallas, Ga. Hospitalized at Pennville, Ky. Arrived at Camp Discharge Sept. 29, 1864, reporting from Louisville, Ky. Mustered out Dec. 12, 1864, expiration of term.

Private Hugh Kennedy, Co. F – Enrolled August 1861 in Phila. at age 15. Also served in 45th Pa Infantry. Wounded May 8, 1864, at Rocky Face Ridge, Ga., "right side-severe." Recorded at Camp Discharge Sept. 29, 1864. Discharged Dec. 10, 1864.

Private Thomas Siatter, Co. H – Transferred from 66th Pa. Infantry March 2, 1862. Prisoner of war March 29-May 5, 1865. Recorded at Camp Discharge May 23, 1865. Discharged by general order June 24, 1865. Joined Veteran Reserve Corps.

Private John W. Glenn, Co. I – Mustered in August 1861 in Phila. at age 19, a laborer. Re-enlisted Jan. 1, 1864, at Lookout Valley, Tenn. Prisoner March 21-May 5, 1865. Present at Camp Discharge May 23, 1865. Discharged by general order June 9, 1865. Joined Veteran Reserve Corps.

Private Dallas Barnholt, Co. E – Mustered in March 1864 in Phila. at age 18, a butcher. Captured at Snow Hill, N.C., March 3, 1865. Paroled at Savannah, Ga., May 5, 1865. Present at Camp Discharge May 26, 1865. Discharged by general order June 14, 1865.

Private John Krouse, Co. C – Mustered in on Aug. 19, 1861, in Phila. at age 19. Captured on Nov. 25, 1863, at Battle of Missionary Ridge, Tenn. Held until Feb. 27, 1865. Recorded at Camp Discharge May 1, 1865. Discharged May 2, 1865.

Private Edward Jones, Co. F – Enrolled Aug. 3, 1861, in Phila. at age 28. Mustered in on Sept. 24, 1861. Deserted; returned. Transferred to Veteran Reserve Corps, date unknown. Hospitalized at Camp Discharge for catarrh on Nov. 24, 1864, for "Horrors" Dec. 29, 1864. Mustered out with company July 14, 1865. Did additional service with 27th Pa. Infantry.

Private Patrick Taggart, Co. F – Enrolled Aug. 3, 1861, in Phila. at age 29. Mustered in on Sept. 24, 1861. Transferred from Co. I on Oct. 1, 1861. Wounded at Kennesaw Mountain, Ga., June 2, 1864. Hospitalized at Camp Discharge to treat gunshot wound of the left groin and neuralgia, Dec. 2, 1864. Mustered out Dec. 21, 1864, expiration of term.

Private John Gilmore, Co. E – Enrolled July 16, 1861, in Phila. at age 20. Mustered in on Aug. 29, 1861. Captured at Missionary Ridge, Tenn., Nov. 25, 1863. Released Dec. 10, 1864, at Charleston S.C. Entered Camp Discharge March 4, 1865. Hospitalized there for catarrh March 6-10, 1865. Discharged from service March 21, 1865, expiration of term.

Sergeant Stephen Bauer, Co. A – Mustered in September 1861 in Phila. as a sergeant, age 34. Recorded present at Camp Discharge Sept. 24, 1864. Discharged Nov. 16, 1864, expiration of term.

Sergeant Henry Brentz, Co. D – Enrolled August 1861 in Phila. at age 26. Recorded at Camp Discharge Sept. 24, 1864. Mustered out Nov. 19, 1864, expiration of term.

Private Patrick Foy, Co. H – Enrolled August 1861 in Phila. at age 27. Transferred from 66th Pa. Infantry March 1862. Present at Camp Discharge Sept. 24, 1864. Mustered out Sept. 27, 1864, expiration of term.

Private Joseph Higginbotham, Co. E – Mustered in on Aug. 3, 1861, in Phila. at age 20. Recorded at Camp Discharge Sept. 26, 1864. Discharged Oct. 17, 1864, expiration of term.

Private George Moore, Co. B – Enrolled August 1861 in Phila. at age 46. Recorded present at Camp Discharge Sept. 27, 1864. Mustered out Nov. 21, 1864, expiration of term.

Private John Fields, Co. G – Mustered in on Oct. 23, 1861, in Phila., at age 23. Recorded at Camp Discharge Oct. 4, 1864. Mustered out Nov. 21, 1864, expiration of term.

Private George Heckmann, Co. A – Mustered in August 1861 in Phila. at age 25. Recorded at Camp Discharge Oct. 16, 1864. Mustered out Nov. 21, 1864, expiration of term.

Private Charles Miller, Co. D – Mustered in September 1861 in Phila. at age 25. Recorded at Camp Discharge Sept. 23-Dec. 1, 1864. Mustered out Nov. 21, 1864, expiration of term.

Sergeant George Kellerman, Co. G – Mustered into service Oct. 10, 1861, in Phila. at age 30. Entered Camp Discharge Oct. 14, 1864. Mustered out Nov. 23, to date Nov. 19, 1864, expiration of term.

Sergeant Peter Cassel, Co. C – Mustered in August 1861 in Phila. at age 44. Transferred from 27th Pa. Infantry. Recorded at Camp Discharge Sept. 23, 1864. Mustered out Nov. 10, 1864, expiration of term.

Sergeant James Murren, Co. H – Mustered in on Aug. 17, 1861, in Phila. at age 23. Transferred from 66th Pa. Infantry March 1, 1862. Promoted to sergeant. Wounded at Pine Knob, Ga., June 15, 1864. Recorded present at Camp Discharge Sept. 22, 1864. Mustered out Dec. 3, 1864, expiration of term.

Corporal Patrick McEnany, Co. A – Mustered in on Aug. 27, 1861, in Phila. at age 24. Captured Nov. 25, 1863. Entered Camp Discharge Jan 5, 1865. Discharged by general order Jan. 16, 1865.

Private Joseph Fortescue, Co. I – Mustered in on Aug. 26, 1861, in Phila. at age 18. Transferred from 66th Pa. Infantry March 1, 1862. Captured at Missionary Ridge, Tenn., Nov. 25, 1863. Held at Andersonville. Sent to Millen, Ga., Nov. 11, 1864. Mustered out Jan. 20, 1865. Entered Veteran Reserve Corps.

75th Pa. Infantry

The regiment was organized in 1861 in Philadelphia from German-speaking recruits. It was attached to the Army of the Potomac, then Army of the Cumberland. The men saw action in nine combat operations, including Second Bull Run, Chancellorsville, and Gettysburg. From its ranks, 161 enlisted men and officers died of wounds or sickness. The regiment mustered out Sept. 1, 1865. *Thirty of its men passed through Camp Discharge, including 19 Andersonville survivors.*

Private John Pfleger, Co. H – Mustered in on Oct. 7,1861, in Phila. at age 42, a gardener; born in Germany. At Camp Discharge from Oct. 6, 1864 to May 22, 1865. Discharged by general order May 22, 1865.

Private George V. Puder, Co. H – Mustered in on Sept. 30, 1861, in Phila. at age 24, a cabinetmaker born in Germany. Recorded at Camp Discharge Oct. 13, 1864, coming from Camp Distribution, Va. Discharged March 31, 1865.

Private Solomon Guelden, Co. E – Mustered in on Feb. 12, 1864, in Phila. Captured Nov. 30, 1864, at Franklin, Tenn. Held at Andersonville and survived. Recorded present at Camp Discharge May 23, 1865. Hospitalized there for colic June 3, 1865. Discharged from service by general order June 14, 1865.

Private Charles Buxbaum, Co. E – Mustered in on Sept. 6, 1861, in Phila. at age 36, a weaver. Captured Nov. 30, 1864, at Franklin, Tenn. Imprisoned at Andersonville. Freed April 28, 1865. Recorded at Camp Discharge May 23, 1865. Discharged by general order June 5, 1865. Joined Veteran Reserve Corps.

Corporal John Guenther, Co. E – Mustered in on Aug. 31, 1861, in Phila. at age 18, a cigar maker. Re-enlisted Jan. 1, 1864, at Chattanooga. Promoted to a musician. Captured Nov. 30, 1864, at Franklin, Tenn. Held at Andersonville. Exchanged April 15, 1865. Recorded at Camp Discharge May 23, 1865. Hospitalized there for diarrhea May 27-28, 1865. Discharged by general order June 13, 1865. Joined Veteran Reserve Corps.

Corporal Francis Miller, Co. I – Mustered in on Oct. 16, 1861, in Phila. at age 18. Promoted to corporal Nov. 1, 1862. Deserted April 6, 1864. Returned Aug. 9, 1864. Recorded at Camp Discharge May 2, 1865. Hospitalized there for ecthyma July 2, 1865. Discharged July 15, 1865, expiration of term.

Private John Eife, Co. E – Mustered in on Sept. 2, 1861, in Phila. at age 21, a tailor. Re-enlisted Jan. 1, 1864, at Chattanooga. Captured Nov. 30, 1864, at Franklin, Tenn. Imprisoned at Andersonville. Paroled April 23, 1865, at Vicksburg, Miss. Recorded at Camp Discharge May 18, 1865. Discharged by general order June 10, 1865. Entered Veteran Reserve Corps.

Private William. Hamburg/Homburg, Co. E – Mustered in on Aug. 2, 1862, in Phila. Captured Nov. 30, 1864, at Franklin, Tenn. Held at Andersonville prison. Exchanged April 15, 1865. Recorded at Camp Discharge May 22, 1865. Discharged June 10, 1865.

Private Stephen Hettel, Co. E – Mustered in on Feb. 16,1864, in Phila. Captured Nov. 30, 1864, at Franklin, Tenn. Held at Andersonville and survived. Exchanged April 15, 1865. Recorded present at Camp Discharge May 22, 1865. Discharged by general order June 14, 1865.

Private Charles Schmidt, Co. E – Mustered in on Aug. 30, 1861, in Phila. at age 36, a barkeeper. Re-enlisted Jan. 1, 1864, at Chattanooga. Recorded present at Camp Discharge May 23, 1865. Discharged by general order June 10, 1865.

Private Gottlieb Eberhart/Everhart, Co. E – Mustered in on Aug. 29, 1861, in Phila. at age 25, a butcher. Re-enlisted Jan. 1, 1864, at Chattanooga. Captured Nov. 30, 1864. Imprisoned at Andersonville. Exchanged April 1, 1865. Recorded at Camp Discharge May 29, 1865. Discharged by general order June 13, 1865. Joined Veteran Reserve Corps.

Corporal Joseph Siegwarth/Siegmuth, Co. E – Mustered in on Aug. 27, 1861, in Phila. at age 42, a cooper. Re-enlisted Jan. 1, 1864, at Chattanooga. Captured Nov. 30, 1864. Recorded at Camp Discharge May 25, 1865. Discharged by general order June 13, 1865. Joined Veteran Reserve Corps.

Sergeant Frederick Bock, Co. E – Mustered in on Aug. 31, 1861, in Phila. at age 29, a carpenter. Re-enlisted Jan. 1, 1864, at Chattanooga. Captured Nov. 30, 1864, at Franklin, Tenn. Held at Andersonville and survived. Exchanged April 1865. Recorded at Camp Discharge May 25, 1865. Discharged by general order June 13, 1865. Entered Veteran Reserve Corps.

Private John Viehman, Co. E – Mustered in August 1862 in Phila. at age 37. Captured Nov. 30, 1864, at Franklin, Tenn. Held at Andersonville prison. Exchanged April 1, 1865. Recorded at Camp Discharge May 25, 1865. Discharged by general order June 13, 1865.

Corporal John Haag, Co. E – Mustered in on Aug. 31, 1861, in Phila. at 28, a shoemaker. Re-enlisted Jan. 1, 1864, at Chattanooga. Captured Nov. 30, 1864, at Franklin, Tenn. Held at Andersonville. Entered Camp Discharge May 25, 1865. Discharged by general order June 13, 1865. Joined Veteran Reserve Corps.

Sergeant Joseph Hinger, Co. E – Mustered in on Aug. 27, 1861, in Phila. at age 31, a carpenter. Wounded at Gettysburg July 4, 1863. Re-enlisted Jan. 1, 1864. Captured Nov. 30, 1864, at Franklin, Tenn. Held at Andersonville. Released April 21, 1865, at Vicksburg, Miss. Recorded at Camp Discharge May 25, 1865. Discharged by general order June 13, 1865. Joined Veteran Reserve Corps.

Private Anton Armbruster Co. E – Mustered in on Aug. 31, 1861, in Phila. at age 26, a driver. Re-enlisted Jan. 1, 1864, at Chattanooga. Captured, held at Andersonville. Exchanged April 1865. Recorded at Camp Discharge May 25, 1865. Discharged by general order June 10, 1865. Joined Veteran Reserve Corps.

Private John Deuschle, Co. E – Mustered in on Feb. 13, 1864, in Phila. Captured Nov. 30, 1864. Recorded at Camp Discharge May 26, 1865. Discharged by general order June 13, 1865.

Sergeant Franz Niebling, Co. E – Mustered in on Aug. 27, 1861, in Phila. at age 26, a tailor. Re-enlisted Jan. 1, 1864, at Chattanooga. Captured Nov. 30, 1864. Recorded at Camp Discharge May 25, 1865. Discharged by general order June 13, 1865. Entered Veteran Reserve Corps.

Private John Beiter, Co. E – Mustered in on Aug. 27, 1861, in Phila. at age 20, a shoemaker. Re-enlisted Jan. 1, 1864, at Chattanooga. Captured Nov. 30, 1864, at Franklin, Tenn. Imprisoned at Andersonville. Exchanged April 1865. Recorded at Camp Discharge May 25, 1865. Discharged by general order June 13, 1865. Entered Veteran Reserve Corps.

Private John Hirschmann, Co. E – Mustered in on Feb. 23, 1864, in Phila. Captured Nov. 30, 1864, at Franklin, Tenn. Imprisoned at Andersonville. Recorded at Camp Discharge May 25, 1865. Discharged by general order June 13, 1865.

Private Charles Leirer/Larue, Co. E – Mustered in on Feb. 11, 1864, in Phila. Captured Nov. 30, 1864, at Franklin, Tenn. Held at Andersonville prison. Exchanged April 1, 1865. Recorded at Camp Discharge May 25, 1865. Discharged by general order June 13, 1865.

Private Michael Steck, Co. E – Mustered in on Sept. 6, 1861, in Phila. at age 43, a laborer. Re-enlisted Jan. 1, 1864, at Chattanooga. Captured Nov. 30, 1864, at Franklin, Tenn. Taken to Andersonville prison. Exchanged April 1, 1865. Reached Camp Discharge June 6, 1865. Discharged by general order June 13, 1865. Joined Veteran Reserve Corps.

Sergeant Charles Preusch, Co. E – Mustered in on Aug. 31, 1861, in Phila. at age 26, a shoemaker. Re-enlisted Jan. 1, 1864, at Chattanooga. Captured Nov. 30, 1864, at Franklin, Tenn. Held at Andersonville. Exchanged April 1, 1865. Recorded at Camp Discharge June 7, 1865. Discharged by general order June 13, 1865. Entered Veteran Reserve Corps.

Corporal Jacob Ullman, Co. E – Mustered in on Aug. 31, 1861, in Phila. at age 25, a shoemaker. Re-enlisted Jan. 1, 1864, at Chattanooga. Captured Nov. 30, 1864, at Franklin, Tenn. Held at Andersonville and survived. Exchanged April 1, 1865. Reached Camp Discharge June 7, 1865. Discharged by general order June 13, 1865. Joined Veteran Volunteer Corps.

Private Charles Laipple, Co. E – Mustered in on Aug. 31, 1861, in Phila. at age 30, a baker. Re-enlisted Jan. 1, 1864, at Chattanooga. Captured Nov. 30, 1864, at Franklin, Tenn. Imprisoned at Andersonville. Exchanged April 1, 1865. Recorded at Camp Discharge June 12, 1865. Discharged by general order June 13, 1865. Entered Veteran Reserve Corps.

Private Gottlieb Hofman, Co. E – Enrolled Sept. 5,1861, in Phila. at age 28, a shoemaker. Promoted to corporal. Recorded at Camp Discharge Sept. 26, 1864. Mustered out Oct. 4, 1864, expiration of term.

Private Lorenz Stocker, Co. H – Enrolled Sept. 25, 1861, in Phila. at age 37, a barber, born in Germany. Wounded at Gettysburg July 1, 1863. Shot in left bicep during afternoon assault. Healed after lengthy hospitalization. Recorded at Camp Discharge on Sept. 28, 1864. Discharged Oct. 1, 1864, expiration of term.

Private George Weigand, Co. B – Mustered into service Aug. 16, 1861, in Phila. at age 35, a gardener. Mustered out Jan. 20, 1865, expiration of term. Recorded present at Camp Discharge Jan. 25, 1865. Did additional service with the 17th Pa. Infantry.

Private Ferdinand Lender, Co. E – Mustered into service Aug. 31, 1861, in Phila. at age 24, a shoemaker. Deserted; returned. Entered Camp Discharge March 10, 1865. Discharged March 21, 1865.

76th Pa. Infantry

The regiment ('Keystone Zouaves') was recruited in 1861 in Lawrence, Mercer, Blair, York, Bedford, Westmoreland, Luzerne, Beaver, Allegheny, and Schuylkill Counties. It was assigned to the Department of the South. The men took part in 14 combat operations, including Fort Wagner, Cold Harbor, Petersburg, the Crater, Chaffin's Farm, Fair Oaks, and Carolinas Campaign. The toll was 364 enlisted men and officers lost to injury and disease. The regiment mustered out July 15, 1865. *One of its men passed through Camp Discharge.*

Private James E. Atwell, Co. F – Drafted, mustered in on Aug. 27, 1863, in Waterford at age 22. Absent, sick. Recorded present at Cap Discharge June 10-22, 1865. Discharged by general order June 22, 1865.

77th Pa. Infantry

The regiment was recruited in 1861 in Franklin, Allegheny, Huntingdon, Mercer, Fulton, Blair, Luzerne, Franklin, Beaver, Dauphin, and Lancaster Counties. It was assigned to the Army of the Ohio, then the Army of the Cumberland. The men engaged in 13 combat operations, including Shiloh, Corinth, Chickamauga, Chattanooga, Kennesaw Mountain, and Franklin. They lost 319 enlisted men and officers to wounds and sickness. Thirty-one died at Andersonville. The regiment mustered out on Dec. 6, 1865. *Four of its men transited Camp Discharge, two of them Andersonville survivors.*

Private Henry Ruth, Co. K – Mustered in on Feb. 22, 1864, in Lancaster at age 21, a brick maker. Wounded at Battle of Franklin, Tenn., Nov. 30, 1864. Recorded at Camp Discharge May 29-June 1, 1865. Discharged June 1, 1865.

Sergeant John Obreiter, Co. K – Enrolled Oct. 23, 1861, in Lancaster, mustered in on Dec. 8, 1861, in Camp Negley, Ky, at age 19. Promoted from corporal December 1862. Captured at Chickamauga, Ga., Sept. 19, 1863. Escaped from Danville, Va., prison twice (December 1863 and February 1864), from Richmond May 1864, and Andersonville prison September 1864. Reached Union lines at Atlanta and was again captured en route to Chattanooga in October 1864. Prisoner to April 1, 1865. Recorded at Camp Discharge May 31, 1865. Discharged June 21, 1865.

Private Augustus Brighton, Co. K – Enrolled Oct. 16, 1861, in Lancaster at age 24. Mustered in on Dec. 8, 1861, in Camp Negley, Ky. Captured at Chickamauga, Ga., Sept. 19, 1863. Held at Andersonville. Freed at Vicksburg, Miss., April 21, 1865, and discharged the next day. Recorded present at Camp Discharge June 6, 1865. Hospitalized there for constipation on June 13, 1865.

Private Matthias Kaley, Co. F – Mustered in on April 4, 1865, in Lancaster at age 19, a laborer. Discharged from service Dec. 6, 1865.

79th Pa. Infantry

The regiment ('Lancaster Rifles') was recruited in 1861 in Lancaster and Washington Counties. It was attached to the Army of the Ohio and the Army of the Cumberland. The men engaged in 14 combat operations, including Chickamauga, Chattanooga, Kennesaw Mountain, Atlanta, Sherman's March to the Sea, and the Carolinas Campaign. In total, 268 enlisted men and officers died of injury or illness. Nineteen died at Andersonville, one at Florence. The regiment mustered out July 12, 1865. *One of its men passed through Camp Discharge.*

Private Robert C. Smeltz, Co. B – Recruit, muster-in information not given. Absent at regimental muster out. Recorded at Camp Discharge July 17-31, 1865.

81st Pa. Infantry

The regiment was recruited in 1861 in Philadelphia, Carbon, and Luzerne Counties. It was attached to the Army of the Potomac (II Corps). The men took part in 23 combat operations, including Seven Pines, Antietam, Fredericksburg, Chancellorsville, Gettysburg, Wilderness, Spotsylvania, Cold Harbor, and Petersburg. From its ranks, 306 enlisted men and officers succumbed to injury or illness. Three men died at Andersonville. The regiment mustered out on June 29, 1865. *Twelve of its men transited Camp Discharge, including one Andersonville survivor.*

1st Lieutenant James H. Walker, Co. E – Mustered in on Sept. 20, 1861, in Phila. at age 24, a machinist born in Ireland. Re-enlisted Jan. 2, 1864, in Stevensburg, Va. Promoted from sergeant March 24, 1864. Commissioned as adjutant April 23, 1864, as captain Oct. 5, 1864, but not mustered. Recorded at camp Nov. 12, 1864, as being "absent without authority." Dismissed Feb. 27, 1865, by special order. Also dismissed from service July 25, 1865, dating to July 17, per instructions of mustering officer; date of discharge July 18.

Sergeant Michael Mahady, Co. D – Mustered in on Aug. 23, 1862, in Phila. at age 23. Recorded present at Camp Discharge on Nov. 12, 1864, relieved from recruiting service 605 Arch St., Phila. Hospitalized at camp for pyrosis (heartburn) Nov. 17-20, 1864. Discharged from service by general order June 1, 1865.

Private Thomas J. Morgan, Co. H – Mustered in on Aug. 2, 1861, at age 24. Deserted Oct. 9, 1861. Recorded at Camp Discharge April 12, 1865. Hospitalized there for scabies on April 19, 1865. Discharged from service April 27, 1865.

Corporal Josiah Houseworth, Co. C – Mustered in on June 21, 1864, in Frankford at age 38. Promoted to corporal Sept. 1, 1864. Wounded April 7, 1865. Absent, wounded, at regimental muster out. Recorded at Camp Discharge May 25, 1865. Discharged by general order June 21, 1865.

Private Conrad Baker, Co. G – Mustered in on Sept. 16, 1861, in Mauch Chunk at age 24, a cooper. Wounded June 30, 1862, and at Fredericksburg, Va., Dec. 13, 1862. Recorded at Camp Discharge Oct. 4-Dec. 24, 1864. Hospitalized there for a gunshot wound of back Nov. 15, 1864. Discharged Dec. 24, 1864, to the expiration of term.

Private Patrick O'Brien, Co. A/D – Mustered in on Sept. 24, 1861, in Phila. at age 29, a jeweler born in Ireland. Recorded at Camp Discharge from Oct. 4 to Dec. 22, 1864. Hospitalized there for catarrh Nov. 15, 1864. Not accounted for on regimental roster.

Private Isaac Kenvin, Co. K – Mustered in on Oct. 27, 1861. Re-enlisted December 1863 in Stevensburg, Va., at age 26, a laborer. Wounded June 3, 1864. Absent, wounded, at regimental muster out. Recorded present at Camp Discharge July 1865. Also served in Veteran Reserve Corps.

Private Dennis Murphy, (Unassigned Company) – Mustered in August 1864 in Hollidaysburg at age 18, a substitute. Recorded at Camp Discharge July 7-10, 1865. Discharged by general order July 10, 1865.

Private Charles Graver, Co. C – Mustered in on March 9, 1864, in Phila. Captured June 3, 1864, at Cold Harbor, Va. Held at Andersonville prison. Freed April 28, 1865. Recorded at Camp Discharge June 12-27, 1865. Hospitalized there for scabies June 23, 1865. Discharged by general order June 27, 1865.

Private George Thomas, Co. I – Mustered into service Sept. 24, 1861, in Phila. at age 21, a butcher. Entered Camp Discharge Jan. 25, 1865. Hospitalized there for catarrh Feb. 27, 1865. Discharged from service March 3, 1865.

Private Charles Wiley, Co. D – Mustered in September 1861 in Phila. at age 21, a farmer. Recorded at Camp Discharge Sept. 26, 1864, and mustered out the following day, expiration of term.

Sergeant Charles E. Warren, Co. E – Mustered in October 1861 as a sergeant. Deserted Oct. 29, 1861. Recorded at Camp Discharge Nov. 12, 1864, listed as Charles Wilson. Forwarded to regiment Nov. 19, 1864. Not accounted for on regimental muster.

82nd Pa. Infantry

The regiment was recruited in 1861 in Philadelphia and Allegheny Counties. It was assigned to the Army of the Potomac (IV Corps, VI Corps) and the Army of the Shenandoah. The men engaged in 27 combat operations, including Seven Pines, Savage Station, Antietam, Fredericksburg, Chancellorsville, Gettysburg, Spotsylvania, Cold Harbor, and Petersburg. In total, 178 enlisted men and officers died of wounds or sickness. Three died at Andersonville. The regiment mustered out July 13, 1865. *Seven of its men passed through Camp Discharge, including one Andersonville survivor.*

Private William Wise, Co. G – Mustered in on Sept. 22, 1862, in Phila. at age 42, a carpenter from Lycoming County. Transferred from Co. D Sept. 4, 1864. Recorded at Camp Discharge June 17-July 31, 1865. Discharged by general order June 17, 1865.

Private William A. Machett, Co. K – Mustered into service on Sept. 4, 1861, in Phila. at age 22. Absent at muster out of the company, detached to corps headquarters as teamster per special order. Entered Camp Discharge Feb. 17, 1865. Discharged by general order March 30, 1865.

Private Theodore H. Eberhart, Co. I – Mustered in on Sept. 2, 1861, in Phila. at age 18. Prisoner from June 1, 1864, to Feb. 20, 1865. Mustered out April 21, 1865. Held at Andersonville prison and survived. Recorded at Camp Discharge April 20, 1865, and discharged the following day.

Corporal Henry H. Wise, Co. G – Mustered in on Aug. 24, 1861, in Phila. at age 19, an umbrella cutter. Re-enlisted Dec. 20, 1863, at Brandy Station, Va. Wounded at Sailors Creek, Va., April 5, 1865, and absent at regimental muster-out. At Camp Discharge July 20-22, 1865. No discharge furnished. Joined Veteran Reserve Corps.

Private Cornelius Cunningham, Co. D – Mustered in on Aug. 10, 1861, in Phila. at age 20. Captured October 1863, details not given. Entered Camp Jan. 9, 1865. Discharged Jan. 23, 1865. Did additional service with 31st Pa. Infantry.

Private Reese E. Lewis, Co. G – Mustered into service on Aug. 24, 1861, in Phila. at age 21. Entered Camp: Discharge Jan. 4, 1865. Mustered out Jan. 28, 1865.

Private Arthur Davis, Co. C – Mustered into service Sept. 9, 1861, in Pittsburgh. Wounded, circumstance not listed. Entered Camp Discharge March 1, 1865. Discharged March 6, 1865, expiration of term. Did additional service with 23rd Pa. Infantry.

87th Pa. Infantry

The regiment was recruited in 1861 in York, Dauphin, Adams, Allegheny, Lawrence, Washington, Lebanon, and Franklin Counties. It was attached to Middle Department, then the Army of the Potomac (III Corps, VI Corps), and the Army of the Shenandoah. The men were in 13 combat operations, including Wilderness, Spotsylvania, Cold Harbor, and Petersburg. The toll was 202 enlisted men and officers lost to injury or illness. Twelve died at Andersonville. The regiment mustered out June 29, 1865, in Alexandria, Va. *Two of its men transited Camp Discharge.*

Private John Snyder, Co. G – Mustered in on Sept. 25, 1861, in York at age 42, a laborer. Re-enlisted March 30, 1864, at Brandy Station, Va. Wounded in the right forearm at Winchester, Va., Sept. 19, 1864. Forearm was amputated the same day. Absent, in hospital at Sandy Hook, Md., at regimental muster out. Recorded at Camp Discharge Dec. 3, 1864, and admitted to camp hospital the next day to treat amputated arm. Discharged from camp Jan. 6, 1865.

Private A. Lewis, Co. C – No such listing in Bates or Pa. Veterans Index, but is entered on the Camp Discharge Hospital Register as hospitalized for syphilis May 15, 1865.

88th Pa. Infantry

The regiment was recruited in 1861 in Philadelphia and Berks County. It was attached to the Army of the Potomac (I Corps, V Corps). The men took part in 19 combat operations, including Second Bull Run, Antietam, Fredericksburg, Chancellorsville, Gettysburg, Wilderness, Cold Harbor, Petersburg, and Five Forks. From its ranks, 181 enlisted men and officers died of injury and sickness. Two died at Andersonville. The unit took part in Grand Review in D.C., then mustered out June 30, 1865. *Sixteen of its men transited Camp Discharge.*

Private Joseph W. Hanaman, Co. K – Mustered in on Sept. 30, 1861, in Phila. at age 21. Recorded present at Camp Discharge Oct. 8-Dec. 7, 1864. Hospitalized at camp for rheumatism Nov. 29, 1864. Mustered out Dec. 7, 1864, expiration of term.

Private Michael Ruth, Co. D – Mustered in on Sept. 10, 1861, in Phila. at age 44. Recorded at Camp Discharge Sept. 23-Dec. 8, 1864. Hospitalized there for rheumatism on Nov. 29, 1864. Mustered out Dec. 8, 1864, expiration of term.

Sergeant Gabriel Hill, Co. A – Mustered in as sergeant Aug. 23, 1861, in Phila. at age 30. Discharged Aug. 23, 1864, expiration of term, but recorded at Camp Discharge Oct. 6, 1864, and hospitalized there for "colic pains for cold" Dec. 22, 1864.

Private John Zeiber, Co. A – Mustered in on Sept. 3, 1861, in Harrisburg at age 19, from Reading. Wounded at Antietam Sept. 17, 1862. Recorded at Camp Discharge Sept. 20-Nov. 30, 1864. Discharged Nov. 30, 1864.

Private Alexander Keys, Co. F – Mustered in on Sept. 30, 1861, in Phila. at age 24, a laborer. Recorded present at Camp Discharge Oct. 18, 1864, arriving from Camp Parole, Md. Mustered out April 14, 1865, to date Dec. 6, 1864.

Private James Wharton, Co. A – Mustered in on Aug. 23, 1861, in Phila. at age 19. Taken prisoner at Gettysburg July 1, 1863. Entered Camp Discharge Jan. 20, 1865. Discharged by general order Feb. 4, 1865.

Private Jacob Drexel, Co. B – Mustered in on Sept. 12, 1861, in Phila. at age 40. Taken prisoner Aug. 17, 1864, and held until March 13, 1865. Entered Camp Discharge April 22,

1865. Hospitalized there the next day for "Deb fr. M.D." (debility from miasmatic disease). Discharged by general order May 2, 1865.

Private William Hutchinson, Co. H – Mustered in on Sept. 10, 1861, in Phila. at age 27. Captured at Weldon Railroad Aug. 19, 1864. Released Feb. 22, 1865, at Aikens Landing, Va. Discharged by general order March 31, 1865.

Private William Carey, Co. H – Mustered in on Sept. 10, 1861, in Phila. at age 40. Prisoner of war Sept. 19, 1864, to March 24, 1865. Recorded at Camp Discharge May 4, 1865. Discharged by general order May 15, 1865.

Private Joseph Grant, Co. A – Mustered in on Sept. 24, 1864, in West Chester at age 35, a substitute. Recorded at Camp Discharge June 1-14, 1865. Discharged by general order June 14, 1865.

Private Meltzer Hughston, Co. A – Mustered in on Aug. 27, 1861, in Phila. at age 25, a miner standing 5-foot-3. Recorded at Camp Discharge Oct. 25, 1864. Hospitalized there to treat secondary syphilis Nov. 16, 1864. Mustered out Nov. 21, 1864, expiration of term.

Private Henry Thompson, Co. D – Mustered in on Sept. 16, 1861, in Phila. at age 28. Recorded at Camp Discharge Sept. 26-Dec. 5, 1864. Discharged by special order Dec. 5, 1864.

Private Joseph McDowell, Co. C – Mustered in on Sept. 10, 1861, in Phila. at age 28. Recorded at Camp Discharge Sept. 27-Oct. 4, 1864. Mustered out Oct. 4, 1864, expiration of term.

Private Michael Conover, Co. K – Mustered in on Sept. 28, 1861, in Phila. at age 19. Wounded at Antietam, Md., Sept. 17, 1862. Recorded at Camp Discharge Oct. 11-Dec. 2, 1864. Also served with 7th US Veteran Volunteers.

Private George W. Green, Co. C – Mustered in on Sept. 13, 1861, in Phila. at age 18, occupation roller. Recorded present at Camp Discharge Oct. 13, 1864. Discharged from service Dec. 3, 1864.

Private Samuel Burkhart, Co. B – Mustered in on Sept. 12, 1861, in Phila. at age 26. Wounded Sept. 17, 1862, and June 25, 1864. Entered Camp Discharge Sept. 22, 1864. Discharged on surgeon's certificate Nov. 3, 1864.

90th Pa. Infantry

The regiment was organized in 1861 in Philadelphia. It was assigned to the Army of the Potomac (I Corps, then V Corps). The men were in 16 combat operations, including Second Bull Run, Chantilly, Antietam, Fredericksburg, Chancellorsville, Gettysburg, and Wilderness. In total, 230 of its enlisted men and officers succumbed to injury and illness. Ten died at Andersonville, one at Florence. The unit merged with the 11th Pa. Infantry on Nov. 26, 1864. *Thirty-six of its men went through Camp Discharge, including two Andersonville survivors.*

Sergeant John Robson, Co. F – Mustered in on Feb. 11, 1862, in Phila. at age 19, a weaver born in Ireland. Promoted to sergeant, date unknown. Sick at Lookout Hospital, date unknown. Transferred to 11th Pa. Infantry, Co. F, Nov. 26, 1864. Recorded at Camp Discharge Feb. 11, 1865.

Private George Smith, Co. G – Drafted; mustered in on Sept. 16, 1863, in Norristown at age 26, a farmer. Deserted July 12, 1864. Recorded present at Camp Discharge June 7, 1865. Discharge status and date not recorded.

Corporal Neil Deacon, Co. I – Mustered in on Feb. 20, 1862, in Phila. at age 30, a laborer. Transferred to 11th Pa. Infantry, Co. G, Nov. 26, 1864. Wounded, in hospital, at regimental muster out. Recorded at Camp Discharge Jan. 20, 1865.

Private John Howell, Co. B – Mustered in on Feb. 13, 1962, in Phila. at age 18, a shoemaker born in England. Transferred to 11th Pa. Infantry, Co. B, Nov. 26, 1864. Recorded at Camp Discharge Feb. 15, 1865.

Private William A. Orr, Co. D – Drafted; mustered in September 1863 in Norristown at age 20, an engineer. Captured May 25, 1864, at North Anna, Va. Held at Andersonville prison. Exchanged April 1, 1865, freed April 29, 1865. Recorded at Camp Discharge May 31, 1865. Charged with desertion, the charge was withdrawn. Discharged from service July 21, 1865.

Sergeant William H. Morris, Co. I – Mustered in on Oct. 24, 1861, in Phila. at age 23. Transferred from Co. B and promoted to sergeant, date unknown. Recorded at Camp Discharge Oct. 28, 1864. Discharged Nov. 2, 1864, expiration of term.

Private Alfred Genay, Co. B – Mustered in September 1861 in Phila. at age 21. Recorded at Camp Discharge Sept. 23, 1864. Discharged from service Nov. 15, 1864.

Private William G. Large, Co. K – Mustered in November 1861 in Phila. at age 20, a machinist. Wounded in right leg April 20, 1863. Underwent surgery April 29, 1863, to amputate right leg at thigh, leaving flap. Transferred to 11th Pa. Infantry, Co. K, Nov. 26, 1864. Recorded at Camp Discharge Nov. 25, 1864, reporting from Broad & Cherry St. Hospital, Phila. Hospitalized at camp to treat amputated leg Dec. 1, 1864. Mustered out Dec. 13, 1864.

Private Robert Torry, Co. K – Drafted; mustered in September 1863 in Reading at age 20, a newsdealer born in Germany. Captured Oct. 14, 1863, at Bristoe, Va. Held at Andersonville and survived. Released Nov. 20, 1864. Recorded at Camp Discharge June 23, 1865. Charged with desertion, the charge was withdrawn. Discharged from service July 18, 1865.

Private John Fineran, Co. D – Mustered in September 1863 in Norristown at age 27, a laborer. Captured at Rappahannock Station, Va., on Nov. 29, 1863. Recorded at Camp Discharge June 12, 1866. Discharged by general order July 27, 1865.

Private John C. Bowen, Co. A – Mustered in on Feb. 10, 1862, in Phila. at age 21, a pattern maker. Captured at Weldon Railroad Aug. 19, 1864. Transferred to 11th Pa. Infantry, Co. A, Nov. 26, 1864. Recorded at Camp Discharge June 1986.

Private Harvey Hastings, Co. G – Mustered in on Nov. 22, 1861, in Phila. at age 26. Recorded at Camp Discharge Oct. 18, 1864-Jan. 10, 1865. Discharged from service Feb. 2, 1865.

Private John Leopold, Co. F – Mustered in on Jan. 8, 1862, in Phila. at age 20, a cabinet maker born in Germany. Absent, sick in hospital since July 1, 1862. Transferred to 11th Pa. Infantry, Co. F, Nov. 26, 1864. Recorded at Camp Discharge Jan. 14, 1865. Muster-out not recorded.

Private George W. Saxer, Co. C – Mustered into service as corporal Feb. 26, 1862, in Phila. at age 21. Captured at Weldon Railroad, Va., Aug. 19, 1864. Held until Sept. 24, 1864. Transferred to 11th Pa. Infantry, Co. C, Nov. 26, 1864. Entered Camp Discharge March 21, 1865. Discharged April 8, 1865.

Private Stephen L. Kane, Co. A – Mustered in on Jan. 20, 1862, in Phila. at age 23, a packer. Transferred to 11th Pa. Infantry, Co. D, Nov. 26, 1864. Recorded at Camp Discharge April 27, 1865. Discharged May 30, 1865.

Private Thomas McKenna, Co. G – Mustered in on Dec. 20, 1861, in Phila. at age 19, a farmer born in Ireland. Prisoner of war Aug. 19, 1864, to March 2, 1865. Recorded at Camp Discharge April 3, 1865. Hospitalized there for acute diarrhea on April 9, 1865. Discharged from service April 14, 1865.

Corporal Thomas F. Fenlin, Co. F – Mustered in on April 18, 1862, in Phila. at age 24, a plumber. Promoted to corporal. Captured at Weldon Railroad Aug. 19, 1864. Transferred to 11th Pa. Infantry, Co. F, Nov. 26, 1864. Recorded at Camp Discharge May 1, 1865. Discharged from service May 5, 1865.

Sergeant Henry F. Bonfield, Co. D – Mustered in on Nov. 29, 1861, in Phila. at age 19, a painter. Prisoner of war Aug. 19, 1864, to Feb. 27, 1865. Transferred to 11th Pa. Infantry, Co. D, Nov. 26, 1864. Recorded at Camp Discharge April 10, 1865. Discharged April 15, 1865.

Sergeant Christopher C. Crouch, Co. B – Mustered in on Feb. 26, 1862, in Phila. at age 24, a coffee roaster. Held as a prisoner of war, dates not listed. Transferred to 11th Pa. Infantry, Co. B, Nov. 26, 1864. Recorded at Camp Discharge April 12, 1865. Discharged from service April 14, 1865.

Sergeant John Logue, Co. B – Mustered in on Feb. 24, 1862, in Phila. at age 18, a coffee roaster. Promoted to sergeant. Transferred from Cos. K and F. Deserted Oct. 25, 1862, at Camp Chase, Ohio. Prisoner Aug. 19, 1864, to Feb. 28, 1865. Transferred to 11th Pa. Infantry, Co. B, Nov. 26, 1864. Recorded at Camp Discharge April 24, 1865. Discharged from service the next day.

Private David B. Hughes, Co. C – Mustered in on Jan. 21, 1862, in Phila. at age 21, a hatter. Missing in action at Wilderness May 4, 1864. Transferred to 11th Pa. Infantry, Co. C, Nov. 26, 1864. Recorded at Camp Discharge on April 18, 1865, and admitted to camp hospital for "Deb fr Fever" the next day. Discharged from service April 22, 1865.

Private Edward Steinmetz, Co. B – Mustered in on Feb. 20, 1862, in Phila. at age 18, a plumber. Captured at Weldon Railroad, Va., Aug. 19, 1864. Transferred to 11th Pa. Infantry, Co. B, Nov. 26, 1864. Released from captivity Feb. 28, 1865, at Wilmington, N.C. Recorded at Camp Discharge May 3, 1865. Admitted to camp hospital with diarrhea May 24, 1865. Discharged from service June 30, 1865.

Private Edward A. Wilday, Co. D – Mustered in on May 3, 1862, in Belle Plain, Va., at age 21, a tinsmith. Prisoner of war Aug. 19, 1864, to Feb. 2, 1865. Transferred to 11th Pa. Infantry, Co. D, Nov. 26, 1864. Recorded at Camp Discharge April 25, 1865. Discharged April 27, 1865.

Private Nathan P. Riley, Co. A – Mustered in April 1861 in Phila. Deserted Jan. 21, 1862. Returned Feb. 25, 1864. Missing in action at Weldon Railroad, Va., Aug. 10, 1864. Recorded at Camp Discharge June 5, 1865. Discharge date was not given.

Private James Garron, Co. G – Mustered in on Jan. 30, 1862, in Phila. at age 24, a laborer born in Ireland. Deserted Aug. 1, 1864. Discharge date was not given.

Private Thomas S. Kimble, Co. K – Mustered in on Oct. 6, 1862, in Chester County at age 21. Recorded at Camp Discharge Oct. 3, 1864. Discharged from service Nov. 19, 1864. Admitted to Camp Discharge Hospital for constipation Nov. 20-21, 1864.

Private William O'Keefe, Co. E – Mustered in on Sept. 17, 1861, in Phila. at age 22. Captured Aug. 19, 1864, at Weldon Railroad, Va., and held to Feb. 28, 1865. Recorded at Camp Discharge April 5, 1865. Hospitalized there for diarrhea on April 13, 1865. Discharged from service the following day.

Corporal Joseph M. Bonsall, Co. K – Mustered in on Sept. 23, 1861, in Phila. at age 23. Promoted to corporal from Co. I, date unknown. Recorded at Camp Discharge Sept. 28, 1864. Discharged Sept. 30, 1864, expiration of term.

Private George L. Bohem/Boehm, Co. H – Mustered in on Sept. 28, 1861, in Phila. at age 42. Transferred from Co. I, date unknown. Recorded at Camp Discharge Oct. 5, 1864. Discharged from service Oct. 7, 1864.

Private John Hood, Co. F – Mustered in on Oct. 25, 1861, in Phila. at age 37. Entered Camp Discharge Dec. 12, 1864. Discharged the following day, expiration of term.

Private William A. Wood, Co. I – Mustered in on Dec. 14, 1861, in Phila. at age 41, a painter. Transferred to 11th Pa. Infantry, Co. I, Nov. 26, 1864. Entered Camp Discharge Dec. 18, 1864. Discharged Dec. 26, 1864.

Private Thomas Ward, Co. C – Mustered in on Dec. 16, 1861, in Phila. at age 40, from England. Sick in hospital, date unknown. Transferred to 11th Pa. Infantry, Co. C, Nov. 26, 1864. Entered Camp Discharge Dec. 28, 1865. Discharged Jan. 4, 1865.

Corporal William Cunningham, Co. I – Mustered in to service Dec. 13, 1861, in Phila. at age 31, a blacksmith. Transferred to 11th Pa. Infantry, Co. D, Nov. 26, 1864. Absent, sick in hospital, at regimental muster out. Entered Camp Discharge Jan 10, 1865. Discharged Jan. 28, 1865. Did additional service with 23rd Pa. Infantry, Co. I, and 3rd US Veteran Reserves, Co. G.

Sergeant Robert Earley, Co. G – Mustered in on Jan. 22, 1862, at age 18. Transferred to 11th Pa. Infantry, Co. G, Nov. 26, 1864. Wounded May 8, 1864. Entered Camp Discharge Jan. 19, 1865. Discharged the following day.

Musician/Sergeant William H. Faaet, Co. C – Mustered into service on Nov. 12, 1861, in Phila. at age 17, a clerk. Captured at Weldon Railroad, Va., Aug. 19, 1864. Entered Camp Discharge on Jan. 27, 1865. Discharged Jan. 28, 1865.

1st Sergeant Christian Gossman, Co. H – Mustered into service Sept. 19, 1861, in Phila. at age 23. Prisoner of war Aug. 19, 1864, to Feb. 24, 1865. Entered Camp Discharge March 17, 1865. Discharged March 20, 1865.

91st Pa. Infantry

The regiment was recruited in 1861, solely in Philadelphia. It was part of the Army of the Potomac. The men fought in 14 engagements, including Fredericksburg, Chancellorsville, Gettysburg, Spotsylvania Courthouse, Cold Harbor, Petersburg, and Hatcher's Run. Two hundred of its enlisted men and officers succumbed to wounds and sickness. Three died at Andersonville. The regiment took part in the Grand Review in D.C., then mustered out July 10, 1865. *Twelve of its men transited Camp Discharge.*

Private James O'Kain/O'Keane, Co. I – Mustered in on Jan. 23, 1862, in Washington, D.C., at age 30. Recorded present at Camp Discharge Jan. 25, 1865. Hospitalized there for scabies Feb. 20-27 and constipation March 1-3, 1865. Discharged from service March 9, 1865.

Private William Egan, Co. H – Mustered in on Jan. 20, 1862, in Phila. at age 33. Prisoner June 1, 1863, to Aug. 1, 1864. Wounded at Hatchers Run, Va., Oct. 28, 1864. Recorded at Camp Discharge Feb. 27, 1865. Discharged by general order March 13, 1865.

Private William Warford, Co. A – Mustered in September 1861 in Phila. at age 22, a conductor. Re-enlisted in Phila. April 7, 1864. Wounded at Spotsylvania Courthouse, Va., June 18, 1864. Recorded at Camp Discharge June 13, 1865. Discharged by general order the next day.

Private Oscar Foust, Co. F – Mustered in on Oct. 25, 1861, in Phila. at age 18. Promoted to corporal March 4, 1862. Entered Camp Discharge March 23, 1865. Discharged from service April 8, 1865.

Private Johnson Agnew, Co. A – Mustered in on Sept. 10, 1861, in Phila. at age 19. Wounded at the Wilderness May 6, 1864. Recorded at Camp Discharge Sept. 23, 1864. Hospitalized there for gonorrhea and rheumatism Dec. 1, 1864. Mustered out Dec. 8, 1864, expiration of term.

Private Samuel C. Simpson, Co. C – Mustered in on Aug. 20, 1861, in Phila. at age 27. Wounded at Chancellorsville, Va., May 3, 1863. Recorded at Camp Discharge Oct. 16, 1864. Discharged Dec. 5, 1864, expiration of term.

Private William R. Cooper, Co. K – Mustered in on Dec. 21, 1861, in Phila. at age 32. Wounded May 2, 1864. Convalesced at Portsmouth Grove Hospital, R.I., from "gunshot wound through the body." Recorded present at Camp Discharge Dec. 27, 1864. Discharged Jan. 6, 1865. Did additional service with 25th Pa. Infantry.

Private Daniel I. Garn, Co. G – Mustered in on Sept. 21, 1864, in Chambersburg at age 20, a one-year draftee. Recorded at Camp Discharge June 16, 1865. Discharged by general order July 12, 1865.

Private George C. Cross, Co. A – Mustered in on Feb. 28, 1865, in Chambersburg, a draftee aged 25. Recorded present at Camp Discharge July 14, 1865. Discharged by general order Nov. 4, 1865, to date July 10, 1865.

Private James Wright, Co. C – Mustered in on Sept. 27, 1864, in Harrisburg at age 43, a one-year draftee. Recorded at Camp Discharge June 12, 1865. Discharged by general order June 21, 1865.

Private R.H. Houston, Co. G – Mustered in on Sept. 9, 1861, at age 36. Recorded at Camp Discharge Sept. 24-Oct. 1, 1864. Mustered out Nov. 2, 1864. Expiration of term.

Sergeant Adrien A. Beaugereau, Co. B – Mustered in on Dec. 23, 1861, in Phila. at age 28. Entered Camp Discharge Dec. 26, 1865. Mustered out Dec. 29, 1864, expiration of term.

93rd Pa. Infantry

The regiment was organized in 1861 with men from Lebanon, Berks, Clinton, Centre, Dauphin, and Montour Counties. Co. G from Montgomery County. It was assigned to the Army of the Potomac (IV Corps, VI Corps), then the Army of the Shenandoah. The men were in 27 engagements, including Seven Pines, Malvern Hill, Antietam, Fredericksburg, Chancellorsville, Gettysburg, Wilderness, Spotsylvania Courthouse, Cold Harbor, Petersburg, and Hatcher's Run. By war's end, 274 of its enlisted men had died from wounds or illness. One died at Andersonville, one at Florence. The regiment mustered out on June 27, 1865. *Two of its men passed through Camp Discharge.*

Corporal John Byerly, Co. H – Mustered into service on Oct. 21, 1861, in Lebanon at age 22, a Danville resident. Recorded present at Camp Discharge on Oct. 3, 1864, and hospitalized there for gleet (gonorrheal infection) Dec. 6. Discharged from service Dec. 17, 1864, to date expiration of term.

Private Benneville Wise, Co. D – Enrolled Sept. 18, 1861, in Lebanon at age 20, a furnacer (tending a mill furnace). Mustered in on Oct. 12 in Lebanon. Recorded at Camp Discharge Oct. 12, 1864. Hospitalized at camp for diarrhea Dec. 2, 1864. Mustered out of service Oct. 28, 1864, expiration of term.

95th Pa. Infantry

"Gosline's Zouaves" formed in 1861 by Philadelphia volunteers. Co. E was from Montgomery County. The regiment attached to the Army of the Potomac, then the Army of the Shenandoah. The men fought at Antietam, Fredericksburg, Chancellorsville, Gettysburg, Wilderness, Spotsylvania Courthouse, Cold Harbor, Petersburg, and New Market. In all, 255 enlisted men and officers succumbed to injuries and illness. One died at Andersonville, two at Florence. The regiment mustered out July 17, 1865. *Twenty-two of its men transited Camp Discharge, six of them Andersonville survivors.*

Private Walter Kenney/Keeny, Co. H – Mustered in on Jan. 27, 1862, in Pottsville at age 20, a miner born in Ireland. Transferred from 96th Pa. Infantry, Co. I, Oct. 10, 1864. Wounded at Cedar Creek, Va., Oct. 19, 1864. Entered Camp Discharge Jan. 28, 1865. Discharged Feb. 2, 1865. Did additional service with 96th Pa. Infantry, Co. G.

Corporal Thomas J. Cross, Co. K – Mustered in on Oct. 15, 1861, in Phila. at age 22. Wounded at Salem Heights, Va., May 3, 1863. Recorded present at Camp Discharge Oct. 17, 1864. Mustered out with company Nov. 2, 1864.

Private Elias H. Hough, Co. C – Mustered in on Feb. 17, 1864, in Phila. at age 18, a farmer from Bucks County. Wounded in action at Petersburg, Va., March 25, 1865. Recorded at Camp Discharge May 23, 1865. Discharged by general order May 29, 1865.

Private Paul Leach/Leech, Co. G – Mustered in on Sept. 30, 1861, in Phila. at age 20. Captured at Spotsylvania, Va., May 14, 1864. Imprisoned at Andersonville. Freed Feb. 26, 1865. Recorded at camp March 30, 1865. Discharged April 1, 1865.

Private George W. Kennedy, Co. G – Mustered in on Sept. 19, 1861, in Phila. at age 19. Captured at Spotsylvania May 14, 1864. Imprisoned at Andersonville. Released March 1, 1865. Recorded at Camp Discharge April 3, 1865. Discharged April 4, 1865.

Private Daniel L. Stanton, Co. D – Mustered in on April 7, 1862, in Phila. at age 22, a trimmer. Transferred from Co. K, Oct. 14, 1864. Prisoner of war, date unknown. Discharged from service April 13, 1865, expiration of term. Entered Camp Discharge April 24, 1865, left April 25.

Corporal William A. Boyle, Co. A – Mustered in September 1861 in Phila. at age 22. Captured at Spotsylvania Courthouse May 14, 1864. Held at Andersonville. Exchanged April 1865. Entered Camp Discharge May 22, 1865. Discharged by general order June 14, 1865.

Private John R. Williamson, Co. D – Mustered in on Jan. 27, 1864, in Phila. at age 30, a nailer. Wounded at Petersburg, Va., March 25, 1865. Discharged by general order May 19, 1865.

Private John W. Darnel, Co. B – Mustered in on Jan. 22, 1864. Discharged by general order May 24, 1865.

Private William H. Phillips, Co. B – Mustered in on Aug. 22, 1861, in Phila. at age 37. Recorded present at Camp Discharge Oct. 28, 1864. Discharged Nov. 2, 1864.

Sergeant John Welsh, Co. K – Mustered in on Sept. 12, 1861, in Phila. at age 25. Promoted to sergeant July 6, 1862. Recorded at Camp Discharge Oct. 27, 1864. Mustered out Nov. 2, 1864.

Private Edward W. Miles, Co. E – Mustered in on March 10, 1864, in Phila. at age 31, a tailor born in Ireland. Wounded in action at Sailor's Creek, Va., April 6, 1865. Recorded at Camp Discharge July 10-31, 1865. Discharged by general order Aug. 3, 1865.

Private Edwin B. Green, Co. F – Mustered in on Sept. 18, 1861, in Phila. at age 19. Recorded at Camp Discharge Nov. 2, 1864. Discharged Nov. 2, 1864.

Corporal John L. Casper, Co. C – Mustered in on Sept. 18, 1861, in Phila. at age 29. Promoted to corporal Jan. 1, 1863. Recorded at Camp Discharge Sept. 24-27, 1864. Discharged Oct. 17, 1864, expiration of term.

Private William A. Powers, Co. D – Mustered in on Sept. 17, 1861, in Phila. at age 18; discharged Sept. 28, 1864. Recorded at Camp Discharge Sept. 20, 1864. Discharged Sept. 28, 1864, expiration of term.

Private Moses Hewett, Co. F – Mustered in on Sept. 14, 1861, in Phila. at age 18. Wounded at Salem Heights, Va., May 3, 1863. Recorded at Camp Discharge Sept. 29-Oct. 4, 1864. Discharged Oct. 6, 1864.

Private Edward R. Jones, Co. K – Mustered in on Oct. 5, 1861, in Phila. at age 19. Wounded at New Market, Va., Sept. 24, 1864. Recorded at Camp Discharge on Oct. 10, 1864, coming from Convalescent Camp, Va. Mustered out with the company on Nov. 2, 1864.

Private Lewis Bender, Co. D – Mustered in on Sept. 16, 1861, in Phila. at age 25. Arrived at Camp Discharge Nov. 11, 1864. Discharged Dec. 2, 1864, expiration of term.

Private John Whealon, Co. F – Mustered into service Sept. 14, 1861, in Phila. at age 23. Captured at Spotsylvania Courthouse, Va., May 14, 1864. Imprisoned at Andersonville. Entered

Camp Discharge on Jan. 30, 1865. Discharged Jan. 31, 1865, expiration of term. Did additional service with 24th Pa. Infantry and 7th US Veteran Volunteers.

Private William Westerman, Co. F – Mustered into service Sept. 6, 1861, in Phila. at age 25. Captured at Spotsylvania Courthouse, Va., May 14, 1864. Entered Camp Discharge Feb. 1, 1865. Discharged Feb. 14, 1865, expiration of term.

Private Timothy A. Clark, Co. G – Mustered into service Sept. 21, 1861, in Phila. at age 20. Deserted Aug. 26, 1862. Returned Feb. 24, 1864, and arrested. Captured at Spotsylvania Courthouse May 12, 1864. Imprisoned at Andersonville. Entered Camp Discharge Feb. 6, 1865. Discharged Feb. 8, 1865.

Private George H. Prickett, Co. B – Mustered into service Aug. 22, 1861, in Phila. at age 24. Captured May 14, 1864, at Spotsylvania Courthouse. Held at Andersonville and survived. Released Dec. 14, 1864. Entered Camp Discharge March 13, 1865. Discharged March 18, 1865.

96th Pa. Infantry

The regiment was recruited in 1861 from Schuylkill, Berks, Luzerne, and Dauphin Counties. It was attached to the Army of the Potomac, the Army of the Rappahannock, and the Army of the Shenandoah. The men took part in 23 actions, including Malvern Hill, Antietam, Fredericksburg, Chancellorsville, Gettysburg, Wilderness, Spotsylvania Courthouse, and Cold Harbor. In total, 219 of its enlisted men and officers died of injury or sickness. Three died at Andersonville. The unit mustered out Oct. 21, 1864. *Twenty-one of its men passed through Camp Discharge, none of them Andersonville survivors.*

Private James Keesey, Co. B – Mustered in on Sept. 23, 1861, in Pottsville. Transferred from 95th Pa. Infantry, Co. E, date unknown. Deserted July 2, 1863, then returned and transferred to Co. E, 95th Pa. Infantry Oct. 18, 1864. Recorded present at Camp Discharge Feb. 6, 1865, and hospitalized for scabies Feb. 20-22, 1865. Discharged from service by general order June 18, 1865.

Private John Billy, Co. C – Mustered in on Sept. 23, 1861, in Pottsville at age 21. Captured Aug. 21, 1864, and held until Feb. 21, 1865. Recorded at Camp Discharge March 24, 1865, and hospitalized there for chronic diarrhea the next day. Forwarded to the provost marshal. Discharged June 14, 1865.

Musician John Price, Co. D – Mustered in on Sept. 23, 1861, in Pottsville at age 14. Captured July 21, 1864, at Danville, Va. Prisoner until Feb. 22, 1865. Discharged from service March 31, 1865.

Private Jonathan Erdman, Co. H – Mustered in on Sept. 25, 1861, in Pottsville at age 20, a plasterer. Re-enlisted Feb. 15, 1864, at Brandy Station, Va. Captured at Spotsylvania Courthouse May 14, 1864. Imprisoned at Andersonville. Exchanged April 5 and released April 20, 1865. Recorded at Camp Discharge May 24, 1865. Discharged by general order June 13, 1865. Joined Veteran Reserve Corps.

Private William Prosser, Co. D/E – Mustered in on Sept. 25, 1861, in Pottsville at age 20. Captured at Spotsylvania Courthouse May 14, 1864. Held at Andersonville and survived. Recorded at Cap Discharge May 19, 1865. Discharged by general order June 24, 1865.

Private William Franey, Co. K – Mustered in on Feb. 24, 1864, in Pottsville, an Irish-born laborer. Captured at Spotsylvania Courthouse May 12, 1864. Held at Andersonville, then sent to Millen, Ga., Nov. 11, 1864. Recorded present at Camp Discharge May 19, 1865. Discharged from service June 14, 1865.

Corporal Michael Larkin, Co. A – Mustered in on Sept. 23, 1861, in Pottsville at age 18. Captured May 12, 1864, at Spotsylvania Courthouse. Held at Andersonville. Freed April 9, 1865. Recorded at Camp Discharge May 20, 1865. Discharged May 27, 1865.

Private Jeremiah Curran, Co. K – Mustered in on Dec. 15, 1861, in Pottsville at age 31, a miner. Transferred to 95th Pa. Infantry, Co. G, date unknown. Deserted Jan. 8, 1863. Captured Aug. 21, 1864, and held until Feb. 28, 1865. Recorded at Camp Discharge May 4, 1865. Discharged May 8, 1865. Joined Veteran Reserve Corps.

Sergeant David C. Prichard, Co. A – Mustered in on Sept. 23, 1861, in Pottsville at age 19. Captured May 12, 1864, at Spotsylvania Courthouse. Imprisoned at Andersonville. Freed April 9, 1865. Recorded at Camp Discharge May 20, 1865. Discharged May 27, 1865.

Corporal Edward McCormick, Co. A – Mustered in on Sept. 23, 1861, in Pottsville at age 21. Captured May 14, 1864, at Spotsylvania Courthouse. Held at Andersonville. Exchanged April 15, 1865. Recorded at Camp Discharge May 20 and discharged May 27, 1865.

Private Michael Moran, Co. F – Mustered in on Sept. 23, 1861, in Pottsville at age 27. Prisoner of war June 8, 1864, to April 15, 1865, primarily at Andersonville. Recorded at Camp Discharge May 20, 1865. Discharged May 27, 1865.

Private Sylvester Maddock, Co. F – Mustered in on Oct. 8, 1861, in Pottsville at age 21. Captured May 14, 1864, at Spotsylvania Courthouse. Held at Andersonville and survived. Exchanged April 15, 1865. Recorded at Camp Discharge May 20, 1865. Discharged May 27, 1865.

Private Patrick Laddie/Laddy, Co. K – Mustered in on Oct. 10, 1861, in Pottsville at age 35. Recorded present at Camp Discharge Nov. 1, 1864. Discharged from service Dec. 7, 1864.

Private Matthew H. Morrell, Co. A – Mustered in on Sept. 23, 1861, in Pottsville at age 18, a miner born in England. Deserted Sept. 11, 1862, at White Orchard Church, Va. Returned Sept. 19, 1863. Wounded in action at Spotsylvania Courthouse May 10, 1864. Recorded at Camp Discharge Nov. 4, 1864. Hospitalized there to treat gunshot wound of right arm Dec. 2, 1864. Discharged March 9, 1865.

Private Thomas Caden, Co. I – Mustered in on Sept. 24, 1861, in Pottsville at age 24. Deserted July 26, 1864. Recorded at Camp Discharge, under arrest at the stockade, Oct. 22, 1864. Treated at the camp hospital for constipation Nov. 22, 1864. Desertion charge was withdrawn on Feb. 27, 1865. Discharged April 1, 1865.

Corporal Thomas Gribbin, Co. K – Mustered in on Dec. 15, 1861, in Pottsville. Transferred to Co. E, 95th Pa. Infantry, Oct 18, 1864. Recorded at Camp Discharge, hospitalized for catarrh, Jan. 3, 1865. Discharged from service Jan. 28, 1865.

Private John Sammon, Co. I – Mustered in on Sept. 13, 1861, in Pottsville at age 18, a teamster. Recorded at Camp Discharge Oct. 7, 1864. Mustered out with company Oct. 21, 1864.

Corporal John Simpson Jr., Co. C – Mustered in on Sept. 23, 1861, in Pottsville at age 21. Promoted to corporal May 10, 1864. Recorded at Camp Discharge Oct. 7, 1864. Mustered out with company Oct. 21, 1864.

Private Daniel Hartline, Co. A – Mustered in on Sept. 23, 1861, in Pottsville at age 20. Recorded at Camp Discharge Oct. 20, 1864. Mustered out with company Oct. 21, 1864.

Private James McDevitt, Co. I – Mustered into service Sept. 23, 1861, in Pottsville at age 18. Captured at Spotsylvania Court House, Va., May 14, 1864. Entered Camp Discharge Jan. 18, 1865. Discharged Jan. 21, 1865.

Private Emanuel Saylor, Co. C – Mustered into service Sept. 23, 1861, in Pottsville at age 27. Captured at Spotsylvania Court House May 20, 1864. Imprisoned at Andersonville and survived. Transferred to Co. E, 95th Pa. Infantry Oct. 18, 1864. Entered Camp Discharge Feb. 3, 1865. Discharged Feb. 4, 1865.

97th Pa. Infantry

The regiment was formed in 1861, comprising men from Chester and Delaware Counties. It was assigned to the Department of the South. The men were in 14 engagements, including Fort Wagner, Cold Harbor, Petersburg, the Crater, Fair Oaks, and the Carolinas Campaign. In all, 322 of its men died from wounds or sickness. Six died at Andersonville. The regiment mustered out Aug. 28, 1865, in Weldon, N.C. *Twenty-five of its men transited Camp Discharge.*

Private William Agg, Co. C – Mustered in on Sept. 18, 1861, in West Chester, at age 18, a farmer. Wounded in action at Bermuda Hundred, Va., May 20, 1864, again severely in the arm by a shell in trenches near Cemetery Hill, Va., Aug. 29, 1864. Recorded at Camp Discharge Feb. 24, 1865. Hospitalized there for burns March 10, 1865. Discharged from hospital March 20, 1865, to date from Sept. 17, 1864, expiration of term.

Private John Sharp, Co. E – Mustered in on March 3, 1865, in Williamsport, at age 25, a laborer. Recorded present at Camp Discharge the next day. Deserted July 29, 1865.

Private Charles Sharp, Co. E – Mustered into service Feb. 15, 1862, in West Chester at age 33, a laborer. Recorded at Camp Discharge March 4, 1865. Dropped from rolls by order of chief mustering office. Discharged April 4, 1865.

Private Hugh Hale, Co. F – Mustered in on Oct. 15, 1861, in West Chester at age 28, a foundryman. Also served in 9th Pa. Infantry. Wounded in action (ankle dislocated) at James Island, S.C., June 10, 1862. Discharged from Camp Discharge Oct. 15, 1864, expiration of term. Recorded present at camp until Nov. 10, 1864.

Corporal Jeremiah Hennessey, Co. E – Mustered in October 1861 in West Chester at age 37, a carpenter. Promoted to corporal June 1862. Recorded at Camp Discharge Oct. 25, 1864. Hospitalized there for 'Chronic Valv. Dis. Heart' Nov. 15, 1864. Discharged from service Dec. 7, 1864, expiration of term.

Private Henry H. Cloud, Co. D – Mustered in on Sept. 6, 1861, in West Chester at age 19, a spinner from Brandywine Village, Del. Was one of five Clouds in Company D. Wounded in action Aug. 16, 1864, at Deep Bottom, Va., Absent, from wounds, at regimental muster out. Present at Camp Discharge Oct. 18, 1864, arriving from Convalescent Camp, Va. Discharged Dec. 1, 1864.

Private Edward Worrell, Co. G – Mustered in on Oct. 7, 1861, in West Chester at age 32, a mason from Marple. One of four Worrells in Company G. Recorded at Camp Discharge Oct. 16, 1864. Hospitalized there for chronic diarrhea Nov. 17, 1864. Discharged Dec. 2, 1864.

Private Burrows Jermyn/Germain, Co. K – Mustered in on Sept. 28, 1861, in West Chester at age 21, a farmer from Spread Eagle. Discharged Oct. 28, 1864, expiration of term. Present at Camp Discharge Nov. 1, 1864, and hospitalized there for gleet Nov. 22, 1864. Left camp Dec. 9, 1864.

Private John W. Edwards, Co. F – Mustered in on Sept. 23, 1861, in West Chester at age 18, a farmer from Hayesville. Severely wounded March 31, 1864, and again at Petersburg, Va., June 15, 1864. Reported to Camp Discharge from Harrisburg Nov. 5, 1864. Hospitalized at camp on Nov. 22 for a gunshot wound of the left arm. Discharged from service Dec. 1, 1864.

Private James McMannus, Co. D – Mustered in on Sept. 6, 1861, in West Chester at age 23, a blacksmith. Wounded May 18, 1864, near Crescent Plains, Va. Recorded at Camp Discharge Sept. 24, 1864. Under arrest there, dates and circumstances are not recorded. Discharged Jan. 10, 1865.

Private George Jones, Co. F – Mustered in on Nov. 19, 1864, in Reading at age 18, a substitute. Reported to Camp Discharge Dec. 28, 1864. Mustered out with company Aug. 28, 1865.

Corporal George Ellam, Co. A – Mustered in on March 16, 1864, at age 21, a wood turner from Coatesville. Captured Sept. 29, 1864, at Fort Gilmer, Va. Prisoner until May 29, 1865. Recorded at Camp Discharge June 7, 1865. Discharged by general order July 27, 1865. Joined Veteran Reserve Corps.

Private William D. Atherton, Co. F – Mustered in on Sept. 30, 1864, in Williamsport at age 37, a draftee. Recorded at Camp Discharge June 21, 1865, at its hospital June 22 for a boil on the heel. Discharged by general order June 27, 1865.

Private Collum Duffy, Co. E – Mustered in October 1861 in West Chester at age 16, a laborer. Taken prisoner Aug. 16, 1864, Paroled Sept. 26, 1864. Recorded at Camp Discharge Nov. 17, 1864, coming from Camp Parole, Md. Hospitalized at Camp Discharge for staphyloma and amaurosis of left eye Nov. 23, 1864. Discharged Dec. 2, 1864, expiration of term.

Private Thomas P. Waddell, Co. G – Mustered in on Oct. 15, 1861, in West Chester at age 23, a butcher. Wounded May 30 and June 25, 1864, circumstances not recorded. Discharged from duty Oct. 1864, expiration of term. Entered Camp Discharge Nov. 25, 1864, reporting from Cuyler Hospital in Germantown. Hospitalized at camp for catarrh and diarrhea Dec. 2, 1864.

Private John Bennett, Co. E – Mustered in on Sept. 9, 1861, in West Chester at age 25, a laborer from East Bedford. Recorded at Camp Discharge Oct. 5, 1864. Discharged Oct. 18, 1864, expiration of term.

Private James Keelan, Co. E – Mustered in on Sept. 18, 1861, in West Chester at age 25, a laborer from Baltimore. Recorded at Camp Discharge Oct. 6, 1864. Discharged Oct. 18, 1864, expiration of term.

Private James Waul, Co. E – Mustered in on Sept. 16, 1861, in West Chester at age 19, a painter. Recorded at Camp Discharge Oct. 6, 1864. Discharged Oct. 18, 1864, expiration of term.

Private Alban D. Ingram, Co. F – Mustered in on Oct. 2, 1861, in West Chester at age 22, a machinist from Phila. Discharged Oct. 3, 1864, expiration of term. Recorded at Camp Discharge Oct. 7-22, 1864.

Private Charles Quigley, Co. I – Mustered in on Oct. 26, 1861, in West Chester at age 29, a laborer. Reported to Camp Discharge on Nov. 4, 1864, from Hilton Head, S.C. Discharged Nov. 21, 1864, expiration of term.

Private James Grindrod, Co, G – Mustered into service Oct. 10, 1861, in West Chester at age 24, a clerk from Avondale. Recorded at Camp Discharge Oct. 15, 1864. Discharged Nov. 3, 1864, expiration of term.

Private James Riley, Co. E – Mustered in on Sept. 9, 1861, in West Chester at age 22, a laborer. Entered Camp Discharge Jan. 3, 1865; discharged the following day. Did additional service with 9th Pa. Infantry.

Corporal Evan M. Geary, Co. G – Mustered into service Oct. 22, 1861, in Pottsville at age 20. Captured at Wilderness, Va., May 7, 186. Promoted to corporal, date unknown. Transferred to 95th Pa. Infantry Oct.18, 1864. Entered Camp Discharge Jan. 11, 1865. Discharged Jan. 20, 1865.

Private Christopher P. Kane, Co. C – Mustered in on Sept. 23, 1861, in Pottsville at age 22. Captured at White Plains, Va., July 25, 1863. Entered Camp Discharge Jan. 11, 1865. Discharged Jan. 23, 1865.

Private Jonathan Cross, Co. H – Mustered in on Oct. 17, 1861, in West Chester at age 44, a farmer. Recorded at Camp Discharge Oct. 18, 1864. Discharged Oct. 22, 1864, expiration of term.

98th Pa. Infantry

The regiment was recruited in 1861 solely in Philadelphia. It was assigned to the Army of the Potomac (IV Corps, VI Corps). The men fought at Seven Pines, Malvern Hill, Antietam, Fredericksburg, Chancellorsville, Gettysburg, Wilderness, Spotsylvania Courthouse, Cold Harbor, and Petersburg. From its ranks, 194 enlisted men and officers succumbed to injury or illness. The unit mustered out on June 29, 1865. *Eighteen of its men passed through Camp Discharge, including one Andersonville survivor.*

Private Hugh Miulkare, Co. E – Mustered in on Sept. 13, 1861, in Phila. at age 21. Wounded June 3, 1864, at Cold Harbor; Va. Present at Camp Discharge Sept. 24, 1864. Discharged Jan. 6, 1865.

Private Cornelius Schaab, Co. F – Mustered in on Aug. 22, 1861, in Phila. at age 31. Wounded at Battle of Wilderness, Va., May 6, 1864. Officially discharged Aug. 27, 1864, expiration of term. Recorded at Camp Discharge Oct. 28, 1864.

Corporal Frederick Lenz, Co. H – Mustered in on Sept. 18, 1861, in Phila. at age 30. Absent, sick in General Hospital in Newark N.J., Aug. 15, 1862. Wounded June 3, 1864, at Cold Harbor, Va. Discharged from duty Oct. 13, 1864, expiration of term. Entered Camp Discharge Jan. 28, 1865, and hospitalized for a gunshot wound of left leg Jan. 29, 1865. Discharged Feb. 8, 1865.

Private John Brough/Braush, Co. G – Mustered in Phila on March 12, 1864. at age 21, a laborer born in Germany. Captured May 26, 1864. Held at Andersonville prison, then sent to Millen, Ga., Oct. 31, 1864, and exchanged April 21, 1865. Recorded at Camp Discharge May 23, 1865. Discharged by general order June 12, 1865.

Private Gottlieb/Guadalupe Bower, Co. E – Mustered in Phila on Sept. 7, 1861. at age 45. Discharged Sept. 15, 1864, expiration of term. Hospitalized at Camp Discharge for a gunshot wound of right leg Dec. 14, 1864.

Private Robert Cavanaugh, Co. A – Mustered in on Aug. 22, 1861, in Phila. at age 20. Hospitalized at Camp Discharge for a gunshot wound of left leg May 4, 1865 (listed as 'W. Cavanaugh, Co. L'). Discharged Aug. 28, 1864, expiration of term.

Private George Trapp, Co. I – Mustered in on Aug. 17, 1861, in Phila. at age 43. Discharged Aug.28, 1864, expiration of term. Recorded present at Camp Discharge Sept. 23-Nov. 7, 1864.

Private Albert Schlosser, Co. F – Mustered in on Aug. 22, 1861, in Phila. at age 35. Wounded June 3, 1864, at Cold Harbor, Va. Discharged Aug. 27, 1864, expiration of term. Recorded at Camp Discharge Sept. 24-Nov. 7, 1864.

Private Lewis/Louis Teichman, Co. F – Mustered in on Aug. 22, 1861, in Phila. at age 35. Not on regimental muster out roll. Recorded at Camp Discharge Sept. 24-Nov. 8, 1864.

Private Henry Schultz, Co. F – Mustered in on Aug. 28, 1861, in Phila. at age 35. Wounded June 3, 1864, at Cold Harbor, Va. Discharged Aug. 27, 1864, expiration of term. Recorded at Camp Discharge Sept. 24-Oct. 31, 1864.

Private Charles Koelble, Co. F – Mustered in on Aug. 22, 1861, in Phila. at age 19, a native of Paris, France. Deserted May 3, 1863, in Phila. Not on regimental muster out roll. Recorded at Camp Discharge Sept. 26-27, 1864.

Private Christian Wiltz/Wilz, Co. C – Mustered in on Sept. 6, 1861, in Phila. at age 27. Discharged Sept. 3, 1864, expiration of term. Recorded present at Camp Discharge Oct. 1, 1864, reporting from Harpers Ferry, Va. Dropped Dec. 5, 1864.

Private Michael Kuntzman, Co. D – Mustered in on Aug. 22, 1861, in Phila. at age 36. Wounded at Cold Harbor, Va., June 3, 1864. Discharged Aug. 28, 1864, expiration of term. Recorded at Camp Discharge Oct. 4-Nov. 5, 1864.

Corporal William Aberle, Co. D – Mustered in on Aug. 22, 1861, in Phila. at age 23. Promoted to corporal Oct. 3, 1861. Wounded at Fort Stevens, D.C., July 12, 1864. Discharged Aug. 28, 1864, expiration of term.

Private Peter Degrace/Degrass, Co. G – Mustered in on Nov. 25, 1861, in Phila. at age 44. Wounded at Cedar Creek, Va., Oct. 19, 1864. Recorded at Camp Discharge Dec. 8, 1864, and discharged Dec. 9, expiration of term.

Private Martin Huhn, Co. F – Mustered in on Aug. 22, 1861, in Phila. at age 25. Detached on hospital duty in Washington, D.C., Jan. 29, 1862. Discharged from service Aug. 27, 1864, expiration of term. Recorded at Camp Discharge Sept. 22, 1864.

(Two other men were listed on the Camp Discharge ledger as belonging to the 98th, but their names did not jibe with the official records. A **Martin Fulmer** was recorded on Sept. 23, 1864, as being a private in Company D. A **William Bosen** arrived on May 19, 1865, claiming to be a private as Company E.)

99th Pa. Infantry

The regiment was organized in 1861 solely in Philadelphia. It was attached to the Army of the Potomac (II Corps, III Corps). The men took part in 25 operations, including Second Bull Run, Fredericksburg, Chancellorsville, Gettysburg, Wilderness, Spotsylvania Courthouse, Cold Harbor, and Petersburg. In all, 235 of its enlisted men and officers died of injury or illness. Eleven died at Andersonville. The regiment was in Grand Review in D.C., then mustered out July 1, 1865. *Thirty-two of its men transited Camp Discharge, three of them Andersonville survivors.*

Private John Kline, Co. E – Mustered in to service Aug. 31, 1861, in Phila. at age 38. Recorded at Camp Discharge Aug. 28, 1864. Discharged from military Aug. 31, 1864, expiration of term.

Corporal Robert Trotter, Co. K – Mustered in on Aug. 21, 1861, in Phila. at age 31. Wounded May 15, 1864, at Spotsylvania Courthouse, Va. Discharged from duty Aug. 20, 1864, expiration of term. Recorded present at Camp Discharge Sept. 23, 1864. Departed camp on Nov. 12, 1864.

Private Robert Thomas, Co. C – Mustered in on Sept. 1, 1861, in Phila. at age 18. Present at Camp Discharge Sept. 22, 1864. Hospitalized there for diarrhea Jan. 3-5, 1865. Discharged from duty Jan. 6, 1865, expiration of term.

Private John Smith, Co. F – Mustered in on Sept. 16, 1861, in Phila. at age 40, a shoemaker. Missing on retreat from Culpepper, Va., Sept. 10, 1864. Recorded present at Camp Discharge Sept. 21, 1864. Hospitalized there for dyspepsia Nov. 15-Dec.3, 1864. Discharged by general order Jan. 17, 1865.

Private John Dimm, Co. G – Mustered in on Sept. 16, 1861, at Lancaster at age 38. Captured Nov. 10, 1862, circumstances not given. Officially discharged Sept. 16, 1864, expiration of term. At Camp Discharge Sept. 23-Dec. 5, 1864, by authority of provost marshal.

Private James McGee, Co. G – Mustered in on Oct. 15, 1861, in Phila. at age 35. Missing in action, captured Sept. 10, 1864, near Petersburg, Va. Paroled Sept. 15, 1864. Present at Camp Discharge Nov. 18, 1864, coming from Camp Parole, Md. Admitted to Camp Discharge Hospital for catarrh on Nov. 20, 1864. Discharged from service Dec. 3, 1864, expiration of term.

Private Charles Whitmyer, Co. C – Mustered in on Sept. 7, 1861, in Washington, D.C., at age 18. Wounded at Chancellorsville, Va., May 2, 1863. Reached Camp Discharge Nov. 22, 1864, reporting from Harrisburg. Admitted to Camp Discharge Hospital to treat gunshot wound of left thigh Nov. 28, 1864. Discharged from service Dec. 13, 1864.

Private Charles E. Stewart, Co. H – Mustered in on Nov. 11, 1861, in Phila. at age 23. Present at Camp Discharge Dec. 5, 1864. Hospitalized there to convalesce from typhoid fever Dec. 9,

1864, and rheumatism Dec. 25, 1864. Discharged from duty Jan. 19, 1865, expiration of term. Did additional service with 29th Pa. Infantry and 2nd Eastern Shore Md. Infantry.

Private Richard M. Watson, Co. I – Mustered in on Dec. 20, 1861, in Phila. at age 23. Entered Camp Discharge Dec. 23, 1864. Hospitalized there for constipation on Dec. 25, 1864. Discharged from duty Jan. 13, 1865, expiration of term.

Private John Baldwin, Cos. F/H – Mustered in on Sept. 19, 1861, in Phila. at age 30. Entered Camp Discharge Dec. 24, 1864. Hospitalized there for contusion from fall Dec. 25, 1864, March 1, 1865. Discharged from duty March 18, 1865. Did additional service with 22nd Veteran Reserve Corps.

Private Hugh Bradley, Co. K – Mustered in on Jan. 4, 1864, at Brandy Station, Va., at age 42, a shoemaker born in Ireland. Wounded in action May 1864 at Tolopotomy, Va. Absent, sick at regimental muster out. Recorded present at Camp Discharge July 22-31, 1865. Went on to join Veteran Volunteer Corps.

Corporal Edward Allen, Co. A – Mustered in on July 26, 1861, in Phila. at age 31, a weaver born in Ireland. Re-enlisted Jan. 4, 1864, at Brandy Station, Va. Wounded July 27, 1864, at Deep Bottom, Va. Promoted to corporal. Absent, in hospital, at muster out. Recorded present at Camp Discharge July 20-31, 1865. Joined Veteran Volunteer Corps.

Private Andrew Hamilton, Co. E – Mustered in May 1861 in Phila. at age 22, a clerk born in Ireland. Captured May 29, 1864. Held at Andersonville and survived. Absent at regimental muster out. Recorded at Camp Discharge June 23-July 31, 1865. Joined Veteran Volunteer Corps.

Private Andrew J. Marshall, Co. K – Mustered in on June 12, 1861, in Phila. at age 21. Transferred from 26th Pa. Infantry. Absent, sick at regimental muster-out. Present at Camp Discharge July 1865.

Private George J. Shane, Co. K – Mustered in on June 1, 1861, at age 21, a laborer. Re-enlisted Feb. 18, 1864, at Brandy Station, Va.; transferred from 26th Pa. Infantry May 29, 1864. Wounded in action Nov. 7, 1864. Absent, sick at regimental muster out. Present at Camp Discharge July 1865. Joined Veteran Volunteer Corps.

Private David S. Hunsburger, Co. A – Mustered in on July 26, 1861, in Phila. at age 19, a wheelwright. Re-enlisted Jan. 1, 1864, at Brandy Station, Va. Promoted to corporal, then sergeant, then reduced to ranks Jan. 1, 1865. Absent, sick at regimental muster out. Present at Camp Discharge July 1865. Joined Veteran Volunteer Corps.

Private William Retherser/Rettihiser, Co. K – Drafted, mustered in on Aug. 20, 1863, in Norristown at age 21. Captured at Cold Harbor, Va., June 1, 1864. Held at Andersonville prison, then exchanged April 1 and freed April 29, 1865. At Camp Discharge June 16, 1865. Discharged by general order June 29, 1865.

Private Thomas Smith, Co. B – Mustered in on Dec. 13, 1861, in Phila. at age 20. Captured at Mine Run, Va., Dec. 2, 1863. Returned to company, date unknown. At Camp Discharge, hospitalized for "Tertian Inter" (probably malaria) June 3, 1865. Discharged from duty by general order June 21, 1865.

Private James Morris, Co H – Mustered in on May 31, 1861, at age 25. Captured and held at Andersonville prison. Exchanged April 1, 1865. Recorded present at Camp Discharge June 15, 1865. Discharged by General Order, June 21, 1865.

Private Amos Barr, Co. C – Mustered in on March 4, 1864, in Lancaster at age 18, a farmer. Wounded at Petersburg, Va., March 25, 1865. Present at Camp Discharge May 22, 1865. Discharged by general order June 1, 1865.

Private William Taylor, Co. B – Mustered in on March 10, 1862, in Washington, D.C., at age 24. Wounded at Petersburg, Va., June 18, 1864, and absent in hospital. Recorded at Camp

Discharge May 3, 1865. Hospitalized there to treat gunshot wound May 4, 1865. Discharged from service May 5, 1865.

Private James H. McElwee, Co. G – Mustered in on Feb. 27, 1865, in Chambersburg at age 25, a draftee. Missing in action April 6, 1865, at Sailor's Creek, Va. Absent, sick, at regimental muster out. Present at Camp Discharge June 29-July 22, 1865.

Private John (Josephus) W. Hull, Co. A – Mustered in on Nov. 3, 1861, in Lancaster at age 27. Wounded at Wilderness, Va., May 5, 1864. Recorded present at Camp Discharge Nov. 2, 1864. Hospitalized there for leg ulcer Nov. 19, 1864. Mustered out, Nov. 23, 1864, expiration of term.

Sergeant Stephen C. Deveney, Co. G – Mustered in on Nov. 11, 1861, in Phila. at age 21. Present at Camp Discharge Dec. 20, 1864. Hospitalized there to convalesce from "T.F." (tertian fever or malaria) Dec. 3, 1864. Discharged Dec. 20, 1864.

Private Peter D. Grass, Co. G – Mustered in on Nov. 25, 1861, in Phila. Hospitalized at Camp Discharge for a gunshot wound to toes Dec. 9, 1864. Discharged same day by order of Maj. Gilbert.

Private William Harbison, Co. K – Mustered in on Aug. 20, 1861, in Phila. at age 20. Wounded at Wilderness May 5, 1864. Recorded present at Camp Discharge Sept. 23, 1864. Discharge received Nov. 11, 1864.

Private David Thorne, Co. G – Mustered in on Nov. 9, 1861, in Phila. at age 19. Wounded in action at Spotsylvania Courthouse, Va., May 12, 1864. Present at Camp Discharge Nov. 11, 1864, arriving from Broad & Cherry Street Hospital, Phila. Was discharged Nov. 9, 1864, expiration of term.

Private Joseph T. Taylor, Co. H – Mustered in on Sept. 4, 1861, in Phila. at age 16. Transferred from 66th Pa. Infantry. Wounded at Gettysburg July 2, 1863. Discharged Aug. 29, 1864. Recorded present at Camp Discharge Sept. 24-Nov. 25, 1864.

Private Benjamin Kirk, Co. D – Mustered in July 1861 in Phila. Wounded at Gettysburg July 2, 1863. Discharged July 26, 1864, expiration of term. Arrived at Camp Discharge with hospital papers Sept. 27, 1864, and departed Dec. 5, 1864.

Corporal Samuel W. Ewing, Co. E – Mustered in on Aug. 24, 1861, in Phila. at age 23. Discharged Aug. 24, 1864, expiration of term. Recorded present at Camp Discharge Sept. 28-Nov. 16, 1864.

Private Samuel Sparks, Co. E – Mustered into service March 13, 1862, in Phila. at age 24. Wounded at Petersburg, Va., Oct. 11, 1864. Entered Camp Discharge March 16, 1865. Discharged March 22, 1865, expiration of term. Did additional service with 109th Pa. Infantry and 141st Pa. Infantry.

Private John Shilling, Co. K – Mustered in on Nov. 15, 1861, in Phila. at age 18. Recorded at Camp Discharge Hospital to treat ecthyma Dec. 4, 1864. Not on muster out roll.

100th Pa. Infantry

The regiment formed in 1861 with men from Washington, Lawrence, Butler, Beaver, and Westmoreland Counties. It was attached to the Army of the Potomac (IX Corps) and the Army of the Tennessee. 'The Roundheads' took part in 22 engagements, including Second Bull Run, Antietam, Fredericksburg, Vicksburg, Wilderness, Spotsylvania Courthouse, Cold Harbor, Petersburg, and the Crater. They lost 409 enlisted men and officers to wounds and illness. Eleven died at Andersonville, one at Florence. The regiment was in Grand Review in D.C., then mustered out July 24, 1865. *Three of its soldiers transited Camp Discharge.*

Private Robert Gordon, Co. A – A substitute recruit mustered in on Jan. 26, 1865. Wounded at Petersburg, Va. March 25, 1865. Recorded at Camp Discharge May 24, 1865, where he was hospitalized to treat a scalp wound May 25-29. Discharged from service by general order June 2, 1865.

Private Edward F. Eberlee, Co. F – A substitute, mustered in on March 10, 1865, at Reading at age 17. Prisoner March 25-30, 1865. Recorded at Camp Discharge May 17, 1865. Hospitalized there for debility from diarrhea May 22, 1865. Discharged from service June 17, 1865.

Private Martin Moon, Co. A – A substitute recruit mustered in on Feb. 1, 1865, at age 19, a laborer. Wounded March 1, 1865. Recorded at Camp Discharge May 18, 1865. Discharged by general order May 24, 1865.

104th Pa. Infantry

The regiment was recruited in 1861 in Bucks, Blair, Dauphin, Schuylkill, Luzerne, and Allegheny Counties. Its men fought at Seven Pines, Savage Station, Fair Oaks, Malvern Hill, Fort Wagner, and Petersburg. By the end, 185 of its enlisted men and officers died from injury or disease. The unit mustered out on Aug. 25, 1865. *Five of its men passed through Camp Discharge.*

Corporal Joseph Biddle, Co. I – Mustered in on Oct. 8, 1861, in Doylestown at age 22. Wounded; transferred to Company D, Sept. 24, 1864. Recorded as present at Camp Discharge Oct. 8-Dec. 5, 1864. Discharged Nov. 12, 1864, expiration of term. Joined Veteran Volunteer Corps.

Private John Dilliard, Co. D – Mustered in on Sept. 23, 1861, in Doylestown at age 21. Transferred to battalion Sept. 24, 1864. At Camp Discharge Nov. 3, 1864, coming from Harrisburg. Admitted to Camp Discharge Hospital with "Int. Fever Tertian" (possibly malaria) Nov. 24, 1864. Muster-out date not recorded.

Private Jacob Hoover, Co. D – Mustered in on Dec. 16, 1861, in Washington, D.C., at age 29. Listed "absent, sick at Reg mustering out." Recorded at Camp Discharge Dec. 14, 1864, and discharged Jan. 19, 1865.

Private Anthony D. Murphy, Co. D – Enrolled Dec. 21, 1861, in Morrisville, Pa., at age 20. Mustered in on Dec. 28, 1864, in Washington, D.C. Recorded at Camp Discharge Dec. 24, 1864. Discharged from service April 24, 1865, expiration of term.

Private Adolphus H. Palmer, Co. D – Mustered in on Oct. 14, 1861, in Doylestown at age 26. Recorded at Camp Discharge Dec. 24, 1864. Discharged April 24, 1865, expiration of term.

105th Pa. Infantry

The regiment was recruited in 1861, primarily in Jefferson County. Known as the Wildcats, it saw combat at Fair Oaks, Seven Days, Bull run, Fredericksburg, Chancellorsville, Gettysburg, Wilderness, Spotsylvania, Cold Harbor, and Petersburg. It lost 384 men to mortal wounds and illness. *Two of its men passed through Camp Discharge.*

Private Hardman Allabrand, Co. A – Mustered in on Sept. 9, 1861, in Pittsburgh at age 18. Wounded at Gettysburg July 2, 1863, and Petersburg, Va., June 18, 1864. Discharged Sept. 9, 1864, expiration of term. Recorded at Camp Discharge Sept. 28-Oct. 4, 1864.

Private Jonathan Keiser, Co. K – Mustered in on Aug. 28, 1863, at age 27. DIscharged Sept. 27, 1864, expiration of term. Recorded at Camp Discharge Sept. 30-Oct. 5, 1864.

106th Pa. Infantry

The regiment was recruited in 1861, mostly from Philadelphia firemen. Also in Montgomery (Co. G), Bradford, and Lycoming Counties. It was part of the famed Philadelphia Brigade that helped to repulse Pickett's Charge. The men fought in nine engagements, including Savage Station, Malvern Hill, Antietam, and Gettysburg. They lost 197 enlisted men and officers to fatal wounds or illnesses. Twelve died at Andersonville, one at Florence. The regiment took part in Grand Review in D.C., then mustered out June 30, 1865. *Thirty-four of its men passed through Camp Discharge, including 18 Andersonville survivors.*

Private Benjamin F. Newell, Co. C – Mustered in to service on Oct. 13, 1861. Transferred to Co. F date unknown. Recorded present at Camp Discharge Oct. 14, 1864, from the hospital in Washington, D.C. Discharged from service Dec. 1, 1864, expiration of term.

Private Robert Glass, Co. H – Mustered in on Oct. 31, 1861. Recorded at Camp Discharge Oct. 30, 1864. Discharged by special order Dec. 3, 1864.

Corporal Joseph A. Pedrick, Co. H – Mustered in to service on Oct. 31, 1861. Recorded present at Camp Discharge on Nov. 7, 1864, reporting from Camp Distribution, Va. Admitted to Camp Discharge Hospital with conjunctivitis on Nov. 14, 1864. Discharged from the military by special order Dec. 5, 1864.

Private James Rowbottom, Co. A – Mustered in on Aug. 17, 1861. Deserted July 1862, but returned, date unspecified. Recorded present at Camp Discharge Dec. 8, 1864. Hospitalized there for diarrhea Dec. 13, 1864. Discharged from service Jan. 26, 1865.

Private James Thompson, Co. H – Mustered in on Oct. 31, 1861. Captured June 22, 1864, paroled June 25. Recorded at Camp Discharge Nov. 11, 1864, arriving from Camp Parole, Md. Discharged Jan. 17, 1865.

Sergeant James J. Foy, Co. H – Mustered in on Oct. 31, 1861. Prisoner June 22, 1864, to Dec. 11, 1864. Recorded present at Camp Discharge March 13, 1865. Discharged by special order March 31, 1865.

Private Denny Keene, Co. B – Mustered in on Aug. 28, 1861. Captured at Petersburg, Va., June 22, 1864. Held at Andersonville prison and survived. Sent to Millen prison, Ga., Nov. 11, 1865. Recorded present at Camp Discharge Jan. 21, 1865. Hospitalized there for catarrh Feb. 4, 1865. Discharged from military by general order Feb. 14, 1865.

Private Daniel Green, Cos. A & K – Mustered in on Aug. 17, 1861. Captured, sent to Andersonville prison, then to Millen prison, Ga., Nov. 11, 1864. Entered Camp Discharge Jan. 28, 1865. Discharged June 12, 1865, expiration of term.

Private Francis Kelly/Kelley, Co. H – Mustered in on Oct. 31, 1861. Captured at Petersburg, Va., June 22, 1864. Held at Andersonville and survived, then sent to Millen prison, Ga., Nov. 11, 1864. Recorded at Camp Discharge Feb. 23, 1865. Discharged by general order June 26, 1865.

Private William Fleming, Co. F – Mustered in on Sept. 17, 1861. Captured and held at Andersonville prison. Exchanged Nov. 14, 1864. Recorded at Camp Discharge Feb. 24, 1865. Discharged by special order March 3, 1865.

Private Burton W. Trout, Cos. D & K – Mustered in on Aug. 27, 1861. Captured at Petersburg June 66, 1864. Held at Andersonville and survived. Freed Feb. 28, 1865. Recorded at camp March 30, 1865. Discharged April 1, 1865.

Private Thomas O'Donnell, Cos. C & F – Mustered in on Sept. 17, 1861, in Phila. at age 34. Captured June 22, 1864. Held at Andersonville prison. Freed April 28, 1865. Recorded at Camp Discharge May 23, 1865. Discharged by general order June 5, 1865. Joined Veteran Volunteer Corps.

Sergeant James B. Marshal, Co. B – Mustered in on Aug. 28, 1861. Captured June 22, 1864, at Petersburg, Va. Held at Andersonville prison. Freed April 9, 1865. Recorded at Camp Discharge May 22, 1865. Discharged by general order June 5, 1865.

Corporal Frederick W. Lucke, Co. F – Mustered in on Aug. 14, 1861. Captured at Petersburg June 22, 1864, and taken to Andersonville prison. Exchanged April 1, 1865. Recorded at Camp Discharge May 17, 1865. Hospitalized there for ecthyma May 28-29, 1865. Discharged from the army by general order June 15, 1865.

Private Samuel N. Black, Co. F – Mustered in on Aug. 14, 1861. Captured June 22, 1864, at Petersburg, Va. Sent to Andersonville, then Millen prison, Ga., Nov. 11, 1864. Freed April 1865. Recorded at Camp Discharge May 18, 1865. Hospitalized there for venereal warts May 27, 1865. Discharged by general order June 17, 1865. Joined Veteran Volunteer Corps.

Private George Hallem, Co. C – Mustered in on Aug. 20, 1861. Wounded and captured at Petersburg June 22, 1864. Held at Andersonville. Exchanged April 1, 1865. Recorded at Camp Discharge May 18, 1865. Hospitalized there for constipation May 21, 1865. Discharged from the army by general order June 16, 1865.

Private Francis X. Schluttenhofer, Cos. C & F – Mustered in on April 13, 1864. Taken prisoner June 22, 1864, at Petersburg, Va. Held at Andersonville. Released April 28, 1865, and exchanged at Jacksonville, Fla. Recorded at Camp Discharge May 20, 1865. Discharged by general order June 22, 1865.

Corporal Charles A. Rubright, Co. F – Mustered in on Aug. 28, 1861. Captured June 22, 1864, at Petersburg, Va. Imprisoned at Andersonville. Released April 28, 1865. Recorded present at Camp Discharge May 23, 1865. Discharged by general order June 5, 1865. Joined Veteran Volunteer Corps.

Private Thomas O'Donnell, Cos. C & F – Mustered in on Sept. 17, 1861, in Phila. at age 34. POW June 22, 1864, to April 28, 1865. Recorded at Camp Discharge May 23, 1865. Discharged by general order June 5, 1865. Joined Veteran Volunteer Corps.

Private Patrick McGreal, Co. B – Mustered in on Aug. 28, 1861. Captured at Petersburg June 22, 1864. Held at Andersonville. Exchanged April 1, 1865. Recorded at Camp Discharge May 26, 1865. Discharged by general order June 1, 1865.

Private James Mitchell, Cos. C & F – Mustered in on Aug. 28, 1861. Captured June 22, 1864. Held at Andersonville and survived. Sent to Millen prison, Ga., Nov. 11, 1864. Released from captivity on April 29, 1865. Discharged by general order May 31, 1865.

Private Patrick Kennedy, Cos. C & F – Mustered in on Aug. 28, 1861. Prisoner June 22, 1864, to April 28, 1865. Held at Andersonville prison. After release, recorded at Camp Discharge June 5, 1865. Discharged by general order June 8, 1865. Joined Veteran Volunteer Corps.

Private William Kephart, Co. F – Bates: Mustered in on Aug. 28, 1861. Recorded at Camp Discharge June 1865. Discharged by general order June 12, 1865.

Private Robert Wilson, Co. H – Mustered in on Oct. 31, 1861. Taken prisoner June 25, 1864. Paroled June 26, 1864. Recorded at Camp Discharge Nov. 17, 1864, from Camp Parole, Md. Admitted to Camp Discharge Hospital with cephalalgia (head pain) Nov. 24, 1864. Discharged from military Dec. 7, 1864, expiration of term.

Private James Warren, Co. F – Mustered in on Oct. 16, 1861. Recorded at Camp Discharge Oct. 4, 1864. Hospitalized there for diarrhea Dec. 5, 1864. Discharged from service by special order Dec. 14, 1864.

Sergeant Jonathan Barnes, Cos. C & F – Mustered in on Sept. 24, 1861. Recorded at Camp Discharge Sept. 26, 1864. Discharged Sept. 27, 1864, expiration of term.

Private Jonathan C. Hallowell, Co. H – Mustered in on Oct. 31, 1861. Captured June 22, 1864. Paroled June 25, 1864. Recorded at Camp Discharge Nov. 11, 1864. Discharged by special order Dec. 6, 1864.

Private Francis E. Stewart, Co. K – Mustered in on Nov. 30, 1861. Entered Camp Discharge Nov. 29, 1864. Discharged Dec. 9, 1864, expiration of term.

Corporal Jefferson Arthur, Cos. I & H – Mustered in on Aug. 26, 1861. Captured at Petersburg, Va., June 22, 1864. Held at Andersonville and survived. Entered Camp Discharge Jan. 25, 1865. Discharged Jan. 28, 1865. Did additional service with 7th US Veteran Reserves, likely on garrison duty at Camp Discharge.

Private James Crowl, Cos. I & H – Mustered in on Aug. 28, 1861. Captured at Petersburg, Va., June 22, 1864. Imprisoned at Andersonville and then Millen, Ga. Entered Camp Discharge Jan. 25, 1865. Discharged from army Jan. 28, 1865.

Sergeant William H. Kitchen, Co. F – Mustered in on Oct. 1, 1861. Recorded at Camp Discharge Feb. 6, 1865. Discharged Feb. 11, 1865, expiration of term.

Sergeant David Jamison, Co. G – Mustered into service in Phila. Aug. 27, 1861. Recorded at Camp Discharge Feb. 25, 1865. Did additional service with Veteran Reserve Corps.

Private Harvey Rue, Cos. I & H – Mustered in on Aug. 26, 1861. Captured June 22. 1864, at Petersburg, Va., and taken to Andersonville. Exchanged Dec. 5, 1864. Entered Camp Discharge March 1, 1865. Discharged March 6, 1865.

Private George Waldron, Co. A – Mustered in on Aug. 17, 1861. Captured May 12, 1865, at Spotsylvania Courthouse, Va. Held at Andersonville and survived. Freed Dec. 14, 1864. Recorded at Camp Discharge March 6, 1865. Discharged by special order March 15, 1865. Did added service with the 20th Pa. Infantry.

107th Pa. Infantry

The regiment was recruited in 1862 in York, Luzerne, Berks, Franklin, Cumberland, Sullivan, Wyoming, Lycoming, Schuylkill, Mifflin, Lancaster, and Bradford Counties. The men were in 20 engagements, including Second Bull Run, Antietam, Fredericksburg, Chancellorsville, Gettysburg, Wilderness, Spotsylvania Courthouse, Cold Harbor, Petersburg, and Five Forks. In the end, 251 of its enlisted men and officers died of injury or sickness. One died at Andersonville. The unit was in Grand Review in D.C., then mustered out July 13, 1865. *Three of its men passed through Camp Discharge.*

Private Adolph Knigher, Co. D – Mustered in on Aug. 19, 1864, in West Chester at age 31, a substitute. Recorded present at Camp Discharge July 15, 1865. Discharged by general order July 26, 1865.

Private Joseph Walters, unassigned – Mustered in on Feb. 27, 1865, for one year. Recorded at Camp Discharge July 15, 1865. Discharged by general order July 26, 1865.

Private Enos Reifsnyder, Co. B – Enrolled Aug. 27, 1862, in Shippensburg at age 21. Mustered in on Sept. 2, 1862, in Harrisburg. Recorded present at Camp Discharge June 29, 1865. Discharged July 11, to date July 1, 1865.

109th Pa. Infantry

The regiment was recruited in 1862 in Philadelphia and Allegheny Counties. The men served in 14 engagements, including Chancellorsville, Gettysburg, Lookout Mountain, Missionary Ridge, and Sherman's March to the Sea. From its ranks, 135 enlisted men and officers died from wounds and illness. Two died at Andersonville. The regiment merged with the 111th Pa. Infantry on March 31, 1865. *Sixteen of its men spent time at Camp Discharge.*

Corporal John Laycock, Co. I – Mustered in on Jan. 29, 1862. Admitted June 4, 1864, to Cumberland Hospital, Tenn., with pneumonia, transferred June 21 to Murfreesboro. Recorded at Camp Discharge Jan. 11, 1865. Discharged from service Feb. 16, 1865.

Corporal Jesse Hellam/Hallman, Co. G – Mustered in on March 3, 1862. Treated at Nashville Hospital No. 1 for dyspepsia and gunshot wound to left arm in 1864, date unspecified. Recorded at Camp Discharge Feb. 4, 1865. Discharged June 6, 1865.

Corporal John E. Antrim, Co. H – Mustered in on March 25, 1862. Recorded at Camp Discharge March 31, 1865. Discharged April 1, 1865.

Corporal Alfred Walter, Co. E – Mustered in on March 14, 1862. Wounded in the right hand at Battle of Resaca, Ga., May 15, 1864. Promoted to corporal June 1, 1864. Recorded present at Camp Discharge April 8, 1865. Discharged April 10, 1865.

Private George G. Stewart, Co. K – Mustered in on March 7, 1862. Recorded at Camp Discharge April 17, 1865. Discharged April 26, 1865. Joined Veteran Volunteer Corps.

Private William H. Amberson, Co. D – Mustered in on March 1, 1862. Treated at Cumberland Hospital, Tenn., for "measels" in 1864. Recorded at Camp Discharge May 2, 1865. Discharged by general order June 1, 1865.

Private Louis Mattocks, Co. D – Mustered in on May 2, 1862. Hospitalized twice in 1864, according to Nashville Hospitals report. Recorded at Camp Discharge May 8, 1865. Discharged there May 25, 1865.

Private Robert Johnston, Co. G – Mustered in on May 28, 1862. Transferred to 11th Pa. Infantry March 31, 1865.

Private Thomas J. Hooven, Co. C – Mustered in on Feb. 19, 1864. Recorded at Camp Discharge July 20-31, 1865. Absent, on detached service, at muster out.

Private Jacob Fuchs, Co. E – Mustered in on Sept. 12, 1862. Recorded at Camp Discharge June 29, 1865. Discharged July 1865.

Private William F. Wyant, Co. B – Mustered in on March 8, 1862. Recorded at Camp Discharge July 31, 1865. Joined Veteran Volunteer Corps.

Private John F. Henry, Co. E – Mustered in on Jan. 17, 1862. Recorded at Camp Discharge Jan. 18, 1865, and hospitalized there for ascites (abdominal swelling). Discharged from service Jan. 19, 1865, expiration of term.

Private Charles Seiger, Co. E – Mustered in on Feb. 19, 1862. Wounded at Wauhatchie, Tenn., Oct. 29, 1863. Entered Camp Discharge Feb. 4, 1865. Discharged Feb. 14, 1865, expiration of term.

Private William Aloways, Co. B – Mustered in on March 7, 1862. Entered Camp Discharge March 7, 1865. Discharged from service March 13, 1865, expiration of term.

Private Robert N. Baylie, Co. E – Mustered in on Feb. 15, 1862. Discharged March 22, 1865. Entered Camp Discharge March 21, 1865. Discharged from service March 22, 1865.

Private John B. Maggie, Co. A – Mustered in on Dec. 3, 1861. Recorded at Camp Discharge March 27, 1865. Hospitalized there for "delirium Tremens" March 28, 1865. Discharged from service by special order March 30, 1865. Did additional service with 19th Pa. Infantry. Dead by the end of 1865.

110th Pa. Infantry

The regiment was formed in 1861 with men from Philadelphia, Blair, Huntingdon, Centre, and Clearfield Counties. The men fought in 25 engagements, including Second Bull Run, Fredericksburg, Chancellorsville, Gettysburg, Wilderness, Spotsylvania Courthouse, Cold Harbor, and

Petersburg. By war's end, 196 enlisted men and officers died from wounds or sickness. Seven died at Andersonville, one at Florence. The regiment took part in Grand Review in D.C., then mustered out Jun 28, 1865. *Eight of its men transited Camp Discharge.*

Private John R. Cooper, Co. D – Mustered in on March 26, 1862, in Phila. at age 35, a cooper. Transferred to Veteran Reserve Corps Nov. 30, 1864. Entered Camp Discharge March 24, 1865. Discharged April 21, 1865.

Sergeant Hiram H. Foster, Co. F – Mustered in August 1861 in Phila. at age 26, a farmer from Bradford County. Re-enlisted on Nov. 19, 1863, at Portsmouth, Va. Prisoner of war on June 29, 1864, to April 29, 1865. Recorded at Camp Discharge May 23, 1865. Discharged by general order June 5, 1865. Joined Veteran Volunteer Corps.

Private John M. Dunsmore, Co. E – Mustered in on March 2, 1862, in Paw Paw, Va., at age 18, a salesman. Recorded at Camp Discharge May 1, 1865. Discharged by general order May 3, 1865.

Private Patrick McLaughlan Jr., Co. E – Enrolled at age 37, a baker, 5-foot-5. Deserted date unknown; not on muster-out roll. Recorded at Camp Discharge Oct. 8, 1864. Discharged Nov. 15, 1864.

Private John Daly, Co. E – Mustered in on Sept. 20, 1861, in Phila. at age 31, a mill hand. Recorded at Camp Discharge Nov. 22, 1864, reporting from Douglas Hospital, Washington, D.C. Admitted to Camp Discharge Hospital for rheumatism Nov. 23, 1864. Discharged Dec. 1, 1864, expiration of term.

Private Thomas Gallegan, Co. D – Mustered into service Feb. 10, 1862, in Phila. at age 30, a laborer. Wounded at Chancellorsville, Va., May 3, 1863. Transferred from 115th Pa. Infantry June 1864. Entered Camp Discharge Jan. 13, 1865. Discharged Jan. 16, 1865.

Private James Curren, Co. F – Mustered into service Jan. 18, 1862, at age 24, a miner. Wounded at Spotsylvania Courthouse, Va., May 12, 1864. Transferred from 115th Pa. Infantry June 22, 1864. Entered Camp Discharge Jan. 19, 1865. Discharged Jan 20, 1865.

Private Henry J. Murray, Co. F – Mustered into service Dec. 31, 1861, in Phila. at age 31. Transferred from 115th Pa. Infantry June 22, 1864. Entered Camp Discharge Jan. 20, 1865. Discharged Jan. 21, 1865, expiration of term.

114th Pa. Infantry (Corps D'Afrique Zouaves)

The regiment was recruited in 1862 in Philadelphia. Known as "Collis' Zouaves," it was in seven engagements: Fredericksburg, Chancellorsville, Gettysburg, Wilderness, Spotsylvania Courthouse, Cold Harbor, and Petersburg. During the war, 111 enlisted men and officers died from wounds or sickness. The regiment mustered out May 29, 1865. *One of its men passed through at Camp Discharge.*

Private H.A. Manderfield, Co. A – Mustered into service on Aug. 17, 1861, in Phila. at age 22, a printer. Deserted in August 1862. Transferred to 190th Pa. Infantry, date unknown. Entered Camp Discharge March 14, 1865. Hospitalized there for sore mouth March 17-19, 1865. Awaiting trial for desertion when discharged from service April 5, 1865.

115th Pa. Infantry

The regiment was recruited in January 1862 in Philadelphia and Harrisburg. The men saw action at Fredericksburg, Bristoe Station, Chancellorsville, Gettysburg, Wilderness, Spotsylvania, Cold Harbor, and Petersburg. The regiment lost 80 men to fatal wounds and illness. It consolidated with 110th Pa. Infantry in June 1864.

Private Michael Sullivan Sr., Co. B – Mustered in on Nov. 11, 1861, in Phila. at age 40, a weaver. Admitted to Camp Discharge Hospital for diarrhea Dec. 31, 1864. Discharged from service Jan. 4, 1865, expiration of term.

Sergeant John Peters, Co. I – Mustered in on April 9, 1862, in Phila. at age 24, a courier. Commissioned 2d lieutenant Jan. 26, 1863, but not mustered. Wounded at Chancellorsville May 3, 1863. Admitted to Camp Discharge Hospital to treat gunshot wound of left thigh April 12, 1865.

116th Pa. Infantry

The regiment formed in 1862, mostly with men from Philadelphia, Montgomery (Co. G), Chester, Schuylkill, and Fayette Counties. It was part of the famed Irish Brigade. The men saw action in eight engagements, including Fredericksburg, Chancellorsville, Gettysburg, Spotsylvania Courthouse, Cold Harbor, and Petersburg. Injury and illness killed 145 of its enlisted men and officers. Fifteen died at Andersonville. The regiment was in Grand Review in D.C., then mustered out June 3 & July 14, 1865. *Two of its men spent time at Camp Discharge; both were Andersonville survivors.*

Private William A. Young, Co. C – Mustered in on Aug. 19, 1862. Captured May 5, 1864, at Battle of Wilderness. Held at Andersonville prison. Freed April 21, 1865. Recorded at Camp Discharge May 18, 1865. Discharged by general order Aug 11, 1865.

Corporal J. Carrigan, Co. I – Mustered in on March 26, 1864, in Pittsburgh at age 19, a gas fitter, born in Canada. Captured June 22, 1864, at Petersburg, Va. Held at Andersonville and survived. Freed April 1865. Recorded at Camp Discharge May 21, 1865. Absent, sick, at regimental muster out. Discharged by general order June 3, 1865.

118th Pa. Infantry

The regiment recruited in 1862 in Philadelphia and was known as the Corn Exchange Regiment, referring to its sponsor. The men fought in seven engagements, including Fredericksburg, Chancellorsville, Gettysburg, Wilderness, and Spotsylvania Courthouse. In the end, 141 enlisted men and officers died from injury or sickness. Thirty-six died at Andersonville. The regiment was in Grand Review in D.C., then mustered out June 1, 1865. *Twelve of its men passed through Camp Discharge, including five Andersonville survivors.*

Corporal Frederick Bubeck, Co. F – Mustered in on Aug. 14, 1862. Captured June 2, 1864, at Cold Harbor, Va. Held at Andersonville prison. Released April 27, 1865. Recorded as present at Camp Discharge May 24, 1865. Discharged by general order June 8, 1865.

Private Frederick Raw, Co. C – Mustered in on Aug. 9, 1862. Captured June 2, 1864, at Cold Harbor, Va. Held at Andersonville and survived. Released April 27, 1865. Recorded at Camp Discharge May 24, 1865. Discharged by general order June 5, 1865.

Private Isaac J. Shuler, Co. C – Mustered in on Aug. 7, 1862. Captured June 2, 1864, at Cold Harbor, Va. Held at Andersonville prison. Released April 29, 1865. Recorded at Camp Discharge May 29, 1865. Discharged by general order June 8, 1865.

Private Tobias Eshleman, Co. G – Mustered in on Aug. 11, 1862. Wounded and captured at Battle of Wilderness May 8, 1864. Held at Andersonville prison. Released April 28, 1865. Recorded at Camp Discharge May 30, 1865. Discharged by general order May 15, 1865.

Private John C. Crowley, Co. C – Mustered in on Sept. 24, 1863, as a substitute. Captured June 2, 1864, at Cold Harbor. Held at Andersonville and survived. Released April 29, 1865. Recorded at Camp Discharge May 31, 1865. Discharged by general order June 5, 1865.

Corporal George W. Brown, Co. F – Mustered in on Aug. 6, 1862. Captured at Weldon Railroad, Va., Aug. 21, 1864. Recorded as present at Camp Discharge July 26, 1865. Discharged July 31, 1865.

Private Christian J. Cole, Co. K – Mustered in on Aug. 15, 1862. Wounded at Shepherdstown, W. Va., Sept. 20, at Fredericksburg, Va., Dec. 13, 1862, and at Wilderness, May 8, 1864. Recorded at Camp Discharge May 24, 1865. Discharged by general order June 22, 1865.

Sergeant David T. Hassinger, Co. D – Mustered in on Aug. 12, 1862. Recorded at Camp Discharge June 7, 1865. Discharged by general order June 22, 1865.

Musician Simon C. Shannon, Co. I – Mustered in on Aug. 15, 1862. Admitted to Camp Discharge Hospital for phthisis (tuberculosis) May 15, 1865. Discharged from service by general order May 18, 1865.

Private Andrew Browning, Co. I – Mustered in on July 22, 1863, as a substitute. Deserted April 23, 1864. Recorded at Camp Discharge June 1, 1865, disposition unclear.

Private Jacob L. Parker, Co. I – Mustered in on July 15, 1863, as a substitute. Captured at Beverly Ford, Va., April 23, 1864. Discharged by general order July 26, 1865.

Corporal Arthur Paul, Co. K – Mustered in on Aug. 11, 1862. Not accounted for on regimental rolls. Recorded at Camp Discharge June 8, 1865.

119th Pa. Infantry

They recruited in 1862 in Philadelphia. Known as "the Gray Reserves," it fought in 17 engagements, including Fredericksburg, Chancellorsville, Gettysburg, Wilderness, Spotsylvania Courthouse, Cold Harbor, and Petersburg. Wounds and illnesses killed 213 enlisted men and officers. The regiment mustered out on June 19, 1865. *Four of its men transited Camp Discharge.*

Private Thomas Blakey, Co. B – Mustered in on June 9, 1863. Recorded at Camp Discharge May 29, 1865. Hospitalized there the next day for "paraplegia for sunstroke" (heat-related ailment). Discharged from service by general order June 2, 1865.

Private A. D. Cowperthwait, Co. F – Mustered in on Aug. 8, 1862. Deserted Nov. 14, 1862. Returned March 18, 1863. Wounded April 1, 1865. Discharged by general order May 19, 1865.

Private Bernard Duffey, Co. F – Mustered in on Aug. 29, 1863, a draftee. Captured, returned, dates unspecified. Deserted on May 7, 1864. Returned June 16, 1865, and recorded present at Camp Discharge. Mustered out with company June 19, 1865.

Sergeant Samuel M. Marsh, Co. C – Mustered in on Aug. 18, 1862. Transferred to Veteran Reserve Corps, 2nd Battalion, Nov. 15, 1863. Admitted to Camp Discharge Hospital for diarrhea Nov. 23-24, 1864. Discharge date not recorded.

121st Pa. Infantry

The regiment was recruited in 1862 in Philadelphia and Venango Counties. The men fought at Fredericksburg, Chancellorsville, Gettysburg, and Petersburg. From its ranks, 175 enlisted men and officers died of injuries or ailments. Two men died in Florence. The unit took part in Grand Review in D.C., then mustered out June 2, 1865. *One of its men went through Camp Discharge.*

Private Henry B. Harp, Co. C – Mustered in on Aug. 28, 1862. Deserted Oct. 30, 1862. Returned. Recorded at Camp Discharge June 20, 1865. Discharged by special order June 29, 1865.

128th Pa. Infantry

The regiment was recruited in 1862 in Berks, Bucks, and Lehigh Counties. The men took part in the Battles of Antietam and Chancellorsville. Fifty-nine enlisted men and officers succumbed to wounds or disease. At Chancellorsville, 234 of its men were captured. The regiment mustered out May 19, 1863. *One of its men passed through Camp Discharge.*

Private James Albright, Co. D – Mustered in on Aug. 13, 1862, in Harrisburg at age 21. Deserted Sept. 17, 1862. Surrendered April 22, 1865; no charges preferred. Recorded at Camp Discharge June 21, 1865. Discharged from service July 7, 1865.

138th Pa. Infantry

The regiment was recruited in 1862 in Montgomery (Cos. A, C, & I), Bucks, Adams, and Bedford Counties. The men took part in 13 engagements, including Wilderness, Spotsylvania Courthouse, Cold Harbor, and Petersburg. Injury and illness claimed 167 enlisted men and officers. The regiment mustered out on June 23, 1865. *One of its men passed through Camp Discharge.*

Private John Hennig, Co. B – Mustered in on Aug. 16, 1862, in Harrisburg at age 20, a printer. Recorded as present at Camp Discharge May 23, 1865. Discharged by general order May 25, 1865.

145th Pa. Infantry

The regiment was recruited in 1862 in Erie, Warren, and Mercer Counties. The men took part in 16 engagements, including Antietam, Fredericksburg, Chancellorsville, Gettysburg, Wilderness, Spotsylvania Courthouse, Cold Harbor, Petersburg, and Appomattox. In total, 422 enlisted men and officers died from wounds or illnesses. Forty-nine died at Andersonville, six at Florence. The unit mustered out May 31, 1865. *One of its men, an Andersonville survivor, transited Camp Discharge.*

Private James Boyle, Co. G – Mustered in on Sept. 19, 1863, a draftee. Missing in action at Spotsylvania Courthouse May 10, 1864. Held at Andersonville prison and survived. Exchanged April 1865. Recorded present at Camp Discharge May 23, 1865. Discharged by general order June 17, 1865.

147th Pa. Infantry

The regiment was organized in the field in 1862 with Philadelphia, Berks, Lehigh, Carbon, Allegheny, Huntingdon, Luzerne, Carbon, and Snyder County men. They took part in 16 engagements, including Chancellorsville, Gettysburg, Lookout Mountain, Missionary Ridge, Kennesaw Mountain, and Sherman's March to the Sea. From its ranks, 142 enlisted men and officers died from injury and sickness. One died at Andersonville. The regiment mustered out June 6 and July 15, 1865. *Two of its men passed through Camp Discharge.*

Private Samuel J. Hart, Co. E – Mustered in on Sept. 17, 1861, in Phila. at age 34, a carpenter. Recorded as present at Camp Discharge Sept. 20, 1864. Hospitalized at camp for catarrh Dec. 16, 1864. Discharged from service Dec. 22, 1864, expiration of term.

Corporal James Robb, Co. I – Mustered in on March 31, 1864, in Phila. at age 24. Absent at regiment's July 15, 1865, muster out; sick at Satterlee Hospital. Recorded at Camp Discharge July 20, 1865. Hospitalized there for scrofula July 21, 1865. Discharged from service July 31, 1865.

183rd Pa. Infantry

The regiment recruited 1863-64 in Philadelphia. Nicknamed the Fourth Union League Regiment, it took part in 16 engagements, including Wilderness, Spotsylvania Courthouse, Cold Harbor, Petersburg, and Appomattox. Its toll was 187 enlisted men and officers dead from wounds and disease during service. Nineteen died at Andersonville. The regiment was in Grand Review in D.C., then mustered out July 13, 1865. *Fifteen of its men passed through Camp Discharge, two of them Andersonville survivors.*

Private James J. Deveney, Co. A – Mustered in on Oct. 15, 1861. Prisoner Aug. 16, 1864, to March 9, 1865. Recorded present at Camp Discharge April 4, 1865. Discharged by general order April 15, 1865.

Private Robert Moore, Co. A – Mustered in on Aug. 10, 1861. Transferred from 72nd Pa. Infantry. Recorded at Camp Discharge April 26, 1865. Discharged May 16, 1865. Mustered out with company July 13, 1865.

Private Robert Smiley, Co. A – Mustered in on Oct. 10, 1861. Recorded at Camp Discharge Oct. 17, 1864. Hospitalized at camp for sunstroke (heat-related ailment) Nov. 15, 1864. Discharged by general order Dec. 29, 1864, expiration of term. Also served with the 72nd Pa.

Private Charles Kappis, Co. G – Mustered in on Sept. 17, 1861. Recorded at Camp Discharge Oct. 30, 1864. Discharged Nov. 5, 1864, expiration of term.

Private Benjamin Bechtel, Co. F – Mustered in on Oct. 31, 1861. Recorded at Camp Discharge Oct. 31, 1864. Discharged from service March 28, 1865.

Private Richard D. Cooper, Co. A – Mustered in on Jan. 13, 1864. Absent, sick, on July 13, 1865, muster out. Recorded at Camp Discharge July 20, 1865. Discharged July 31, 1865. Joined Veteran Volunteer Corps.

Private Samuel S. Walters, Co. F – Mustered in on Sept. 16, 1861. Recorded at Camp Discharge July 20, 1865. Discharged by general order Aug. 19, 1865. Joined Veteran Volunteer Corps.

Private Frank Alexander, Co. K – Mustered in on Jan. 5, 1864. Recorded at Camp Discharge July 19, 1865. Discharged Aug. 31, to date, July 13, 1865.

Private Hugh McKay, Co. B – Mustered in on Feb. 9, 1864. Prisoner of war Aug. 16, 1864, to March 17, 1865. Recorded at Camp Discharge July 1865. Discharged by general order July 12, 1865.

Private Robert O'Neil, Co. C – Mustered in on Aug. 10, 1861. Captured at Petersburg, Va., June 22, 1864. Discharged by general order June 26, 1865. Recorded at Camp Discharge July 1865. Joined Veteran Volunteer Corps.

Private William Nugent, Co. E – Mustered in on Feb. 3, 1864. Captured May 12, 1864, at Spotsylvania Courthouse. Held at Andersonville prison and survived. Released April 17, 1865. Recorded at Camp Discharge June 21, 1865. Discharged by general order June 27, 1865.

Corporal George W. Smith, Co. H – Mustered in on Jan. 21, 1864. Captured June 3, 1864, at Cold Harbor, Va. Held at Andersonville prison. Exchanged April 1, 1865. Recorded at Camp Discharge May 26, 1865. Discharged by general order June 8, 1865.

Private John Gorman, Co. G – Mustered in on Jan. 21, 1864. Prisoner Aug. 28, 1864, to April 5, 1865. Recorded present at Camp Discharge June 1, 1865. Discharged by general order June 21, 1865.

Private William F. Weed, Co. F – Mustered in on Oct. 3, 1861. Recorded at Camp Discharge Oct. 31, 1864. Hospitalized at camp for diarrhea Dec. 17, 1864. Discharged by special order Dec. 28, 1864.

Corporal David S. Bechtel, Co. D – Mustered in on March 13, 1862. Wounded at Deep Bottom, Va., Aug. 16, 1864; prisoner Aug. 16-Dec. 20, 1864. Entered Camp Discharge March 17, 1865. Discharged March 18, 1865, expiration of term. Did additional service with 72nd Pa. Infantry.

188th Pa. Infantry

The regiment was organized in the field in 1864 with men from Philadelphia and eight other counties. The men took part in seven operations, including Cold Harbor, Petersburg, Richmond, New Market Heights, and Fair Oaks. In total, 192 enlisted men and officers succumbed to wounds and sickness during service. *One died at Andersonville. Four of its men transited Camp Discharge.*

Private Francis Baxter, Co. F – Mustered in on May 7, 1863, in Phila. at age 35, a Scottish-born laborer. Recorded present at Camp Discharge May 10, 1865. Discharged by general order May 13, 1865.

Private Joseph D. Hampton, Co. E – Mustered in on Feb. 29, 1864, in Frankford at age 21, a clerk. Had been an unassigned recruit in 3rd Pa. Artillery. Discharged by general order May 15, 1865.

Private John Bodine, Co. B – Mustered in on Sept. 2, 1864, in Williamsport at age 29. Recorded present at Camp Discharge May 19, 1865. Discharged by general order May 27, 1865.

Private James H. Jeffers, Co. F – Mustered in on Feb. 11, 1862, in Phila. at age 29, a blacksmith. Hospitalized at Camp Discharge for variola (smallpox). Died on Feb. 15, 1865, at US Hospital in Phila.

190th Pa. Infantry

The regiment was organized in the field in 1864 with men from Philadelphia, across the state, and in Prince William County, Va. The men took part in 11 actions, including Cold Harbor, Petersburg, Appomattox, and Five Forks. During service, 214 men died from wounds and illnesses. Three men died at Florence Prison. The regiment took part in Grand Review in D.C. *One of its men passed through Camp Discharge.*

Corporal William C. Albright, Co. B – Mustered in September 1861 at age 29. Captured at Weldon Railroad Aug. 19, 1864. Paroled September 1864. Recorded at Camp Discharge Oct. 20, 1864, coming from Camp Parole, Md. Discharged Dec. 23, 1864. Additional service with 17th Pa., 100th Pa., and 190th Pa.

191st Pa. Infantry (2nd Veteran Volunteers)

The regiment was organized in the field in 1864 with men from eight Pa. counties, including Philadelphia and Prince William County, Va. The men took part in 11 actions, including Cold Harbor, Petersburg, Appomattox, and Five Forks. By the war's end, 201 enlisted men and officers died of wounds and sickness. Two died at Andersonville. The regiment took part in Grand Review in D.C. *Nine of its men passed through Camp Discharge.*

Corporal Samuel S. Wilson, Co. I – Recorded at Camp Discharge Nov. 25, 1864, reporting from Camp Parole, Md. Discharged Dec. 12, 1864; expiration of term.

Private John Everett, Co. A – Mustered in to service on July 11, 1862, in Phila. at age 44. Captured Aug. 19, 1864, at Weldon Railroad Va. Logged at Camp Discharge June 28, 1865. Discharged by general order June 30, 1865.

Sergeant Thomas Fitzsimmons, Co. B – Prisoner of war from Aug. 19, 1864, to March 22, 1865. Logged at Camp Discharge April 24, 1865. Discharged April 27, 1865.

Private Abraham Maurer, Co. A – Mustered in on Aug. 27, 1861. Prisoner of war Aug. 19, 1864, to March 2, 1865. Recorded at Camp Discharge April 20, 1865. Discharged May 2, 1865, expiration of term.

Private William Wallace, Co. C – Absent, sick at regimental muster out. Logged at Camp Discharge on April 20, 1865. Discharged April 22, 1865.

Private Joseph C. Curtman, Co. A – Mustered in on April 4, 1862. Recorded present at Camp Discharge April 7, 1865. Hospitalized there for acute diarrhea on April 9, 1865. Discharged from service April 10, 1865, expiration of term.

Private William Hess/Hesse, Co. A – Mustered in on April 7, 1864. Present at Camp Discharge April 8, 1865. Discharged April 12, 1865, expiration of term.

Corporal David Cassidy, Co. A – Mustered in on Aug. 27, 1861. Prisoner of war Aug. 19, 1864, to Feb. 28, 1865. Recorded at Camp Discharge May 3, 1865. Discharged from service May 15, 1865, expiration of term.

Corporal Joseph G. Kline, Co. A – Mustered in on Feb. 13, 1862. Prisoner of war from Aug. 19, 1864, to March 1, 1865. Recorded at Camp Discharge May 21, 1865. Discharged May 27, 1865, expiration of term.

196th Pa. Infantry

The regiment was recruited in July 1864 under the auspices of the Union League Association of Philadelphia to serve for one hundred days. They were known as the Fifth Union League Regiment; it guarded Confederate prisoners in Chicago, then served provost duty at Fort Delaware. Mustered out of service at Philadelphia Nov. 17, 1864.

Private James Kenworthy/Kinsworthy, Co. E – Mustered in on July 20, 1864. Mustered out with the company Nov. 17, 1864. Entered Camp Discharge Dec. 12, 1864. Admitted to Camp Discharge Hospital for sore throat Dec. 13, 1864. Discharged Dec. 14, 1865.

197th Pa. Infantry

The regiment was recruited in Philadelphia, Delaware, and Lancaster Counties in 1864 as a 100-day regiment. Known as the 3rd Coal Exchange Regiment, it spent time guarding Confederate prisoners at Rock Island. Six men died of disease during service. The bulk of the regiment was discharged Nov. 11 or 12, 1864. *Forty-four of its men were at Camp Discharge.*

Colonel John R. Haslett – Mustered in on July 22, 1864. Mustered out with regiment Nov. 11, 1864.

Lieutenant Colonel Charles D. Kenworthy – Mustered in on July 22, 1864. Mustered out with regiment Nov.11, 1864.

Major John Woodcock – Mustered in on July 14, 1864. Promoted from captain, Co. I, July 22, 1864. Mustered out with regiment Nov. 11, 1864.

Major Thomas Dinan – Mustered in on July 22, 1864. Mustered out with regiment Nov.11, 1864.

Quartermaster Spencer M. Janney – Mustered in on July 22, 1864. Mustered out with regiment Nov. 11, 1864.

Surgeon David P. Boyer – Mustered in on July 22, 1864. Mustered out with regiment Nov. 11, 1864.

Assistant Surgeon Joseph H. Gallagher – Mustered in on July 22, 1864. Mustered out with regiment Nov. 11, 1864.

Assistant Surgeon James Shaw – Mustered in on July 29, 1864. Mustered out with regiment Nov. 11, 1864.

1st Lieutenant James C. Hinkson, Co. A – Mustered in on July 15, 1864. Mustered out with company Nov. 11, 1864.

2nd Lieutenant Thomas H. Berry, Co. A – Mustered in on July 15, 1864. Mustered out with company Nov. 11, 1864.

Captain Enoch C. Gilbert, Co. B – Mustered in on July 16, 1864. Mustered out with company Nov. 11, 1864.

1st Lieutenant Joseph J. Babcock, Co. B – Mustered in on July 16, 1864. Mustered out with company Nov. 11, 1864.

2nd Lieutenant Edwin Montgomery, Co. B – Mustered in on July 16, 1864. Mustered out with company Nov. 11, 1864.

Captain John K. Landis, Co. C – Mustered in on July 15, 1864. Mustered out with company Nov. 11, 1864.

1st Lieutenant Henry S. Reinhold, Co. C – Mustered in on July 15, 1864. Mustered out with company Nov. 11, 1864.

2nd Lieutenant Benjamin O. Conn, Co. C – Mustered in on July 15, 1864. Mustered out with company Nov. 11, 1864.

Captain George W. Williams, Co. D – Mustered in on July 25, 1864. Mustered out with company Nov. 11, 1864.

1st Lieutenant Charles E. Clark, Co. D – Mustered in on July 25, 1864. Mustered out with company Nov. 11, 1864.

2nd Lieutenant John B. Fryer, Co. D – Mustered in on July 25, 1864. Mustered out with company Nov. 11, 1864.

Captain Bernard T. Janney, Co. E – Mustered in on July 22, 1864. Mustered out with company Nov. 11, 1864.

1st Lieutenant Joseph W. Patton, Co. E – Mustered in on July 22, 1864. Mustered out with company Nov. 11, 1864.

2nd Lieutenant David T. St. John, Co. E – Mustered in on July 22, 1864. Mustered out with company Nov. 11, 1864.

Captain Harry H. Shantz, Co. F – Mustered in on July 18, 1864. Mustered out with company Nov. 11, 1864.

1st Lieutenant Eugene M. Washburne, Co. F – Mustered in on July 18, 1864. Mustered out with company Nov. 11, 1864.

2nd Lieutenant Frederick W. Carpenter, Co. F – Mustered in on July 18, 1864. Mustered out with company Nov. 11, 1864.

Captain John C. Snyder, Co. G – Mustered in on July 22, 1864. Mustered out with company Nov. 11, 1864.

1st Lieutenant Charles S. Jones, Co. G – Mustered in on July 22, 1864. Mustered out with company Nov. 11, 1864.

2nd Lieutenant Wilmer Atkinson, Co. G – Mustered in on July 22, 1864. Mustered out with company Nov. 11, 1864.

Captain William Wrigley, Co. H – Mustered in on July 22, 1864. Mustered out with company Nov. 11, 1864.

1st Lieutenant John M. Hassan, Co. H – Mustered in on July 22, 1864. Mustered out with company Nov. 11, 1864.

2nd Lieutenant Howard Deacon, Co. H – Mustered in on July 23, 1864. Mustered out with company Nov. 11, 1864.

Captain Ralph Buckley, Co. I – Mustered in on July 14, 1864. Mustered out with company Nov. 11, 1864.

1st Lieutenant Roswell T. Williams, Co. I – Mustered in on July 14, 1864. Mustered out with company Nov. 11, 1864.

2nd Lieutenant James Carrick, Co. I – Mustered in on July 14, 1864. Mustered out with company Nov. 11, 1864.

Captain William Babe, Co. K – Mustered in on July 23, 1864. Mustered out with company Nov. 11, 1864.

1st Lieutenant James L. Molineaux, Co. K – Mustered in on July 19, 1864. Mustered out with company Nov. 11, 1864. Died soon after leaving Camp Discharge in December 1864. Presumably sick at camp.

2nd Lieutenant Martin L. Littlefield, Co. K – Mustered in on July 19, 1864. Mustered out with company Nov. 11, 1864.

Corporal Stewart Smith, Co. D – Mustered in on July 23, 1864. Deserted in Phila. July 28, 1864. Entered Camp Discharge Oct. 30, 1864. Charge of desertion removed and "absence without proper authority" substituted. Mustered out with company Nov. 11, 1864.

Private William Jordan, Co. D – Mustered in on July 23, 1864. Deserted in Phila. July 28, 1864. Entered Camp Discharge Oct. 30, 1864. Charge of desertion removed and "absence without proper authority" substituted. Mustered out with company Nov. 11, 1864.

Private James Albany, Co. D – Mustered in on July 23, 1864. Deserted in Phila. July 28, 1864. Entered Camp Discharge Oct. 30, 1864. Charge of desertion removed. Discharged Nov. 2, 1864.

Private Charles Shaw, Co. D – Mustered in on July 23, 1864. Deserted in Phila. July 28, 1864. Entered Camp Discharge Oct. 30, 1864. Mustered out with company Nov. 11, 1864.

Private Henry Walker, Co. G – Mustered in on July 18, 1864. Deserted same day. Returned, July 28, 1864. Entered Camp Discharge Nov. 18, 1864. Charge of desertion withdrawn Dec. 8, 1864. Discharged Dec. 21, 1864.

Private Robert Wharton, Co. D – Mustered in on July 23, 1864. Deserted at Phila. July 28, 1864. Entered Camp Discharge Nov. 4, 1864. Mustered out with company Nov. 11, 1864.

Private Roswell Corbett, Co. E – Mustered in on Sept. 5, 1864. Recorded at Camp Discharge on Nov. 24, 1864, and admitted same day to the camp hospital for "Int. Fever Quotid." and for vaccinia (cowpox) Dec. 27-29, 1864. Discharged by general order, June 6, 1865.

198th Pa. Infantry

The regiment recruited in Montgomery, Philadelphia, Berks, Cambria, Monroe, and Luzerne Counties. The men were in 11 actions, including Petersburg, Appomattox, and Five Forks. By the end, 117 enlisted men and officers succumbed to wounds and illness during service. The regiment took part in Grand Review in D.C. and mustered out June 3, 1865, in northern Virginia. *Ten of its men passed through Camp Discharge.*

Private Daniel N. Kimble, Co. M – Mustered in on Feb. 15, 1864. Wounded at Lewis Farm, Va., March 29, 1865. Logged at Camp Discharge May 23, 1865. Discharged by general order June 1, 1865.

Private Jacob B. Schmehl, Co. D – Mustered in on Sept. 6, 1864. Wounded at Lewis Farm, Va., March 29, 1865. Recorded at Camp Discharge May 25, 1865. Discharged by general order June 2, 1865.

Corporal Henry Martin, Co. L – Mustered in on Sept. 17, 1864. Wounded at Lewis Farm, Va., March 29, 1865. Recorded at Camp Discharge May 22, 1865, and hospitalized there for a gunshot wound. Discharged from service June 1, 1865.

Private William Scragg, Co. D – Mustered in on Sept. 13, 1864. Wounded at Lewis' Farm, Va., March 29, 1865. Recorded at Camp Discharge May 31, 1865. Discharged by general order June 8, 1865.

Private David S. Griffith, Co. F – Mustered in on Sept. 2, 1864. Logged at Camp Discharge May 31, 1865.

Private William Martin, Co. N – Mustered in on Oct. 5, 1864. Wounded at Lewis' Farm, Va., March 29, 1865. Recorded at Camp Discharge May 26, 1865. Discharged by general order June 8, 1865.

Private John Fies, Co. D – Mustered in on Sept. 6, 1864. Wounded at White Oak Road, Va., March 31, 1865. Discharged by general order. June 22, 1865.

Private William Cavanaugh, Co. L – Mustered in on Sept. 14, 1864. Wounded at White Oak Road, Va., March 31, 1865. Logged in at Camp Discharge June 3, 1865. Discharged June 22, 1865.

Private David Huston, Co. B – Mustered in on Sept. 8, 1864. Recorded at Camp Discharge July 11, 1865. Discharged by general order July 17, 1865.

Private Frederick Kraft, Co. K – Mustered in on Sept. 10, 1864. Not accounted for on regimental rolls. Recorded at Camp Discharge June 23, 1865, departing June 27, 1865.

199th Pa. Infantry

The regiment was raised in 1864 with men from Philadelphia, Montgomery, Lancaster, Dauphin, Crawford, Allegheny, Lycoming, and Erie Counties. Also known as the Commercial Regiment, it fought at Petersburg and Appomattox. Eighty-four enlisted men and officers succumbed to wounds and disease during service. The unit mustered out in Richmond in June 1865. *Four of its men passed through Camp Discharge.*

Private Samuel Ruff, (unassigned) – Mustered in on Sept. 27, 1864, in Harrisburg at age 25. Transferred from 99th Pa. Infantry. Captured at Boydton Plank Road, Va., Oct. 27, 1864. Recorded at Camp Discharge 1865. Discharge by general order July 18, 1865.

Corporal John A. Hopkins, Co. H – Mustered in on Sept. 26, 1864, in Harrisburg at age 37, an engineer. Recorded at Camp Discharge June 20, 1865. Mustered out with company June 28, 1865.

Private Israel S. Meredith, Co. H – Mustered in on Sept. 29, 1864, in Harrisburg at age 29, a gas fitter. Recorded at Camp Discharge June 20, 1865. Mustered out with company June 28, 1865.

Private Edward Hillier, Co. C – Mustered in on Sept. 26, 1864, in Harrisburg at age 30, a blacksmith born in England. Absent, sick in hospital since June 3, 1865. Recorded at Camp Discharge June 20, 1865. Discharged by general order July 10, 1865.

203rd Pa. Infantry

The regiment was organized in 1864 with men from Philadelphia, Delaware, Chester, Lancaster, Lycoming, Tioga, and Luzerne Counties. The men saw action at Richmond, Fair Oaks, Fort Fisher, and Wilmington, N.C. By the end, 146 enlisted men and officers to fatal injury or ailments. The regiment mustered out on June 22, 1865. *Fourteen of its men spent time at Camp Discharge.*

Private David Abrams, Co. E – Mustered in on Sept. 7, 1864. Wounded at Fort Fisher, N.C., Jan. 15, 1865. Absent at muster out. Discharged at Camp Discharge July 1865.

Private Robert Carr, Co. I – Mustered in on Sept. 2, 1864. Absent, on detached service, at muster out. Recorded at Camp Discharge June 16, 1865. Discharged July 1865.

Private George W. Cronk, Co. I – Mustered in on Sept. 2, 1864. Absent, on detached service, at muster out. Recorded at Camp Discharge June 16, 1865. Discharged July 1865.

Corporal Roscoe Loomis, Co. I – Mustered in on Sept. 2, 1864. Wounded near Wilmington, N.C., Feb.21, 1865. Absent, in hospital, at muster out. Recorded at Camp Discharge June 9, 1865. Discharged July 1865.

Private George Packer, Co. G – Mustered in on Sept. 5, 1864. Recorded at Camp Discharge June 16, 1865. Mustered out with company June 22, 1865. Departed Camp Discharge July 1865.

Private John T. Bridgens, Co. G – Mustered in on Sept. 5, 1864, at age 26. Recorded at Camp Discharge June 16, 1865. Mustered out with company June 22, 1865. Departed Camp Discharge July 1865.

Private Henry Newcomer, Co. K – Mustered in on Aug. 30, 1864, in Lancaster at age 33, a carpenter, 5-foot-4. Absent at muster out, on furlough since May 11, 1865. Recorded at Camp Discharge June 21, 1865. Discharged June 30, 1865.

Private Jabez I. Miller, Co. E – Mustered in on Sept. 5, 1864. Absent, on furlough, at muster out. Recorded at Camp Discharge June 10, 1865. Departed July 1865.

Private William Burgess, Co. E – Mustered in on Sept. 6, 1864. Recorded at Camp Discharge June 10, 1865. Mustered out with company June 22, 1865. Departed Camp Discharge July 1865.

Private Elmer. R. Burgess, Co. C – Mustered in on Aug. 30, 1864. Recorded at Camp Discharge June 10, 1865. Mustered out with company June 22, 1865. Departed Camp Discharge July 1865.

Private Newell Williams, Co. D – Mustered in on Sept. 14, 1864. Absent, on detached service, at muster out. Recorded at Camp Discharge June 16, 1865. Departed camp in July 1865.

Corporal Hiram H. Robinson, Co. C – Mustered in on Aug. 30, 18643. Promoted to corporal Feb. 11, 1865. Recorded at Camp Discharge June 11, 1865. Mustered out with the company and departed camp on June 22, 1865.

Private Rollin Sturdevant, Co. E – Mustered in on Sept. 5, 1864. Discharged by general order May 22, 1865.

Corporal Cyrus D. Alton, Co. G – Mustered in on Sept. 5, 1864. Recorded at Camp Discharge June 7, 1865. Mustered out with the company and left camp on June 22, 1865.

210th Pa. Infantry

The regiment was organized in 1864 with men from Dauphin, Bradford, Columbia, Franklin, Potter, Mercer, and Mifflin Counties. They took part in nine actions, including Petersburg, Appomattox, and Five Forks. Eighty-five enlisted men and officers succumbed to wounds or illnesses during service. The unit took part in Grand Review in D.C., then mustered out May 30, 1865. *One of its stray men passed through Camp Discharge.*

Private Charles Spillner, Co. K – Mustered in to service on Jan. 31, 1864. Entered Camp Discharge May 29, 1865. Discharged by general order June 20, 1865, to date May 30, 1865.

CAVALRY REGIMENTS

1St Pa. Cavalry (44th Pa. Regiment)

The regiment was recruited in 1861 in Athensville, Montgomery County (Co. B), and 13 other counties. The men were in 24 operations, including Second Bull Run, Antietam, Fredericksburg, Chancellorsville, Gettysburg, Cold Harbor, Petersburg, and Appomattox. From its ranks, 201 enlisted men and officers died of injuries or illness. The regiment took part in Grand Review in D.C. *Twenty of its men passed through Camp Discharge, twelve of them Andersonville survivors.*

Sergeant William Patterson, Co. A – Mustered in to service as corporal Aug. 1, 1861, in Harrisburg at age 24, a Mifflinburg tanner. Promoted from corporal. Captured June 21, 1864. Held at Andersonville and survived; sent to Millen Nov 14, 1864. Mustered out at Camp Discharge Feb. 4, 1865.

Sergeant William S. Miller, Co. A – Mustered in August 1861 in Harrisburg at age 24, a farmer from Juniata County. Promoted from corporal. Wounded at Whitehouse, Va., June 21, 1864. Recorded at Camp Discharge Nov. 2, 1864. Admitted to the camp hospital to treat gunshot wound of right leg Nov. 15. Mustered out Nov. 16.

Sergeant John H. Fertig, Co. A – Mustered in on Aug. 1, 1861, in Harrisburg at age 21, a clerk. Promoted to sergeant. Captured June 21, 1864, at Whitehouse, Va., and sent to Andersonville. Released Feb. 28, 1865, at Wilmington, N.C. Recorded at Camp Discharge April 3. Mustered out April 5.

Private Aaron E. Bachman, Co. L – Mustered in July 1861 in Reading. Captured Dec. 1, 1863. Held at Andersonville. Recorded at Camp Discharge May 18, 1865. Mustered out May 31, 1865.

Private James Handlin, Co. H – Mustered in September 1861 in Washington, D.C., at age 22. Captured at Whitehouse, Va., June 13, 1864. Held at Andersonville. Released March 13, 1865. Recorded at Camp Discharge May 16. Admitted to camp hospital for ecthyma July 2. Mustered out July 31.

Private Franklin Breneiser, Co. L – Mustered in on Feb. 2, 1864, in Reading at age 22, a trimmer. Captured June 21, 1864. Held at Andersonville. Sent to Millen, Ga., Oct. 31, 1864. Mustered out July 31, 1865.

Private Thomas Martin, Co. M – Mustered in February 1864 in Harrisburg at age 19, a laborer born in Ireland. Missing at Todds Tavern, Va., June 1864. Transferred to Battalion Sept. 9, 1864. At Camp Discharge July 14-31, 1865.

Private Thomas W. Grant, Co. E – Mustered in August 1861 in Washington, D.C., at age 27, a shoemaker. Re-enlisted Jan. 1, 1864. Captured July 16, 1864. Transferred to Battalion Sept. 9, 1864. At Camp Discharge June 29-July 15, 1865, when mustered out—joined Veteran Reserves.

Private Anthony Frank, Co. F – Mustered in on July 17, 1863, in Harrisburg at age 18, a moulder from York; 5-foot-4. Captured June 23, 1864. Held at Andersonville. Released April 28, 1865. Recorded at Camp Discharge May 25, 1865. Mustered out June 21, 1865.

Private James Benninghoff, Co. G. – Mustered in on Aug. 28, 1861, in Harrisburg at age 20. Wounded and captured Nov. 28, 1863, at Mine Run. Va.; released Nov. 20, 1864, at Savannah, Ga. Entered Camp Discharge Feb. 28, 1865. Discharged March 6, 1865.

Private Joseph E. Nutt, Co. H – Mustered in on Sept. 6, 1861, in Washington, D.C., at age 20. Captured June 21, 1864, at Whitehouse, Va. Held at Andersonville and Millen. Released Feb. 26, 1865, at Wilmington, N.C. Mustered out March 31, 1865.

Private James W. Brown, Co. F – Mustered in August 1861 in Phila. at age 24. Captured August 1862 and Nov. 17, 1863. Held at Andersonville. Exchanged April 1865. Entered Camp Discharge May 19, 1865. At the camp hospital for syphilis May 20 and sprained wrist June 7. Mustered out June 16.

Sergeant Jonas E. Lucas, Co. F – Mustered in as sergeant July 1861 in Harrisburg at age 24. Captured in action Nov. 17, 1863, and held at Andersonville. At Camp Discharge May 19-June 16, 1865, when he was mustered out.

Corporal Joseph A. Shaffer, Co. F – Mustered in August 1861 in Harrisburg at age 17, a farmer from Greene County. Re-enlisted February 1864. Captured at St. Mary's Church, Va., June 24, 1864. Held at Andersonville. Paroled at Jacksonville April 28, 1865. At Camp Discharge May 20, 1865. Discharged June 9, 1865.

Private William Yontz, Co. C – Mustered in on Aug. 7, 1861, in Harrisburg, at age 20, a refiner from Lewistown. Captured July 14, 1864. At Camp Discharge Hospital Feb. 10-11, 1865, for "cyn: parotidea" (mumps). Discharged Feb. 15, 1865.

Private Daniel Wiggins, Co. G. – Mustered in February 1862 in Camp Pierpont, Va. Transferred to Battalion Sept. 1, 1864. At Camp Discharge Hospital for ecthyma March 15-16, 1865. No discharge date recorded.

Private A.B. Rosenberger/Rousenberger, Co. I – Mustered in on Aug. 13, 1861, in Pittsburgh at age 21. Captured and returned, dates unknown. Recorded at Camp Discharge Sept. 20, 1864. Mustered out Sept. 27.

Private Albert H. Arnold, Co. H. – Mustered in on Sept. 6, 1861, in Washington, D.C., at age 20. Captured June 21, 1864. Held at Andersonville; sent to Millen, Ga., Nov. 11, 1864. Entered Camp Discharge Jan. 23, 1865. Discharged Jan. 25. 1865.

Corporal John M. Boyce, Co. K. – Mustered in on Sept. 6, 1861, in Phila. at age 20. Captured June 21, 1864. Held at Andersonville. Entered Camp Discharge Feb. 1, 1865. Discharged Feb. 4, 1865.

Private William H. Manor, Co. K – Mustered into service Oct. 15, 1861, in Pittsburgh at age 24, a farmer. Transferred to Battalion Sept. 1, 1864. Entered Camp Discharge Feb. 2, 1865. Transferred to Co. L, 2nd Provisional Cavalry June 17, 1865.

2nd Pa. Cavalry (59th Pa. Regiment)

The regiment was recruited in 1861 in Philadelphia, Lancaster, Berks, Centre, Crawford, Northampton, Tioga, and Armstrong Counties. The men saw action in 16 engagements, including Second Bull Run, Antietam, Gettysburg, Wilderness, Cold Harbor, and Appomattox. By the war's end, 253 enlisted men and officers died of wounds and ailments. Thirty-three died at Andersonville. The regiment took part in Grand Review in D.C. *Thirty-five of its men were at Camp Discharge, including six Andersonville survivors.*

Sergeant Henry L. Sitter, Co. I. – Mustered in as bugler on Nov. 25, 1861, in Phila. at age 24. Captured June 24, 1864, at St. Mary's Church, Va. Held at Andersonville. Released Nov. 26, 1864. Entered Camp Discharge Jan. 26, 1865. hospitalized there for constipation Feb. 9-14 and ecthyma Feb. 18-28, 1865. Discharged on March 1.

Sergeant Hugh Branghal, Co. G – Mustered in on Jan. 1, 1862. Prisoner Aug. 18, 1864, to March 2, 1865; Recorded at Camp Discharge April 6, 1865. Mustered out April 20, 1865, expiration of term.

Corporal Asa Kirby, Co. A – Mustered in November 1861 at Phila. at age 21. Recorded at Camp Discharge Nov. 3, 1864. Mustered out Jan. 10, 1865, expiration of term.

Corporal Matthew Macklen/MacKline, Co. A – Mustered in on Nov. 6, 1861, in Phila. at age 22. Prisoner Aug. 18, 1864-March 1, 1865. Recorded at Camp Discharge April 4, 1865. Discharged from service April 15.

Private Amos D. Powell, Co. M – Mustered in on Oct. 1, 1861, at Camp Orr (Kittanning, Pa.) at age 22. Captured July 12, 1864, near Petersburg, Va. Held at Andersonville, Libby and Florence S.C. Released March 1, 1865. Recorded at Camp Discharge April 14, 1865. Discharged April 21, 1865.

Farrier John H. Johnson, Co. A – Mustered in November 1861 in Phila. at age 38. Recorded at Camp Discharge Nov. 14, 1865. Hospitalized there for chronic diarrhea Nov. 15, 1864. Mustered out Nov. 16, 1864, expiration of term.

Private John J. H. Truby, Co. M – Enrolled at age 23, a farmer. Re-enlisted Dec. 17, 1863. Prisoner from July 12, 1864, to April 29, 1865. Held at Andersonville. Recorded at Camp Discharge May 29, 1865. Discharged by general order June 5, 1865. Joined Veteran Reserve Corps.

Private Amos M. Benner, Co. D – Mustered in on Oct. 17, 1861, in Phila. at age 21. Not accounted for on regimental roster. Recorded at Camp Discharge Oct. 28, 1864.

Private Michael Zeaner/Zehner, Co. B – Mustered in on Aug. 28, 1861, in Phila. at age 29. Recorded at Camp Discharge Nov. 2, 1864. Discharged Dec. 29, 1864.

Corporal Ira Kennedy, Co. B/C – Mustered in on Sept. 13, 1861, in Phila. at age 28. Promoted to corporal. Recorded at Camp Discharge Sept. 22, 1864. Hospitalized there for diarrhea Dec. 20, 1864. Mustered out Jan. 6, 1865, expiration of term.

Corporal Lewis Mawry, Co. E – Mustered in November 1861 in Phila. at age 18. Reported to Camp Discharge Nov. 4, 1864, from Broad & Cherry Street Hospital. Hospitalized at camp to treat gunshot wound of left forearm Nov. 15, 1865. Discharged Dec. 6, 1864.

Private Asa M. Sprigg, Co. E – Mustered in on Nov. 4, 1861, in Phila. at age 25, a blacksmith. Deserted June 1, 1862, in Washington, D.C. Recorded at Camp Discharge Dec. 14, 1864. Discharged from service Feb. 16, 1865.

Private Josiah Buskirk, Co. H – Mustered in January 1864 in Bealton, Va., at age 42, a shoemaker. Re-enlisted Jan. 15, 1864. Transferred to 1st Provisional Cavalry June 17, 1865; Vet. Recorded at Camp Discharge July 20, 1865. Hospitalized there for fractured ankle July 21, 1865. Mustered out July 31, 1865.

Private H. P. Jones, Co. B – Mustered in on Nov. 11, 1861, in Phila. at age 27, a schoolteacher. Captured June 24, 1864. Held at Andersonville. Exchanged April 15, 1865. Hospitalized June 29 at Camp Discharge for chronic diarrhea. Discharged by General Order, July 7, 1865.

Private Charles A. Newman, Co. I – Mustered in January 1862 in Phila. at age 35, a laborer. Re-enlisted Dec. 25, 1863, at Bealton, Va. Prisoner from July 12, 1864, to April 29, 1865. Recorded at Camp Discharge May 25, 1865. Discharged June 10, 1865. Joined Veteran Reserves.

Private Abraham L. Hershey, Co. G – Mustered in March 1864 in Phila. at age 20. Captured June 24, 1864, at Charles City, Va. Held at Andersonville. Released April 28, 1865. Recorded at Camp Discharge May 25, 1865. Discharged by general order June 14, 1865.

Private William Crowley, Co. E – Mustered in on March 5, 1864, in Phila. Prisoner of war, dates not known. Recorded at Camp Discharge May 26, 1865. Discharged by general order June 14, 1865.

Private Henry M. Brannon/Brannan, Co. E – Mustered in on Dec. 2, 1861, in Phila. at age 22. Captured, held at Andersonville. Exchanged at Savannah, Ga., Nov. 14, 1864. Entered Camp Discharge Jan. 24, 1865. Discharged Feb. 14, 1865.

Private Charles Elwell, Co. B – Mustered in on Feb. 7, 1862. Prisoner June 24-Dec. 11, 1864. Recorded at Camp Discharge April 8, 1865. Hospitalized there for a contusion of finger April 9-11, 1865. Discharged from service April 15, 1865.

Private Orris J. Coats, Co. A/I – Enrolled in service Oct. 6, 1861, in Summit, Pa., at age 33; mustered in on Nov. 25, 1861, in Phila. as sergeant. At Camp Discharge, hospitalized for diarrhea Nov. 29, 1864. Mustered out Dec. 2, 1864.

Private Michael Zeaner/Zehner, Co. B – Mustered in August 1861 in Phila. at age 29. Recorded at Camp Discharge Nov. 2, 1864. Hospitalized at camp for catarrh and rheumatism Dec. 1, 1864. Mustered out Dec. 29, 1864, expiration of term.

Private John Madara, Co. K – Mustered in on Aug. 21, 1861, in Phila. at age 44. Entered Camp Discharge Dec. 8, 1864. Hospitalized there for asthma Dec. 9. Mustered out Dec. 24, 1864, expiration of term.

Sergeant Conrad Seidentopf, Co. C – Mustered in as private Oct. 2, 1861, in Phila. at age 36, an engineer. Entered Camp Discharge Jan. 25, 1865. Hospitalized there for fever Feb. 4, 1865. Mustered out Feb. 14, 1865, expiration of term.

Private August Zimmerman, Co. H. – Enrolled in service Feb. 20, 1862, in Scranton at age 19. Entered Camp Discharge March 4, 1865. Hospitalized there to treat gunshot wound on March 12, 1865. Mustered out of service March 18, 1865.

Private Robert Porter, Co. A – Mustered in on Oct. 23, 1861, in Phila. at age 18, a gardener; deserted Jan. 14, 1862, at Phila. Entered Camp Discharge Sept. 30, 1864. Discharged Oct. 3, 1864.

Private Charles Stackhouse, Co. B – Mustered in on Sept. 4, 1861, in Phila. at age 18. Recorded at Camp Discharge Oct. 10, 1864. Mustered out Dec. 29, 1864, expiration of term.

Saddler Samuel Z. Heitz, Co. C – Mustered in October 1861 in Phila. at age 27. Recorded at Camp Discharge Nov. 5, 1864. Mustered out Nov. 10, 1864, expiration of term.

Private Thomas White, Co. C – Mustered in on Sept. 2, 1861, in Phila. at age 22. Not accounted for in Bates regimental history. Entered Camp Discharge Dec. 4, 1864. Discharged Dec. 7.

Private William Crothers, Co. C – Mustered in on Nov. 6, 1861, in Phila. at age 38, a dairyman. Deserted May 10, 1863, at Fairfax Court House, Va. Entered Camp Discharge Dec. 2, 1864. Ordered to Regiment Dec. 29, 1864.

Private John Rushton, Co. A – Mustered in on Dec. 16, 1861, in Phila. at age 40. Entered Camp Discharge Dec. 16, 1864. Mustered out Dec. 30, 1864.

Private Peter Davidson, Co. G – Mustered in on Dec. 23, 1861, in Phila. at age 35. Entered Camp Discharge Dec. 21, 1864. Discharged from service Dec. 27, 1864.

Corporal Abandon S. Moyer, Co H – Mustered into service on Jan. 15, 1862, in Phila. at age 18. Promoted from private. Entered Camp Discharge Jan. 16, 1865. Discharged Jan. 19, 1865.

Private John R. Williams, Co. L – Mustered into service on Jan. 1, 1862, in Phila. at age 24. Entered Camp Discharge Jan. 16, 1865. Discharged Jan. 19, 1865.

Corporal James M. Long, Co. K – Mustered into service on March 5, 1862, in Phila. at age 24. Captured, dates unknown. Entered Camp Discharge March 6, 1865. Discharged by General Order. June 28, 1865.

Private James White, Co. G – Mustered into service on March 25, 1862, at age 37. Entered Camp Discharge March 25, 1865. Discharged March 30, 1865.

3rd Pa. Cavalry (60th Pa. Volunteers)

The regiment was organized in 1861 with men from Philadelphia, Allegheny, Cumberland, and Schuylkill Counties, plus Washington, D.C. Also known as Young's Kentucky Light Cavalry, it took part in eight engagements, including Manassas, Antietam, Fredericksburg, Gettysburg, and Petersburg. In total, 169 enlisted men and officers succumbed to wounds and disease. *Twenty-seven of its men passed through Camp Discharge, including nine Andersonville survivors.*

Private Martin F. Flaherty, Co. A – Mustered in on July 18, 1861, in Phila. at age 24, a boilermaker. Captured, date uncertain—possible Andersonville survivor. Recorded at Camp Discharge Jan. 9, 1865. Mustered out Feb. 15, 1865, expiration of term.

Private James Johnson/Johnston, Co. K – Mustered in on Aug. 19, 1861, in Phila. at age 21, a teamster. Captured, date and whereabouts uncertain. Recorded at Camp Discharge Jan. 11, 1865. Mustered out Feb. 15, 1865, expiration of term.

Private Willis Brown, Co. K – Mustered in on Aug. 19, 1861, in Phila. at age 19, a farmer standing 5-feet-3. Captured at Parker's Store, Va., Nov. 29, 1863. Recorded at Camp Discharge Jan. 11, 1865. Hospitalized there for scabies Feb. 10-17, 1865. Mustered out Feb. 15, 1865, expiration of term.

Private John Rourke, Co. A – Mustered in on Aug. 12, 1861, in Phila. at age 41, a laborer. Captured, date and whereabouts uncertain. Hospitalized at Camp Discharge for "Horrors" Jan. 30, 1865. Mustered out Feb. 16, 1865, expiration of term.

Private George Wiegand/Wigand, Co. F – Mustered in on Aug. 16, 1861, in Phila. at age 19, a bricklayer. Captured at Catlett's Station, Va., Oct. 5, 1863, and taken to Andersonville prison. Entered Camp Discharge Jan. 24, 1865. Mustered out Feb. 14, 1865, expiration of term.

Corporal Charles Bickley, Co. L – Enrolled Aug. 19, 1861, in Pottsville at age 20, an engineer; mustered in on Aug. 22, 1861, in Washington, D.C. Promoted to corporal. Captured by guerrillas near Black Water, Va., in either June or July 1864. Entered Camp Discharge Feb. 25, 1865. Mustered out March 3, 1865.

Private Henry S. Roberts, Co. E – Mustered in on July 23, 1861, in Phila. at age 24, a sawyer. POW June 29, 1864, to Feb. 27, 1865. Survived Andersonville. Recorded at Camp Discharge March 29, 1865. Mustered out April 1, 1865, expiration of term.

Private John Sterling, Co. L – Enrolled in service on Aug. 19, 1861, in Pottsville at age 23, a miner. Mustered in on Aug. 22, 1861, in Washington, D.C. Captured Jan. 7, 1864, whereabouts uncertain. Recorded at Camp Discharge May 18, 1865. Discharged June 21, 1865, expiration of term.

Private Albert. C. Fuller, Co. G – Mustered in August 1861 in Washington, D.C., at age 25, a farmer from Armstrong County. Captured at Culpepper, Va., May 3, 1864. Survived

Andersonville. Exchanged April 5, 1865. Recorded at Camp Discharge May 19, 1865, and hospitalized there for ecthyma May 24. Mustered out June 16, 1865, expiration of term.

Sergeant Thomas J. Wier/Weir, Co. D – Mustered in August 1861 in Washington, D.C., at age 31, a coach maker. Captured Nov. 11, 1863, fate uncertain. Recorded at Camp Discharge May 21, 1865. Hospitalized there for "debility from dysentery in prison" May 24-29. Mustered out June 21, 1865, expiration of term.

Private William West, Co. F/I – Mustered in August 1861 in Washington, D.C., at age 22, a blacksmith. Captured Nov. 27, 1863, fate uncertain. Recorded at Camp Discharge May 22, 1865. Mustered out June 21, 1865, expiration of term.

Private Alexander T. High, Co. H – Enrolled August 1861 at Newville, Pa., at age 23, a carpenter. Captured at Realton Station, Va.; POW from Nov. 21, 1864, to April 9, 1865. Recorded at Camp Discharge May 20, 1865. Mustered out May 27, 1865, expiration of term.

Private Nicholas E. Bloom, Co. B – Mustered in July 1861 in Phila. at age 21, a shoemaker. Prisoner Nov. 21, 1863, to April 9, 1865. Captured near Bealton Station, Va. Survived Andersonville and Pemberton prisons. Paroled at Bealton, Fla. Recorded at Camp Discharge May 22, 1865. Mustered out May 27, 1865, expiration of term.

Private John Springbitt, Co. G – Mustered in August 1861 in Washington, D.C., at age 25, a tobacconist. Was a prisoner of war from May 3, 1864, to April 9, 1865, surviving Andersonville. Recorded at Camp Discharge May 23, 1865. Mustered out May 27, 1865, expiration of term.

Private John M. Bowers, Co. D – Enrolled July 28, 1861, in Washington, D.C., at age 20, a soldier. Mustered in on Aug. 13, 1861, in D.C. Sick in hospital in Baltimore since June 3, 1863. Hospitalized at Camp Discharge Hospital for "night sweats" Dec. 9, 1864. Sick at muster-out.

Private John W. Artley, Co. B – Mustered in on July 23, 1861, in Phila. at age 19, a shoemaker. Captured on Sept. 20, 1863, while on scout patrol near Warrenton, Va. Survived Andersonville. Recorded at Camp Discharge Jan. 7, 1865. Hospitalized there for jaundice Jan. 8-Feb. 2; for catarrh Jan. 26-30. Mustered out Jan. 31, 1865, expiration of term.

Private Joseph G. Emery, Co. F – Mustered in on Aug. 16, 1861, in Phila. at age 24. Transferred, no further record. Hospitalized at Camp Discharge for constipation May 22, 1865.

Private Alex Thompson, Co. E – Mustered in as a farrier Aug. 22, 1861, in Washington, D.C., at age 29, a laborer. Recorded at Camp Discharge Sept. 24, 1864. Discharged Oct. 3, 1864.

Private John Briscoe/Briscal, Co. D – Mustered in August 1861 in Washington, D.C., at age 22, a tailor. Deserted, then returned. Recorded at Camp Discharge Nov. 10, 1864. Mustered out Nov. 14, expiration of term.

Private Thomas T. Hurdle, Co. D – Mustered in August 1861 in Washington, D.C., at age 22. Deserted, then returned. Recorded at Camp Discharge Nov. 11. Mustered out Nov. 14, 1864, expiration of term.

Private John Bowen, Co. L – Mustered in on Aug. 22, 1861, in Washington, D.C., at age 20, a painter. Captured Jan. 7, 1864, at Warrenton, Va. Survived Andersonville. Entered Camp Discharge Dec. 10, 1864. Mustered out Dec. 13, 1864. Another service in 136th Pa. Infantry, Co. B, and 5th Pa. Cavalry, Co. L.

Private William Winterbottom, Co. E – Mustered into service on Aug. 16, 1861, in Phila. at age 18, working in manufacturing. Captured July 26, 1863, whereabouts uncertain. Mustered out, Jan. 23, 1865, expiration of term. Additional service with the US Veteran Volunteers.

Private William Frost, Co. I – Mustered in on Aug. 17, 1861, in Washington, D.C., at age 17, a farmer. Captured Dec.12, 1863. Survived Andersonville. Entered Camp Discharge Jan. 10, 1865. Mustered out Jan. 23, 1865, expiration of term. Additional service with 2nd Pa. Infantry, Co. I, and 3rd W.S, Veteran Volunteers, Co. A.

Private Willis Brown, Co. K – Mustered into service Aug. 19, 1861, in Phila. at age 19, a farmer standing 5-feet-3. Captured at Parker's Store, Va., Nov. 29, 1863. Survived Andersonville. Exchanged Nov. 14, 1864, at Savannah, Ga. Entered Camp Discharge Jan. 11, 1865. Mustered out Feb. 15, 1865, expiration of term.

Private John S. Smith, Co. B -- Mustered into service Aug. 23, 1861, in Phila. at age 22, a farmer. Captured near Waterloo, Va., Sept. 25, 1863. held at Andersonville and survived. Entered Camp Discharge Jan. 20, 1865. Mustered out Jan. 25, 1865, expiration of term.

Private William J. Burch/Birch, Co. D – Mustered into service Aug. 13, 1861, in Washington, D.C., at age 19, a farmer. Captured Jan. 7, 1864, whereabouts uncertain. Entered Camp Discharge Jan. 25, 1865. Mustered out Jan. 28, 1865, expiration of term. Additional service with 5th Battalion D.C. Infantry, Co. A.

Private James York, Co. L – Mustered into service Aug. 22, 1861, in Washington, D.C., at age 22, a laborer. Captured near Black Water, Va., June 15, 1864, fate uncertain. Entered Camp Discharge Feb. 20, 1865. Discharged Feb. 25, 1865

4th Pa. Cavalry (64th Pa. Regiment)

The regiment was recruited in 1861 in Northampton, Allegheny, Indiana, Westmoreland, Lebanon, Venango, and Luzerne Counties. The men saw action at Seven Days, Mechanicsville, Malvern Hill, Antietam, Sharpsburg, Fredericksburg, Chancellorsville, Gettysburg, Cold Harbor, Petersburg, and Five Forks. They lost 358 enlisted men and officers to disease and injury. *Six of its men transited Camp Discharge.*

Private William Thompson, Co. I – Mustered in on March 25, 1864, in Meadville at age 21. Deserted Feb. 21, 1865, before Petersburg, Va. Recorded at Camp Discharge May 16, 1865. No discharge date recorded.

Private Ezra Dickerson, Co. M – Mustered in April 1864 in Scranton at age 22, a mason. Wounded in action. Recorded at Camp Discharge on May 16, 1865. Discharged by general order May 24, 1865.

Private F. Weaver, Co. C – Hospitalized at Camp Discharge for a gunshot wound of right foot on Nov. 30, 1864. Muster-in and muster-out dates not recorded.

Private William J. Boyd, Co. A – Enlisted Aug. 7, 1861, in Bethlehem at age 23. Mustered in on Aug. 15, 1861, in Phila. Recorded at Camp Discharge Sept. 24, 1864. Discharged Oct. 26, 1864.

Corporal Anthony Allen, Co. G – Mustered in on Oct. 21, 1861, in Harrisburg at age 21. At Camp Discharge Oct. 1-Oct. 28, 1864, although mustered out Oct. 20 upon expiration of term.

Private Abraham Barr, Co. A – Mustered in August 1861 in Phila. at age 23, from Bethlehem. Mustered out Aug. 15, 1864, upon expiration of term. Entered Camp Discharge Oct. 18, 1864, coming from Washington, D.C. Dropped Dec. 5, 1864.

5th Pa. Cavalry (65th Pa. Volunteers)

Known as the Cameron Dragoons, the regiment recruited in 1861 from Philadelphia, Allegheny, Lycoming, and Venango Counties. The men took part in seven engagements, including Seven Days, Petersburg, Appomattox, and Five Forks. They lost 293 enlisted men and officers to wounds or ailments during service. The unit mustered out August 1865 in Philadelphia. *Eighteen of its men were at Camp Discharge, thirteen of them Andersonville survivors.*

Private William J. Skerrett, Co. D – Mustered in September 1862 in Phila. at age 22, a farmer. Captured at Stony Creek, Va., June 29, 1864. Held at Andersonville. Released May 3,

1865. At Camp Discharge June 12–June 30, 1865. Hospitalized at camp for injury from fall 24 feet through the roof. Discharged by general order, June 30, 1865.

Corporal Bentley Gaul, Co. G – Mustered in on Sept. 12, 1862, in Phila. at age 23, a carpenter. Promoted to corporal May 1, 1864. Captured June 29, 1864, at Reams Station, Va. Survived Andersonville. Recorded at Camp Discharge May 24, 1865. Discharged by general order June 22, 1865.

Corporal Oliver K. Lewis, Co. C – Mustered in on July 26, 1861, in Phila. at age 21, a clerk. Captured June 29, 1864, at Reams Station, Va. Survived Andersonville. Released Dec. 13, 1864. Entered Camp Discharge Feb. 27, 1865. Discharged March 3, 1865.

Corporal James Cornett, Co. F – Mustered in on Aug. 20, 1861, in Phila., at age 32, from Phoenixville. Served as a nurse in a regimental hospital. Captured at Reams Station, Va., June 29, 1964. Held in Andersonville. At Camp Discharge, hospitalized for chronic diarrhea Feb. 27, 1865. Mustered out March 30, 1865, expiration of term.

Private Garl Moendler/Charles Mandler, Co. A – Mustered in on July 18, 1861, in Phila. at age 40, a shoemaker. Captured at Reams Station, Va., June 29, 1864. Held at Andersonville. Released March 3, 1865. Recorded at Camp Discharge March 31 and hospitalized with fever April 8. Mustered out April 15, 1865, expiration of term.

Corporal John J. Yorgey, Co. K – Enrolled July 20, 1861, in Milton, Pa., at age 19, a blacksmith. Mustered in on Aug. 19, 1861, in Phila. Captured June 29, 1864, at Reams Station, Va. Released Dec. 16, 1864. Recorded at Camp Discharge Feb. 20, 1865. Discharged March 6, 1865, expiration of term.

Private Isaac Palm/Palmer, Co. K – Mustered in on Aug. 10, 1861, in Phila. at age 25, a farmer. Captured June 29, 1864, at Stoney Creek Station, Va. Held at Andersonville. Released Feb. 27, 1865. Recorded at Camp Discharge April 1, 1865. Hospitalized there for scabies April 3-7. Discharged April 15, 1865.

Private John Durkin, Co. G – Mustered in August 1861 in Phila. at age 21, a miner from Schuylkill County. Re-enlisted Dec. 1, 1863. Captured June 29, 1864, at Reams Station, Va. Held in Andersonville. At Camp Discharge May 23-June 3, 1865. Discharged by general order June 17, 1865. Joined Veteran Reserve Corps.

Private William Stewart, Co. G – Mustered in on Feb. 7, 1864, in Meadville at age 18, a hatter. Captured, dates of imprisonment unknown. Held in Andersonville. Paroled, date unknown. Recorded at Camp Discharge May 22, 1865. Discharged June 21, 1865, by general order.

Private James Salmon, Co. G – Mustered in August 1861 in Phila. at age 22, a miner from Pottsville. Re-enlisted Jan. 1, 1864. Captured at Reams Station, Va., June 29, 1864. Held at Andersonville. Sent to Millen, Ga., Oct. 31, 1864. Exchanged April 1, 1865. At Camp Discharge May 22-June 17, hospitalized for diarrhea May 25. Discharged by general order June 17, 1865. Joined Veteran Reserve Corps.

Private Joseph Bowers, Co. M – Mustered in February 1864 in Phila. at age 18, a laborer. Captured April 9, 1864, at Stony Creek, Va. Held at Andersonville and survived. Exchanged April 29, 1865. Recorded at Camp Discharge May 22, 1865. Discharged by general order June 7, 1865.

Private William T. Wise, Co. D – Mustered in July 1861 in Phila. at age 27, a seaman. Captured June 29, 1864, at Reams Stations, Va. Held at Andersonville. Paroled April 28, 1865. Recorded at Camp Discharge May 25, 1865. Mustered out June 5, 1865, expiration of term.

Private Herman Claudius, Co. B – Mustered in July 1861 in Phila. at age 30, a butcher from Reading. Captured June 5, 1864, at Piedmont, Va. Held in Andersonville. Released March 20, 1865. Recorded at Camp Discharge May 10, 1865. Mustered out May 15, 1865, expiration of term.

Private Frank P. Gamble, Co. C – Mustered in on Aug. 19, 1861, in Phila. at age 21, a laborer. Captured June 29, 1864, at Reams Station, Va. Held at Andersonville. Released Feb. 28, 1865. Mustered out May 16, 1865.

Private Isaac Paulin, Co. K – Mustered in on Aug. 10, 1861, in Phila. at age 25. At Camp Discharge, hospitalized for scabies April 1-7, 1865. Not on muster-out roll.

Sergeant Henry Biss, Co. E – Mustered in on July 30, 1861, in Phila. at age 30, a cabinet-maker. Promoted from corporal. Captured June 29, 1864, at Reams Station, Va. Released Aug. 22, 1864. Entered Camp Discharge Feb. 16, 1865. Discharged Feb. 24, 1865.

Private Jacob Grunner, Co. B – Mustered in on July 23, 1861, in Phila. at age 23, a baker. Captured June 29, 1864, at Reams Station, Va. Held at Andersonville. Released Dec. 14, 1864. Entered Camp Discharge March 2, 1865. Mustered out, March 9, 1865, expiration of term.

Corporal William M. McKinney, Co. F – Mustered in on Aug. 5, 1861, in Phila. at age 31, a gardener. Promoted to corporal. Captured June 29, 1864. Entered Camp Discharge March 27, 1865. Mustered out March 30, 1865, expiration of term.

6th Pa. Cavalry (70th Pa. Volunteers)

The regiment was organized in 1861 with men from Philadelphia, Chester, Berks, and Luzerne Counties. Also known as Rush's Lancers for their early use of 9-foot lances, they saw action in 12 operations, including Antietam, Fredericksburg, Chancellorsville, Gettysburg, Cold Harbor, and Petersburg. By the war's end, 167 enlisted men and officers were dead from injuries or illness. The regiment took part in Grand Review in D.C. *Twenty of its men moved through Camp Discharge, including two Andersonville survivors.*

Private Richard J. Gibbs, Co. E – Mustered in September 1861 in Phila. at age 18. Wounded in action June 1, 1864. Absent, sick at regimental muster-out. Recorded at Camp Discharge Oct. 28, 1864. Discharge date not listed.

Private Daniel Leech/Leach, Co. B – Mustered in August 1861 in Phila. at age 19. Recorded at Camp Discharge Sept. 22, 1864. Mustered out Dec. 14, 1864, expiration of term. Remained hospitalized at camp Dec. 16 to treat gunshot wound of the back and ecthyma.

Private James Campbell, Co. K – Mustered in September 1861 in Phila. at age 43. At Camp Discharge Oct. 4-Dec. 21, 1864. Discharged Dec. 21, 1864.

Private Anthony Aberle, Co. G – Mustered in October 1861 in Phila. at age 34. Transferred to Veteran Reserve Corps, date unknown. Returned by special order dated Aug. 2, 1864. Recorded at Camp Discharge Nov. 1, 1864. Mustered out Dec. 7, 1864, expiration of term.

Corporal Roland N. Kidder, Co. E – Mustered in September 1861 in Phila. at age 19. Captured April 29, 1864, at Trevilian Va. Survived Andersonville. Paroled April 29, 1865, at Jacksonville, Fla. Recorded at Camp Discharge May 26, 1865. Discharged by general order June 28, 1865.

Sergeant John J. Huntzinger, Co. G – Mustered in as sergeant on Nov. 29, 1861, in Phila. at age 32, from Reading. Entered Camp Discharge Dec. 8, 1864. Filed a formal complaint about camp conditions. Discharged Dec. 17, 1864, by order of Major Gilbert.

Bugler Matthew F. Greeley, Co. C – Mustered in September 1861 in Phila. at age 24. Promoted to bugler, date unknown. Captured, a prisoner from July 27, 1864, to March 2, 1865. Recorded at Camp Discharge April 20, 1865. Discharged April 21, 1865.

Private George McEvoy, Co. F – Mustered in September 1861 in Phila. at age 22. Captured at Spotsylvania Courthouse, Va., May 12, 1864. Held at Andersonville but escaped, date unknown. Recorded at Camp Discharge May 8, 1865. Discharged from service May 25, 1865.

Private H. Everly, Co. G – Listed on Camp Discharge Hospital Register as admitted for tetter, a skin disease. No regimental information about him could be found.

Private John Moyer, Co. G – Mustered in January 1864 in Phila. at age 27, a clerk from Schuylkill County. Camp Discharge Hospital Register lists him as hospitalized to treat a gunshot wound of the left hip on Dec. 6, 1864. No mustering-out information is available.

Sergeant Wilmer H. Foard, Co. K – Mustered in on Dec. 9, 1861, in Phila. as quartermaster sergeant, at age 18. Wounded in action Aug. 29, 1864. Discharged Dec. 9, 1864, expiration of term. On Dec. 13, he had a gunshot wound of the left shoulder treated at Camp Discharge Hospital.

Saddler Hugh Osborne, Co. B – Mustered in on Aug. 29, 1861, in Phila. at age 24. Shot and captured June 1864 and held at Danville prison. Recorded at Camp Discharge Sept. 27, 1864. Mustered out Oct. 19, 1864, expiration of term.

Private Charles H. Masland, Co. E – Mustered in September 1861 in Phila. at age 19. Absent, sick at the expiration of term. Recorded at Camp Discharge Sept. 28, 1864. Discharged Oct. 26, 1864.

Private Willoughby Deitrick, Co. I – Mustered in on Oct. 2, 1861, in Phila. at age 19. Recorded at Camp Discharge Oct. 4, 1864. Discharged Oct. 7, 1864, expiration of term.

Private John L. Westley, Co. I – Mustered into service Oct. 3, 1861, in Phila. at age 18. Recorded at Camp Discharge Oct. 3, 1864. Discharged Oct. 15, 1864, expiration of term.

Private Henry Crox, Co. K – Mustered in November 1861 in Phila. at age 24. Recorded at Camp Discharge Nov. 10, 1864. Discharged Nov. 20, 1864, expiration of term.

Corporal Thomas B. Barnes/Baines, Co. H – Mustered in on Oct. 10, 1861, in Phila. at age 24. Wounded in action June 11, 1864. Recorded at Camp Discharge Oct. 14-22, 1864.

Private George W. Fox, Co. I – Mustered in Oct. 3, 1861, in Phila. at age 19. Entered Camp Dec. 5, 1864, and was discharged the same day, expiration of term.

Private Frederick Smith, Co. G – Mustered in on Dec. 12, 1861, in Phila. at age 18. Wounded during service, specifics unrecorded. Entered Camp Discharge Dec. 8, 1864. Discharged Dec. 12, 1864, expiration of term.

Private Samuel Roberts, Co. I – Mustered into service Feb. 5, 1862, in Phila. as a sergeant. Prisoner from Aug. 13, 1864, to Feb. 23, 1865. Reduced to the rank of private for absence without leave to date March 13, 1865. Entered Camp Discharge March 21, 1865. Discharged March 25, 1865.

7th Pa. Cavalry (80th Pa. Volunteers)

The regiment was organized in 1861 with men from Philadelphia, Chester, and a dozen other Pa. counties. The men were in eight operations, including Chickamauga and the Siege of Atlanta. They lost 292 enlisted men and officers to wounds or illness. The regiment mustered out in Nashville in August 1865. *One of its men, an Andersonville survivor, passed through Camp Discharge.*

Private Alfred Hummel, Co. A – Mustered in February 1864 in Reading at age 18, a 5-foot-4 laborer. Captured at Carters Creek Station, Tenn., Oct. 1, 1864. Held at Andersonville. Released at Vicksburg March 27, 1865. Recorded at Camp Discharge May 31, 1865. Discharged by general order July 29, 1865.

8th Pa. Cavalry (89th Pa. Volunteers)

The regiment was recruited in 1861 in Montgomery (Co. M), Philadelphia, Bucks, Chester, and Lycoming Counties. The men took part in 28 operations, including Antietam, Fredericksburg,

Chancellorsville, Gettysburg, Wilderness, Spotsylvania Courthouse, Cold Harbor, and Petersburg. They lost 188 enlisted men and officers to wounds or sickness. *Fifty-seven of its men were at Camp Discharge, including fifteen Andersonville survivors.*

Corporal William Galloway, Co. D – Mustered in on Aug. 19, 1861, in Phila. at age 22. Promoted to corporal. POW Nov. 2, 1863-Dec. 11, 1864. At Camp Discharge, hospitalized for scabies Feb. 14-18, 1865. Discharged March 2, 1865.

Private Alexander Wilson, Co. K – Mustered in on Sept. 17, 1861, in Phila. at age 23. Prisoner of war May 12 to November 1864, whereabouts uncertain. Entered Camp Discharge Jan. 30, 1865. Discharged Feb. 2, 1865.

Private John H. Ward, Co. C & H – Mustered in on Aug. 19, 1861, in Phila. at age 21. Captured Oct. 3, 1863, at Sulphur Springs, Va. Imprisoned at Andersonville. Released Nov. 20, 1864. Recorded at Camp Discharge Feb. 14, 1865. Discharged from service March 6, 1865.

Sergeant Daniel Slawter, Co. H – Mustered in on Aug. 19, 1861, in Phila. at age 19. Promoted to sergeant. Captured Oct. 12, 1863, at Sulphur Springs, Va. Held at Andersonville. Released Feb. 26, 1865. Recorded at Camp Discharge April 17, 1865. Discharged April 25, 1865.

Sergeant Eldridge J. Gouring/Growing, Co. K – Captured Oct. 12, 1863. Imprisoned at Andersonville. Exchanged April 1, 1865. Recorded at Camp Discharge May 24, 1865. Discharged June 5, 1865.

Private William Wentzel, Co. K – Mustered in on Sept. 27, 1861, in Phila. at age 18. Captured Oct. 12, 1863. Prisoner at Andersonville. Exchanged April 1, 1865. Recorded at Camp Discharge May 24, 1865. Discharged June 5, 1865.

Private Samuel C. Hopper, Co. H – Mustered in on Aug. 27, 1861, in Phila. at age 28. Captured Oct. 12, 1863. Imprisoned at Andersonville. Exchanged April 1, 1865. Recorded at Camp Discharge May 24, 1865. Discharged by general order. June 8, 1865.

Private Samuel F. Tomlinson, Co. H – Mustered in September 1861 in Phila. at age 19. Captured Oct. 12, 1863. Held at Andersonville. Released April 28, 1865. Recorded at Camp Discharge May 22, 1865. Discharged June 5, 1865.

Sergeant George Hinkson, Co. H – Mustered in September 1861 in Phila. at age 27. Captured Oct. 12, 1863. Imprisoned at Andersonville. Released April 28, 1865. Recorded at Camp Discharge May 22, 1865. Discharged June 8, 1865.

Corporal David Dickey, Co. F – Mustered in August 1861 at age 35, a storekeeper born in Ireland. Re-enlisted Dec 31, 1863. POW June 24, 1864, to April 25, 1865, whereabouts unknown. Recorded at Camp Discharge May 22, 1865. Hospitalized there for scorbutus (scurvy) May 25, 1865. Discharged by general order June 8, 1865. Went on to join Veteran Reserve Corps.

Private Thomas Nelson/Neilson, Co. H – Mustered in August 1861 in Phila. at age 21. Captured at Sulphur Springs, Va., Oct. 12, 1863. Survived Andersonville. Recorded at Camp Discharge May 22, 1865. Discharged June 21, 1865.

Private Richard M. Rockwell, Co. K – Mustered in on Sept. 21, 1861, in Phila. at age 18. Captured Oct. 12, 1863, at Sulphur Springs, Va. Imprisoned at Andersonville. Exchanged April 1, 1865. Recorded at Camp Discharge May 22, 1865. Discharged by general order June 21, 1865.

Private John H. Smith, Co. H – Mustered in September 1861 in Phila. at age 22. Recorded at Camp Discharge Sept. 26, 1864. Discharged from service Nov. 29, 1864, expiration of term.

Private Henry H. Smith, Co. A – Mustered in on Sept. 9, 1861, in Phila. at age 18. Captured June 30, 1864. Survived Andersonville. Recorded at Camp Discharge Dec. 12, 1864. Discharged Dec. 28, 1864.

Corporal Edwin Goodwin, Co. D – Mustered in September 1861 in Phila. at age 28, a weaver. Re-enlisted Nov. 31, 1863. Captured at Dinwiddie Courthouse, Va., March 31, 1865. Paroled April 9, 1865. Recorded at Camp Discharge June 26, 1865. Discharged Aug. 8, 1865. Joined Veteran Volunteer Corps.

Private Joseph Diggle, Co. B – Mustered in on Feb. 16, 1865, in Phila. at age 19, a spinner. Prisoner of war April 7-9, 1865. Paroled. Recorded at Camp Discharge June 26, 1865. Discharged Aug. 10, 1865.

Private Timothy Mooney (Saddler), Co. D – Mustered in August 1861 in Phila. at age 27, a carpenter. Re-enlisted Dec. 31, 1863. POW April 7-9, 1865. Recorded at Camp Discharge June 26, 1865. Discharged Aug. 14, 1865. Went on to join Veteran Volunteer Corps.

Private John B. Dandois (Saddler), Co. B – Mustered in July 1861 in Phila. at age 31, a saddler. Re-enlisted Feb. 1, 1864. POW April 7-9, 1865. Paroled. Recorded at Camp Discharge June 26, 1865. Transferred to 16th Cavalry July 24, 1865. Discharged July 26, 1865. Joined Veteran Volunteer Corps.

Private William Miller, Co. I – Mustered in on Feb. 21, 1865, in Phila. at age 25, a machinist. Prisoner April 7-9, 1865. Recorded at Camp Discharge June 26, 1865. Discharged by general order July 15, 1865.

Private Francis Miller, Co. I – Promoted to corporal Nov. 1, 1862. Deserted April 6, 1864. Demoted. Returned Aug. 9, 1864. Recorded at Camp Discharge July 1865. Discharged July 15, 1865, expiration of term.

Private Henry Tanner, Co. G – Mustered in on Feb. 14, 1865, in Williamsport at age 25, a roller, 5-foot-4. Prisoner of war April 7-9, 1865. Recorded at Camp Discharge June 26, 1865. Discharged by general order July 15, 1865.

Private Lawrence Anderson, Co. B – Mustered in August 1864 in Lancaster at age 21, a laborer, 5-foot-2. Prisoner April 7-9, 1865. Recorded at Camp Discharge June 26. Discharged July 12, 1865.

Private Eugene Bush, Co. A – Mustered in on Feb. 9, 1865, in Williamsport at age 18, a clerk. Wounded in action April 7, 1865, at Farmdale, Va. Recorded at Camp Discharge June 29, 1865. Discharged July 1865.

Private John Cassady, Co. E – Mustered in on Aug. 21, 1861, in Phila. at age 24, a saddler. Bugler after transfer to Co. E and then 16th Pa. Cavalry. Re-enlisted Jan. 1, 1864. At Camp Discharge July 1865. Mustered out Aug. 11, 1865.

Private John M. Vanderslice, Co. D – Mustered in February 1864 in Phila. at age 18, a clerk, 5-foot-5. Received Medal of Honor for leading a successful charge at Hatchers Run, Va., Feb. 6, 1865. Captured at Farmville, Va., and held April 7-9, 1865. Paroled. Recorded at Camp Discharge June 26, 1865. Discharged July 12, 1865.

Private John Haines, Co. I – Prisoner April 7-9, 1865. Recorded at Camp Discharge June 26, 1865. Discharged by general order July 8, 1865.

Private John Kemp, Co. D – Mustered in February 1865 in Phila. at age 21, a miner. Wounded at Dinwiddie Courthouse, Va., March 31, 1865. Entered Camp Discharge May 26 and hospitalized May 27-28 to treat gunshot wound of the left shoulder. Discharged by general order July 6, 1865.

Private Theodore Yocum, Co. I – Mustered in on Feb. 25, 1865, in West Chester at age 21, a wheelwright; POW April 7-9, 1865. Recorded at Camp Discharge June 26, 1865. Discharged by general order July 8, 1865.

Private Henry Pugh, Co. D – Mustered in on March 31, 1864, in Phila. at age 18, a laborer. Captured at Appomattox Courthouse April 7, 1865. Paroled April 9, 1865. Recorded at Camp Discharge June 26, 1865. Discharged by general order July 8, 1865.

Private William Platt, Co. B – Mustered in on Feb. 13, 1865, in Lancaster at age 26, a sawyer, 5-foot-4. Captured April 7, 1865. Paroled April 9, 1865. Discharged by general order July 8, 1865.

Private George Gilchrist, Co I – Mustered in November 1864 in Frankford at age 24, a seaman. Prisoner April 7-9, 1865. Recorded at Camp Discharge June 26, 1865. Discharged by general order July 8, 1865.

Private J. Murray, Co. F – No regimental or state veteran information found. Recorded at Camp Discharge May 31, 1865, with muster-out listed in June 1865.

Corporal John Keefe, Co. L – Mustered in September 1861 in Phila. at age 25, an Irish-born laborer. Transferred to Company I. Prisoner of war Sept. 7, 1863, to April 28, 1865, location not known. Recorded at Camp Discharge June 8, 1865. Discharged June 17, 1865.

Private William W. Benjamin, Co. B – Mustered in March 1864 in Williamsport, a farmer, 5-foot-4. Wounded in action on Dec. 8, 1864. Recorded at Camp Discharge May 29, 1865, and hospitalized for catarrh on June 7, 1865. Discharged by general order June 8, 1865.

Private Jonathan M. Smiley, Co. A – Mustered in July 1861 in Phila. at age 21. Captured June 30, 1864. Held at Andersonville and survived. Exchanged April 1, 1865. Recorded at Camp Discharge May 29, 1865. Discharged June 14, 1865.

Private John Levan, Co. G – Mustered in February 1864 in Williamsport at age 18, a laborer. Captured June 24, 1864. Imprisoned at Andersonville. Exchanged April 1, 1865. Recorded at Camp Discharge May 31, 1865. Discharged by General Order June 17, 1865.

Private Richard Marston, Co. H – Mustered in February 1864 in Phila. at age 30, a ship carpenter. Sent to hospital March 9, 1865. Recorded at Camp Discharge May 26, 1865. Discharged by general order June 14, 1865.

Private William Brown, Co. I – Mustered in on Oct. 5, 1861, at age 32, a rope-maker born in England. Captured near Charles City July 16, 1864. Recorded at Camp Discharge May 4, 1865. Discharged May 5, 1865. Admitted to Camp Discharge Hospital for treatment of scorbutus May 25, 1865.

Private Wm. F. Harmstead, Co. D – Mustered in February 1864 in Phila. at age 25, a printer. Prisoner April 7-9, 1865. Recorded at Camp Discharge June 26, 1865. Discharged July 12, 1865.

Private James Campbell, Co. K – Mustered in on Sept. 30, 1861, in Phila. at age 43. Recorded at Camp Discharge Oct 4, 1864. Admitted to camp hospital to treat diarrhea Nov. 24, 1864. Discharged Dec. 21, 1864.

Corporal Henry J. Reifsnyder, Co. M – Enlisted Sept. 24, 1861, mustered in on Oct. 5, 1861, in Phila. at age 21. Captured Oct. 12, 1863, at Sulphur Springs, Va. Held at Andersonville and survived. Admitted to Camp Discharge Hospital with impetigo Jan. 7, 1865. Discharged by general order Jan. 30, 1865. Joined Veteran Reserve Corps.

Sergeant David Wolf, Co. H – Mustered in on Sept. 9, 1861, in Phila. at age 22. Prisoner Oct. 12, 1863, to Nov. 20, 1864. Held at Andersonville. Hospitalized for scabies at Camp Discharge Hospital Jan. 19-30, 1865. Discharged Feb. 14, 1865.

Sergeant William Hunter, Co. H – Mustered in on Aug. 19, 1861, in Phila. at age 25. Captured Nov. 12, 1863. Held at Andersonville and survived. Hospitalized for ecthyma at Camp Discharge Feb. 8-14, 1865. Discharged from service Feb. 14, 1865.

Private James Galloway, Co. D – Mustered in on Feb. 7, 1862, in Phila. at age 27. Discharged Feb. 7, 1865, expiration of term.

Corporal Henry Howarth, Co. D – Mustered in August 1861 in Phila. at age 33, a painter born in England. Wounded in 1864 at Richmond, Va., date and details not given. Recorded at Camp Discharge Sept. 23-Dec. 5, 1864. Officially discharged Sept. 10, 1864, upon expiration of term.

Corporal Jonathan Knight, Co. M – Mustered in on Sept. 24, 1861, in Phila. at age 21. Promoted to corporal. Recorded at Camp Discharge Sept. 24, 1864. Discharged from service Sept. 27, 1864, expiration of term.

Private Edward Fried, Co. H – Mustered in August 1861 in Phila. at age 19. Recorded at Camp Discharge Sept. 24-Nov. 21, 1864. Not accounted for on regimental rolls.

Corporal William Calloway, Co. M – Recorded at Camp Discharge Oct. 1-Oct. 29, 1864. Not accounted for on regimental rolls.

Sergeant Major Charles E. Fellows, regimental staff – Mustered in on Sept. 4, 1861, in Phila. at age 32 as private in Co. A. Promoted to sergeant, sergeant major, second lieutenant, first lieutenant, and, finally, to captain. Recorded at Camp Discharge Sept. 20, 1864. Mustered out Sept. 22, 1864. Dropped Dec. 5, 1864.

Private Thompson A. Corson, Co. M – Deserted March 8, 1863, according to deserters roll. Recorded present at Camp Discharge Oct. 14, 1864. Came from Camp Cadwalader. Absent beginning Oct. 16, 1864. No entry on regimental rolls.

Private Alfred Oat, Co. D – Mustered in on Sept. 16, 1861, in Phila. at age 20, a laborer. Promoted to corporal, then to sergeant. Discharged Sept. 15, 1864. Recorded at Camp Discharge Sept. 21, 1864, listed as sergeant. Not accounted for on regimental rolls.

Private Peter Reidenaur, Co. M – Mustered in on Oct. 5, 1861, in Phila. at age 21. Recorded at Camp Discharge Dec. 12, 1864. Mustered out Dec. 14, 1864, expiration of term.

Private Joseph Renfried, Co. K – Mustered in on Oct. 1, 1861, in Phila. at age 21. Prisoner July 4-September 1863, and Oct. 12, 1863-November 1864. Present at Camp Discharge Jan. 5, 1865. Discharged Jan. 7, 1865.

Farrier Augustus Gleik, Co. K – Mustered in on Aug. 24, 1861, in Phila. at age 23, a farrier. Enlisted in Co. A but transferred to Co. K. Prisoner Oct. 12, 1863, to November 1864. Recorded at Camp Discharge Jan. 5, 1865. Discharged Jan. 7, 1865.

Private Charles Williamson, Co. H – Mustered in on Aug. 19, 1861, in Phila. at age 21. Transferred from Co. C. Recorded at Camp Discharge Jan. 7, 1865. Discharged Feb. 2, 1865.

Private William Eckenbrine, Co. L – Mustered into service Sept. 4, 1861, in Phila. at age 23. Captured June 17, 1864, circumstances unclear. Transferred to 8th Cavalry, Co. I, Nov. 15, 1864. At Camp Discharge Feb. 1, 1865. Discharged Feb. 15, 1865.

Private Charles McPherson, Co. K – Mustered in on Sept. 27, 1861, in Phila. at age 23. Prisoner Oct. 12, 1863-November 1864, details unknown. Recorded at Camp Discharge Feb. 21, 1865. Discharged Feb. 25, 1865.

11th Pa. Cavalry (108th Pa. Volunteers)

The regiment was organized in 1861 with men from Philadelphia, Chester, and seven other Pa. counties, plus Iowa, New York, and New Jersey. Dubbed "Harlan's Light Cavalry," It saw action in 13 engagements, including Seven Pines, Petersburg, and Appomattox. In total, 290 enlisted men and officers died of injury or illness during service. The unit mustered out in August 1865 in Richmond. *Twenty-three of its stray men went through Camp Discharge, including 16 Andersonville survivors.*

Sergeant Hiram H. Foster, Co. F – Enrolled Aug. 24, 1861, in Troy, Pa., at age 26, a farmer, mustered in three days later in Phila. Promoted to corporal, then sergeant. Re-enlisted Nov. 19, 1863. Captured at Reams Station, Va., June 29, 1864. Imprisoned at Andersonville. Exchanged April 5, 1865. Discharged by general order May 3, 1865. Mustered out June 5, 1865.

Corporal Wyatte W. Watson, Co. M – Mustered in August 1861 at Camp Chase, Ohio, at age 21, a farmer, 5-foot 1½. Captured May 6, 1863, near South Mills, N.C., then captured June 29, 1864, at Reams Station, Va. Held at Andersonville and survived. Discharged June 5, 1865.

Private John Elser, Co. D – Enrolled Aug. 14, 1861, in Chambersburg at age 19, a butcher. Mustered in a week later in Phila. Re-enlisted Nov. 20, 1863. Captured June 15, 1864. Held at Andersonville and survived. Exchanged April 5, 1865. Recorded at Camp Discharge May 24, 1865. Discharged by general order June 5, 1865. Joined Veteran Volunteers.

Private Orin M. Fletcher, Co. F – Enrolled Aug. 24, 1861, in Troy at age 26, a farmer. Mustered in three days later in Phila. Re-enlisted Jan. 1, 1864. Captured June 29, 1864, at Reams Station, Va. Held at Andersonville. Exchanged April 1865. Recorded at Camp Discharge May 24, 1865. Discharged by general order June 5, 1865. Joined Veteran Volunteer Corps.

Private Benjamin Deibler, Co. L – Captured June 24, 1864, at Stoney Creek, Va. Imprisoned at Andersonville and Millen, Ga. Recorded at Camp Discharge May 24, 1865. Discharged by general order June 5, 1865. Joined Veteran Volunteers.

Private William Tompkins, Co. F – Enrolled Aug. 24, 1861, in Troy at age 22, a farmer. Mustered in three days later in Phila. Re-enlisted Nov. 19, 1863. Captured June 9, 1864, at Petersburg. Imprisoned at Andersonville. Released April 21, 1865. Returned to Annapolis May 3, 1865. Recorded at Camp Discharge May 24, 1865. Admitted to camp hospital with diarrhea May 27, 1865. Discharged by general order June 21, 1865. Joined Veteran Volunteers.

Private William Johnson, Co. C – Mustered in August 1861 in Phila at age 23, a finisher. Promoted to corporal May 1863. Captured at Reams Station, Va., June 29, 1864. Prisoner June 29, 1864-April 29, 1865, at Andersonville and Millen, Ga. Recorded at Camp Discharge May 25, 1865. Discharged by general order June 5, 1865.

Private John J. Lavery, Co. L – Mustered in August 1862 in Harrisburg at age 32. Captured at Ream's Station, Va., June 29, 1864. Held at Andersonville and survived. Recorded at Camp Discharge May 19, 1865. Hospitalized for boils at camp hospital. Discharged by general order June 16, 1865.

Hospital Steward James T. Harnit – Captured at Ream's Station, Va., June 29, 1864. Recorded at Camp Discharge May 20, 1865. Hospitalized at camp for bronchitis May 21, 1865. Discharged by general order June 21, 1865. Joined Veteran Volunteer Corps.

Private William H. Sturges, Co. C – Mustered in September 1861 in Phila. at age 28, a 5-foot-3½ waterman. Captured at Petersburg June 29, 1864. Paroled at Jacksonville April 29, 1865. Recorded at Camp Discharge May 26, 1865. Discharged June 8, 1865.

Corporal William H. Simon, Co. C – Mustered in on Sept. 25, 1861, in Phila. at age 21, a gardener. Promoted to corporal. Wounded and captured at Reams Station, Va., June 29, 1864. Exchanged Aug. 28, 1864, at Annapolis, Md. Recorded at Camp Discharge Oct. 20, 1864. Discharged Nov. 3, 1864.

Corporal David B. Zilafro, Co. L – Mustered in September 1861 in Phila. at age 21, a farmer. Recorded at Camp Discharge Oct. 27, 1864. Discharged Nov. 9, 1864, expiration of term.

Private John Flicker, Co. C – Mustered in November 1862 in Phila. at age 20. Captured June 29, 1864, at Reams Station, Va. Imprisoned at Andersonville. Exchanged April 3, 1865. Recorded at Camp Discharge May 30, 1865. Hospitalized at Camp Discharge for diarrhea June 12, acute diarrhea June 21, 1865. Discharged by general order June 26, 1865.

Private Charles Gantz, Co. C – Mustered in August 1861 in Phila. at age 21, a gardener. Captured June 29, 1864, at Stony Creek, Va. Imprisoned at Andersonville. Paroled April 11, 1865, at Vicksburg, Miss. Recorded at Camp Discharge June 1865. Discharged June 26, 1865.

Private William H. Guie, Co. B – Mustered in on Aug. 19, 1861, in Phila. at age 20, a paper maker. Captured at Reams Station, Va., June 29, 1864. Held at Andersonville. Discharged May 13, 1865.

Private William Thompson, Co. E – Mustered in on Sept. 2, 1861, in Phila. at age 21, a laborer. Deserted Nov. 27, 1861, in Annapolis, Md.

Private John Keltner, Co. D – Mustered in October 1861 in Washington, D.C., at age 18, a farmer from Franklin County. Re-enlisted Nov. 11, 1863. Captured June 29, 1864, at Reams Station, Va. Survived Andersonville. Released May 9, 1865. Recorded at Camp Discharge May 27, 1865. Discharged June 8, 1865. Joined Veteran Volunteer Corps.

Private James R. Vandivort, Co. L – Enrolled Sept. 16, 1861, in Clarion at age 23, a laborer. Mustered in nine days later in Phila. Captured June 29, 1864. Held at Andersonville and Millen, Ga. Prisoner, date unknown. Discharged by general order June 21, 1865.

Private David Williams, Co. L – Mustered in August 1862 in Pittsburgh at age 21. Captured June 29, 1864. Held at Andersonville. Released April 28, 1865. Recorded at Camp Discharge May 31, 1865. Discharged June 21, 1865.

Private George H. Bishop, Co. B – Mustered in on Aug. 29, 1861, in Phila. at age 19, a music teacher from London, England. Captured at Reams Station, Va., June 29, 1864. Held at Andersonville. Released Nov. 23, 1864. Recorded at Camp Discharge Feb. 1, 1865. Hospitalized at camp for enlarged tonsils Feb. 8, 1865. Discharged Feb. 18, 1865.

Corporal Alvin H. Ingalls, Co. F – Enrolled Aug. 24, 1861, in Troy at age 21, a farmer. Promoted to corporal. Wounded and captured at Petersburg June 9, 1864. Recorded at Camp Discharge Oct. 1, 1864. Discharged Oct. 8, 1864, expiration of term.

Private Adam Hosbaugh, Co. C – Enlisted in Washington, D.C., Oct. 2, 1861, a whipmaker. Recorded at Camp Discharge Oct. 4, 1864. Discharged Oct. 6, 1864, expiration of term.

Sergeant William Fulton, Co. E – Mustered in on Aug. 21, 1861, in Phila. at age 19, a laborer. Promoted to corporal Feb. 19, 1862, to sergeant April 1, 1864. Captured June 29, 1864, at Reams Station, Va. Imprisoned at Andersonville. Released Jan. 7, 1865. Recorded at Camp Discharge Feb. 18, 1865. Discharged Feb. 24, 1865. Additional service with 17th Pa. Infantry, Co. C.

12th Pa. Cavalry (113th Pa. Infantry)

The regiment was recruited in 1861 in Philadelphia, Chester, and six other Pa. counties, plus West Virginia. It was involved in three engagements: Second Bull Run, Antietam, and Second Winchester. By the war's end, 142 enlisted men and officers succumbed to wounds or illness. Thirteen died at Andersonville. *Twenty-one of its men spent time at Camp Discharge, including five Andersonville survivors.*

Corporal John F. Gardner, Co. G – Mustered in on Feb. 14, 1865, in Phila. at age 21. Promoted to corporal. Captured Feb. 3, 1864. Imprisoned at Andersonville. Recorded at Camp Discharge April 2, 1865. Discharged by special order April 15, 1865. Join Veteran Volunteer Corps.

Private William Sullivan, Co. H – Mustered in on Feb. 18, 1862, at Harrisburg at age 22, a recruit. Captured Nov. 22, 1864, at Charleston, Va. Released Feb. 2, 1865, at Wilmington, N.C. Recorded at Camp Discharge April 1, 1865. Discharged by general order April 12, 1865.

Private A. Hotchkins, Co. B – Mustered in April 1864 in Meadville at age 22, a farmer. Captured at Halltown, Va., June 29, 1864. Recorded at Camp Discharge May 22, 1865. Discharged by general order June 23, 1865.

Corporal William H. Bowers, Co. I – Mustered in on Sept. 2, 1864, in Harrisburg at age 23, a clerk. Promoted to corporal, date unknown. Recorded at Camp Discharge May 31, 1865. Discharged June 20, 1865.

Private Rufus Cameron, Co. B – Mustered in May 1864 in Harpers Ferry at age 18, a printer from Altoona. Recorded at Camp Discharge May 31, 1865. Discharged by general order June 27, 1865.

Private John Peters, Co. I – Mustered in on Feb. 24, 1862, in Phila. at age 22. Recorded at Camp Discharge April 11, 1865, listed as sergeant. Not on regimental muster-out roll. Discharged April 14.

Private William Card, Co. A – Mustered in on April 25, 1864, in Meadville at age 19. Captured at Harpers Ferry June 29, 1864. Held at Andersonville, then sent to Millen (Ga.) prison on Nov. 11, 1864. Paroled at Dalton, Va., May 7, 1865. Recorded at Camp Discharge May 26, 1865. Hospitalized at camp for acute diarrhea June 3, 1865. Discharged by general order July 5, 1865.

Private Christian/Charles Speece, Co. G – Mustered in February 1864 in Harrisburg at age 22. Captured June 29, 1864, at Reams Station, Va. Held at Andersonville, then to Millen, Ga., on Nov. 11, 1864. Paroled at Resaca, Ga., May 14, 1865. Recorded at Camp Discharge May 26, 1865. Discharged by general order June 5, 1865.

Private Jacob Walters, Co. G – Mustered in January 1862 in Phila. at age 18. Taken prisoner June 29, 1864. At Reams Station, Va. Sent to Andersonville, then to Millen Nov. 11, 1864. Paroled at Savannah May 7, 1865. Recorded at Camp Discharge May 25, 1865. Discharged by general order June 5, 1865.

Private William F. Johnson, Co. E – Mustered in February 1864 in Harrisburg, age 21, a machinist. POW held at Andersonville, then sent to Millen, Ga., Nov. 11, 1864. Recorded at Camp Discharge May 26, 1865. Discharged June 2, 1864.

Private Charles P. Johnson, Co. I – Mustered in on Feb. 13, 1862, in Phila. at age 35. Discharged by general order April 20, 1865.

Private David McWilliams, Co. E – Mustered in on Nov. 11, 1861, in Phila. at age 42. Recorded at Camp Discharge Nov. 28, 1864. Hospitalized at camp for "Int. Fever Tertian" (malarial fever) Nov. 29, 1864. Discharged March 1, 1865.

Private Anton Wentzel, Co. E – Mustered in on Dec. 31, 1861, in Phila., a recruit from Lancaster. Sick in hospital in York at muster out. Recorded at Camp Discharge March 2, 1865. Hospitalized at camp for "Cyavel" March 25, 1865. Forwarded to Camp Cadwalader. Discharged July 24, 1865.

Private Thomas F. Brady, Co. F – Mustered in April 1864 in Harrisburg at age 21, a boatman born in Dublin. Captured Nov. 13, 1864, at Reys Ford, Va. Paroled at Washington, Ga., May 8, 1865. Recorded at Camp Discharge June 12, 1865. Discharged June 30, 1865.

Private W. H. Flaherty, Co. A – Hospitalized at Camp Discharge for scorbutus Jan. 12, 1865. Not listed on regimental rolls.

Private Robert W. Hodson, Co. K – Mustered in on Jan. 8, 1862, in Phila. at age 34. Recorded at Camp Discharge Feb. 24, 1865. Hospitalized at camp for bronchitis Feb. 26-28, 1865. Discharged by general order March 7, 1865.

Private John Scheiber/Shiber, Co. E – Mustered in on Nov. 11, 1861, in Phila. at age 31. Recorded at Camp Discharge Dec. 8, 1864. Discharged by general order Dec. 10, 1864.

Corporal Marzellus Jeleniewski, Co. A – Mustered in on Dec. 17, 1861, in Phila. at age 37. Promoted to corporal, date unknown. Reported sick in hospital at Phila. Recorded at Camp Discharge Jan. 4, 1865. Discharged by special order Jan. 4, 1865.

Private David T. Little, Co. M – Mustered into service March 3, 1862, in Loreto, Pa., at age 25. Recorded at Camp Discharge March 3, 1865. Discharged March 15, 1865.

Private John Whelan, Co. F – Mustered into service March 5, 1862, in Phila. at age 36. Absent, sick at muster out. Recorded at Camp Discharge March 7, 1865. Discharged March 15, 1865.

Private William McGinty, Co. K – Mustered into service March 15, 1862, in Phila. at age 30. Recorded at Camp Discharge March 25, 1865. Discharged March 29, 1865.

13th Pa. Cavalry (117th Pa. Volunteers)

Also known as the Irish Dragoons, the regiment was organized in 1861 with men from Philadelphia, Cumberland, Lycoming, Pike, and Wayne Counties. Saw action in 14 operations, including Wilderness, Spotsylvania Courthouse, Cold Harbor, and Petersburg. It lost 290 enlisted men and officers to wounds or sickness during service. They mustered out July 1865 in Raleigh, N.C. *Thirteen of its separated men, including four Andersonville survivors, passed through Camp Discharge.*

Private Daniel O'Leary, Co. A – Mustered in on Oct. 29, 1861. Recorded at Camp Discharge Oct. 31, 1864. Hospitalized there for "Int. Fever Tertian" (malarial fever) Nov. 16, 1864. Discharged Dec. 3, 1864, expiration of term.

Private Charles Williams, Co. A – Mustered in on May 24, 1864. Prisoner of war Sept. 29, 1864, to May 1, 1865. Treated at Camp Discharge Hospital for ecthyma May 30-June 1, 1865. Discharged by general order June 24, 1865.

Private Daniel Egan/Eagan, Co. E – Mustered in on Dec. 9, 1861. Captured June 24, 1864, at St. Mary's Church, Va. Held at Andersonville. Released from captivity Nov. 20, 1864. Recorded at Camp Discharge March 28, 1865. Hospitalized at camp for 'D. fr. M Disease' (debility from miasmatic disease) March 29-April 21, 1865. Discharged by special order April 22, 1865.

Private John Lowery, Co. B – Drafted. Wounded at Peeble's Farm, Va., Sept. 30, 1864. Transferred to 91st Pa. Infantry, Co. F, June 1, 1865.

Private Michael Dougherty, Co. B – Mustered in August 1862 in Phila. Held at Andersonville and survived. Exchanged April 5, 1865. Recorded at Camp Discharge May 24, 1865. Discharged June 24, 1865. Awarded Medal of Honor.

Sergeant John M. Lafferty, Co. L – Mustered in on Nov. 9, 1861. Captured June 17, 1864, at Trevilian Station, Va. Held at Andersonville and survived. Exchanged April 1, 1865. Recorded at Camp Discharge May 19, 1865.

Sergeant Walter Webb, Co. B – Mustered in on Oct. 24, 1861. Held at Andersonville and survived. Exchanged April 1, 1865. Recorded May 20, 1865, at Camp Discharge.

Private George W. Huth, Co. A – Mustered in on Dec. 21, 1861. Recorded at Camp Discharge May 26, 1865. Discharged by general order June 1, 1865.

Private John J. Weaver, Co. M – Mustered in on Aug. 18, 1863. Recorded at Camp Discharge May 11, 1865. Discharged by general order May 22, 1865.

Private Charles W. Johnson, Co. I – Mustered in on April 27, 1862. Prisoner June 12-Dec. 13, 1864, whereabouts not listed. Recorded at Camp Discharge May 18, 1865. Discharged by general order May 27, 1865.

Private Michael Norton, Co. A – Mustered in on Feb. 16, 1861. Prisoner of war March 9-Nov. 30, 1864. Entered Camp Discharge March 11, 1865. Hospitalized at camp for chronic diarrhea March 12, 1865. Discharged by general order March 15, 1865.

Private W. Sullivan, Co. E? – On Camp Discharge Hospital Register as treated for constipation April 3-7, 1865. Not on regimental rolls.

Private Charles B. Capewell, Co. I – Mustered in on April 10, 1862. Recorded at Camp Discharge April 11, 1865. Discharged by special order April 12.

19th Pa. Cavalry (180th Pa. Regiment)

The regiment was organized in 1863 with men from Philadelphia and a few from Huntingdon County. The men took part in the Battle of Nashville and 30 smaller actions. They lost 124 enlisted men and officers to injury or disease during service. *Thirty-two of its men passed through Camp Discharge, including twenty-two Andersonville survivors.*

Private John Feehan, Co. D – Mustered in on Aug. 15, 1863. Captured Dec. 17, 1864. Captured Dec. 17, 1864. Held at Andersonville and survived. Exchanged April 15, 1865. Recorded at Camp Discharge May 24, 1865. Discharged by general order June 5, 1865.

Private William Jacobs, Co. M – Mustered in on Oct. 17, 1863. Captured Dec. 19, 1864. Held at Andersonville and survived. Exchanged April 15, 1865. Recorded at Camp Discharge May 25, 1865. Discharged by general order June 5, 1865.

Sergeant James F. Foster, Co. M – Mustered in on Aug. 24, 1864. Captured at Nashville, Tenn., Dec. 17, 1864. Held at Andersonville. Recorded at Camp Discharge May 19, 1865. Discharged by general order June 16, 1865.

Private Henry Mason, Co. K – Absent, sick at muster out. Recorded at Camp Discharge Oct.18, 1864-July 31, 1865.

Private Henry McKnight, Co. E – Mustered in on Sept. 15, 1863. Recorded at Camp Discharge June 26, 1865-July31, 1865. Discharged by general order July 28, 1865.

Sergeant Samuel Baker, Co. C (Co. L) – Captured at Hollow Tree Gap, Tenn., Dec. 17, 1864. Andersonville survivor (wrongly listed as "Pvt. Saml Baker of 19th Pa. Infantry"). Recorded at Camp Discharge June 26, 1865. Discharged by general order July 19, 1865. Joined Veteran Volunteer Corps.

Private Calvin Morrison, Co. G – Mustered in on Aug. 12, 1863. Recorded at Camp Discharge May 22, 1865. Immediately hospitalized for diarrhea. Died at Camp Discharge Hospital July 31, 1865.

Private Andrew C. Patterson, Co. H – Mustered in on Sept. 2, 1863. Prisoner Feb. 16, 1864-March 30, 1865. Held at Andersonville and survived. Exchanged April 1, 1865. Recorded at Camp Discharge June 17, 1865. Discharged by general order June 27, 1865.

Private Francis M. Primm, Co. M – Mustered in on Aug. 9, 1863. Captured Nov. 23, 1864, at Franklin, Tenn. Held at Andersonville and survived. Released April 4, 1865. Recorded at Camp Discharge June 15, 1865. Discharged by general order June 24, 1865.

Private John Barton, Co. F – Enrolled Aug. 4, 1863. Recorded at Camp Discharge June 1, 1865. Discharged by general order June 24, 1865.

Corporal John R. Brainard, Co. F – Mustered in on July 8, 1863. Captured, held at Andersonville. Recorded at Camp Discharge May 31, 1865. Discharged by general order June 27, 1865.

Private Benjamin O. Carpenter, Co. A – Mustered in on June 23, 1863. Captured Dec. 26, 1864, at Nashville. Held at Andersonville. Exchanged April 5, 1865. Paroled in Jacksonville on April 28, 1865. Recorded at Camp Discharge May 20, 1865. Discharged by general order June 5, 1865.

Private John Corbett, Co. A – Mustered in on June 23, 1863. Captured Nov. 24, 1864. Held at Andersonville. Paroled April 28, 1865. Recorded at Camp Discharge May 20, 1865. Discharged by general order June 5, 1865.

Private Edward Mullen, Co. C – Enrolled July 7, 1863. Captured, held at Andersonville, and survived. Exchanged April 1, 1865. Recorded at Camp Discharge May 20, 1865. Discharged by general order June 5, 1865.

Private Charles Austin Co. E/D – Enrolled Aug. 21, 1863. Captured Nov. 24, 1864. Held at Andersonville and survived. Paroled April 28, 1865. Recorded at Camp Discharge May 22, 1865. Discharged by special order June 8, 1865.

Private William Taylor Co. L – Mustered in on Aug. 17, 1863. Captured Dec. 17, 1864. Held at Andersonville. Exchanged April 1, 1865. Paroled April 28, 1865. Recorded at Camp Discharge May 22, 1865. Discharged by general order June 5, 1865.

Private Jacob Snyder, Co. E – Mustered in Oct. 19, 1862. Captured Dec. 24, 1864. Held at Andersonville and survived. Exchanged April 1, 1865. Paroled April 28, 1865. Recorded at Camp Discharge May 22, 1865. Hospitalized at camp for diarrhea May 23, 1865. Discharged by general order June 8, 1865.

Corporal Joseph Martin, Co. D – Enrolled Aug. 8, 1863. Recorded at Camp Discharge May 22, 1865. Dishonorably discharged April 26, 1865.

Private John A. Whiteman, Co. M – Mustered in on Aug. 18, 1864. Captured Nov. 24, 1864. Held at Andersonville and survived. Exchanged April 1, 1865. Paroled April 28, 1865. Recorded at Camp Discharge May 22, 1865. Discharged by general order June 27, 1865.

Private Miles M. Hampson/Hampton, Co. M – Mustered in on Dec. 17, 1863. Captured at Memphis Nov. 23, 1864. Held at Andersonville and survived. Recorded at Camp Discharge May 22, 1865. Hospitalized there for headache May 28-29, 1865. Discharged by general order June 16, 1865.

Private Darius Thomas, Co. G – Mustered in on Sept. 10, 1863. Captured at Guntown, Miss., June 10, 1864. Held at Andersonville and survived. Recorded at Camp Discharge May 22, 1865. Discharged by general order June 16, 1865.

Sergeant John Smeigh, Co. D – Mustered in on July 14, 1863. Captured Nov. 24, 1864, at Franklin, Tenn. Held at Andersonville. Recorded at Camp Discharge May 22, 1865. Camp's hospital register might list him as "J.S. Mead, 17th Pa. Cavalry, Co. F." (no such person). Discharged by general order June 16, 1865.

Sergeant Charles H. Hunt, Co. M – Mustered in on Aug. 9, 1863. Taken prisoner at Nashville Dec. 17, 1864. Held at Andersonville and survived. Recorded at Camp Discharge May 22, 1865. Hospitalized there for ringworms June 8, 1865. Discharged by general order June 16, 1865.

Private William Robson, Co. K – Mustered in September 1863 in Phila. at age 18. Captured March 10, 1864. Held at Andersonville and survived. Recorded at Camp Discharge May 30, 1865. Mustered out June 16, 1865.

Sergeant James Martin, Co. E – Mustered in on July 8, 1863. Captured at Guntown, Miss., June 13, 1864. Held at Andersonville. Exchanged April 15, 1865. Recorded at Camp Discharge May 22, 1865. Hospitalized there for scabies May 31 and abscess of hand June 7, 1865. Discharged by general order June 16, 1865.

Private John Havens, Co. L – Mustered in on Sept. 24, 1863. Taken prisoner June 11, 1864. Held at Andersonville. Sent to Millen Oct. 31, 1864. Exchanged April 1, 1865. Paroled April 29, 1865. Recorded at Camp Discharge May 26, 1865. Discharged by general order June 5, 1865.

Sergeant Frederick R. Plfander, Co. D – Mustered in on July 25, 1863. Taken prisoner Dec. 17, 1864. Held at Andersonville and survived; exchanged April 15, 1865. Paroled April 28, 1865. Recorded at Camp Discharge May 26, 1865. Discharged by general order June 8, 1865.

Private Hamilton Connor, Co. E – Enrolled Sept. 17, 1863. Recorded at Camp Discharge June 7, 1865. Discharged by general order July 3, 1865.

Private Victor V. Dougherty, Co. M – Enrolled Aug. 25, 1863. Deserted. Returned. Recorded at Camp Discharge June 26, 1865. Discharged by general order Nov. 24, 1865.

Private Joseph B. Jones, Co. H – Enrolled Sept. 30, 1863. Recorded at Camp Discharge June 27, 1865. Discharged by general order July 28, 1865.

Quartermaster Sergeant Henry Moser, Co. B – Enrolled June 30, 1863. Recorded at Camp Discharge June 27, 1865. Hospitalized there for glaucoma June 29, 1865. Discharged by general order July 26, 1865.

Private Henry M. Lahr, Cos. L, C, H – Enrolled Aug. 23, 1864. Recorded at Camp Discharge June 26, 1865. Discharged by general order July 25, 1865.

20th Pa. Cavalry (181st Pa. Regiment)

The regiment was organized in 1863 as a six-month regiment, drawn from Philadelphia and six counties, including Montgomery, Chester, and Bucks. The men fought at New Market, Berkeley Springs, and Lynchburg. In total, 128 enlisted men and officers succumbed to injury or illness. The unit was in Grand Review in D.C. *Five of its men passed through Camp Discharge.*

Private Vernon B. Thomas, Co. F (Bugler) – Enrolled Jan. 15, 1864. Recorded at Camp Discharge June 20, 1865. Discharged by special order June 23, 1865.

Corporal George W. Derrick, Co. M – Wounded April 30. 1865. Recorded at Camp Discharge May 26, 1865. Hospitalized there for a gunshot wound of right hip May 27-29, 1865. Discharged by general order June 2, 1865.

Private James Neville, Co. G – Recorded at Camp Discharge Oct. 8, 1864. Discharged by special order Jan. 6, 1864.

Private Alexander Knepp, Co. B – Enrolled Jan. 27, 1864. Absent, sick at regimental muster out. Recorded at Camp Discharge July 21-31, 1865.

Private Thomas F. Amos, Co. B – Enlisted July 24, 1863. Recorded at Camp Discharge Oct. 10, 1864. Dropped Dec. 5, 1864.

ARTILLERY

1st Pa. Light Artillery (43rd Pa. Volunteers)

The regiment was recruited in 1861 in Philadelphia and numerous Pa. counties. Saw action in 11 engagements, including Malvern Hill, Second Bull Run, Antietam, Fredericksburg, and Fair Oaks. In total, 277 enlisted men and officers succumbed to injury or sickness during service. *Three of its men passed through Camp Discharge.*

Private Martin Sullivan, Co. H – Mustered in May 1864 in Phila. at age 39. Recorded at Camp Discharge July 6, 1865. Immediately hospitalized there for debility from asthma. Mustered out July 7, 1865, but remained at camp through July 31.

Private John Leidy, Co. H – Mustered in February 1864 in Phila. at age 20. Mustered out with battery June 27, 1865. Recorded at Camp Discharge beginning June 30, 1865.

Private Jacob Fremoyer, Co. G – Mustered into service Sept. 15, 1861, at Camp Tennally, Washington, D.C. Entered Camp Discharge Sept. 23, 1864. Died on Dec. 2, 1864, at Haddington Hospital in Philadelphia.

2nd Pa. Heavy Artillery (112th Pa. Regiment)

The regiment was recruited in 1862 from Philadelphia and Allegheny, Franklin, and Monroe Counties. With over 5,000 men, it was the largest regiment in the Union Army. The men saw action at Petersburg and Chaffin's Farm. By the war's end, 616 enlisted men and officers died of injuries or illness. The unit mustered out at City Point., Va., in January 1866. *Thirty-five of its men were at Camp Discharge.*

Private Samuel B. Watson, Co. H – Mustered in on Nov. 11, 1861, in Phila. at age 22, from White Haven. Captured Sept. 29, 1864. Paroled March 20, 1865. Recorded at Camp Discharge March 22, 1865. Discharged by special order April 5, 1865.

Private Gilbert Roehm, Co. G – Mustered in on Dec. 9, 1861, in Phila. at age 19. Captured Sept. 29, 1864, at Chaffin's Farm, Va. Returned March 1, 1865. Recorded at Camp Discharge April 12, 1865. Discharged April 27, 1865.

Private John B. Fletcher, Co. L – Mustered in January 1864 in Phila. at age 18. POW Sept. 29, 1864-April 28, 1865. Recorded at Camp Discharge May 24, 1864. Discharged by general order June 30, 1865.

Private George A. Campbell, Co. H – Mustered in September 1862 in Phila. at age 20. Captured July 29, 1864. Paroled March 20, 1865. Absent, sick at regimental muster out. Recorded at Camp Discharge May 29, 1865. Hospitalized there for scurvy May 30, 1865. Discharged by general order June 14, 1865.

Sergeant John Fassett, Co. G – Enrolled November 1861 in Phila. at age 21. Promoted to sergeant June 1, 1863. Wounded in action at Chaffin's Farm, Va., Sept. 29, 1864. Sent to US Hospital, Portsmouth Grove, R.I. Recorded at Camp Discharge Nov. 21, 1864. Hospitalized at camp for a gunshot wound of left knee Nov. 29, 1864. Discharged from service Dec. 3, 1864, expiration of term.

Sergeant William Franklin, Co. A – Mustered in on Aug. 24, 1862, in Phila. at age 28. Recorded at Camp Discharge May 10, 1865. Discharged by general order May 13, 1865.

Private John J. Vaney/Viney, Co. H – Mustered in December 1862 in Phila. at age 23. Entered Camp Discharge May 10, 1865. Discharged by general order May 13, 1865.

Private Edward Reading, Co. H – Mustered in February 1864 in Phila. at age 27. Promoted to corporal, then sergeant. Wounded at Chaffin's Farm, Va., Sept. 29, 1864. Recorded at Camp Discharge May 11, 1865. Discharged by general order May 12, 1865.

Private Daniel Dougherty, Co. D – Mustered in on Nov. 25, 1861, in Phila. at age 21. Recorded at Camp Discharge Dec. 27, 1865. Discharged Jan. 6, 1865, expiration of term.

Private Paul Weber, Co. B – Mustered in July 1864 in Phila. at age 19. Captured at Chaffin's Farm, Va., Sept. 29, 1864. Absent, in hospital, at expiration of term. Recorded at Camp Discharge July 14, 1865. Discharged July 31, 1865.

Private Charles M. Ditslear, Co. C – Mustered in April 1864 in Harrisburg at age 22, a laborer from Franklin County. Recorded at Camp Discharge June 29, 1865. Hospitalized there for constipation July 2, 1865. Discharged by general order July 21, 1865.

Private Elliand Romig, Co. A – Mustered in February 1864 in Frankford at age 29. Captured at Cold Harbor, Va., June 2, 1864. Recorded at Camp Discharge June 29, 1865. Discharged by general order July 7, 1865.

Private Samuel Cassiday, Co. A – Mustered in February 1864 in Hollidaysburg at age 25, a laborer. Reported missing in action June 2, 1864. Recorded at Camp Discharge June 29, 1865. Discharged by general order July 12, 1865.

Private John W. Chesser, Co. G – Mustered in November 1861 in Phila. at age 28. Recorded at Camp Discharge Nov. 21, 1864, reporting from US Hospital, Portsmouth Grove, R.I. Admitted to Camp Discharge Hospital to convalesce from typhoid fever Nov. 22, 1864. Discharged from service Dec. 3, 1864, expiration of term.

Private Charles B. Skinner, Co. L – Mustered in October 1861 in Phila. at age 43. Absent, sick in confinement, at regimental muster out. Recorded at Camp Discharge Nov. 21, 1864, reporting from Washington, D.C. Admitted to camp hospital for constipation Nov. 22, 1864, for erysipelas of left arm Dec.1, 1864. Discharged from service by special order Dec. 3, 1864.

Private Frederick Lantz, Co. H – Mustered in on Nov. 6, 1861, in Phila. at age 31. At Camp Discharge, hospitalized for gunshot wound of left leg Dec. 3, 1864. Discharged from service Dec. 8, 1864, expiration of term.

Private Leonard Dorwarth, Co. A – Mustered in on Nov. 1, 1861, in Phila. at age 28. Hospitalized at Camp Discharge for catarrh and enlarged tonsil Dec. 20, 1864. Discharged from service Dec. 29, 1864, expiration of term.

Sergeant Samuel Neely, Co. G – Mustered in on Dec. 2, 1861, in Phila. at age 35. Promoted to corporal, then sergeant. Wounded at Chaffin's Farm, Va., Sept. 29, 1864. Admitted to Camp Discharge Hospital to treat gunshot wound of left thigh Dec. 22, 1864. Discharged Dec. 22, 1864, expiration of term.

Private John Kerr, Co. G – Mustered in on Dec. 23, 1861, in Phila. at age 23. Transferred from Battery E. Deserted April 14, 1862. Returned March 30, 1863. Discharged Nov. 22, 1864. Entered Camp Dec. 28, 1864, and hospitalized there for gonorrhea Jan. 3-14, 1865.

Private Joshua H. Wallens, Co. I – Mustered in as sergeant Dec. 30, 1861, in Phila. at age 21, a blacksmith. At Camp Discharge, hospitalized to treat gunshot wound of left forearm Feb. 9, 1865. Discharged from service Feb. 11, 1865, expiration of term.

Sergeant William H. Cox, Co. K – Mustered in February 1864 in Phila. at age 20. Captured at Cold Harbor, Va., June 2, 1864. Held at Andersonville and survived. Paroled at Vicksburg, Miss., April 12, 1865. Recorded at Camp Discharge May 10, 1865. Hospitalized there for constipation May 20-24 and ecthyma May 24, 1865. Discharged from service by general order June 10, 1865.

Private David Robertson, Co. L – Mustered in on Nov. 25, 1861, in Phila. at age 28. Promoted to corporal, then sergeant. Reduced to ranks Jan. 20, 1864. At Camp Discharge, hospitalized for sprain Dec. 3, 1864. Discharged from service by special order Dec. 10, 1864.

Private William Aregood, Co. H – Mustered in on Dec. 6, 1861, in Phila. at age 33. Wounded at Petersburg June 18, 1864. Admitted to Camp Discharge Hospital for catarrh Dec. 14, 1864. Discharged from service Dec. 14, 1864, expiration of term.

Private Henry J. Reifsnyder, Co. M – Mustered in on Oct. 5, 1861, in Phila. at age 21, a farmer. Captured Oct. 12, 1863, at Sulphur Springs, Va. Admitted to Camp Discharge Hospital for impetigo Jan. 6, 1865. Discharged Jan. 29, 1865. Joined Veteran Volunteer Corps.

Private Richard S. Lewis, Co. D – Mustered in on Sept. 24, 1861, in Doylestown at age 33. Recorded at Camp Discharge Sept. 24, 1864. Discharged Oct. 4, 1864, expiration of term.

Private Henry L. Buck, Co. D – Mustered in on Sept. 24, 1861, in Doylestown at age 23. Recorded at Camp Discharge Sept. 24, 1864. Discharged Oct. 4, 1864, expiration of term.

Private Charles T. G. Ruley, Co. G – Mustered into service Nov. 19, 1864, in Phila. at age 18. Recorded at Camp Discharge Dec. 3, 1864. Discharged Dec. 10, 1864, expiration of term.

Private James Straun, Co. E – Mustered in on Nov. 21, 1861, in Phila. at age 43. Recorded at Camp Discharge Dec. 7, 1864. Discharged Dec. 12, 1864, expiration of term.

Private Christian F. Hanson, Co. G – Mustered in on Dec. 9, 1861, in Phila. at age 33. Entered Camp Discharge Dec 15, 1864. Discharged Dec. 16, 1864, expiration of term.

Private Frank C. Miner, Co. H – Mustered in on Dec. 10, 1861, in Phila. at age 21. Entered Camp Discharge Dec. 16, 1864. Discharged Dec. 19, 1864, expiration of term. Additional service with 6th Pa. Infantry.

Private Henry Jones, Co. D – Mustered in on Dec. 2, 1861, in Phila. at age 27. Deserted June 4, 1863. Returned. Entered Camp Discharge Dec. 17, 1864. Discharged Dec. 21, 1864, expiration of term.

Private John Saier, Co. B – Mustered in on Dec. 20, 1861, in Phila. at age 38, a machinist born in Germany. Entered Camp Discharge Jan. 4, 1865. Discharged Jan. 6, 1865, expiration of term.

Private Frank Anderson, Co. E – Mustered in on Jan. 11, 1862, in Phila. at age 18. Entered Camp Discharge Jan. 11, 1865. Discharged Jan. 16, 1865, expiration of term. Discharged for disability.

Private William H. Cunningham, Co. K – Enrolled Jan. 17, 1862, in Watsontown, Pa., at age 34. Mustered in Jan. 29, 1862, in Phila. Recorded at Camp Discharge Jan. 18, 1865. Discharged from service Jan. 28, 1865, expiration of term.

Private Samuel Mathews, Co. E – Mustered into service Dec. 24, 1861, in Phila. at age 42. Absent, sick in hospital, at regimental muster out. Entered Camp Discharge Jan. 18, 1865. Discharged Jan. 19, 1865.

3rd Pa. Heavy Artillery (152nd Pa. Volunteers)

The regiment was organized in 1863 with men from Philadelphia and various Pa. counties. They saw action at Suffolk, Gettysburg, and Petersburg. After the war, the unit provided the guard for Jefferson Davis's imprisonment at Fortress Monroe. By war's end, 234 enlisted men and officers succumbed to wounds or ailments. *Nine of its men were at Camp Discharge, including two Andersonville survivors.*

Private John Kelly, Co. A – Mustered in on Jan. 11, 1862, in Phila. at age 20, a brick maker. Captured at Smithfield, Va., Feb. 1, 1864. Released Nov. 18, 1864, at Savannah. Recorded at Camp Discharge Feb. 10, 1865. Discharged by special order March 1, 1865.

Private William Rutz, Co. A – Mustered in on Jan. 18, 1862, in Phila. at age 35, a butcher. Captured Feb. 1, 1864, at Smithfield, Va. Held at Andersonville and survived. Released at Charleston, S.C., Dec. 11, 1864. Recorded at Camp Discharge Feb. 14, 1865. Discharged by special order March 3, 1865.

Private Morris Miller, Co. A – Mustered in on Jan. 18, 1862, in Phila. at age 20, a farmer. Captured at Smithfield, Va., Feb. 1, 1864. Released at Charleston, S.C., Dec. 10, 1864. Recorded at Camp Discharge Feb. 24, 1865. Discharged by special order March 7, 1865.

Private Robert W. Hodson, Co. K – Recorded at Camp Discharge Feb. 24, 1865. No record on Bates or Pa. Veteran Card.

Corporal James M. Emory/Emery, Co. A – Mustered in October 1862 in Phila. at age 18. Captured at Smithfield, Va., Feb. 1, 1864. Imprisoned at Andersonville. Recorded at Camp Discharge May 19, 1865. Hospitalized there for scorbutus June 1, 1865. Discharged from service by general order June 16, 1865.

Private John M. Sowers, Co. F – Mustered in on Feb. 24, 1864, in Carlisle at age 40. Recorded at Camp Discharge May 10, 1865. Discharged by general order May 13, 1865.

Private William L. Van Horn, Co. H – Mustered in December 1862 in Phila. at age 25. Recorded at Camp Discharge May 16, 1865. Discharged by general order May 22, 1865.

Private William Romaine, Co. A – Mustered into service Dec. 6, 1861, in Phila. at age 34, a mechanic. Recorded at Camp Discharge Jan. 10, 1865. Also discharged Jan. 10, 1865, expiration of term.

Private Jacob Christian, Co. B – Mustered into service Jan. 20, 1862, in Phila. at age 20, an ivory carver, 5-feet-3. Recorded at Camp Discharge Feb. 4, 1865. Discharged by special order, Feb. 8, 1865.

Durell's Independent Light Artillery Battery D

The regiment was recruited in Berks and Bucks Counties and organized in Doylestown. The first men were mustered in on Sept. 24, 1861. They saw action at Bull Run, South Mountain, Fredericksburg, Vicksburg, and Petersburg. Twenty-four died in the line of duty. The unit disbanded and mustered out June 13, 1865, in Philadelphia. *Nine of its men transited Camp Discharge.*

Private William G. Ganster – Mustered in on Dec. 18, 1861. Hospitalized at Camp Discharge to treat amputated right leg Jan.5, 1865. Discharged from service Jan. 6, 1865, expiration of term.

Private William Arnold – Mustered in on Aug. 23, 1864. Hospitalized at Camp Discharge for constipation June 8, 1865. Mustered out with battery June 13, 1865.

Private Asa W. Clark – Mustered in on Feb. 20, 1864. Hospitalized at Camp Discharge for acute diarrhea June 8, 1865. Mustered out with battery June 13, 1865.

Private Charles Kennedy – Mustered in on March 23, 1864. Hospitalized at Camp Discharge for acute diarrhea June 8, 1865. Mustered out with battery June 13, 1865.

Private Anton Kerfies/Kerfus – Mustered in on Sept. 21, 1864. Substitute recruit. Hospitalized at Camp Discharge for congestive liver June 8, 1865. Mustered out with battery June 13, 1865.

Private George B. W. Neiman – Mustered in on Jan. 19, 1864. Hospitalized at Camp Discharge for enteritis June 8, 1865. Mustered out with battery June 13, 1865.

Private Daniel D. Hart – Mustered in on March 17, 1864. Hospitalized at Camp Discharge for constipation June 8, 1865. Mustered out with battery June 13, 1865. Joined Veteran Volunteer Corps.

Private Eli Yeager – Mustered in on Aug. 25, 1864. Hospitalized at Camp Discharge for acute diarrhea June 11, 1865. Mustered out with battery June 13, 1865.

Sergeant Elias K. Cooper – Mustered in on Sept. 24, 1861. Hospitalized at Camp Discharge for constipation June 12, 1865. Mustered out with battery June 13, 1865. Joined Veteran Volunteer Corps.

PART II

The garrison guards, in order of their units' arrival at Camp Discharge.

186th Pa. Infantry (Co. G)

The regiment was recruited in 1864 in Philadelphia for three-year terms. Its colonel was appointed as the city's provost marshal, and the regiment was assigned provost duty. It saw no combat. Company G was assigned to guard Camp Discharge beginning in November 1864, and most of its men spent time in the camp hospital. Company G's full roster of 108 officers and enlisted men is shown here.

Captain David P. Billington – Mustered into service June 22, 1864. Treated at Camp Discharge Hospital for hemorrhoids November 1864. Mustered out with company Aug. 15, 1865.

2nd Lieutenant Joseph A. Kauffman – Mustered in on May 30, 1864. Mustered out with company Aug. 15, 1865.

Sergeant William N. Nycum – Mustered in on March 24, 1864. Promoted from corporal Dec. 1, 1864. Mustered out with company Aug. 15, 1865.

Sergeant R.H. Magill – Mustered in on March 24, 1864. Admitted to Camp Discharge Hospital for balanitis (genital inflammation) Nov. 25–Dec. 2, 1864. Mustered out with company Aug. 15, 1865.

Sergeant Clarence A. Nourse – Mustered into service March 24, 1864. Promoted from corporal Dec. 1, 1864. Mustered out with company Aug. 15, 1865.

Sergeant John Jacobs – Mustered in on March 24, 1864. Admitted to Camp Discharge Hospital for scabies Jan. 13-20, 1865. Mustered out with company Aug. 15, 1865.

Sergeant William H. Rambo – Mustered in on March 21, 1864. Admitted to Camp Discharge Hospital for hand abscess Jan. 16-20, 1865. Mustered out with company Aug. 15, 1865.

Corporal T.L. Kirkwood – Mustered in on March 24, 1864. Promoted to corporal Dec. 1, 1864. Hospitalized at Camp Discharge for contusion of leg Jan. 2-12, 1865. Mustered out with company Aug. 15, 1865.

Corporal John Harris – Mustered in on March 24, 1864. Promoted to corporal Dec. 1, 1864. Admitted to Camp Discharge Hospital for "inter fev tertian" Feb. 20-March 8, 1865, and constipation May 23, 1865. Mustered out with company Aug. 15, 1865.

Corporal Lewis K. Todd – Mustered into service March 24, 1864. Mustered out with company Aug. 15, 1865.

Corporal J. Hogentogler – Mustered in on March 24, 1864. Hospitalized at Camp Discharge for gonorrhea Nov.14-Dec. 2, 1864, and catarrh Dec.19, 1864-Jan. 2, 1865.Mustered out with company Aug. 15, 1865.

Corporal Lamb'n F. Thomas – Mustered into service March 24, 1864. Promoted to corporal Oct. 1, 1864. Mustered out with company Aug. 15, 1865.

Corporal William Farthing – Mustered in on March 24, 1864. Mustered out with company Aug. 15, 1865. Admitted to Camp Discharge Hospital for catarrh Dec. 14-21 and ecthyma Dec. 29, 1865.

Corporal Abram Shaffer – Mustered into service March 24, 1864. Promoted to corporal Oct. 1, 1864. Mustered out with company Aug. 15, 1865.

Musician Edward Shiffert – Mustered in on April 11, 1864. Hospitalized at Camp Discharge for ecthyma Dec. 13-23, 1864, erysipelas Feb. 8-14, 1865, catarrh March 9-11, 1865, diarrhea March 19-25, 1865, hand-wound April 21, 1865, erysipelas May 22, 1865. Mustered out with company Aug. 15, 1865.

Musician Austin M. Fithian – Mustered in on March 24, 1864. Mustered out with company Aug. 15, 1865.

Private W. Pearson – Mustered in on July 19, 1864. Admitted to Camp Discharge Hospital for "intermittent f. Tert." Nov. 13, 1864, intermittent fever Dec. 7-11, 1864, catarrh Feb. 11, 1865, and ague March 4, 1865. Mustered out with company Aug. 15, 1865.

Private James Riley/Reily – Mustered in on March 24, 1864. Hospitalized at Camp Discharge for ecthyma intertrigo (skin inflammation) Nov. 13-14, 1864, secondary syphilis Dec. 4-9, 1864, and constipation March 24 and April 12, 1865. Mustered out with company Aug. 15, 1865.

Private Dennis Kelley – Mustered in on March 24, 1864. Admitted to Camp Discharge Hospital for lumbago Nov. 13-17, 1864. Deserted Aug. 4, 1865.

Private Charles Fraser – Mustered in on March 24, 1864. Hospitalized at Camp Discharge for nonsyphilitic bubo (inflamed node) Nov. 13-28, 1864, cynanche (sore throat) Feb. 14-18, 1865. Mustered out with company Aug. 15, 1865.

Private William Overaker – Mustered in on March 24, 1864. Admitted to Camp Discharge Hospital for jaundice Nov.13-Dec. 4, 1864. Mustered out with company Aug. 15, 1865.

Private David T. Romig – Mustered in on March 24, 1864. Hospitalized at Camp Discharge for catarrh Nov.13-17, Dec. 20-22, 1864, and Feb. 23-April 3, 1865. Mustered out with company Aug. 15, 1865.

Private Joel J. Greenfield – Mustered in on July 29, 1864. Hospitalized at Camp Discharge for "intermittent f tertian" Nov. 15-23, 1864. Mustered out with company Aug. 15, 1865.

Private James Warner – Mustered in on March 24, 1864. Hospitalized at Camp Discharge for catarrh Nov16-18, 1864. Mustered out with company Aug. 15, 1865.

Private James Rodgers – Mustered in on March 24, 1864. Admitted to Camp Discharge Hospital for tertiary syphilis Nov. 18, 1864. Deserted Dec. 17, 1864, resolution not recorded. Mustered out with company Aug. 15, 1865.

Private George Miller – Mustered in on Aug. 2, 1864. Hospitalized at Camp Discharge for catarrh Nov. 20-21, 1864, for stomatitis (mouth inflammation) Feb. 26, 1865. Mustered out with company Aug. 15, 1865.

Private George Eschleman – Mustered in on March 24, 1864. Admitted to Camp Discharge Hospital "for int. Fever tertian" Nov. 21-25, 1864. Mustered out with company Aug. 15, 1865.

Private Martin Zell – Mustered in on March 24, 1864. Admitted to Camp Discharge Hospital for gonorrhea Nov. 21, 1864-Dec. 7, 1865, for catarrh Dec. 28-29, 1865, for gonorrhea Feb. 24 and May 1-23, 1865. Mustered out with company Aug. 15, 1865.

Private William Stubbs – Mustered in on March 24, 1864. Admitted to Camp Discharge Hospital for catarrh Nov. 22-27, 1864. Deserted Feb. 14, 1865, disposition unrecorded.

Private John W. Fisher – Mustered in on March 24, 1864. Hospitalized at Camp Discharge for ecthyma Nov. 23-4, 1864, for catarrh Dec. 9-12, 1864. Mustered out with company Aug. 15, 1865.

Private John Collum – Mustered in on March 24, 1864. Admitted to Camp Discharge Hospital for gonorrhea Nov. 25-Dec. 6, 1864, and for rheumatism and conjunctivitis Dec. 9, 1864. Deserted Aug. 4, 1865.

Private Lucius Foor – Mustered in on March 24, 1864. Admitted to Camp Discharge Hospital for "conv. From typhoid fever" Nov. 26, 1864. Mustered out with company Aug. 15, 1865.

Private John Vanhorn – Mustered in on Aug. 5, 1864. Hospitalized at Camp Discharge for pleurisy Nov. 27-Dec. 17, 1864. Mustered out with company Aug. 15, 1865.

Private James McCartney – Mustered in on March 24, 1864. Admitted to Camp Discharge Hospital for gonorrhea Nov. 27-Dec. 1, 1864. Absent, in arrest, at muster out.

Private Henry Glazier – Mustered in on March 24, 1864. Hospitalized at Camp Discharge for "tert. Int" (fever) Nov. 29-Dec. 5, 1864. Mustered out with company Aug. 15, 1865.

Private John Rhoads – Mustered in on June 22, 1864. Admitted to Camp Discharge Hospital for sore throat Nov. 29-Dec. 6, 1864. Mustered out with company Aug. 15, 1865.

Private John Riday – Mustered in on March 24, 1864. Admitted to Camp Discharge Hospital for pleuralgia Nov. 30-Dec. 9, 1864, catarrh Jan. 12–13, 1865, and tertiary syphilis Feb. 27, 1865. Mustered out with company Aug. 15, 1865.

Private John W. Rudy – Mustered in on March 24, 1864. Admitted to Camp Discharge Hospital for diarrhea Nov. 30-Dec. 3, 1864, catarrh Jan.12-13, 1865, and bronchitis Feb. 1-20, 1865. Mustered out with company Aug. 15, 1865.

Private Mahlon L. Ironside – Mustered in on July 20, 1864. Hospitalized at Camp Discharge for ecthyma Dec. 1-2, 1864, and catarrh March 6-11, 1865. Mustered out with company Aug. 15, 1865.

Private Michael Karney – Mustered in on March 24, 1864. Admitted to Camp Discharge Hospital for catarrh Dec.1-12, 1864, sore throat Dec.19-20, 1864, diarrhea March 12-14, 1865, and sore throat May 25, 1865. Mustered out with company Aug. 15, 1865.

Private John A. Herman – Mustered in on March 24, 1864. Hospitalized at Camp Discharge for leg ulcer Dec. 3-22, 1864. Mustered out with company Aug. 15, 1865.

Private James Reily – Mustered in on March 24, 1864. Admitted to Camp Discharge Hospital for secondary syphilis Dec. 5-9, 1864, and constipation March 24-25 and April 12, 1865. Mustered out with company Aug. 15, 1865.

Private Oliver Guthrie – Mustered in on July 30, 1864. Hospitalized at Camp Discharge for ecthyma Dec. 6-7, 1864, ague March 4-7, 1865, and catarrh April 1-6 and May15-18, 1865. Mustered out with company Aug. 15, 1865.

Private Josiah Zembower – Mustered in on July 26, 1864. Admitted to Camp Discharge Hospital for "sore throat subj to diphtheria" Dec. 9-15, 1864, and catarrh May 24, 1865. Mustered out with company Aug. 15, 1865.

Private William Miller – Mustered in on March 24, 1864. Hospitalized at Camp Discharge for ecthyma Dec. 9-21, 1864, conjunctivitis Jan. 20-28, 1865, and catarrh May 21, 1865. Mustered out with company Aug. 15, 1865.

Private John Cox – Mustered in on March 24, 1864. At Camp Discharge, hospitalized for ecthyma Dec. 13-20, 1864. Deserted Feb. 14, 1865. Returned from desertion under presidential proclamation April 19, 1865. Mustered out with company Aug. 15, 1865.

Private James Lake – Mustered in on March 24, 1864. Admitted to Camp Discharge Hospital for ecthyma Dec. 13–23, 1864, and pleurodynia (chest pain) Jan. 25-28, 1865. Mustered out with company Aug. 15, 1865.

Private Charles Hosback – Mustered in on Aug. 5, 1864. At Camp Discharge, hospitalized for rheumatism Dec. 15-16, 1864, furunculus (boil) Dec. 27, 1864-Jan. 2, 1865, sore throat March 4-6, 1865, and constipation April 11-14, 1865. Mustered out with company Aug. 15, 1865.

Private Israel K. Briggs – Mustered in on March 24, 1864. Hospitalized at Camp Discharge for "int. Fever" Dec. 15-27, 1864, ecthyma Jan. 20-24, 1865, balanitis (genital inflammation) Jan. 25-27, 1865, and ecthyma March 15-16, 1865. Mustered out with company Aug. 15, 1865.

Private Frank Foesig – Mustered in on March 24, 1864. Admitted to Camp Discharge Hospital for ecthyma Dec17-26, 1864. Mustered out with company Aug. 15, 1865.

Private Matthew McDaniels – Mustered in on March 4, 1864. Hospitalized at Camp Discharge for ecthyma Dec. 20-24, 1864, diarrhea Jan. 21-26, 1865, and "intermittent tert" (fever) Feb. 23, 1865. Mustered out with company Aug. 15, 1865.

Private Silas H. Sparks – Mustered in on March 24, 1864. Admitted to Camp Discharge Hospital for ecthyma Dec. 22, 1864-Jan. 2, 1865. Mustered out with company Aug. 15, 1865.

Private John Q.A. Nycum – Mustered in on March 24, 1864. While at Camp Discharge, hospitalized for ecthyma Dec. 23-24, 1864. Absent, in arrest, at muster out.

Private Lewis B. Hixeon – Mustered in on March 24, 1864. Admitted to Camp Discharge Hospital for ecthyma Dec. 23-24, 1864. Mustered out with company Aug. 15, 1865.

Private William Weight – Mustered in on March 24, 1864. At Camp Discharge, hospitalized for catarrh Dec. 25-6, 1864. Mustered out with company Aug. 15, 1865.

Private William R. Rogers – Mustered in on March 24, 1864. Hospitalized at Camp Discharge for catarrh Dec. 25-6, 1864, and Jan. 1-13, 1865. Mustered out with company Aug. 15, 1865.

Private Thomas Stailey – Mustered in on March 24, 1864. Admitted to Camp Discharge Hospital for colic and constipation Dec.28, 1864-Jan. 3, 1865. Mustered out with company Aug. 15, 1865.

Private Adam K. Bottenfield – Mustered in on March 24, 1864. At Camp Discharge, hospitalized for colic Dec. 28–29, 1864, and lumbago Jan. 25-31 and April 12-17, 1865. Mustered out with company Aug. 15, 1865.

Private William H. Thomas – Mustered in on March 24, 1864. Admitted to Camp Discharge Hospital for catarrh Dec. 28-29, 1864. Mustered out with company Aug. 15, 1865.

Private Thomas O'Brien – Mustered in on March 24, 1864. Hospitalized at Camp Discharge for diarrhea and catarrh Jan. 9-11, 1865, and catarrh May 14-17, 1865. Mustered out with company Aug. 15, 1865.

Private Jacob B. Leahman – Mustered in on March 24, 1864. At Camp Discharge, hospitalized for contusion Jan. 11, 1865, and "tertian int" (fever) Jan. 17, 1865. Mustered out with company Aug. 15, 1865.

Private Daniel Kauffman – Mustered in on March 24, 1864. At Camp Discharge, hospitalized for bronchitis Jan. 15-30, 1865, and catarrh May 14-17, 1865. Mustered out with company Aug. 15, 1865.

Private William Stubbs – Mustered in on March 24, 1864. Hospitalized at Camp Discharge for sore throat Jan. 17-21, 1865. Deserted Feb. 14, 1865, disposition not given.

Private Michael Karney – Mustered in on March 24, 1864. Admitted to Camp Discharge Hospital for sore throat Jan. 19-20, 1865. Mustered out with company Aug. 15, 1865.

Private Israel Evans – Mustered in on March 24, 1864. At Camp Discharge, hospitalized for diarrhea Jan. 19, 1865, and scrofula (tuberculosis of neck) March 6, 1865. Mustered out with company Aug. 15, 1865.

Private Jacob W. Barndollar – Mustered in on Aug. 5, 1864. Hospitalized at Camp Discharge for catarrh Jan. 21-Feb. 1, 1865. Mustered out with company Aug. 15, 1865.

Private Joseph O'Neill – Mustered in on March 24, 1864. Admitted to Camp Discharge Hospital for pleurodynia Jan. 25-30, 1865, and conjunctivitis Feb. 20-24, 1865. Mustered out with company Aug. 15, 1865.

Private Alex Carpenter – Mustered in on March 24, 1864. At Camp Discharge, hospitalized for bronchitis Jan. 30-Feb.2, 1865, and constipation Feb. 28-March 2, 1865. Mustered out with company Aug. 15, 1865.

Private Job Stewart – Mustered in on March 24, 1864. Admitted to Camp Discharge Hospital for sprain Jan. 30-Feb. 10, 1865. Mustered out with company Aug. 15, 1865.

Private Jacob H. King – Mustered in on March 24, 1864. Hospitalized for cyanche (inflamed throat) Feb. 3-6, 1865. Mustered out with company Aug. 15, 1865.

Private Joseph Ritchey – Mustered in on March 24, 1864. At Camp Discharge, hospitalized for catarrh Feb. 6-21, 1865, sore throat Feb. 27, 1865, and catarrh May 27. Mustered out with company Aug. 15, 1865.

Private William Pearson – Mustered in on July 19, 1864. Admitted to Camp Discharge Hospital for catarrh Feb. 9-10, 1865. Mustered out with company Aug. 15, 1865.

Private John Holt – Mustered in on July 19, 1864. At Camp Discharge, hospitalized for bronchitis Feb. 12-20, 1865. Mustered out with company Aug. 15, 1865.

Private William Peifer – Mustered in on March 24, 1864. Hospitalized at Camp Discharge for catarrh Feb. 12-18, 1865. Mustered out with company Aug. 15, 1865.

Private Charles Fraser – Mustered in on March 24, 1864. At Camp Discharge, Hospitalized for cyanche (inflamed throat) Feb. 14-18, 1865. Mustered out with company Aug. 15, 1865.

Private David Veach – Mustered in on March 21, 1864. Hospitalized at Camp Discharge for catarrh Feb. 15, 1865. Mustered out with company Aug. 15, 1865.

Private John K. Hanna – Mustered in on July 20, 1864. While at Camp Discharge, hospitalized for catarrh March 9, 1865. Mustered out with company Aug. 15, 1865.

Private David Atherholdt – Mustered in on March 24, 1864. Deserted Dec. 1, 1865, disposition not given.

Private Israel T. Benson – Mustered in on March 24, 1864. Mustered out with company Aug. 15, 1865.

Private Theodore Estricker – Mustered in on March 24, 1864. Mustered out with company Aug. 15, 1865.

Private George Foesig – Mustered in on March 24, 1864. Mustered out with company Aug. 15, 1865.

Private Thomas Fleming – Mustered in on March 24, 1864. Mustered out with company Aug. 15, 1865.

Private Richard T. Foor – Mustered in on March 24, 1864. Mustered out with company Aug. 15, 1865.

Private William Fry – Mustered in on July 20, 1864. Mustered out with company Aug. 15, 1865.

Private John Fralich – Mustered in on March 24, 1864. Deserted. Returned. Discharged by special order Sept. 5, 1865.

Private G.L. Grammar – Mustered in on March 24, 1864. Mustered out with company Aug. 15, 1865.

Private John H. Greenfield – Mustered in on March 24, 1864. Deserted Nov. 4, 1864.

Private Thomas E. Howard – Mustered in on March 24, 1864. Mustered out with company Aug. 15, 1865.

Private George Himes – Mustered in on March 24, 1864. Mustered out with company Aug. 15, 1865.

Private Henry Holt – Mustered in on Aug. 2, 1864. Mustered out with company Aug. 15, 1865.

Private Charles T. Hallowell – Mustered in on July 18, 1864. Mustered out with company Aug. 15, 1865.

Private John S. Kauffman – Mustered in on March 24, 1864. Mustered out with company Aug. 15, 1865.

Private William Kreitz – Mustered in on March 24, 1864. Mustered out with company Aug. 15, 1865.

Private Jacob Kline – Mustered in on March 24, 1864. Mustered out with company Aug. 15, 1865.

Private Amos Longenecker – Mustered in on March 24, 1864. Mustered out with company Aug. 15, 1865.

Private Daniel Lukens – Mustered in on Aug. 5, 1864. Mustered out with company Aug. 15, 1865.

Private John H. Moyer – Mustered in on March 24, 1864. Mustered out with company Aug. 15, 1865.

Private William Mahaney – Mustered in on July 30, 1864. Mustered out with company Aug. 15, 1865.

Private Benjamin F. Murphy – Mustered in on March 24, 1864. Discharged on surgeon's certificate June 20, 1865.

Private Ephraim Reitzel – Mustered in on March 24, 1864. Mustered out with company Aug. 15, 1865.

Private Albert M. Sheble – Mustered in on March 24, 1864. Mustered out with company Aug. 15, 1865.

Private Charles M. Soladay – Mustered in on March 24, 1864. Mustered out with company Aug. 15, 1865.

Private William Sickel – Mustered in on March 24, 1864. Mustered out with company Aug. 15, 1865.

Private Charles M. Thomas – Mustered in on July 18, 1864. Discharged by general order July 24, 1865.

Private Charles Tarrence – Mustered in on July 18, 1864. Discharged by general order July 24, 1865.

Private William Walter – Mustered in on March 24, 1864. Mustered out with company Aug. 15, 1865.

Private Rudy F. Wolf – Mustered in on March 24, 1864. Mustered out with company Aug. 15, 1865.

Private William R. Wilson – Mustered in on March 24, 1864. Deserted Nov. 14, 1864.

187th Pa. Infantry

The regiment was formed in 1864 in Philadelphia and became part of the Army of the Potomac. The men underwent combat at Cold Harbor and during the Siege of Petersburg. They lost 136 enlisted men and officers to battle and disease. Companies C, H, G, and K were sent to Camp Discharge as provost guards in May 185. The regiment mustered out in August 1865. *Three hundred fifty-eight of its men were garrisoned at Camp Discharge.*

COMPANY C (88 MEN)

Captain William Young – Mustered in on Feb. 26, 1864. Mustered out with company Aug. 3, 1865.

First Lieutenant Orville D. Harder – Mustered in on Feb. 26, 1864. Mustered out with company Aug. 3, 1865.

Second Lieutenant George G. Lovett – Mustered in on Feb. 26, 1865. Mustered out with company Aug. 3, 1865.

Second Lieutenant James R. Johnson – Mustered in on May 11, 1864. Mustered out with company Aug. 3, 1865.

Sergeant Alfred B. Patton – Mustered in on Jan. 22, 1864. Hospitalized at Camp Discharge for ecthyma May 28-June 1, 1865. Mustered out with company Aug. 3, 1865. Joined Veteran Reserve Corps.

Sergeant John S. Ware – Mustered in on Jan 29, 1864. Hospitalized at Camp Discharge for constipation and vomiting May 29, 1865. Mustered out with company Aug. 3, 1865. Joined Veteran Reserve Corps.

Sergeant Seth K. Sharpless – Mustered in on June 20, 1864. Mustered out with company Aug. 3, 1865.

Sergeant William H. Cool – Mustered in on June 20, 1864. While at Camp Discharge, hospitalized for pneumonia May 27, 1865. Mustered out with company Aug. 3, 1865.

Sergeant Frank Rockafeller – Mustered in on June 25, 1864. Mustered out with company Aug. 3, 1865.

Corporal Amos Garman – Mustered in on Jan. 19, 1864. Admitted to Camp Discharge Hospital to treat ecthyma May 23, 1865. Mustered out with company Aug. 3, 1865. Then joined Veteran Reserve Corps.

Corporal John Harder – Mustered in on June 20, 1864. Mustered out with company Aug. 3, 1865.

Corporal John C. Irvin – Mustered in on June 20, 1864. Mustered out with company Aug. 3, 1865.

Corporal Hugh P. Libhart – Mustered in on June 20, 1864. Mustered out with company Aug. 3, 1865.

Corporal William E. Mohr – Mustered in on Feb. 3, 1864: Mustered out with company Aug. 3, 1865.

Musician James B. Forrest – Mustered in on Jan. 29, 1864. Hospitalized at Camp Discharge for hand-wound June 5, 1865. Mustered out with company Aug. 3, 1865. Joined Veteran Reserve Corps.

Musician Charles P. Harder – Mustered in on April 14, 1864. Mustered out with company Aug. 3, 1865.

Private Arthur Alward – Mustered in on Jan. 29, 1864. Admitted to Camp Discharge Hospital for gonorrhea May 23, 1865. Mustered out with company Aug. 3, 1865.

Private John R. Beatty – Mustered in on Jan. 26, 1864. Hospitalized at Camp Discharge for ecthyma May 24, 1865, and congestive liver June 16, 1865. Mustered out with company Aug. 3, 1865.

Private Charles S. Beaver – Mustered in on Jan. 22, 1864. Mustered out with company Aug. 3, 1865.

Private George W. Berdaniel – Mustered in on Jan. 29, 1864. Mustered out with company Aug. 3, 1865.

Private Henry E. Brace – Mustered in on Jan. 26, 1864. Hospitalized at Camp Discharge to treat syphilis May 23, 1865. Mustered out with company Aug. 3, 1865.

Private Benton B. Brown – Mustered in on Jan. 24, 1864. Admitted to Camp Discharge Hospital for constipation June 19, 1865. Mustered out with company Aug. 3, 1865.

Private George W. Brown – Mustered in on Jan. 20, 1864. While at Camp Discharge, hospitalized for gonorrhea May 13, 1865, and for ecthyma and gonorrhea May 24, 1865. Mustered out with company Aug. 3, 1865.

Private William Bryant – Mustered in on Jan. 30, 1864. Hospitalized at Camp Discharge for hemorrhoids May 19-23, 1865, and constipation June 4, 1865. Mustered out with company Aug. 3, 1865.

Private Andrew Campbell – Mustered in on Jan. 29, 1864. Admitted to Camp Discharge Hospital to treat laceration of leg May 13, 1865. Mustered out with company Aug. 3, 1865.

Private Nelson B. Case – Mustered in on Jan. 22, 1864. Mustered out with company Aug. 3, 1865.

Private Michael Caslin – Mustered in on Jan. 29, 1864. Hospitalized at Camp Discharge to treat catarrh June 20, 1865. Mustered out with company Aug. 3, 1865.

Private Charles Cutair – Mustered in on Jan. 22, 1864. Hospitalized at Camp Discharge for gonorrhea May 14-17, 1865, ecthyma May 28, 1865, and gonorrhea June 15, 1865. Mustered out with company Aug. 3, 1865.

Private John C. Devine – Mustered in on Jan. 29, 1864. At Camp Discharge, hospitalized for indecipherable ailment May 13, 1865. Mustered out with company Aug. 3, 1865.

Private James S. Easten – Mustered in on Jan. 26, 1864. Hospitalized at Camp Discharge for ecthyma May 22, 1865. Mustered out with company Aug. 3, 1865.

Private Samuel Eckert – Mustered in on June 20, 1864. Admitted to Camp Discharge for hand-wound June 1, 1865. Mustered out with company Aug. 3, 1865.

Private William Elliott – Mustered in on Jan. 21, 1864. Mustered out with company Aug. 3, 1865.

Private Charles W. Eyerly – Mustered in on Jan. 29, 1864. Mustered out with company Aug. 3, 1865.

Private Osman Foreman – Mustered in on Jan. 5, 1864. At Camp Discharge, hospitalized for boils May 13, 1865. Mustered out with company Aug. 3, 1865.

Private John Fox – Mustered in on Jan. 29, 1864. Mustered out with company Aug. 3, 1865.

Private Joseph L. Frame – Mustered in on Jan. 29, 1864. Mustered out with company Aug. 3, 1865.

Private William H. Fribley – Mustered in on Feb. 3, 1864. Mustered out with company Aug. 3, 1865.

Private Charles Funston – Mustered in on June 20, 1864. Hospitalized at Camp Discharge for cough May 16-20, 1865, for venereal warts May 24, 1865, and foot wound June 15, 1865. Mustered out with company Aug. 3, 1865.

Private Joseph Gandiblue – Mustered in on June 20, 1864. Admitted to Camp Discharge Hospital for sprained ankle May 17-22, 1865. Mustered out with company Aug. 3, 1865.

Private James H. Gibbons – Mustered in on Jan. 29, 1865. Mustered out with company Aug. 3, 1865.

Private Charles H. Gibbs – Mustered in on Sept. 17, 1864. Discharged by general order May 30, 1865.

Private James M. Gibbs – Mustered in on Jan. 22, 1864. Mustered out with company Aug. 3, 1865.

Private Ephraim K. Hale – Mustered in on Sept. 8, 1864. Discharged by general order July 5, 1865.

Private Jacob W. Heffler – Mustered in on June 20, 1864. Hospitalized at Camp Discharge for catarrh June 2, 1865, and ecthyma July 19, 1865. Mustered out with company Aug. 3, 1865.

Private John Henry – Mustered in on June 20, 1864: Mustered out with company Aug. 3, 1865.

Private William F. Hullihen – Mustered in on Sept. 21, 1864. Hospitalized at Camp Discharge for scabies May 23-June 1, 1865. Discharged by general order July 14, 1865.

Private John Ickus – Mustered in on Jan. 29, 1864. Mustered out with company Aug. 3, 1865.

Private Henry Ickus – Mustered in on Jan. 29, 1864. Mustered out with company Aug. 3, 1865.

Private Caleb Jackson – Mustered in on Jan. 20, 1864. Mustered out with company Aug. 3, 1865.

Private George W. Jackson – Mustered in on Jan. 29, 1864. Mustered out with company Aug. 3, 1865.

Private Gottlieb Kercher – Mustered in on Jan. 26, 1864. While at Camp Discharge, hospitalized for rheumatism May 25, 1865. Mustered out with company Aug. 3, 1865. Joined Veteran Volunteer Corps.

Private Joseph Levers – Mustered in on Jan. 20, 1864. Mustered out with company Aug. 3, 1865.

Private William Lewis – Mustered in on June 20, 1864. Admitted to Camp Discharge Hospital for diarrhea July 15, 1865. Mustered out with company Aug. 3, 1865.

Private Patrick Maney – Mustered in on May 25, 1864. Hospitalized at Camp Discharge for boils June 4, 1865, and acute diarrhea June 21, 1865. Mustered out with company Aug. 3, 1865.

Private Oscar Mellin – Mustered in on Sept. 13, 1864. Discharged by general order July 5, 1865.

Private John Miller – Mustered in on Jan. 22, 1864. Hospitalized at Camp Discharge for erysipelas (skin infection) May 30, 1865. Mustered out with company Aug. 3, 1865.

Private William Milner – Mustered in on Jan. 26, 1864. Admitted to Camp Discharge Hospital for gonorrhea May 13, 1865, and for "cons. syphilis" and rheumatism June 7, 1865. Discharged on surgeon's certificate July 4, 1865.

Private Thomas P. Morgan – Mustered in on Jan. 29, 1864. Mustered out with company Aug. 3, 1865.

Private Watkin Morgan – Mustered in on Jan. 29, 1864. Mustered out with company Aug. 3, 1865.; Vet.

Private John O'Brien – Mustered in on Jan. 22, 1864. Mustered out with company Aug. 3, 1865.

Private Irwin T. Patton – Mustered in on Jan. 22, 1864. Hospitalized at Camp Discharge for scabies May 20-June 21, 1865. Mustered out with company Aug. 3, 1865.

Private Henry Powley – Mustered in on Jan. 22, 1864. Hospitalized at Camp Discharge for bubo (genital inflammation) May 20-21, 1865. Mustered out with company Aug. 3, 1865.

Private David H. Rank – Mustered in on Jan. 21, 1864. Sent to Camp Discharge Hospital to treat ecthyma May 28, 1865. Mustered out with company Aug. 3, 1865.

Private Isaac Rantz – Mustered in on Jan. 29, 1864. Hospitalized at Camp Discharge for ulcer of leg May 31, 1865. Mustered out with company Aug. 3, 1865. Joined Veteran Reserve Corps.

Private Peter M. Reed – Mustered in on Jan. 20, 1864. Admitted to Camp Discharge Hospital for ecthyma June 4, 1865. Mustered out with company Aug. 3, 1865.

Private Warren M. Ridgway – Mustered in on Jan. 26, 1864. Hospitalized at Camp Discharge for hand-wound May 24, 1865. Mustered out with company Aug. 3, 1865.

Private Charles Rishel – Mustered in on Jan. 29, 1864. Hospitalized at Camp Discharge for sore leg May 13-23, 1865, and sore throat May 24, 1865. Mustered out with company Aug. 3, 1865. Joined Veteran Reserve Corps.

Private George Rishel – Mustered in on Jan. 29, 1863. Admitted to Camp Discharge Hospital for gonorrhea and ecthyma May 24, 1865. Mustered out with company Aug. 3, 1865.

Private John Roberts – Mustered in on Jan. 29, 1864. Mustered out with company Aug. 3, 1865. Joined Veteran Reserve Corps.

Private John J. Roderick – Mustered in on Jan. 29, 1864. Mustered out with company Aug. 3, 1865.

Private John Sechler – Mustered in on Jan. 29, 1864. Mustered out with company Aug. 3, 1865.

Private Jacob Slack – Mustered in on Jan. 26, 1864. Admitted to Camp Discharge Hospital for catarrh May 23, 1865. Mustered out with company Aug. 3, 1865.

Private Edward D. Smith – Mustered in on Jan. 21, 1864. At Camp Discharge, hospitalized for constipation June 19, 1865. Mustered out with company Aug. 3, 1865. Joined Veteran Reserve Corps.

Private Isaac Snell – Mustered in on Jan. 28, 1864. Hospitalized at Camp Discharge for syphilis May 13, 1865. Mustered out with company Aug. 3, 1865.

Private Peter Spooneberger – Mustered in on Jan. 29, 1864. While at Camp Discharge, hospitalized for syphilis May 13, 1865. Mustered out with company Aug. 3, 1865.

Private Samuel Stahl – Mustered in on Jan. 28, 1864. Mustered out with company Aug. 3, 1865. Joined Veteran Reserve Corps.

Private George W. Vangilder – Mustered in on Jan. 20, 1864. Mustered out with company Aug. 3, 1865.

Private William Vogle – Mustered in on June 25, 1864. Hospitalized at Camp Discharge for sore mouth May 15-17, 1865. Mustered out with company Aug. 3, 1865.

Private John H. Wallace – Mustered in on Jan. 29, 1864. Mustered out with company Aug. 3, 1865.

Private James D. Ware – Mustered in on Jan. 29, 1864. Hospitalized at Camp Discharge for balanitis (genital inflammation) May 19, 1865. Mustered out with company Aug. 3, 1865.

Private George Warren – Mustered in on Jan. 29, 1864. Absent, sick at muster out.

Private Henry Warren – Mustered in on Jan. 25, 1864. At Camp Discharge, hospitalized for leg ulcer May 26 and June 6, 1865. Mustered out with company Aug. 3, 1865.

Private William M. Watts – Mustered in on Jan. 29, 1864. Hospitalized at Camp Discharge for catarrh May 22, 1865. Mustered out with company Aug. 3, 1865.

Private A. B. Werkheiser – Mustered in on Jan. 29, 1864. Admitted to Camp Discharge Hospital for syphilis May 13, 1865, constipation June 9, 1865, and rheumatism June 17, 1865. Mustered out with company Aug. 3, 1865.

Private Elijah Wertman – Mustered in on Jan. 22, 1864. Mustered out with company Aug. 3, 1865.

Private John Wertman – Mustered in on Jan. 26, 1864. Mustered out with company Aug. 3, 1865.

Private William Williams – Mustered in on Jan. 29, 1864. Hospitalized at Camp Discharge for delirium tremens, leg sore, and head wound May 13, 1865. Mustered out with company Aug. 3, 1865. Joined Veteran Reserve Corps.

Private Lewis V. Wray – Mustered in on Jan. 21, 1864. Wounded at Petersburg, Va., June 18, 1864. Hospitalized at Camp Discharge for ecthyma June 2, 1865. Mustered out with company Aug. 3, 1865.

187TH PA., COMPANY G (85 MEN)

Captain W. Henrie Carling – Mustered in on May 11, 1864. Mustered out with company Aug. 3, 1865.

1st Lieutenant Frank J. Deemer – Mustered in on May 11, 1864. Mustered out with company Aug. 3, 1865.

2nd Lieutenant Miles M. Bradford – Mustered in on May 11, 1864. Mustered out with company Aug. 3, 1865.

Sergeant George A. Wolcott – Mustered in on April 7, 1864. At Camp Discharge, hospitalized for erysipelas (skin infection) May 31, 1865. Mustered out with company Aug. 3, 1865. Joined Veteran Reserve Corps.

Sergeant Albert Simpson – Mustered in on April 7, 1864. Mustered out with company Aug. 3, 1865.

Sergeant Stephen M. Whitbeck – Mustered in on April 7, 1864. Admitted to Camp Discharge Hospital for ecthyma May 25, 1865. Mustered out with company Aug. 3, 1865. Joined Veteran Reserve Corps.

Sergeant John W. Marshall – Mustered in on April 7, 1864. While at Camp Discharge, hospitalized for ecthyma June 4, 1865. Mustered out with company Aug. 3, 1865.

Sergeant John S. Jenkins – Mustered in on April 7, 1864. Promoted from corporal Feb. 6, 1865. Hospitalized at Camp Discharge for ecthyma May 17-20, 1865. Mustered out with company Aug. 3, 1865.

Corporal Levi Bennett – Mustered in on April 7, 1864. Mustered out with company Aug. 3, 1865.

Corporal James Hatten – Mustered in on April 7, 1864. At Camp Discharge, hospitalized for "debility from M.D." (miasmatic disease, perhaps cholera) June 4, 1865. Mustered out with company Aug. 3, 1865. Joined Veteran Reserve Corps.

Corporal William Webber – Mustered in on April 7, 1864. Mustered out with company Aug. 3, 1865.

Corporal William H. Daley – Mustered in on April 7, 1864. Mustered out with company Aug. 3, 1865.

Corporal John G. Jones – Mustered in on April 7, 1864. Promoted to corporal Feb. 6, 1865. Mustered out with company Aug. 3, 1865.

Corporal Frank Stanton – Mustered in on May 17, 1864. Promoted to corporal Feb. 19, 1865. Mustered out with company Aug. 3, 1865. Joined Veteran Reserve Corps.

Corporal John Montgomery – Mustered in on May 17, 1865. Bates: Promoted to corporal Feb. 24, 1865. Hospitalized at Camp Discharge for rheumatism May 18, 1865. Mustered out with company Aug. 3, 1865. Joined Veteran Reserve Corps.

Musician Albert Hatten – Mustered in on April 7, 1864. Promoted to corporal Feb. 24, 1865; Mustered out with company Aug. 3, 1865.

Musician Charles Hines – Mustered in on April 7, 1864. Mustered out with company Aug. 3, 1865.

Musician James M. Whitman – Mustered in on April 7, 1864. Admitted to Camp Discharge Hospital for congestive liver June 12, 1865. Mustered out with company Aug. 3, 1865.

Private Henry Arnold – Mustered in on April 7, 1864. Mustered out with company Aug. 3, 1865.

Private Lorsen Akerly – Mustered in on April 7, 1864. Mustered out with company Aug. 3, 1865.

Private Amos H. Adams – Mustered in on April 7, 1864. Mustered out with company Aug. 3, 1865.

Private Joseph O. Boswell – Mustered in on April 7, 1864. Admitted to Camp Discharge Hospital for acute diarrhea June 20, 1865. Mustered out with company Aug. 3, 1865.

Private James O. Benjamin – Mustered in on April 7, 1864. Mustered out with company Aug. 3, 1865.

Private Joseph Bennett – Mustered in on April 7, 1864. Hospitalized at Camp Discharge for scorbutus (scurvy) June 12, 1865. Mustered out with company Aug. 3, 1865.

Private Andrew J. Clark – Mustered in on April 7, 1864. Mustered out with company Aug. 3, 1865.

Private William M. Clark – Mustered in on April 7, 1864. Mustered out with company Aug. 3, 1865.

Private Seth A. Cobb – Mustered in on April 7, 1864. Mustered out with company Aug. 3, 1865.

Private James M. Conrad – Mustered in on April 7, 1864. Mustered out with company Aug. 3, 1865.

Private John Conrad – Mustered in on April 7, 1864. Mustered out with company Aug. 3, 1865.

Private James Conway – Mustered in on April 7, 1864. While at Camp Discharge, hospitalized for boils June 9, 1865. Mustered out with company Aug. 3, 1865.

Private David W. Copeland – Mustered in on April 7, 1864. Mustered out with company Aug. 3, 1865.

Private Lafayette Davis – Mustered in on April 7, 1864. Admitted to Camp Discharge Hospital for cough May 14-22, 1865. Mustered out with company Aug. 3, 1865.

Private Moses Davis – Mustered in on April 7, 1864. Hospitalized at Camp Discharge for scurvy of gums May 14, 1865, for ecthyma June 11, 1865. Mustered out with company Aug. 3, 1865.

Private Nathan Davis – Mustered in on April 7, 1864. Admitted to Camp Discharge Hospital for ecthyma June 12, 1865. Mustered out with company Aug. 3, 1865.

Private Ami D. Dimmick – Mustered in on May 17, 1864. Mustered out with company Aug. 3, 1865.

Private Peter Eckerson – Mustered in on April 7, 1864. Mustered out with company Aug. 3, 1865. Joined Veteran Reserve Corps.

Private James Farnam – Mustered in. on April 7, 1864. Hospitalized at Camp Discharge for "endocard. and red hepatization lungs" (pneumonia) May 14, 1865. Discharged on surgeon's certificate June 17, 1865.

Private John Felts – Mustered in on May 17, 1864. At Camp Discharge, hospitalized for conjunctivitis June 2, 1865. Mustered out with company Aug. 3, 1865.

Private Henry Fisk – Mustered in on May 17, 1864. Hospitalized at Camp Discharge for gonorrhea June 15, 1865. Mustered out with company Aug. 3, 1865.

Private Mer. W. Goodrich – Mustered in on April 7, 1864. Admitted to Camp Discharge Hospital for diarrhea May 14-18, 1865. Mustered out with company Aug. 3, 1865.

Private Andrew Halstead – Mustered in on April 7, 1864. While at Camp Discharge, hospitalized for "testicle problem" June 2, 1865. Mustered out with company Aug. 3, 1865.

Private Charles J. Hayden – Mustered in on April 7, 1864. Hospitalized at Camp Discharge for diarrhea May 26, 1865. Mustered out with company Aug. 3, 1865.

Private Francis F. Hayden – Mustered in on April 7, 1864. Mustered out with company Aug. 3, 1865.

Private Harvey Hayden – Mustered in on April 7, 1864. Mustered out with company Aug. 3, 1865.

Private H. B. Hitchcock – Mustered in on April 7, 1864. Mustered out with company Aug. 3, 1865.

Private William Hollenback – Mustered in on April 7, 1864. Mustered out with company Aug. 3, 1865.

Private William J. Hughes – Mustered in on April 7, 1864. Admitted to Camp Discharge Hospital for endocarditis (heart valve inflammation) and sunstroke May 14-17, 1865. Mustered out with company Aug. 3, 1865.

Private Douglass J. Jay – Mustered in on April 7, 1864. Promoted to sergeant major May 1, 1865.

Private Michael Kelly – Mustered in on April 7, 1864. Mustered out with company Aug. 3, 1865. Joined Veteran Reserve Corps.

Private Martin V. Kennedy – Mustered in on April 7, 1864. Hospitalized at Camp Discharge for "erythema scrot." (genital disease) June 5, 1865. Mustered out with company Aug. 3, 1865. Joined Veteran Reserve Corps.

Private Christ Kindrew – Mustered in on April 7, 1864. Admitted to Camp Discharge Hospital for scorbutus May 24, 1865. Mustered out with company Aug. 3, 1865.

Private John Kindrew – Mustered in on April 7, 1864. Admitted to Camp Discharge Hospital for gunshot wound May 14, 1865. Discharged on surgeon's certificate June 24, 1865.

Private Norman T. Kirk – Mustered in on April 7, 1864. Hospitalized at Camp Discharge for constipation June 9, 1865. Mustered out with company Aug. 3, 1865.

Private John LaFrance – Mustered in on April 7, 1864. At Camp Discharge, hospitalized for constipation June 18, 1865. Deserted Nov. 17, 1864. Returned April 26, 1865. Mustered out with company Aug. 3, 1865.

Private George Lampman – Mustered in on April 7, 1864. Mustered out with company Aug. 3, 1865.

Private Emery B. Larribee – Mustered in on April 7, 1864. Mustered out with company Aug. 3, 1865.

Private George Markley – Mustered in on April 7, 1864. Mustered out with company Aug. 3, 1865.

Private James McConnell – Mustered in on May 17, 1864. Hospitalized at Camp Discharge for sore throat May 28, 1865. Mustered out with company Aug. 3, 1865.

Private Byron McDonald – Mustered in on April 7, 1864. Mustered out with company Aug. 3, 1865.

Private Henry W. Miller – Mustered in on April 7, 1864. Mustered out with company Aug. 3, 1865.

Private Levi W. Miller – Mustered in on April 7, 1864. Mustered out with company Aug. 3, 1865.

Private Sydney Miller – Mustered in on April 7, 1864. Mustered out with company Aug. 3, 1865.

Private Minor Nogle – Mustered in on April 7, 1864. Mustered out with company Aug. 3, 1865.

Private William Nogle – Mustered in on April 7, 1864. Mustered out with company Aug. 3, 1865.

Private John G. Oetzel – Mustered in on April 7, 1864. Mustered out with company Aug. 3, 1865.

Private Francis W. Payne – Mustered in on April 7, 1864. Mustered out with company Aug. 3, 1865.

Private John C. Peck – Mustered in on April 7, 1864. Hospitalized at Camp Discharge for pneumonia May 14-30, 1865. Mustered out with company Aug. 3, 1865.

Private Norman D. Riker – Mustered in on April 7, 1864. Mustered out with company Aug. 3, 1865. Joined Veteran Reserve Corps.

Private William R. Sayer – Mustered in on April 7, 1864. Mustered out with company Aug. 3, 1865.

Private Philip B. Sears – Mustered in on April 7, 1864. Mustered out with company Aug. 3, 1865.

Private Peter Seigle – Mustered in on April 7, 1864. Mustered out with company Aug. 3, 1865.

Private Thomas M. Stewart – Mustered in on April 7, 1864. Mustered out with company Aug. 3, 1865.

Private Thomas Swartz – Mustered in on April 7, 1864. Mustered out with company Aug. 3, 1865.

Private Milton Taylor – Mustered in on April 7, 1864. Mustered out with company Aug. 3, 1865.

Private Henry Tewksberry – Mustered in on April 7, 1864. Mustered out with company Aug. 3, 1865.

Private William Thorn – Mustered in on April 7, 1864. Mustered out with company Aug. 3, 1865.

Private David K. Tooker – Mustered in on April 7, 1864. Mustered out with company Aug. 3, 1865.

Private Michael Walters – Mustered in on April 7, 1864. Mustered out with company Aug. 3, 1865.

Private Frederick M. Westcott – Mustered in on April 7, 1864. Hospitalized at Camp Discharge for "rheumatic calli" May 26, 1865, constipation June 4, 1865, and boils June 13, 1865. Mustered out with company Aug. 3, 1865.

Private George W. Westcott – Mustered in on April 7, 1864. Mustered out with company Aug. 3, 1865.

Private James T. Westcott – Mustered in on April 7, 1864. Mustered out with company Aug. 3, 1865.

Private Lyman F. Westcott – Mustered in on April 7, 1864. Admitted to Camp Discharge Hospital for headache May 16-18, 1865. Mustered out with company Aug. 3, 1865.

Private Reuben G. Westcott – Mustered in on April 7, 1864. At Camp Discharge, hospitalized for constipation June 9, 1865. Mustered out with company Aug. 3, 1865.

Private John W. White – Mustered in on April 7, 1864. Hospitalized at Camp Discharge for catarrh May 14-18, 1865. Discharged on surgeon's certificate July 29, 1865.

Private George E. Yarrington – Mustered in on April 7, 1864. Admitted to Camp Discharge Hospital for ecthyma June 19, 1865. Mustered out with company Aug. 3, 1865.

187TH PA., COMPANY H (96 MEN)

Captain Charles W. Mutchler – Mustered in on May 11, 1864. Admitted to Camp Discharge Hospital for "quotidian int." (fever) Jan. 7-10, 1865, and sore throat March 1-3, 1865. Mustered out with company Aug. 3, 1865.

1st. Lieutenant Charles F. Fenerstein – Mustered in on May 7, 1864. Promoted from 1st sergeant to 2nd lt. March 21, 1865. Promoted to 1st lt. May 17, 1865. Mustered out with company Aug. 3, 1865.

2nd Lieutenant Porter Squires – Mustered in on May 7, 1864. Hospitalized at Camp Discharge for influenza Jan. 5-18, 1865. Promoted from 1st sergeant May 19, 1865. Mustered out with company Aug. 3, 1865.

Sergeant Harrison J. Fickes – Mustered in on May 7, 1864. At Camp Discharge, hospitalized for catarrh Dec. 24, 1864-Jan. 6, 1865. Promoted from sergeant, June 1, 1865. Mustered out with company Aug. 3, 1865.

Sergeant William Clemens – Mustered in on May 7, 1864. Hospitalized at Camp Discharge for otalgia (ear pain) Dec. 9-10, 1864, and thigh fracture Jan. 19, 1865. Mustered out with company Aug. 3, 1865. Joined Veteran Reserve Corps.

Sergeant Eldridge D. Davis – Mustered in on May 7, 1864. Promoted from corporal June 1, 1865. Mustered out with company Aug. 3, 1865. Joined Veteran Reserve Corps.

Sergeant Philip D. Edwards – Mustered in on April 8, 1864. Promoted from Corporal, March 24, 1865. Hospitalized at Camp Discharge for constipation May 14-18, 1865, and catarrh June 1865. Mustered out with company Aug. 3, 1865.

Sergeant Tobias D. Yoder – Mustered in on May 7, 1864. Mustered out with company Aug. 3, 1865.

Corporal John C. Allen – Mustered in on May 7, 1864. Mustered out with company Aug. 3, 1865.

Corporal Samuel D. Bortel – Mustered in on May 7, 1864. Hospitalized at Camp Discharge for "mercurialism" (mercury poisoning) June 2, 1865. Mustered out with company Aug. 3, 1865.

Corporal John Butt – Mustered in on May 7, 1864. Mustered out with company Aug. 3, 1865.

Corporal William C. Dively – Mustered in on May 7, 1864. Mustered out with company Aug. 3, 1865.

Corporal Ira S. Gordon – Mustered in on May 7, 1864. Mustered out with company Aug. 3, 1865.

Corporal Asher T. Hinds – Mustered in on May 7, 1864. At Camp Discharge, hospitalized for vaccinia (cowpox) Dec. 27, 1865, and catarrh Jan. 11-13, 1865. Promoted to corporal, June 1, 1865. Mustered out with company Aug. 3, 1865.

Corporal William H. Seiders – Mustered in on May 7, 1864. Bates: Promoted to corporal June 1, 1865. Mustered out with company Aug. 3, 1865.

Corporal Charles Stubbins – Mustered in on May 7, 1864. Promoted to corporal March 21, 1865. Mustered out with company Aug. 3, 1865.

Corporal Willard M. Whitney – Mustered in on May 7, 1864. Promoted to corporal June 1, 1865. Mustered out with company Aug. 3, 1865.

Private H. B. Alexander – Mustered in on May 7, 1864. Hospitalized at Camp Discharge for chilblains Dec. 15-27, 1865, syphilis May 14, 1865, and diarrhea July 20, 1865. Mustered out with company Aug. 3, 1865.

Private George H. Baldwin – Mustered in on May 7, 1864. Admitted to Camp Discharge Hospital for a contusion of thigh Dec. 2-19, 1864. Mustered out with company Aug. 3, 1865. Joined Veteran Reserve Corps.

Private James T. Baldwin – Mustered in on May 7, 1864. At Camp Discharge, hospitalized for vaccinia (cowpox) Dec. 27-Jan. 11, 1865, catarrh Feb. 11-14, 1865, gonorrhea and bubo (genital inflammation) May 25, 1865, bubo June 16, 1865. Mustered out with company Aug. 3, 1865. Joined Veteran Reserve Corps.

Private Jonathon M. Balwin – Mustered in on May 7, 1864. Hospitalized at Camp Discharge for "int. fever tert." Nov. 18-22, 1864, and Dec. 22, 1864. Mustered out with company Aug. 3, 1865.

Private Romanus Baldwin – Mustered in on May 7, 1864. Hospitalized at Camp Discharge for pleurodynia (chest pain) Feb. 11-13, 1865, and catarrh May 19-23, 1865. Mustered out with company Aug. 3, 1865.

Private John Beebes – Mustered in on May 7, 1864. At Camp Discharge, hospitalized for influenza Jan. 5-10, 1865. Mustered out with company Aug. 3, 1865.

Private Alex J. Berkey – Mustered in on May 7, 1864. Hospitalized at Camp Discharge for sore throat Jan. 14-19, 1865. Mustered out with company Aug. 3, 1865.

Private John Berkey – Mustered in on May 7, 1864. Admitted to Camp Discharge Hospital for wrist sprain Dec. 13-23, 1864, and catarrh Dec. 27-29, 1864. Mustered out with company Aug. 3, 1865.

Private Jacob Bogner – Mustered in on May 7, 1864. Hospitalized at Camp Discharge Hospital for ecthyma Nov. 30, 1864. Mustered out with company Aug. 3, 1865.

Private George W. Cantebury – Mustered in on May 7, 1864. Admitted to Camp Discharge Hospital for lumbago Feb. 6-15, 1865, and constipation June 16, 1865. Mustered out with company Aug. 3, 1865.

Private John O. Collier – Mustered in on May 7, 1864. Mustered out with company Aug. 3, 1865.

Private Henry W. Conrad – Mustered in on Aug. 17, 1864. Hospitalized at Camp Discharge for cephalalgia (head pain) Dec. 11-13, 1864, catarrh and rheumatism Jan. 4-March 1, 1865. Mustered out with company Aug. 3, 1865.

Private Rufus C. Conrad – Mustered in on May 7, 1864. Mustered out with company Aug. 3, 1865.

Private Lewis Custer – Mustered in on May 7, 1864. Hospitalized at Camp Discharge for diphtheria Nov. 27-Dec. 5, 1864, diarrhea Dec. 30-Jan. 2, 1865, and gonorrhea May 13, 1865. Mustered out with company Aug. 3, 1865.

Private Jonathan Dellinger – Mustered in on May 7, 1864. Hospitalized at Camp Discharge for "ophthal: catarrh" July 15, 1865. Mustered out with company Aug. 3, 1865.

Private Richard W. Derr – Mustered in on May 7, 1864. Died Nov. 30, 1864, at Camp Discharge.

Private George M. Dunn – Mustered in on May 7, 1864. Hospitalized at Camp Discharge for "bilious headache" Dec. 2-5, 1854, and influenza Jan. 5-10, 1865. Mustered out with company Aug. 3, 1865.

Private Franklin Finnecy – Mustered in on May 7, 1864. Hospitalized at Camp Discharge for vaccinia (cowpox) Jan. 2-5, 1865, erysipelas (skin infection) Jan. 19-Feb. 5, 1865, and constipation May 2-23, 1865. Mustered out with company Aug. 3, 1865.

Private Jeremiah Flegle – Mustered in on May 7, 1864. Admitted to Camp Discharge Hospital for variola (small pox) Dec. 23, 1864-Jan. 30, 1865. Mustered out with company Aug. 3, 1865. Joined Vet. Reserve Corps.

Private Joseph B. Fletcher – Mustered in on May 7, 1864. At Camp Discharge, hospitalized for constipation May 20-21, 1865. Deserted June 1, 1864. Returned April 27, 1865. Mustered out with company Aug. 3, 1865.

Private Samuel Fritz – Mustered in on May 7, 1864. Mustered out with company Aug. 3, 1865.

Private Barney A. Gardner – Mustered in on May 7, 1864. Admitted to Camp Discharge Hospital for sore throat Dec. 30, 1864-Jan. 7, 1865. Mustered out with company Aug. 3, 1865.

Private Charles Glessner – Mustered in on May 7, 1864. Hospitalized at Camp Discharge for dysphonia (voice disorder) Nov. 13, 1864-Dec. 6, 1865. Mustered out with company Aug. 3, 1865.

Private William S. Hall – Mustered in on May 7, 1864. Hospitalized at Camp Discharge for catarrh Nov. 27-28, 1864. Mustered out with company Aug. 3, 1865.

Private Jeremiah Hartman – Mustered in on May 7, 1864. Discharged on surgeon's certificate Aug. 3, 1865.

Private John H. Hartman – Mustered in on May 7, 1864. Hospitalized at Camp Discharge for catarrh fever Dec. 1-17, 1864, vaccinia (cowpox) Dec. 27-Jan. 5, 1865, and erysipelas (skin infection) Feb. 26, 1865. Mustered out with company Aug. 3, 1865.

Private Simon Hass – Mustered in on May 7, 1864. Admitted to Camp Discharge Hospital for catarrh May 14-18, 1865. Mustered out with company Aug. 3, 1865.

Private Benjamin Hipple – Mustered in on May 7, 1864. Hospitalized at Camp Discharge for paronychia (finger infection) Dec. 11-20, 1864, influenza Jan. 5-14, 1865, and furuncle (boil) Feb. 12-17, 1865. Mustered out with company Aug. 3, 1865.

Private Joseph Hopper – Mustered in on May 7, 1864. Mustered out with company Aug. 3, 1865.

Private John L. Hunt – Mustered in on May 7, 1864. Hospitalized at Camp Discharge for gonorrhea Nov. 13-19, 1864, and catarrh fever Dec. 3-17, 1864. Mustered out with company Aug. 3, 1865. Joined Veteran Reserve Corps.

Private Samuel Ireley – Mustered in on May 7, 1864. Admitted to Camp Discharge Hospital for ecthyma Nov. 13-27, 1864, catarrh Jan. 15-20, 1865, ecthyma July 1, 1865, and "elongated mouth" July 18, 1865. Mustered out with company Aug. 3, 1865.

Private William Johnson – Mustered in on May 7, 1864. Discharged on surgeon's certificate May 6, 1865.

Private Conrad Keene – Mustered in on May 7, 1864. Hospitalized at Camp Discharge for sore throat Dec. 23, 1864-Jan. 16, 1865, and pleurodynia (chest pain) Feb. 15, March 1, 1865. Mustered out with company Aug. 3, 1865. Joined Veteran Reserve Corps.

Private Herman W. Lape – Mustered in on May 7, 1864. Hospitalized at Camp Discharge for catarrh Feb. 4-16, 1865. Mustered out with company Aug. 3, 1865.

Private Benjamin Lauer – Mustered in on May 7, 1864. Mustered out with company Aug. 3, 1865.

Private Levi Leese – Mustered in on May 7, 1864. Hospitalized at Camp Discharge for vaccinia (cowpox) Dec. 27, 1864-Jan. 5, 1865. Mustered out with company Aug. 3, 1865. Joined Veteran Reserve Corps.

Private Henry J. Lehman – Mustered in on May 7, 1864. Mustered out with company Aug. 3, 1865.

Private Philip Lehr – Mustered in on May 7, 1864. Mustered out with company Aug. 3, 1865.

Private Adam Martin – Mustered in on May 7, 1864. Admitted to Camp Discharge Hospital for sore throat Feb. 18-28, 1865, and jaundice March 8, 1865. Mustered out with company Aug. 3, 1865. Joined Veteran Reserve Corps.

Private Thomas B. McCord – Mustered in on May 7, 1864. Hospitalized at Camp Discharge for ecthyma Nov. 20-21, 1864, contusion of hand Dec. 9, 1864-Jan. 7, 1865, vaccinia (cowpox)

Dec. 27, 1864, "sec. syphilis" Jan. 19-Feb. 1, 1865, syphilis May 13, 1865, and "general debility" June 20, 1865. Mustered out with company Aug. 3, 1865.

Private John H. McGinney – Mustered in on May 7, 1864. Admitted to Camp Discharge Hospital for ecthyma Nov. 13-Dec. 17, 1864, ague (perhaps malaria) Feb. 20-25, 1865, and constipation May 13-15, 1865. Mustered out with company Aug. 3, 1865.

Private Andrew J. McReynolds – Mustered in on March 1, 1864. Hospitalized at Camp Discharge for "cyan tonsil" Dec. 24-30, 1864, and April 13-16, 1865. Mustered out with company Aug. 3, 1865.

Private John H. Meily – Mustered in on May 7, 1864. Hospitalized at Camp Discharge for ankle ulcer Nov. 13, 1864-Jan. 17, 1865, gonorrhea and indigestion Feb. 17-21, 1865, and ecthyma May 15-22. Mustered out with company Aug. 3, 1865. Joined Veteran Reserve Corps.

Private Loren Miller – Mustered in on May 7, 1864. Admitted to Camp Discharge Hospital for catarrh Nov. 13-17, 1864, and ecthyma June 11, 1865. Mustered out with company Aug. 3, 1865.

Private William H. Miller – Mustered in on May 7, 1864. Hospitalized at Camp Discharge for syphilis May 13, 1865. Mustered out with company Aug. 3, 1865. Joined Veteran Reserve Corps.

Private Jackson Nagle – Mustered in on May 7, 1864. Hospitalized at Camp Discharge for ecthyma Nov. 30-Dec. 7, 1864, and constipation May 18-20 and June 4, 1865. Mustered out with company Aug. 3, 1865.

Private George Nichols – Mustered in on May 7, 1864. Admitted to Camp Discharge Hospital for variola (smallpox) Dec. 9, 1864, and sunburn and ague (perhaps malaria) June 20, 1865. Mustered out with company Aug. 3, 1865.

Private Christopher Olewiler – Mustered in on May 7, 1864. Hospitalized at Camp Discharge for ecthyma Jan. 14-30, 1865. Mustered out with company Aug. 3, 1865.

Private Charles L. Peck – Mustered in on May 7, 1864. Admitted to Camp Discharge Hospital for catarrh Nov. 18-25, 1864, ecthyma Jan. 7-12, 1865, scabies Feb. 20-27, 1865, "external piles" June 7-8, 1865, and constipation July 19, 1865. Mustered out with company Aug. 3, 1865.

Private Jacob D. Powell – Mustered in on May 7, 1864. Hospitalized at Camp Discharge for sore throat Jan. 3, 1865, and diarrhea July 20, 1865. Mustered out with company Aug. 3, 1865.

Private John Ream – Mustered in on May 7, 1864. Mustered out with company Aug. 3, 1865. Joined Veteran Reserve Corps.

Private John Reed – Mustered in on May 7, 1864. Hospitalized at Camp Discharge for conjunctivitis Dec. 26, 1864-Jan. 5, 1865, indigestion Feb. 15-18, 1865, rheumatism March 28, 1865, and constipation May 22, 1865. Mustered out with company Aug. 3, 1865.

Private Albert G. Reynolds – Mustered in on May 7, 1864. Admitted to Camp Discharge Hospital for vaccinia (cowpox) Dec. 27, 1864, and catarrh June 27, 1865. Mustered out with company Aug. 3, 1865. Joined Veteran Reserve Corps.

Private Joseph W. Reynolds – Mustered in on May 7, 1864. Mustered out with company Aug. 3, 1865.

Private William N. Reynolds – Mustered in on May 7, 1864. Hospitalized at Camp Discharge for catarrh Nov. 20-22, 1864, vaccinia (cowpox) Dec. 27, 1865, bronchitis Jan. 27-Feb. 5, 1865, and ecthyma July 1, 1865. Mustered out with company Aug. 3, 1865.

Private Jefferson Ringler – Mustered in on May 7, 1864. At Camp Discharge, hospitalized for diarrhea Nov. 17-18, 1864, and paronychia (finger infection) Feb. 12-26, 1865. Mustered out with company Aug. 3, 1865.

Private Peter G. Rolls – Mustered in on May 7, 1864. Hospitalized at Camp Discharge for lues veneria (venereal Disease) Nov. 13, 1864. Discharged on surgeon's certificate Feb. 26, 1865.

Private John L. Rosenberger – Mustered in on April 16, 1864. Camp Discharge Hospital Register: hospitalized for scabies May 29, 1865. Mustered out with company Aug. 3, 1865.

Private Cornelius Rynearson – Mustered in on May 7, 1864. At Camp Discharge, hospitalized for headache July 16, 1865. Mustered out with company Aug. 3, 1865.

Private Israel Seiders – Mustered in on May 7, 1864. Hospitalized at Camp Discharge for catarrh Nov. 13-Dec. 19, 1864, "int. fever tertian" Nov. 25-Dec. 7, 1864, paronychia (finger infection) Dec. 15-21, 1864, and chill Dec. 30, 1864. Mustered out with company Aug. 3, 1865. Joined Veteran Reserve Corps.

Private Joseph Seiders – Mustered in on May 7, 1864. Wounded at Petersburg, Va., June 18, 1864, with shell wound to right shoulder. Admitted to Camp Discharge Hospital for sore throat Dec. 27-29,1864. Mustered out with company Aug. 3, 1865. Joined Veteran Reserve Corps.

Private Frank Smith – Mustered in on May 7, 1864. Promoted to quartermaster sergeant May 11, 1864. Muster out date not recorded.

Private John L. Smith – Mustered in on May 7, 1864. Mustered out with company Aug. 3, 1865.

Private Truxton Smith – Mustered in on May 7, 1864. Hospitalized at Camp Discharge for catarrh Dec. 15-16, 1864. Mustered out with company Aug. 3, 1865.

Private John Spangler – Mustered in on May 7, 1864. Mustered out with company Aug. 3, 1865. Joined Veteran Reserve Corps.

Private Levi Stedg – Mustered in on May 7, 1864. Hospitalized at Camp Discharge for catarrh Nov. 26, 1864, "int. fever tert." March 2-17, 1865, and ecthyma May 15-21, 1865. Mustered out with company Aug. 3, 1865.

Private Ebenezer M. Stevens – Mustered in on May 7, 1864. Admitted to Camp Discharge Hospital for gonorrhea May 22 and June 1865. Mustered out with company Aug. 3, 1865.

Private Henry Stevens – Mustered in on May 7, 1864. Admitted to Camp Discharge Hospital for ecthyma May 13-23 and June 6, 1865. Mustered out with company Aug. 3, 1865.

Private Oliver Stout – Mustered in on May 7, 1864. Hospitalized at Camp Discharge for "cyanche tonsils" Jan. 5-30, 1865. Mustered out with company Aug. 3, 1865.

Private Robert C. Titus – Mustered in on May 7, 1864. Admitted to Camp Discharge Hospital for sore throat Dec. 24-31, 1864, diarrhea. Jan. 7-8, 1865, and balanitis (genital inflammation) May 20-23, 1865. Mustered out with company Aug. 3, 1865.

Private Jacob E. Troup – Mustered in on May 7, 1864. Hospitalized at Camp Discharge for "conv. typhoid fever" Dec. 4-16, 1864, catarrh Jan. 18-30, 1865. Mustered out with company Aug. 3, 1865.

Private John Way – Mustered in on May 7, 1864. Mustered out with company Aug. 3, 1865.

Private M.D. Whitebeck – Mustered in on May 7, 1864. Hospitalized at Camp Discharge for sore throat Dec. 3-21, 1864, furunculus (boil) Jan. 6-12, 1864, gonorrhea May 22, 1865, and catarrh June 8, 1865. Mustered out with company Aug. 3, 1865.

Private Ebenezer B. Whitney – Mustered in on May 7, 1864. Admitted to Camp Discharge Hospital for "int. fever tert." Nov. 23, 1864-Feb. 4, 1865. Mustered out with company Aug. 3, 1865.

Private Daniel Will – Mustered in on May 7, 1864. Hospitalized at Camp Discharge for cynanche tonsil Dec. 14-31, 1864, catarrh May 14-17, 1865, and sore throat Jan. 13-16, 1865. Mustered out with company Aug. 3, 1865. Joined Veteran Reserve Corps.

Private Jacob Wilson – Mustered in on May 7, 1864. Hospitalized at Camp Discharge for sore throat Jan. 15-20, 1865, catarrh May 15-18, 1865, ecthyma July 18, 1865. Mustered out with company Aug. 3, 1865. Joined Veteran Reserve Corps.

Private Henry J. Wolf – Mustered in on May 7, 1864. Mustered out with company Aug. 3, 1865.

Private John Wolford – Mustered in on May 7, 1864. Mustered out with company Aug. 3, 1865.

Private John S. Zeigler – Mustered in on May 7, 1864. At Camp Discharge, hospitalized for gonorrhea May 23, 1865. Mustered out with company Aug. 3, 1865.

187TH PA., COMPANY K (89 MEN)

1st Lieutenant Alex Blackburn – Mustered in on May 11, 1864. Mustered out with company Aug. 3, 1865.

2nd Lieutenant George S. Walker – Mustered in on April 12, 1864. Promoted from 1st sergeant Jan. 1, 1865. Mustered out with company Aug. 3, 1865.

Sergeant Lucien Bothwell – Mustered in on May 4, 1864. Promoted to 1st sergeant Jan. 1, 1865. Hospitalized at Camp Discharge for catarrh May 23, 1865, scurvy and mouth ulcers May 29, 1865. Mustered out with company Aug. 3, 1865. Joined Veteran Reserve Corps.

Sergeant Thomas Ramsey – Mustered in on May 4, 1864. Admitted to Camp Discharge Hospital for enteritis June 19, 1865. Mustered out with company Aug. 3, 1865.

Sergeant Charles Wesley – Mustered in on May 4, 1864. Mustered out with company Aug. 3, 1865. Joined Veteran Reserve Corps.

Sergeant Samuel Hook – Mustered in on May 4, 1864. Promoted to sergeant Jan. 1, 1865. Hospitalized at Camp Discharge for ophthalmia (eye inflammation) May 13-18, 1865. Mustered out with company Aug. 3, 1865. Joined Veteran Reserve Corps.

Sergeant George Doane – Mustered in on May 4, 1864. Hospitalized at Camp Discharge for ecthyma June 17, 1865. Promoted to sergeant July 1, 1865. Mustered out with company Aug. 3, 1865.

Sergeant Isaac B. Bowser – Mustered in on May 4, 1864. Admitted to Camp Discharge Hospital for gunshot wound May 13-19, 1865, gunshot wound of left thigh May 24, 1865. Discharged on Surgeon's Certificate, date unknown.

Corporal William Lewars – Mustered in on May 4, 1864. Mustered out with company Aug. 3, 1865.

Corporal Philip Garman – Mustered in on May 4, 1864. Mustered out with company Aug. 3, 1865. Joined Veteran reserve Corps.

Corporal Jay Whitehead – Mustered in on May 4, 1864. Mustered out with company Aug. 3, 1865.

Corporal Stephen Sawyer – Mustered in on May 4, 1864. Mustered out with company Aug. 3, 1865. Joined Veteran Reserve Corps.

Corporal John J. Eowland – Mustered in on May 4, 1864. Mustered out with company Aug. 3, 1865. Joined Veteran Reserve Corps.

Corporal John Dunn – Mustered in on May 4, 1864. Promoted to corporal May 1, 1865. Hospitalized at Camp Discharge for constipation May 13-15, 1865. Mustered out with company Aug. 3, 1865.

Corporal Dewitt C. Johnson – Mustered in on May 4, 1864. Admitted to Camp Discharge Hospital for bronchitis May 1865, for ecthyma June 12, 1865. Promoted to corporal July 1, 1865. Mustered out with company Aug. 3, 1865.

Corporal Edwin Rogers – Mustered in on May 4, 1864. Mustered out with company Aug. 3, 1865.

Musician Samuel Loury – Mustered in on May 4, 1864. Mustered out with company Aug. 3, 1865.

Private Jeremiah Austin – Mustered in on May 4, 1864. Mustered out with company Aug. 3, 1865.

Private Leander Bacon – Mustered in on May 4, 1864. Mustered out with company Aug. 3, 1865.

Private Zach T. Baltowser – Mustered in on May 13, 1864. Hospitalized at Camp Discharge for "dis. Heart" May 26. Discharged on Surgeon's Certificate, date unknown.

Private Alexander E. Case – Mustered in on May 4, 1864. Mustered out with company Aug. 3, 1865.

Private Samuel P. Collins – Mustered in on May 4, 1864. Admitted to Camp Discharge Hospital for dysphagia pharyngitis (throat ailment) May 29, 1865. Mustered out with company Aug. 3, 1865.

Private John A. Cree – Mustered in on May 4, 1864. Mustered out with company Aug. 3, 1865.

Private Jacob B. Cobaugh – Mustered in on May 4, 1864. Mustered out with company Aug. 3, 1865.

Private John C. Connell – Mustered in on May 4, 1864. Mustered out with company Aug. 3, 1865.

Private Henry Culp – Mustered in on May 4, 1864. Hospitalized at Camp Discharge for gonorrhea June 2, 1865. Mustered out with company Aug. 3, 1865.

Private John J. Campbell – Mustered in on May 4, 1864. Mustered out with company Aug. 3, 1865.

Private William Cortright – Mustered in on May 4, 1864. Admitted to Camp Discharge Hospital for hemorrhoids May 20, 1865. Mustered out with company Aug. 3, 1865.

Private Anson Dann – Mustered in on May 4, 1864. Mustered out with company Aug. 3, 1865.

Private Paul Dishong – Mustered in on May 4, 1864. Hospitalized at Camp Discharge for diarrhea July 21, 1865. Mustered out with company Aug. 3, 1865.

Private Thomas M. Davis – Mustered in on May 4, 1864. Hospitalized at Camp Discharge for constipation May 14-16 and June 11, 1865. Mustered out with company Aug. 3, 1865.

Private Edward Doane – Mustered in on May 4, 1864. At Camp Discharge, hospitalized for gunshot wound of hand June 16, 1865. Discharged by general order, date unknown.

Private Jacob Evans – Mustered in on May 4, 1864. Mustered out with company Aug. 3, 1865.

Private Charles B. Ellis – Mustered in on May 4, 1864. Hospitalized at Camp Discharge for catarrh May 14-18, 1865. Mustered out with company Aug. 3, 1865.

Private Benjamin Figart – Mustered in on May 4, 1864. Mustered out with company Aug. 3, 1865.

Private Daniel Fry – Mustered in on May 4, 1864. Mustered out with company Aug. 3, 1865.

Private Winfield S. Geiter – Mustered in on May 4, 1864. Admitted to Camp Discharge Hospital for cephalalgia (headache) May 27, 1865. Mustered out with company Aug. 3, 1865.

Private George Grafius – Mustered in on May 4, 1864. Hospitalized at Camp Discharge for hemorrhoids May 29, 1865. Mustered out with company Aug. 3, 1865.

Private Thomas Graves – Mustered in on May 4, 1864. Mustered out with company Aug. 3, 1865.

Private William Garrison – Mustered in on April 8, 1864. Mustered out with company Aug. 3, 1865.

Private Adam Garman – Mustered in on May 4, 1864. Mustered out with company Aug. 3, 1865.

Private Nathaniel P. Green – Mustered in on May 4, 1864. Admitted to Camp Discharge Hospital for gunshot wounds May 13-19, 1865. Discharged on Surgeon's Certificate, date unknown.

Private Christian Geiter – Mustered in on Sept. 5, 1864. Discharged by general order July 15, 1865.

Private Joseph R. Hollen – Mustered in on May 4, 1864. Mustered out with company Aug. 3, 1865.

Private William Hopkins – Mustered in on May 4, 1864. Mustered out with company Aug. 3, 1865.

Private John Hartman – Mustered in on May 4, 1864. Mustered out with company Aug. 3, 1865. Joined Veteran Reserve Corps.

Private John J. Jones – Mustered in on May 4, 1864. Admitted to Camp Discharge Hospital for headache May 26, 1865. Mustered out with company Aug. 3, 1865.

Private James Kennelly – Mustered in on May 10, 1864. Hospitalized at Camp Discharge for gonorrhea May 26, 1865. Mustered out with company Aug. 3, 1865.

Private Daniel Kennelly – Mustered in on May 10, 1864. Mustered out with company Aug. 3, 1865.

Private George W. Kuhn – Mustered in on May 10, 1864. Discharged by general order July 3, 1865.

Private Emanuel Louder – Mustered in on May 4, 1864. Mustered out with company Aug. 3, 1865.

Private William N. Lovell – Mustered in on May 4, 1864. Mustered out with company Aug. 3, 1865.

Private Josiah Lenig – Mustered in on May 4, 1864. Hospitalized at Camp Discharge for catarrh May 20-21 and May 28, 1865. Died at Philadelphia, Pa., Sept. 20, 1865.

Private Benjamin F. Myers – Mustered in on May 4, 1864. Mustered out with company Aug. 3, 1865.

Private John Malanophy – Mustered in on May 4, 1864. Mustered out with company Aug. 3, 1865.

Private Jacob Miller – Mustered in on April 4, 1864. Admitted to Camp Discharge Hospital for catarrh June 12, 1865. Mustered out with company Aug. 3, 1865.

Private William Morgan – Mustered in on May 4, 1864. Mustered out with company Aug. 3, 1865. Joined Veteran Reserve Corps.

Private John W. Minnich – Mustered in on May 4, 1864. Mustered out with company Aug. 3, 1865.

Private Hiram Miller – Mustered in on May 4, 1864. Mustered out with company Aug. 3, 1865.

Private Daniel D. Mead – Mustered in on May 4, 1864. Hospitalized at Camp Discharge for rheumatism May 26, 1865. Discharged on surgeon's certificate, date unknown.

Private Anier McElhose – Mustered in on May 4, 1864. Mustered out with company Aug. 3, 1865.

Private Philip C. McDonald – Mustered in on May 4, 1864. Admitted to Camp Discharge Hospital for constipation May 28, 1865, rheumatism and colic June 11, 1865, ulcer of lip July 21, 1865. Mustered out with company Aug. 3, 1865.

Private Joseph O'Brien – Mustered in on May 4, 1864. Hospitalized at Camp Discharge for constipation May 16, 1865. Deserted. Returned. Mustered out with company Aug. 3, 1865.

Private Thomas M. Reese – Mustered in on May 4, 1864. Hospitalized at Camp Discharge for catarrh May 17-21, 1865, for indigestion June 1, 1865. Mustered out with company Aug. 3, 1865.

Private Elias Rowland – Mustered in on May 4, 1864. At Camp Discharge, hospitalized for back sprain July 15, 1865. Mustered out with company Aug. 3, 1865.

Private Benjamin Rogers – Mustered in on May 4, 1864. Admitted to Camp Discharge Hospital for chancres (syphilitic ulcer) May 25 and May 27, 1865, and orchitis (genital inflammation) July 21, 1865. Mustered out with company Aug. 3, 1865.

Private Cornelius Rhodes – Mustered in on May 4, 1864. Mustered out with company Aug. 3, 1865.

Private Joseph Ross – Mustered in on May 4, 1864. Mustered out with company Aug. 3, 1865. Joined Veteran Reserve Corps.

Private Samuel Simpson – Mustered in on May 4, 1864. Discharged by general order July 31, 1865.

Private W. W. Spaulding – Mustered in on May 4, 1864. Mustered out with company Aug. 3, 1865.

Private Malvin H. Seely – Mustered in on May 4, 1864. Absent, sick at muster out.

Private Webster Spencer – Mustered in on May 4, 1864. Hospitalized at Camp Discharge for sore foot and erysipelas (skin infection) May 27, 1865. Mustered out with company Aug. 3, 1865.

Private Henry Swenck – Mustered in on May 4, 1864. Mustered out with company Aug. 3, 1865.

Private William H. Sowers – Mustered in on May 4, 1864. Admitted to Camp Discharge Hospital for cough and debility May 16, 1865. Mustered out with company Aug. 3, 1865.

Private Philip Smith – Mustered in on May 4, 1864. Admitted to Camp Discharge Hospital for headache June 12, 1865. Mustered out with company Aug. 3, 1865.

Private Thomas L. G. Shearer – Mustered in on May 4, 1864. Hospitalized at Camp Discharge hernia May 26, 1865. Discharged on surgeon's certificate, date unknown.

Private Abram Spare – Mustered in on May 4, 1864. Discharged, date unknown.

Private David Searfoss – Mustered in on May 4, 1864. Deserted July 2, 1865.

Private Jacob Titman – Mustered in on April 8, 1864. Hospitalized at Camp Discharge for enteritis June 8, 1865. Mustered out with company Aug. 3, 1865.

Private Frederick M. Thomas – Mustered in on May 4, 1864. Mustered out with company Aug. 3, 1865.

Private Joseph B. Ulmer – Mustered in on May 4, 1864. Admitted to Camp Discharge Hospital for infection of jaw June 19, 1865. Mustered out with company Aug. 3, 1865.

Private Newell J. Verguson – Mustered in on May 4, 1864. Mustered out with company Aug. 3, 1865. Joined Veteran Reserve Corps.

Private Clark V. Worden – Mustered in on May 4, 1864. Mustered out with company Aug. 3, 1865.

Private Thomas Warfield – Mustered in on May 4, 1864. Mustered out with company Aug. 3, 1865.

Private Daniel Wesley – Mustered in on May 4, 1864. Mustered out with company Aug. 3, 1865.

Private Frederick Weidley – Mustered in on May 4, 1864. Admitted to Camp Discharge Hospital for jaundice May 22, 1865. Mustered out with company Aug. 3, 1865.

Private John Weaver – Mustered in on May 4, 1864. At Camp Discharge, hospitalized for cephalalgia July 20, 1865. Mustered out with company Aug. 3, 1865.

Private Isaac Wissinger – Mustered in on May 4, 1864. Hospitalized at Camp Discharge for constipation July 21, 1865. Mustered out with company Aug. 3, 1865.

Private Michael Wesley – Mustered in on May 4, 1864. Admitted to Camp Discharge Hospital for ankylosis (stiffening) of fingers of right-hand May 25, 1865. Discharged on surgeon's certificate, date unknown.

7th Battalion, US Veteran Volunteers

7th Regiment Infantry

Organized in the District of Columbia in early 1865. Attached to the 3rd Brigade, 1st Division, 1st Veteran Corps, to June 1865. Assigned to duty in Washington, D.C., Virginia, and Pennsylvania until muster-out July 23, 1866.

Captain James Dunn/Dunne, Co. B – Had served in 1st Missouri Engineers, Co. A, and 25th Missouri Infantry, Co. C.

Captain Solomon S. Hovey Jr, Co. K – Had served as captain in 21st Mass., Cos. E, F, D.

1st Lieutenant Edmond English, Co.'s E, K, G, F, S – Had served in 6th US Veteran Volunteers

1st Lieutenant Henry P. Ritzius, Co. K – Had been 2nd Lieut./Major in 52nd N.Y. Infantry, Cos. A, F, G, C.

Lieutenant Peter Byrne, Co. K – Had served in 115th Pa Infantry, Co. A, mustering in as sergeant Nov. 18, 1861, in Phila. at age 28. Promoted to 2nd Lt. May 18, 1862. To captain June 29, 1863. Discharged June 22, 1864, by reason of consolidation. At Camp Discharge, hospitalized for leg ulcer July 31, 1865.

2nd Lieutenant Albert Quigley, Co.'s D, K – Had been in 2nd Pa. Reserves (31st Pa. Infantry, Co. A, mustering in on May 25, 1861, in Phila. at age 26. Mustered out of Pa. Reserves June 16, 1864.

The following enlisted men of the 7th USV.V. had served in Pa. regiments:

Private John Aldworth, Co. B – Had been in 3rd Pa. Reserves (31st Pa. Infantry), Co. K, enrolling May 27, 1861, in Phila. at age 26, a carpenter. Mustered out of Pa. Reserves June 17, 1864.

Private Jefferson Arthur, Co. B – Was in 106th Pa Infantry, Co. I, mustering in on Aug. 26, 1861, as corporal, and was captured at Petersburg, Va., June 22, 1864.

Private John Boyle, Co. B – Had served in 23rd Pa. Infantry, Co. F, joining Aug. 2, 1861, in Phila. at age 21. Mustered out Sept. 8, 1864.

Private Crosby Carlton, Co. K – Was in 36th Pa. Infantry (7th Pa. Reserves), Co. I, joined June 14, 1861, in West Chester, at age 23, a teacher. Captured May 5, 1864, at Wilderness and imprisoned at Andersonville. Went to Camp Discharge, was discharged from 36th Pa. Jan. 28, 1865.

Private John Conway, Cos. F, K – Had been in 36th Pa. Infantry (7th Pa. Reserves), Co. E, enrolling May 31, 1861, in Phila. at age 21, a laborer. Mustered out of 36th Pa. June 16, 1864.

Private Josiah Logenour, Co. B – Had been in 104th Pa. Infantry, Co. E, mustering in on Sept. 12, 1861, in Doylestown at age 20. Captured at Fair Oaks, Va., May 31, 1862. Mustered out with company Sept. 30, 1864.

Private Francis Dashow, Co. B – Had served in 73rd Pa. Infantry, Co. K, mustering in on July 15, 1861, in Phila. at age 43. Discharged Jan. 15, 1862.

Private John Dawling/Dowling, Co. K – Had been in 5th Pa. Infantry, Co. H, mustering in on Aug. 10, 1861, in Phila. at age 30, a draper. Discharged Sept. 7, 1864.

Private Alexander Gillingham, Co. B – Had been in 2nd Pa. Heavy Artillery, Co. D, mustering in on Nov. 22, 1861, in Phila. at age 36. Was a sergeant but discharged on surgeon's certificate Jan. 6, 1863.

Private Robert Goss, Co. B – Was in 69th Pa. Infantry, Co. I, mustering in on Aug. 19, 1861, in Phila. at age 26. Wounded at Ball's Cross Roads, Va., Sept. 29, 1861, and discharged on surgeon's certificate.

Private George W. Hein(m)er, Cos. F, K – Likely in 109th Pa. Infantry, Co. G (as George W. Humer), mustering in on April 4, 1862, in Phila. at age 30.

Private Timothy Lucas, Co. B – Had been in 3rd Pa. Cavalry, Co. E, mustering in on Aug. 16, 1861, in Washington, D.C., at age 30, a shoemaker. Mustered out Aug. 24, 1864.

Teamster Andrew J. McNamee, Co. B—Had been in 72nd Pa. Infantry, Co. H, mustering in on Aug. 10, 1861, in Phila. at age 29. Mustered out Aug. 24, 1864.

Private Lafayette Palmer, Co. B – Had enrolled in 41st Pa. Infantry (12th Pa. Reserves), Co. A., May 30, 1861, in Phila. at age 37, a machinist. Re-enlisted March 14, 1862. Transferred to Veteran Reserve Corps. Sept. 1, 1863.

Private William Ratcliff, Co. B – Was in 110th Pa. Infantry, Co. E, mustering in on Aug. 30, 1861, in Phila. at age 21, a laborer. Discharged Aug. 30, 1864, expiration of term.

Private Augustus Raymon/Reeman, Co. B – Enrolled in 49th Pa. Infantry, Co. A, on Aug. 15, 1861, in Milroy, Pa., at age 19, a laborer. Mustered in at Camp Griffin, Va., Oct. 24, 1861. Captured at Chantilly, Va., Oct. 14, 1863. Released at Savannah, Ga., Nov. 20, 1864. Discharged Jan. 27, 1865.

Private Charles Schneck, Co. B – Had mustered in to 3rd Pa. Cavalry, Co. D, on Aug. 13, 1861, in Washington D.C. at age 24, a cooper. Captured Jan. 7, 1864. Returned to duty Aug. 12, 1864, in Washington. Mustered out Aug. 24, 1864.

Private John Shay, Co. B – Served in 93rd Pa. Infantry, Co. C, having mustered in on Oct. 21, 1861, in Lebanon at age 18, a miner. Wounded at Chancellorsville, Va., May 3, 1863. Transferred to Veteran Reserve Corps, date unknown.

Private Michael Smith, Co. B – Had been in 72nd Pa. Infantry, Co. G, mustering in on Aug. 10, 1861, in Phila. at age 19, a gentleman. Mustered out with company Aug. 24, 1864.

Musician Casper H. Somerdyke/Sumerdike, Co. B – Mustered in to 104th Pa. Infantry, Co. D, on Sept. 17, 1861, as a drummer, in Doylestown at age 15. Mustered out Sept. 30, 1864, expiration of term.

Sergeant Clark Stockdill, Cos. C, K – Had served in 9th Pa. Reserves, Co. F, mustering in on July 28, 1861, in Washington D.C. at age 20, a carpenter. Mustered out May 13, 1864.

Private Henry Timmins, Cos. E, K – Had mustered in to 81st Pa. Infantry, Co. A, on Aug. 6, 1861, at age 37, a laborer.

Private Samuel Wallace, Co. B – Had been in 2nd Pa. Reserves, Co. H, mustering in on Aug. 1, 1864, in Sandy Hook, Md., at age 30, a plasterer. Promoted to 1st sergeant May 1863, and commissioned 2nd lieutenant September 1863. Reduced to sergeant May 1864. Mustered out with company June 16, 1864.

Private Joseph Watson, Co. B – Had enrolled in 3rd Pa. Reserves, Co. K, on May 27, 1861, in Phila. at age 26, a carpenter. Mustered in on July 29, 1861, in Harrisburg. Mustered out with company June 17, 1864.

Private John Whalon/Whealon, Co. B – Mustered in to 95th Pa. Infantry, Co. F, on Sept. 14, 1861, in Phila. at age 23. Captured at Spotsylvania May 14, 1864. Discharged Jan. 31, 1865.

Private Charles H. Williams, Co. B – Had been in 69th Pa. Infantry, as musician in Company C, then promoted to principal musician Field & Staff 1863. Mustered out, expiration of term.

Private John Winnemore, Co. B – Had served in 73rd Pa. Infantry, mustering in on Aug. 3, 1861, in Phila. at age 28, as sergeant. Discharged July 28, 1864. Mustered out July 28, 1864, expiration of term.

Private Lawrence Monroe, Co. B – Had been in 5th Pa Reserves, Co. D, mustering in on June 21, 1861, at Camp Tennally at age 31, a laborer. Mustered out June 11, 1864. Hospitalized at Camp Discharge for gonorrhea Aug. 8, 1865.

Private William Waltemeyer, Co. K – Was in 87th Pa Infantry, Co. C, mustering in on Sept. 16, 1861, in York at age 22. Mustered out Oct. 13, 1864. Treated for syphilis at Camp Discharge Hospital on July 25, 1865.

Non-Pennsylvania men in 7th US Veteran Volunteers, with prior units noted:

Sergeant William E. Cushing, Co. K (Likely with 11th Mass. Infantry, Cos. F, K) – Admitted to Camp Discharge Hospital for foot ulcer on July 20, 1865.

Private William F. Coolidge, Co. K (11th Mass. Infantry) – At Camp Discharge Hospital Register, hospitalized for ecthyma on July 20, 1865.

Private John Bentz, Co. K (103rd N.Y. Infantry) – Admitted to Camp Discharge Hospital for catarrh on July 20, 1865.

Private David B. Gerry, Co. K (Mass. Light Artillery) – Admitted to Camp Discharge Hospital for gastroenteritis on July 20, 1865.

Private Ira A. Bryant, Co. K (17th Vet. Res. Corps) – Admitted to Camp Discharge Hospital for dysphonia (voice problems) on July 20, 1865.

Private Peter Gibney, Co. K (71st N.Y. Volunteers) – Admitted to Camp Discharge Hospital Register for jaundice on July 20, 1865.

Corporal David Hetzell, Co. K (74th N.Y. Volunteers) – Entered Camp Discharge Hospital with constipation on July 21 and Aug. 15, 1865.

Private Patrick White, Co. K (Perhaps Frederick White) – Admitted to Camp Discharge Hospital with constipation on July 21, 1865.

Corporal John T. Garee, Co. B (7th Ohio Volunteers) – Admitted to Camp Discharge Hospital with jaundice on July 21, 1865.

Private Fillippi Pass, Co. B (39th N.Y. Volunteers) – Admitted to Camp Discharge Hospital for bilious catarrh on July 22, 1865.

Private Alfred Seco, Co. B (5th N.Y. Volunteers) – Admitted to Camp Discharge Hospital with gonorrhea on July 22, 1865.

Private David Q.(A) Cole, Or Daniel G. Cole Co. B (US Navy) – Admitted to Camp Discharge Hospital with diarrhea on July 22-31, 1865.

Sergeant (2nd Lieutenant) Leonard Fisler, Co. B (9th Vol. Res. Corps) – Admitted to Camp Discharge Hospital with tertian fever on July 22, 1865.

Private Michael N. Ham, Co. B (11th N.Y. Independent Battery) – Admitted to Camp Discharge Hospital with tertian fever on July 22, 1865.

Private James C. Erwin, Co. B (3rd US Cavalry) – Admitted to Camp Discharge Hospital for ecthyma on July 24, 1865.

Private Lorenzo Fishinger, Co. K (103rd N.Y. Volunteers) – Admitted to Camp Discharge Hospital for constipation on July 25, 1865.

Private Thomas Potts, Co. K (4th N.J. Infantry) – Entered Camp Discharge Hospital with sore feet on July 25, boil on foot Aug. 24, 1865.

Private Thomas Riley, Co. K (VRC 2nd N.J. Cavalry) – Admitted to Camp Discharge Hospital for headache from sunstroke on July 26, 1865.

Sergeant John C. Eichelberger, Co. B (2nd Iowa Infantry) – Admitted to Camp Discharge Hospital for ecthyma on July 27, 1865.

Private William H. Carey/Carry, Co. K (136th Co. 2nd Battery Vet. Res. Corps) – Admitted to Camp Discharge Hospital for diarrhea on July 27, 1865.

Private Moses Ferris, Co. K (Vet. Res. Corps) – Admitted to Camp Discharge Hospital for contusion and hand sprain on July 27, 1865.

Private James Butterworth, Co. K (3rd R.I. Heavy Artillery) – Admitted to Camp Discharge Hospital for chills from sunstroke on July 27, 1865.

Private Eugene Burchenal, Co. B (1st Del. Infantry) – Admitted to Camp Discharge Hospital for indigestion on July 28-31, 1865.

Private Frederick Wilkins, Co. K (39th N.Y. Volunteers) – Admitted to Camp Discharge Hospital for syphilis on July 29, gonorrhea on Aug. 1, constipation on Aug. 19, 1865.

Private Daniel McCarty, Co. B (11th US Infantry) – Admitted to Camp Discharge Hospital for gonorrhea on July 30-31, 1865.

Private Walter Coulter, Co. B (7th N.J. Infantry) – Admitted to Camp Discharge Hospital for "quotidian int." fever on July 31, 1865.

Corporal Joshua Marsan, Co. B (25th Ill. Infantry) – Admitted to Camp Discharge Hospital for sienteria (dysentery) on July 31, 1865.

Private Charles Schmitt, Co. B (34th Co. 2nd Battery Vet. Res. Corps) – Admitted to Camp Discharge Hospital for truritus (skin rash) on July 31-Aug. 31, 1865.

Private John W. Chandler, Co. K (2nd N.J. Infantry) – Hospitalized at Camp Discharge for rheumatism on July 31-Aug. 2, 1865.

Private Asa W. Jaquith, Co. K (9th Maine Infantry) – Admitted to Camp Discharge Hospital for back sprain on July 31-Aug. 2, 1865; chancre Aug. 12, 1865.

Private George Lang, Co. K (39th N.Y. Infantry) – Admitted to Camp Discharge Hospital for gonorrhea on July 31, gonorrhea Aug. 8, bubo Aug. 16, 1865.

Private James Green, Co. B (1st Tenn. Cavalry) – Admitted to Camp Discharge Hospital for debility on Aug. 1, 1865.

Private Morris Stack, Co. K (71st N.Y. Volunteers) – Hospitalized at Camp Discharge for swelled face on Aug. 1-2, 1865.

Private Thomas Potts, Co. K (4th N.J. Infantry) – Hospitalized at Camp Discharge for orchitis (inflamed genitals) on Aug. 1, 1865.

Private Isaac Coe, Co. K (90th N.Y. Infantry) – Treated at Camp Discharge Hospital for diarrhea on Aug. 3, 1865.

Corporal David Lee, Co. K (29th Mass Infantry) – Admitted to Camp Discharge Hospital for diarrhea on Aug. 3-4, chronic intermittent ecthyma on Aug. 24, 1865.

Private William Moody, Co. B (2nd D.C. Volunteers) – Treated at Camp Discharge Hospital for chancre (genital ulcer) on Aug. 5, 1865.

Private Abraham Johndrew, Co. K (2nd N.J. Volunteers) – Admitted to Camp Discharge Hospital for ecthyma on Aug. 5, 1865.

Sergeant John C. Steinbauer, Co. K (8th N.J. Volunteers) – Treated at Camp Discharge Hospital for constipation on Aug. 6-7, 1865.

Private Napoleon DeBuc, Co. K (8th N.J. Volunteers) – Admitted to Camp Discharge Hospital for otitis (inflamed ear) on Aug. 9, 1865.

Private Richard M. Blake, Co. K (2nd N.J. Infantry) – Admitted to Camp Discharge Hospital for diarrhea on Aug. 9 and Aug. 16, 1865.

Private Edward W. Pratt, Co. K (2nd Mass Light Artillery) – Treated at Camp Discharge Hospital for cough on Aug. 14, 1865.

Private John Daley, Co. K (23rd Mass. Volunteers) – Admitted to Camp Discharge Hospital for "chronic int. sudamina" (akin to heat rash) on Aug. 12, 1865.

Private Roswell Knowlton, Co. K (2nd US Artillery) – Hospitalized at Camp Discharge for fall from a horse, thigh contusion on Aug. 15, 1865.

Corporal William L. Walker, Co. K – Admitted to Camp Discharge Hospital for chancres on Aug. 16, 1865.

Private Patrick Blunt, Co. K (9th Mass. Infantry) – Hospitalized at Camp Discharge for diarrhea on Aug. 16, 1865.

Private Alva J. Wilson, Co. K (1st Mass. Volunteers) – Treated at Camp Discharge Hospital for diarrhea on Aug. 18, 1865.

Private Richard Warren, Co. K (1st US Cavalry) – Admitted to Camp Discharge Hospital for gonorrhea on Aug. 21, 1865.

Private George W. Carman, Co. K (8th N.J. Infantry) – Hospitalized at Camp Discharge for icterus (jaundice) on Aug. 21, 1865.

Private William McConnell, Co. K (79th N.Y. Infantry) – Hospitalized at Camp Discharge for ecthyma on Aug. 23, 1865.

Private William McKinzie, Co. K (65th N.Y. Infantry) – Hospitalized at Camp Discharge for tertian int. on Aug. 24, 1865.

Corporal Robert W. Jessup, Co. K (17th Mass. Volunteers) – Treated at Camp Discharge Hospital for bruises and cuts from being dragged by horse on Aug. 29, 1865.

Private Isaac R. Babcock, Co. K (2th Mass. Infantry)

Private George W. Baily, Co. K (16th US Infantry)

Private Joseph Barkman, Co. K (1st N.Y. Cavalry)

Private Richard A. Barry, Co. B (3rd Md. Cavalry)

Musician George H. Baylis, Co.'s E, K

Corporal Elias Beaham, Co. K (31st N.Y. Infantry)

Private Samuel Boyd, Cos. D, K (8th Mo. Infantry)

Private William Brennan, Co. B (2nd US Infantry)

Sergeant Robert S. Brown, Co. K (8th N.J. Infantry)

Private Edward Byrne, Co. B (9th Mass. Infantry)

Corporal Horatio Cameron, Co. B (1st Mass. Cavalry)

Private Peter Carr, Cos. I, K (16th Vet. Res. Corps)

Private Edward Colbert, Co. K (4th N.J. Cavalry)

Private David A. Cole, Co. B

Private Charles Crager, Co. B (1st Md. Cavalry)

Private Henry Davis, Co. K (60th N.Y. Volunteers)

Private James Deany/Deary/Dearing, Co. K (71st N.Y. Volunteers)

Private John Douglas, Co. B (5th Wisc. Infantry)

Private Gustav Dreyfus, Co. K (9th N.Y. Volunteers)

Private John Eichman, Co. B (1st N.Y. Cavalry)

Sergeant Elmore Evans, Co. K (42nd Ohio Infantry)

Private Moses Farris, Co. K (6th Conn. Volunteers)

Corporal Joseph Finkelmeyer, Co. K (7th N.Y. Volunteers)

Corporal Lloyd Ford, Cos. G, K (US Navy)

Private Ansel J. Foster, Co.K (12th Mass. Infantry)

Private Charles Grager/Greger/Gregor, Co. B (Vet. Res. Corps. Possibly 12th Maine Infantry)

Private John Hall, Cos. I, K (6th Conn. Volunteers)

Private Daniel Har(r)igan/Horigan, Co. K (95th N.Y. Volunteers)

Musician Robert B. Harris, Co. K ((10th Maine Volunteers)

Private Samuel Harris, Co. B (US Navy)
Corporal Frank B. Hastings, Co. B (13th Mass. Infantry)
Private Charles Hauser, Co. B (1st N.J. "Lincoln" Cavalry)
Private John Hervey, Co. K (99th N.Y. Volunteers)
Corporal David Hertzell, Co. K (74th N.Y. Volunteers)
Private William G. Hilt/Hitt, Cos. I, K (24th Mass. Volunteers)
Private Thomas Howard, Co. B (9th Mass. Infantry)
Private Isaac C. Howell, Co. B (2nd N.J. Volunteers)
Private Augustus Hungerford, Co. B (7th Ohio Vol. Infantry)
Private Andrew Jackson, Co. B (15th N.Y. Volunteers)
Corporal Richard M. James, Co. K (40th N.Y. Volunteers)
Sergeant George Jones, Co. B (9th Battery Wisc. Light Artillery)
Private Frederick Klink, Co. B (5th US Artillery)
Private Ludwig Koch, Co. B (Reg 1" A Corps. Mo.)
Corporal Levin (Samuel) J. (F). Lank, Co. B (1st Del. Infantry)
Private James Linch/Lynch, Co. K (12th Mass. Volunteers)
Musician Augustus A. Lindon/Linton Co. K (11th Mass. Volunteers)
Private Alexander Livingston, Co. B (2nd Ill. Light Artillery, 14th Ill. Infantry)
Private William J. Love, Co. K (28th Mass. Infantry)
Private Silas Marcelle, Co. K (2nd D.C. Infantry)
Private John March/Mertz, Co. K (103rd N.Y. Volunteers)
Private Anthony Mayer/Moyer/Myer, Co. K
Private Samuel/Solomon McAdams Co. B (30th N.Y. Volunteers)
Private Daniel McCann, Co. B (3rd US Artillery)
Corporal James F. McGunigle, Co. K (9th Mass. Volunteers)
Private John McNamara, Co. B (23rd Ill. Volunteers)
Sergeant Nathan L. Meands/Mends, Co. K (22nd Mass. Volunteers)
Private Lewis/Louis L. Mitchell, Co. K (1st N.Y. Volunteers)
Private Charles J. Moore, Co. B (1st Md. Light Artillery)
Corporal Thomas G. Nightengale (11 Mass. Volunteers)
Private Alexander Noble, Co. B (16th N.Y. Volunteers)
Private Hiram G./T. Nourse Co. B (18th Mass. Volunteers)
Private Lewis Pasquay, Co. B (1st Md. Volunteers)
Corporal Joseph Patterson, Co. B (79th N.Y. Infantry)
Sergeant George R. Philipps, Co. B (2nd Mass. Infantry)
Corporal Joseph Rand, Co. B (16th Mass. Volunteers)
Private William Randon, Co. K (45th N.J. Infantry)
Private Edwin Reed, Co. K ((2nd D.C. Volunteers)
Private Thomas Rex, Co. B (51st N.Y. Volunteers)
Private Edward P. Richardson, Co. K (4th US Artillery)
Private Patrick/William Riley, Co. K (8th N.J. Volunteers)
Private William Rotherman, Co. B (7th N.J. Infantry)
Wagoneer Louis J. Shepard, Co. K (1st Mass. Cavalry)
Private Anthony Sherlock, Co. B (3rd N.J. Volunteers)
Private John Shilling, Co. K (103rd N.Y. Volunteers)
Private George W. Spalding, Co. K (4th Mass. Cavalry)
Sergeant John C. Steinbauer, Co. K (8th N.J. Volunteers)
Private Henry Stettler, Co, B (US Navy)

Sergeant Jeremiah Stewart/Stuart, Co. K (13th Mass. Volunteers)
Private William Swift, Co. B (12th US Infantry)
Sergeant John B. Thompson, Co. K (8th N.J. Volunteers)
Private Augustus Trainer, Co. B (5th Md. Volunteers)
Private George H. Upton, Co. K (4th N.H. Volunteers)
Private Jacob Wagner, Co. B (2nd Mass. Infantry)
Private John Walch/Walsh, Co. K (4th US Infantry)
Private Anthony Warsaw, Co. B
Private John Welch, Co. K (8th N.J. Volunteers)
Private Frederick White, Co. K (13th N.Y. Volunteers)
Private Henry Williams, Co. B (2nd Md. Eastern Shore Infantry)
Private Charles Wilson, Co. B (Possibly 95th N.Y. Volunteers)
Private Preston W. Wright, Co. B (1st Md. Light Artillery)

References

Books

Auge, M. *Lives of the Eminent Dead and Biographical Notes of Prominent Living Citizens.* Norristown, PA: self-published, 1879.

Bates, Samuel P. *History of Pennsylvania Volunteers, 1861-5; In Compliance With Acts of the Legislature.* Harrisburg, PA: B. Singerly, 1870.

Billings, John D. *Hardtack and Coffee: The Unwritten Story of Army Life.* Boston, MA: G.M. Smith, 1888.

Board of Editors, *History of the First Troop Philadelphia City Cavalry 1914-1948.* Philadelphia, PA: William F. Fell, 1948.

Denney, Robert E. *Civil War Medicine: Care & Comfort of the Wounded.* New York: Sterling Publishing, 1994.

Dorwart, Bonnie Brice. *Death Is in the Breeze: Disease During the American Civil War.* Frederick, Maryland: National Museum of Civil War Medicine Press, 2009.

Dougherty, Michael. *Prison Diary of Michael Dougherty: While Confined at Pemberton, Barrett's, Libby, Andersonville and Other Southern Prisons.* Bristol, PA: Charles A. Dougherty, 1908.

Ernsberger, Don. *Paddy Owen's Regulars: A History of the 69th Pennsylvania "Irish Volunteers."* Xlibris, 2004.

Faust, Drew Gilpin. *This Republic of Suffering: Death and the American Civil War.* New York: Knopf, 2008.

Flower, Milton E., editor. *Dear Folks at Home. The Civil Letters of Leo W. and John I. Faller, With an Account of Andersonville.* Carlisle, PA: Cumberland County Historical Society, 1963.

Gibbs, James M. *History of the First Battalion Pennsylvania Six Months Volunteers and 187th Regiment Pennsylvania Volunteer Infantry.* Harrisburg, PA: Central Printing and Publishing House, 1905.

Huntington, D.L., and Otis, George A., editors. *The Medical and Surgical History of the War of the Rebellion.* Washington, D.C.: Government Printing Office, 1883.

Lowry, Thomas P. *The Story the Soldiers Wouldn't Tell: Sex in the Civil War.* Mechanicsburg, PA: Stackpole, 1994.

Miller, Francis T. *Prisons and Hospitals: The Photographic History of the Civil War.* Secaucus, NJ: Castle Books, 1957.

Mott, Valentine, chairman of inquiry. *Narrative of Privations and Sufferings of United States Officers and Soldiers While Prisoners of War in the Hands of Rebel Authorities.* Philadelphia, PA: US Sanitary Commission, 1864.

Price, Isaiah. *History of the Ninety-Seventh Regiment, Pennsylvania Volunteer Infantry, During the War of the Rebellion, 1861-65.* Philadelphia, PA: Isaiah Price, 1875.

Roberts, Edward F. *Andersonville Journey: The Civil War's Greatest Tragedy.* Shippensburg, PA: Burd Street Press, 1998.

Stille, Charles J. *History of the United States Sanitary Commission, Being the General Report of Its Work During the War of the Rebellion.* Philadelphia, PA: Lippincott, 1866.

Walker, James D., editor. *Pennsylvania at Andersonville, Georgia: Ceremonies at the Dedication of the Memorial Erected by the Commonwealth of Pennsylvania.* Harrisburg, PA: Pennsylvania Andersonville Memorial Commission, 1905.

Ward, Geoffrey. *The Civil War: An Illustrated History.* New York: Knopf, 1990.

Waskie, Anthony. *Philadelphia and the Civil War: Arsenal of the Union.* Charleston, SC: History Press, 2011.

Wittenberg, Eric J. *Rush's Lancers: The Sixth Pennsylvania Cavalry in the Civil War.* Yardley, Pennsylvania: Westholme, 2006.

Wray, William J. *History of the Twenty Third Pennsylvania Volunteer Infantry: Birney's Zouaves, Three Months and Three Years Service Civil War, 1861-1865.* Philadelphia, PA: Twenty-Third Regiment Survivors Association, 1904.

Articles

Bachman, Aaron Eugene. Civil War memoir. *Ancestry.com.*

Costa, Dora L. "Scarring and Mortality Selection Among Civil War POWs: A Long-Term Mortality, Morbidity and Socioeconomic Follow-Up." *Demography*, November 2012, Vol. 49, No. 4.

Cross, David F. "Why Did the Yankees Die at Andersonville?" *North & South* magazine, September 2003, Vol. 6, No. 6.

Dixon, Ina. "Civil War Medicine: Modern Medicine's Civil War Legacy." *American Battlefield Trust.*

Gorman, Kathleen L. "Civil War Pensions." *Virginia Center for Civil War Studies.*

Holberton, William B. "Demobilization of the Union Army 1865-66." Lehigh University master's thesis, 1993.

Lerwill, Leonard L. "The Personnel Replacement System in the United States Army." *Department of the Army Pamphlet No. 20-211*, 1954.

Nicholson, Kevin S. "After Andersonville: Survivors, Memory and the Bloody Shirt." *The Gettysburg College Journal of the Civil War Era*, Vol. 8, May 2018.

Prechtel-Kluskens, Claire. "A Reasonable Degree of Promptitude: Civil War Pension Application Processing, 1861–1885." *Prologue* magazine of the US National Archives and Records Administration, Spring 2010, Vol. 42, No. 1.

Reilly, Robert F. "Medical and Surgical Care During the American Civil War, 1861-1865." *Baylor University Medical Center Proceedings*, April 2016, Vol. 29, No. 2.

Richards, H.M.M. "In Rebel Prisons: A Tribute to Samuel B. Trafford." Lebanon County, Pa., Historical Society publications, Vol. VIII, No. 8.

Smyth, S. Gordon. "The Land of the Llewellyn and Camp Discharge." *Historical Sketches: A Collection of Papers Prepared for the Historical Society of Montgomery County, Pennsylvania.* Historical Society of Montgomery County, 1905.

Staff, Lower Merion Parks & Recreation Department. "List of Historic and Cultural Resources." Feasibility Study for Schuylkill River West Trail, Appendix 2, 2008.

Wodehouse, Lawrence. "John McArthur, Jr. (1823-1890)." *Journal of the Society of Architectural Historians*, December 1969, Vol. 28, No. 4.

Archival & Unpublished Material

US National Archives and Records Administration, Washington, D.C.: Adjutant General—Records of Posts 1820-1940 (Record group 393), M617 Returns from Military Posts, Reports of Proceedings of Posts, Letters Sent; Quartermaster General—92.16 Cartographic Records (General) 1820-1985, Architectural and Engineering Plans.

Pennsylvania State Archives, Harrisburg, Pa.: Records of the Transportation and Telegraph Department—Series 19.184, Transportation Accounts, 1861–1867; MG 7, Military Manuscripts Collection, 1758–1931; RG 19, Records of the Department of Military and Veterans Affairs, Office of the Adjutant General, Series 19.11, Civil War Muster Rolls and Related Records, 1861–1866.

Corson, Hiram. Unpublished diary. Holdings of Montgomery County Historical Society, Norristown, Pa.

Corson, Joseph K. Unpublished memoir. Courtesy of Ann F. Corson.

Newspapers

Brookville Republican (Brookville, Pa.)—online at newspapers.com

- "How the Troops are to Be Paid and Mustered Out." May 31, 1865, p.2
- Herald & Free Press (Norristown, Pa.)—holdings of Montgomery County Historical Society, Norristown, Pa.
-Untitled item about Camp Discharge. Nov. 8, 1864, p.3

Herald & Republican (Norristown, Pa.)—holdings of Montgomery County Historical Society, Norristown, Pa.

-"Soldier's Funeral." March 9, 1865, p.3
-"More Fruits of Rebel Barbarity." April 6, 1865, p.3
-"Died." May 18, 1865, p.3
-Untitled item about Camp Discharge sale. Dec. 21, 1865, p. 2

Lebanon Daily News (Lebanon, Pa.) – online at newspapers.com

-"A Union Soldier on the Pension List Goes to the Poor House." Jan. 2, 1903, p. 1

Philadelphia Daily News

-"Phila. CC Buys 85 Acres." Dec. 22, 1965, p. 50

Philadelphia Inquirer (Philadelphia, Pa.)—online at newspapers.com

-"Demobilization Report." Dec. 6, 1865, p. 10
-"Employment of Discharged Soldiers." May 10, 1865, p. 2
-"Arrival of the Sick and Wounded," April 7, 1865, p. 8
-"Discharges." May 22, 1865, p. 8

Philadelphia Times (Philadelphia, Pa.)—online at newpapers.com
-"Clerk Dougherty Gone." Jan. 22, 1887, p. 1
Reading Times (Reading, Pa)—online at newspapers.com
-"Accident on the Reading Railroad." March 15, 1865, p. 2
-"Veteran Dead: Albert Thalheimer, Retired Manufacturer, Passes Away." April 19, 1923, p. 3
Star and Enterprise (Newville, Pa.)—online at newspapers.com
-Untitled item about Camp Curtin. May 20, 1865, p. 2
Wilkes-Barre News (Wilkes-Barre, Pa.)—online at newspapers.com
-"Victims of Prison Pens." Nov. 28, 1905, p. 3
-Wilson Long obituary. May 25, 1899, p. 1
Wilkes-Barre Semi-Weekly Record (Wilkes-Barre, Pa.)—online at newspapers.com
-"Local Heroes of Andersonville," Oct. 20, 1903, p. 6
Wilmington News Journal (Wilmington, Del.)—online at newspapers.com
-Untitled item about Collum Duffy. Sept. 2, 1890, p. 3

About the Authors

(Courtesy Harriet Katz)

JIM REMSEN is a journalist and author of three previous books, *The Intermarriage Handbook* (HarperCollins, 1988), *Visions of Teaoga* (Sunbury, 2014), and *Embattled Freedom* (Sunbury 2017). Since retiring as Religion Editor at *The Philadelphia Inquirer*, Jim has pursued his keen interest in history, especially underappreciated aspects of our nation's local histories.

(Courtesy Jacob Long)

BRAD UPP is a board member of the Lower Merion Historical Society and a former educator. His upbringing near Camp Discharge stoked a fascination with history and led him to become a Civil War historian, relic hunter, and re-enactor representing the 69th Pennsylvania Infantry. Brad is a skilled collector of artifacts from various periods of history, a passion that has taken him to a myriad of locations throughout the United States.

Made in the USA
Middletown, DE
19 September 2021

48611128R00149